GAULLISM

GAULLISM

The Rise and Fall of a
Political Movement

ANTHONY HARTLEY

Routledge & Kegan Paul   London

First published in Great Britain in 1972
by Routledge & Kegan Paul Ltd
Broadway House, 68-74 Carter Lane
London EC4V 5EL
Printed in Great Britain by
Lowe & Brydone (Printers) Limited, London

ISBN 0 7100 7316 X

To Rhea who dislikes the subject.

Preface to this Edition

This book was first published in the United States in July 1971. Since then little has occurred which would cause me to modify my view of the Gaullist movement. The immediate past, indeed, has confirmed the pattern of change which has followed de Gaulle's departure from office and subsequent death. President Pompidou has now consented to Great Britain's admission to the Europe Economic Community (EEC) and, as his political success at his meeting with President Nixon in the Azores during December 1971 shows, is also trying to mend his bridges with the United States. It could be maintained that this considerable reversal of de Gaulle's foreign policy was already implicit in the last period of the General's rule, but this does not alter the fact that remarkably little of that ambitious construction has been left standing.

As for the rank and file Gaullists, they continue to display 'moroseness' in their judgements on the outside world and France's domestic affairs. It has become clear just how little Gaullist ambitions corresponded to France's real international power, and the resultant awakening has been a disagreeable one. Another leading Gaullist, Jules Jeanneney, has left the *Union des democrates pour la République* (UDR), and scandals concerning corruption and the doings of the French intelligence service (SDECE) have been bad for party morale. At present the UDR seems to be more than usually divided into factions manipulated with the skill of a virtuoso by the President of the Republic.

To turn to a more properly historical point, the picture of war-time Gaullism and its relations with the British government will soon be changed by research in British documents now becoming available. But it seems probable that this change will consist of gains in complication and subtlety rather than a complete obliteration of the existing picture. For instance, it will be useful to have some idea of the attitude towards the Gaullists held by different parts of the British government. We shall probably have to wait longer for a real history of the Resistance movement—an almost impossibly difficult book to write.

A.H.

Preface

This book began as a short sketch of what the political movement called Gaullism was and is. It gradually grew until the limits of that rather cursory endeavor were exceeded. What I have finally written is a history of certain trends in French political life which have been apparent since before 1940, but which the defeat and the adventure of Free France crystallized around the name of Charles de Gaulle. Since so many scholars have preceded me on this particular road, I would not claim any special originality for my account of it. But I hope I have managed to put together some facts that have not hitherto been gathered into one book and to give a clear account of events which were both dramatic and complicated. I hold views on European politics – and especially on the future of European integration – which are on record and will, doubtless, be clear to my readers. But I have tried to hold the balance even in writing about Gaullism and not to inject my own desires and prejudices into the argument. De Gaulle appears to me as a man of tragically flawed greatness, but no one who was a fifteen-year-old Englishman in 1940 and who was subsequently partially educated in France, could fail to treat him with respect. I should wish to have done so. My theme is not the fascinating one of his character, but some judgment of it will inevitably emerge from these pages.

In writing this book, my obligations have mostly been to other writers who are mentioned in the notes. But I should like to thank my friend Douglas Johnson, with whom I have talked about French politics for more than twenty years now, for agreeing to read some of the chapters. He, of course, is not responsible for my conclusions. My thanks are also due to my publisher and editor, Harris Dienstfrey, who alternately prodded me and then waited patiently for the results.

A.H.

Contents

Preface
vii

Abbreviations
xiii

Introduction
1

Chapter One

De Gaulle's Doctrine:
The Roots of Gaullism
5

Chapter Two

The Third Republic:
Prelude to Failure
35

Chapter Three

The War Years:
The Founding of Gaullism
51

Chapter Four

The Fourth Republic and the RPF
95

Chapter Five

The Founding of the Fifth Republic:
Gaullism and Algeria
147

Chapter Six

Gaullism Abroad: The Foreign Policy
of the Fifth Republic
195

Chapter Seven

Gaullism at Home: The Domestic Policy
of the Fifth Republic
245

Chapter Eight

The Decline of Gaullism:
May and the End of a Régime
275

Conclusion and Aftermath
299

Notes
311

A Selective Bibliographical Note
349

Index
360

Abbreviations

ABM	Antiballistic missile
ALN	Armée de libération nationale
AMGOT	Allied military government
ARS	Action républicaine et sociale
BBC	British Broadcasting Corporation
CAL	Comités d'action lycéens
CD	Centre démocrate
CDL	Comités départementaux de libération
CDR	Comité pour la défense de la République
CFDT	Confédération française démocratique du travail
CFLN	Comité français de libération nationale
CGE	Comité général d'études
CGT	Confédération générale du travail
CII	Compagnie internationale pour l'Informatique
CLER	Comité de liaison des étudiants révolutionnaires
CNI	Centre national des indépendants
CNPF	Confédération nationale du patronat francais
CNR	Conseil national de la Résistance
COMAC	Comité d'action militaire
CPL	Comité parisien de libération
CRS	Compagnies républicaines de sécurité
CSP	Comités de salut publique

DMR	Délégué militaire régional
EDC	European Defense Community
EEC	European Economic Community
ENA	Ecole nationale d'administration
EURATOM	European Atomic Energy Authority
FFI	Forces françaises de l'intérieur
FGDS	Fédération de la gauche démocrate et socialiste
FLN	Front de libération nationale
FNF	Front national français
FTPF	Francs-tireurs et partisans français
GDR	German Democratic Republic
GNP	Gross national product
GPRA	Gouvernement provisoire de la république algérienne
GPRF	Gouvernement provisoire de la république française
ICBM	Intercontinental ballistic missile
IMF	International monetary fund
IRBM	Intermediate-range ballistic missile
IUT	Institut universitaire de téchnologie
JCR	Jeunesse communiste révolutionnaire
MLF	Multilateral force
MNA	Mouvement national algérien
MP	Milice patriotique
MRP	Mouvement républicain populaire
MTLD	Mouvement pour le triomphe des libertés démocratiques
MUR	Mouvements unis de résistance
NADGE	NATO air defense ground environment
NATO	North Atlantic Treaty Organization
NPT	Non-proliferation treaty
OAS	Organisation armée secrète
OCM	Organisation civile et militaire
OEEC	Organization for European Economic Cooperation
ORTF	Office de Radiodiffusion-Télévision française
PDM	Progrès et démocratie moderne
PPF	Parti populaire français
PSF	Parti social français
PSU	Parti socialiste unifié
RGR	Rassemblement des gauches républicaines
RPF	Rassemblement du peuple français
SACEUR	Supreme allied commander Europe
SDECE	Section de documentation extérieure et de contreespionnage
SDR	Special drawing rights

SDS	Sozialistischer deutscher Studentenbund
SEATO	South-East Asia Treaty Organization
SMIG	Salaire minimum interprofessionnel garanti
SNE.SUP	Syndicat national de l'enseignement supérieur
SR	Service de renseignement
TVA	Taxe sur la valeur ajoutée
UD Ve	Union démocratique pour la Ve République
UDCA	Union de défense des commerçants et artisans
UDR	Union des démocrates pour la République
UDR	Union pour la défense de la République
UDT	Union démocratique du travail
UGTT	Union générale des travailleurs tunisiens
UJC-ML	Union des jeunesses communistes (marxistes-léninistes)
U.N.	United Nations
UNEF	Union nationale des étudiants français
UNR	Union pour la nouvelle République
URAS	Union des républicains d'action sociale
USRAF	Union pour le salut et le renouveau de l'Algérie française
WEU	Western European Union

Introduction

What is called Gaullism is at once a political movement and a political doctrine. Both movement and doctrine take their name from one man, Charles de Gaulle, the originality of whose thought and the power of whose personality were for ten years to be the very basis of the Fifth French Republic just as, during the Second World War, they were the basis of the Free French movement in London and imparted to it its intransigent ardor and its oversusceptibility towards affronts from the Allies. In the character of de Gaulle's actions, in the content of his public utterances could be seen the reflection of a coherent view of politics which he seemed to have formed at quite an early stage in his career. What has been called 'le style du Général' was the result in action of a system of thought which, however deeply rooted it may be in certain more or less constant traditions of the French mind, was nonetheless an individual synthesis distinguished both by its inner logic and by its implicit tensions. To define this system is the first task of a student of Gaullism.

But Gaullist political doctrine was not formed and does not exist in a vacuum. In the twenties and thirties, Charles de Gaulle, a professional soldier for whom a great future had been predicted (but who had spent a large part of the First World War in a German prison camp), could see

1

around him the living proof of that need for firm government in France which was to become one of the main themes of his political career. The decadence of the Third Republic, coming as it did after the supreme effort of the war, was to end by alienating men of widely divergent views from the régime. De Gaulle was no exception. When the catastrophe of 1940 arrived it only seemed to him to confirm the sense of foreboding which, as "a reserved but passionate witness of public affairs," he had felt in the years that had gone before. Similarly, between 1940 and 1946, his success in the unwearying assertion of France's right to be considered a great power, in the battle with the German occupier and the more difficult struggle with Anglo-Saxon and Russian Allies, seemed to imply that character and intelligence placed at the service of an inflexible patriotism could achieve the impossible. After his resignation on January 20, 1946, as president of the French provisional government, he once again, during the period of the Fourth Republic, saw fulfilled a prophecy, this one made to the Constituent Assembly on December 31, 1945: "if you do not take into account the absolute necessities of governmental authority, dignity and responsibility, you will find yourselves in a situation which I predict will cause you bitter regret for having taken the way you have chosen." The government found itself in that situation on May 13, 1958, when an unmanageable Algerian crisis culminated in a threat of civil war.

Thus Gaullism and the doctrine behind it were inspired and annealed by forty disastrous years of French history. The character of Gaullism cannot be considered apart from that background—or from the social and economic evolution which has transformed France over half a century. For if the Gaullist Fifth Republic represented a strengthening of the French state and an assertion of traditional French nationalism (just how traditional will become clear in the course of this book), it has also made its own the modernization of France's economy for which the Fourth Republic laid the foundations, but which needed a stable political régime to produce its full results. The lessening isolation of French life (due to entry into the European Economic Community [EEC], better communications and more opportunities for travel), the depopulation of the countryside, the higher standards of living, the weakening of traditional attitudes such as anticlericalism—all these changes have been reflected in France's political structures. The Gaullist political party, under whatever name it has gone—*Union pour la*

Nouvelle République (UNR), *Vème République, Union pour la défense de la République* (UDR) etc.—is no exception. It is not something totally new in French politics, but a development of trends that had already been visible under the Fourth, and even the Third Republic.

Gaullism as seen in the shape taken by the Fifth Republic used to its own advantage an evolution in French political and social life that was already under way. Moreover, the political stability and continuity of administration insured by the Gaullist régime until the events of May 1968, allowed officials to carry out reforms which would otherwise have remained on paper. Plans alternately matured and set aside under the Fourth Republic took their place among the achievements of the Gaullist period when attention could be given to these plans and regular credits voted for them.

To say that the Gaullist Republic reaped what its predecessors had sown is not to denigrate it. There is merit in reaping.

Gaullism, therefore, is not only the result of the impact of a single man on the course of French history; it is also the expression of that history itself. It is an ill-defined phenomenon shifting uneasily between a political movement and a personal clientele. The Gaullist party was always treated by de Gaulle himself in as arbitrary a manner as the earlier organization, *Le Rassemblement du peuple français* (RPF). The phrase attributed to him by a satirist, apocryphal though it may be, expresses well enough his relations with his own party: "This party was founded to serve me . . . not to inconvenience me. It should keep quiet." Will Gaullism survive the silencing of that peremptory voice? Would Gaullist doctrine and style have lasted beyond their originator's withdrawal from politics in 1969? And now that he is dead?

It is not difficult to see that, now that de Gaulle is gone, many things will be changed. But it also seems likely that much of what has been done under the Fifth Republic will prove to have a durable effect on French political life as well as on world politics. To estimate that effect and to make some attempt to predict what France's future is now likely to be must be the theme of a concluding chapter. First must come some analysis of the thought and style that have so shaped France's recent history—an element that seems best called de Gaulle's doctrine, since no other word quite expresses the mixture of intellect and personality which has to be taken into account in understanding the development and influence of Gaullism.

CHAPTER I

De Gaulle's Doctrine:
The Roots of Gaullism

*He felt about France what Pericles felt of
Athens–unique value in her, nothing else
mattering; but his theory of politics was
Bismarck's. He had one illusion–France; and
one disillusion–mankind, including Frenchmen
and his colleagues not least.*
–J. M. Keynes on Clemenceau

At the beginning of de Gaulle's *Mémoires de Guerre* there is a famous
passage where he describes the feeling he had for France:

All my life I have thought of France in a certain way. This is inspired
by sentiment as much as by reason. The emotional side of me tends
to imagine France, like the princess in the fairy stories or the
Madonna in the frescoes, as dedicated to an exalted and exceptional
destiny. Instinctively I have the feeling that Providence has created
her either for complete successes or for exemplary misfortunes. If, in
spite of this, mediocrity shows in her acts and deeds, it strikes me as
an absurd anomaly, to be imputed to the faults of Frenchmen, not to
the genius of the land. But the positive side of my mind also assures
me that France is not really herself unless she is in the front rank;

that only vast enterprises are capable of counter-balancing the ferments of disintegration inherent in her people . . .[1]

In itself this was little different from the exaltation of the nation state to be found in much political literature of the nineteenth and early twentieth centuries. France the princess or Divine Mother took its place alongside Cathleen ni Houlihan or the helmeted goddesses of Teutonic legend as the personification of a national myth. But de Gaulle, heir to a classical civilization and son of a professor in a Catholic college, was to bring to his vision more logic and cohesion than others had done. France was not merely a princess, setting on fire all the chivalrous instincts of a young man; it was also a biological entity, an organism existing in time as well as in space, reaching back into history as well as forward into the future. It is "Old France, weighed down with history, prostrated by wars and revolutions, endlessly vacillating from greatness to decline, but revived, century after century, by the genius of renewal!"[2] And this apostrophe which closes the *Mémoires* is placed side by side with a similar invocation of the earth's power of regeneration. Like a living thing France had its natural rhythms. Like a living thing it ran the danger of death or sterility, but, as in the lands that form it, spring always followed winter, new growth brought back life to the barren fields.

If the nation state was viewed as a living organism, it followed that it had to be regarded as unique. It could neither be assimilated to, nor merged with, any other nation state which in turn would have its own individual set of characteristics. It was these states which were "certainly very different from one another, each of which has its own spirit, its own history, its own language, its own misfortunes, glories and ambitions; but which are the only entities that have the right to order and the authority to act."[3] De Gaulle's opposition to supra-national institutions, whether those of the European Economic Community in Brussels or of the United Nations Organization in New York, was based, therefore, on far more than a mere dislike of his country being submitted to the decisions of such 'aréopages.' Not merely would it have been a weakening of the national organism and a betrayal of a slowly evolved inheritance to accept any outside control beyond what the ordinary play of international power dictates, but also a folly that would end in ruin. For the nation state was the only really dynamic political structure capable of concentrating and expressing human aspirations. Thus "the supreme interest of mankind dictates that each nation be responsible for itself ... "[4] Only in this way could the varying capacities of the different peoples of the world be realized.

Another consequence of this view of the nation state as a self-sufficient organism was that, in relations between states, the accent must be placed on competition rather than on cooperation. "Life is life—in other words a struggle, for a nation as for a man"[5] was a phrase that often recurred on de Gaulle's lips. His book *La France et son armée* (1938) begins with the statement "France was made with strokes of the sword."[6] Throughout the *Mémoires* the truth of the idea that France's allies will take advantage of its weakness to further their own interests, one of the major themes of the book, was taken for granted. The description of Winston Churchill was that of a great ally, but also a great adversary:

> when he saw France in my person as an ambitious state apparently eager to recover her power in Europe and the world, Churchill had *quite naturally* felt something of Pitt's spirit in his own soul.[7] [Italics mine.]

Peoples could, of course, enter into alliances, but these were essentially arrangements of convenience in accordance with immediate national interests. "It is reason which dictates treaties."[8] At most, traditional feelings of sympathy, corresponding perhaps to the recognition of a geo-political basis for alliances, add a little warmth to the relationship. Otherwise all states were potential rivals to be saluted inasmuch as they played their roles with courage and determination, to be respected as contributing to the cultural and political diversity of the world, but also to be suspected and, if the suspicions proved to be true (as usually turned out to be the case), to be vehemently opposed in their attempts to encroach upon France's rights.

This view of international relations has many resemblances with that prevailing in Europe in the eighteenth century, with the policies of the *ancien régime* to whose realism de Gaulle had paid tribute.* The

*In Keynes's portrait of Clemenceau quoted at the head of this chapter the following description is given of the 'Tiger's' view of international relations:

conflicts between states remain limited conflicts for specific ends, because, since the nation state was the foundation of civilization, it would be folly for one of them to try to dominate another. It was this type of *hubris* that brought about the German catastrophe: "Once more it has been proved that for a people, however resolute and powerful it may be, the unbridled ambition of dominating others may snatch more or less brilliant and prolonged successes, but that the outcome is collapse."[9] Similarly de Gaulle's view of the necessary integrity of nations implied a belief in the independence of colonies, and anyone who had read his published works and speeches would have had no illusions about the policies he was likely to follow in Algeria. How could there have been 'integration' between two disparate organisms? As he put it in a press conference on September 5, 1961: "We do not believe that the interest, the honor and the future of France should be . . . based on continuing the domination of populations, the great majority of which is not composed of her people and whom everything leads more and more to free themselves and become their own masters."[10] More brutally, de Gaulle expressed his distaste for 'integration' when he asked the Gaullist deputy Raymond Dronne whether he would allow his daughter to marry a *Bougnoul* (a pejorative expression for an Algerian Moslem).[11]

II

But if there was to be no domination as between states, it nonetheless remained true that the struggle for advantage was constant. It is not surprising, therefore, that de Gaulle should have asserted that "the military body is the most complete expression of the spirit of a social system."[12] For the force at the disposal of a nation was the very palladium of its sovereignty. To allow one's army or nation to be

---

"Nations are real things, of which you love one and feel for the rest indifference—or hatred. The glory of the nation you love is a desirable end—but generally to be obtained at your neighbour's expense. The politics of power are inevitable . . ." The resemblance of this to the more somber side of de Gaulle's philosophy of international relations is striking, but Clemenceau had perhaps less magnanimity than de Gaulle and also less conception of the historic unity of Europe which is liable to be harmed if conflicts between states are carried to extremes.

"integrated!—in other words blotted out" or to deprive oneself of any means of defense possessed by others was to risk harming that sovereignty beyond repair. Thus yet another Gaullist policy, the construction of a French nuclear striking force, stemmed from an integral part of de Gaulle's thinking on international affairs. Without nuclear weapons France would have been threatened in war and at a disadvantage in peace. And integration of a political nature whether in the Atlantic alliance or the European Economic Community was, as we have seen, an unthinkable folly.

This appreciation of the part played by force as the incarnation of the national will corresponded to a more general theory of its role as the supremely dynamic factor in human affairs. *Le fil de l'épée (The Edge of the Sword,* 1932), undoubtedly the most striking general statement of de Gaulle's philosophy of politics and history, begins with a dithyrambic celebration of the necessity of force which, though often quoted, is worth quoting again in view of its importance as a credo:

> Is it possible to conceive of life without force? Only if children cease to be born, only if minds are sterilized, feelings frozen, men's needs anesthetized, only if the world is reduced to immobility, can it be banished. Otherwise, in some form or other, it will remain indispensable, for, without it, thought would have no driving power, action no strength. It is the prerequisite of movement and the midwife of progress. Whether as the bulwark of authority, the defender of thrones, the motive power of revolution, we owe to it, turn and turn about, both order and liberty. Force has watched over civilizations in the cradle; force has ruled empires, and dug the grave of decadence; force gives laws to the peoples and controls their destinies.[13]

At other times, however, this resounding declaration of vitalist belief is attenuated into a melancholy resignation which saw war as inevitable—"an ineluctable element, just as much as birth and death"[14]—but which, while accepting this as a fact of human existence, was prepared to deplore, rather than exult over it. One of the most curious aspects of de Gaulle's thought was implied in the argument which he put forward in *Vers l'armée de métier (The Army of the Future,* 1934) to support his advocacy of a small, highly trained professional army. This type of army, he claimed, would diminish the ravages of war which were at their worst in the clash between whole nations armed in a *levée en masse.* Moreover, since the nation states which composed Europe

were by then too firmly rooted to be eliminated or conquered in any
real sense by their rivals, the limited objectives, which were all that
could be achieved by force of arms, would more easily and appropri-
ately be attained through the use of a military instrument composed of
professionals. "On the whole, no form of battle is more sanguinary than
that of nations-in-arms."[15]

Leaving aside the applicability to the twentieth century of these
arguments (which were published five years before the outbreak of a
war in which the very existence of nation states was seen to be at
stake), what is interesting here is the attempt to moderate evils
otherwise regarded as inevitable. To the limited advantages over rivals
to which nation states can aspire, corresponds a limited and surgically
skilled application of force. To the restrained rivalries of *ancien régime*
diplomacy correspond the professional maneuvers of a small elite army,
whose battles can be decided by a swift measurement of relative skills
rather than by the prolonged bloodbath of grappling conscript armies.
Classical measure once again mitigates the inevitably unpromising raw
material of which the international scene is composed. If some limit can
be set to the damage men do to others and to themselves, then much
will have been achieved. A Lowest Common Multiple of behavior is all
that can be hoped for; a Highest Common Factor is out of the question.
A reasoned pessimism about human nature as manifested in political
action gave to de Gaulle's view of politics its peculiar atmosphere of
weary disillusionment. "The nature of things . . . ," "the force of
things . . . ," "things being what they are"—this type of phrase,
recurring again and again in de Gaulle's writings or speeches, implied a
recognition of the narrow boundaries within which a statesman can
affect events, a realistic appraisal of the intractable hostility of political
phenomena to the well-meaning efforts of idealists and reformers. So,
far from wishing to change the rules of the international chess game, de
Gaulle's desire for reform was confined to producing a more favorable
configuration among the pieces already on the board. In this acceptance
of the human situation he followed the succession of the great French
moralists who have striven for four hundred years to bring within their
own conception of a classic order all the disparate and unruly elements
of man's nature. And the political equivalent of this effort was the
policy of the *ancien régime* which de Gaulle praised for its sense of
reality, its grasp of the concrete:

refraining from abstractions but relishing realities; preferring the useful to the sublime and opportune measures to resounding phrases; seeking for each particular problem, not the ideal solution, but the practical one; unscrupulous as to means, but great, nevertheless, through its observance of a just proportion between the desired end and the forces of the state.[16]

One side of de Gaulle's political thought consists of this kind of measured realism which could border on a brutal cynicism, but which also may have had the effect of keeping political competition between states or parties within the bounds of a civilized tradition. The world postulated by this view of politics may have been a harsh one, but it excluded the worst excesses either of idealistic enthusiasm or atavistic barbarity. De Gaulle was no humanitarian, but his conception of realpolitik was tailored to the measure of humanity—of a humanity, it is true, on which the uttermost demands can be made in the name of the community through which it takes on a corporate existence: the community of the nation state.*

But there was another side to de Gaulle's political thinking than that contained in the careful practice of diplomatic realism. The eulogy of force quoted above has behind it the romanticism of the nineteenth century, and the organic biological quality attributed to France as a natural phenomenon suggests a less limited struggle among nation states than even the unceasing rivalries of an older Europe. The justification of force by its power of creating change derives from a social Darwinism in which "the nature of things" could come to mean "the survival of the fittest." It was one thing to apply this phrase to the instability of Franco-German relations.[18] It was quite another for de Gaulle to speak in his Bayeux speech of "that Sarre to whom the nature of things, *revealed by our victory,* once more indicates its place alongside us."[19] [Italics mine.] Here "the nature of things" was not so much an incentive to moderation as an invitation to *hubris.* A situation created by force was to be exploited without regard to the further political consequences, or, indeed, to France's ability to maintain its

---

*A similar balance can be observed in de Gaulle's military theories. Although, as the advocate of a mechanized striking force, he was a partisan of an offensive strategy, this did not prevent him from describing the advantages of constructing fortified zones to defend France's eastern frontier (see *Rôle historique des places françaises* first published in 1925).[17]

position in the face of local opposition or a restoration of German power which, surely, in terms of any prudent and realistic policy must have also seemed to be in "the nature of things" by June 16, 1946.

Alongside the reasoned pursuit of limited objectives by nations there also existed in de Gaulle's world the romantic quest for fame and glory founded on the psychological necessities of individual men. In *Le fil de l'épée*, de Gaulle insists on the necessity for grandeur in any plan presented by a leader to his followers:

> It must, indeed, respond to the cravings felt by men who, imperfect themselves, seek perfection in the end they are called upon to serve. Conscious of their own limitations and restricted by nature, they give free rein to unlimited hopes and each measuring his own littleness, accepts the need for collective action on condition that it contribute to an end which is, in itself, great.[20]

Grandeur, glory, brilliance, vast enterprises, vast policy – these words of romantic aspiration in de Gaulle's writings form a counterpoint to the classical resignation with which he otherwise accepted the hard facts of international life. And as for individuals, so for peoples:

> it is a moot point whether some great national dream is not necessary to a nation to keep it active and united.[21]

If *raison d'état* played a part here, realism was left far behind or consisted more in concentrating on the relationship of the individual citizen to his nation than in any appraisal of that nation's ability to realize the myth that is its unifying force. A polity based on myth risks becoming a polity of pure prestige in which the idea that a nation has of itself will be more important than its real position in the world or than that "observance of a just proportion between the desired end and the forces of the state" which de Gaulle noted with such approval in the diplomacy of the *ancien régime*. The temptation present in this form of political thinking is that its romanticism may come to dominate its realism so that the appearance of power is accepted as having the same value as the substance, and diplomatic activity is held to be equivalent to international influence. De Gaulle's political thought had a tendency to dissolve the barriers between myth and reality, and, in the resultant mingling, even the author of the confusion may himself have been led to mistake the one for the other.

Such an interpenetration of the world of the imagination and the assessment of everyday events is one sign of a literary bent. De Gaulle was a considerable writer who used words to persuade and inspire and whose ideas can hardly be discussed without reference to the unique rhetorical expression imparted to them. Nor had he escaped the literary influences of his time. The romanticism of action and violence found in his writings was something he had in common with such vitalist French writers of the interwar period as André Malraux and Antoine de Saint-Exupéry. In *Vers l'armée de métier* can even be found the somewhat frantic association of eroticism and violence which was so typical of French writing of the twenties and thirties. De Gaulle described how Frenchmen face danger:

> Their eyes being blindfolded, they strike at empty air, rush aimlessly hither and thither, and hurl themselves heroically against brick walls. Then, discomfited but compensated by their pride, they find themselves face to face with reality and tear aside its veils. Then they embrace it, dominate it, penetrate it, and extract from it all the pleasures of glory.[22]

'Glory' here takes on the unexpected aspect of rape, but this is not so very different from one of Malraux's heroes describing the fascination of standing before life like a naked woman one is about to possess. Malraux's conception of *destiny* also seems to cover much the same concept of creative myth as de Gaulle's "great national dream." From Barrès and Péguy onwards, de Gaulle had certainly been more influenced by the romantic, vitalist writers of the twentieth century and their cult of energy than might be supposed from his classical style and constant references to traditional French culture. Péguy too provided a source in which he would have found the mingling of the French Catholic tradition with that of revolutionary Jacobinism, the same acceptance of the whole of the French past which is so remarkable a feature of his own character. The divergent literary influences to be detected in the style and content of de Gaulle's writing are, indeed, another instance of the same dichotomy between classical and romantic, measure and disproportion, that has been noted in discussing his philosophy of politics.

III

It was in the relationship between de Gaulle and France—the relationship which was so central to his whole life and thought—that these contrasts are best explained and most nearly reconciled. For de Gaulle, France was above all the country of a classic dignity and measure. In the preface of his first book *La discorde chez l'ennemi* (1924) there is a famous passage where the nature of French civilization is defined and implicitly contrasted with German:

> In the French-style garden no tree seeks to stifle others with its shadow, the flower-beds adapt themselves to being geometrically designed, the pool does not covet a waterfall, the statues do not make an exclusive claim to admiration. Sometimes a noble melancholy emanates from it. Perhaps it comes from the feeling that each element by itself would have appeared to greater advantage. But it would have been to the detriment of the whole, and the passer-by is satisfied with the rule that has imparted to the garden its magnificent harmony.[23]

The book itself deals with the errors of the German leadership during the First World War, errors which, according to de Gaulle, sprang from "the characteristic taste for monstrous undertakings, the passion for extending their personal power at any cost, the scorn of limits set by human experience, common sense and the law."[24] Thus the 'vast enterprises' recommended by de Gaulle to men living in society were "monstrous" when carried on by German generals, and the latter were criticized as disciples of Nietzsche, although de Gaulle's own ideas on the role of the leader had much in common with the Nietzschean superman. France, on the contrary, with its "rare and precious harmony," which has imprinted on Frenchmen "her own stamp, making a balanced whole out of their differences and welding their many-sidedness into unity,"[25] France the fairy princess of de Gaulle's imagination, by definition will refuse to lend itself to any project not sanctioned by the classical moderation of its civilization.

Thus it was the classical character of French civilization which justified de Gaulle's romantic insistence on the primacy of France. "Nothing could make us forget that its greatness is the condition *sine qua non* of world peace. There would be no justice, if justice were not done to France!"[26] This kind of claim for France's superiority over other countries, for its essential difference from the egotistical nation states by which it is surrounded, was based on a belief in the innate quality of French life:

> Our country with her tinted sky, her varied contours, her fertile soil, our fields full of fine corn and vines and livestock, our industry of artistic objects, finished products and luxury articles, our gifts of initiative, adaptation and self-respect make us, above all others, a race created for brilliant deeds and picked bodies of specialists.[27]

In de Gaulle's view France's role in the world was one of leadership, and spiritual and cultural supremacy was closely interwoven with the political claim to be *primus inter pares.* For it was the peculiar addiction of Frenchmen to generous ideas, their position as the marching wing of European civilization and as a people in some sense exemplary for the rest of the world, that allowed them to pretend to a certain intangible hegemony over less richly endowed countries. The French sense of order and measure, if reflected in international relations, could only be for the good of all concerned: "The dream of France is, pre-eminently, that of an organized world, where the strictness of the law, the moderateness of desires and the ubiquity of the police would guarantee peace for all and allow everyone to live his own life."[28] Yet this conception too was ambivalent. Spiritual leadership must pay in terms of an accretion to France of power and influence: "To combine the permanent interest of France with a great human ideal would be a great, and at the same time, a very profitable achievement!"[29]

The attitude of de Gaulle towards France was indeed not unlike that of Soviet leaders towards the USSR. Just as a Russian Communist would maintain that foreign Communists, by serving Russian national interests, are also sustaining the cause of world communism in the only way possible, so for de Gaulle France and European civilization were so fused together that any advantage obtained by France, even at the expense of other European states, could only be for the good of the world as a whole. A kind of cultural imperialism—and how many Frenchmen are there who do not instinctively think of their country as culturally superior to other nations?—leads naturally into a claim to political primacy and, from there, into a justification of the measures needed to maintain it. France, the legendary princess, necessarily wears its egotism with a difference. De Gaulle, the romantic lover, could lavish his devotion on a country whose classical civilization carried within itself the *raison d'être* of his passion and provided it with an ethical content. France was still seen by him as a princess, still believed to be more beautiful (and therefore better) than the ugly sisters by which it is surrounded: the other nation states who may be envious of France's exceptional destiny, but who also, in their heart of hearts, desire the revelation afforded by it. "Old world, ever new, which, from century to century, received the deep imprint of France and which is waiting secretly for her to come again and show the road!"[30]

The romantic side of de Gaulle's political thought was, therefore, reconciled with his realistic respect for 'things as they are' by his lasting belief in the 'special' quality of France. It was this special quality which assigned France to a central place in history, to the place of signal honor and signal danger. "That France has been exposed to the greatest possible perils," de Gaulle asserted in a speech to the Consultative Assembly after VE Day, "was unavoidable . . . that conjunction of geographic, material and spiritual factors which has made France what it is . . . doomed it to remain in the center of events and run remarkable dangers."[31] De Gaulle's country appeared to him as a sort of touchstone of history, and his fellow-countrymen as a people with a mission guided by "the eternal law which makes us the vanguard of a civilization founded on the law of peoples and the respect of the human person."[32] He was prepared to enumerate reasons why this should be so—geographical position, historical experience, economic and political power within the European system—but it was clear that the original premise reposes on no very rational foundation. It was rather a matter of faith, and de Gaulle, with his French talent for self-analysis, was undoubtedly conscious of this compulsive belief welling up from the depths of his own being. It was not for nothing that, in the opening passage of the *Mémoires* quoted above, this basic *credo* was associated with childhood and its irrational desire for the certainty of myth. It was not for nothing that, speaking at Vincennes before the graves of those executed by the Germans, he could say of them: "They confessed France, they only confessed France."[33] The religious term (the meaning given to this sense of *confesser* in Littré is "make a public act of adhesion to a doctrine or religion") perfectly expressed de Gaulle's own relationship to his country, as well as the fervor of devotion to the national idea which he expected of other Frenchmen.

IV

The part played by Frenchmen as individuals in the Gaullist scheme
of things was, indeed, small enough, and it has often been remarked
that de Gaulle's opinion of the French was as poor as his opinion of
France was high. His comment on the fact that the continuation of the
war into 1945 was favorable to French interests may serve as an
example of this distinction between eternal France and merely
transitory Frenchmen: "from the viewpoint of France's higher interests—which is something quite different from the immediate advantage of the French . . . "[34] Professor Alfred Grosser has remarked that,
in de Gaulle's writings and speeches, economic and social progress were
strictly subordinated to the real end of Gaullist policy: the maintenance
of France's national interests and power in the world at large.
Individuals were defined in their aspect of being citizens of the French
republic rather by what they contributed to this task than by what they
may have hoped to receive from the state in the way of social services
or a higher standard of living. As President Auriol remarked to an
official of the Quai d'Orsay in 1948, such social and economic
questions, in any case, held little attraction for de Gaulle.[35] And, in
case of a clash between the interests of the individual and the
necessities of the state, there could be no question of the former taking
priority over the latter or of setting aside the claims the state might
have on the citizen. "What feeds them in their hearts is not what they
receive from the wheat. It is what they give to it"—this phrase from
Saint-Exupéry sums up well enough the pressingly paternal invitation to
greatness that de Gaulle extended to Frenchmen.

Collectively, however, the French people were a necessary term in the
Gaullist world of myth. For the 'vast enterprises' to which France's
destiny calls it could not be achieved without their aid—a paradox
expressed in a peculiarly bitter form by André Malraux's remark that,
since 1940, de Gaulle knew that he was "the alibi of millions of
men."[36] For the greatness of France, unity was essential; only "a great
people brought together"[37] could perform the tasks that France
required of them. In war "the cement of French unity is the blood of

Frenchmen ... "[38] In peace "national unity means that ... the common interest must be imposed on everyone."[39] Thus, imperfect though the response of many Frenchmen may have been to the demands made on them by their country—and de Gaulle never ceased to emphasize the harm done to France by the extreme individualism and bitter factiousness of the French—it was on them, when welded into a collective whole, that France had to rely to maintain its just place in the world. The achievements, the 'vast policy' that were required to maintain the activity and cohesion of the French people must be the result of individuals putting their own interests after those of France, but those who did this would be moved to their selfless devotion to the national cause by the mythopoeic power of a dream which they shared, an appeal to which they responded. It was this 'appeal' which gave its title to the first volume of de Gaulle's *Mémoires* and whose necessity he so often underlined:

> Ah! I well know that to spread and maintain in the masses of men and women—so diverse in their characters, activities and interests—of which France is eternally composed, the spirit to which they aspire, there must be a constant powerful appeal, a great movement of souls.[40]

But an appeal to a people implied a voice to make explicit the destiny to which France was called and to which, therefore, in their innermost being Frenchmen aspired even without being fully conscious of doing so. To utter this 'appeal,' to bring up into the consciousness of Frenchmen their own secret desires was the task of leadership to which, after so many great French national leaders, de Gaulle addressed himself.

During the war, on December 16, 1941, an American naval officer, Lieutenant Commander Kittredge, was present at a conversation between de Gaulle and Admiral Stark, the United States Atlantic naval commander, during which the former defined his own view of his historic role. Kittredge reported de Gaulle's words as follows:

> [De Gaulle] was also convinced that French culture, intelligence and capacities of leadership were so widely diffused in France that when any elite or governing class failed France, through decadence or defeatism, new individuals were always projected upward out of the

French masses, to give enlightened and inspired leadership to "eternal France"; that this had been true through the centuries from the time of Charlemagne to that of Hitler. Thus De Gaulle referred to the rise of the Capetian royal house, to Joan of Arc, to Henri IV, to the revolutionary leaders (1789-93), to Napoleon, finally to Poincaré and Clemenceau; De Gaulle added—"perhaps this time I am one of those thrust into leadership by circumstances, and by the failure of other leaders."[41]

"Admiral Stark," continues Kittredge, "was much impressed by this historical and philosophical analysis and suggested that De Gaulle, on meeting Roosevelt . . . should attempt to make the President understand his concepts." (De Gaulle had, in fact, already tried to convey to the American leader his own sense of being chosen for a mission. In a letter to Roosevelt of October 26, 1941, after describing how at first he had tried to influence French politicians by his military ideas and had then appealed to Frenchmen after the armistice purely as a soldier, he went on:

We have seen a sort of mystique created in France of which we are the center and which has united, little by little, all the elements of resistance. It is in this way that, by the force of things, we have become a French moral entity.[42].

There is no evidence that this apologia for his mission had any impact on Roosevelt's deep-rooted prejudice against de Gaulle.)

This was an element in de Gaulle's thought that remained constant. Nearly nineteen years later, at the time of the generals' putsch in Algeria, he told a minister who had returned from Algiers after having been held prisoner by the rebels:

What do you expect . . . ? There is a fact which they have not decided to take into account, an essential fact, however—one which destroys all their calculations. That fact is De Gaulle. I don't always understand it very well myself . . . but I am its prisoner.[43]

The historical role which de Gaulle assumed was, therefore, one greater than the individual on whom it had been thrust "by circumstances, and by the failure of other leaders." The individual Charles de Gaulle became a kind of intermediary between the French people and France. It was his appeal in the name of France that had to stir them into activity. It was his interpretation of the national interest to which they must subordinate their private concerns. It was he even when no longer in office, who, as the moral legatee of the inheritance of French national feeling, represented the continuity of France. When, in a notorious phrase of a speech delivered at the time of the Algerian 'barricades,' on January 29, 1960, de Gaulle spoke of "the national legitimacy that I have embodied for twenty years," he did not mean (as some of his critics maintained that he meant) that he had been the legal government of France throughout that period, but rather that the accumulation of moral and national capital which had been amassed around his person made him the real judge of legal governments and allowed him to weigh their actions in the balance of French national interests.

There was, of course, a strong element of romanticism, not to say mysticism, in de Gaulle's concept of his role as a sort of vicar on earth of an eternal and unchanging France. To hold such a view of his own political leadership required an overwhelming sense of mission and a boundless confidence in the correctness of his own interpretation of the transcendent value which had chosen him as its temporal representative. If such assurance were not originally contained within the "certain idea of France" held by the young de Gaulle, it is easy to see how it might have grown out of the almost miraculous career of the leader of Free France. The whole atmosphere of the *Mémoires* is messianic: it is the tale of a great national leader, like Moses, guiding his people back out of the wilderness into the Promised Land that had once been theirs. De Gaulle's success in leading Free France, in overcoming opposition from other, less 'legitimate,' Frenchmen and in asserting his country's claims before the world could not but have convinced him that his conception of France's destiny was the right one and that his own style of leadership was best fitted to convey the French idea to the world or evoke it from his fellow-countrymen. After that, his belief in his own mission was strengthened by the accuracy of his prophecies in regard to the future of the Fourth Republic. Few political predictions have been fulfilled with more apparent inevitability than that which he made to the Constituent Assembly on December 31, 1945 (see p. 2), three weeks before his resignation as head of the provisional government.

It would have required an almost superhuman modesty for de Gaulle not to draw from his own career the conclusion that his interpretation of the true interest of France was the one most consonant with the nature of French greatness and the lessons of French history. But it is also true to say that the whole bent of his thought and the impulsion of his deepest emotions predisposed him to assume the mantle of national leadership both on the spiritual and on the political plane, De Gaulle's charisma came from the fact that he desired to incarnate France, and some, at least, of his political strength was due to his having incarnated its less admirable, as well as its most valuable qualities.

Conscious of his role as the representative of an enduring France, it is understandable that de Gaulle should always have reserved his sharpest words for those groupings in the state and in society which claimed to be intermediary between himself and the French people. These forces of darkness are usually described in Gaullist language as the "feudal-ities"—the image carrying with it the implication of centrifugal forces determined to assert their own interests above those of a unitary French state and its representative, de Gaulle. "For the feudal-ities . . . have agreed to oppose the establishment of a state which would dominate all of them and hamper their intrigues. Now, it is to a state of this kind that I mean to lead the nation."[44] * Behind the acid criticisms of the 'party régime' which strew de Gaulle's writings lies the supreme reproach that, by definition, the parties cannot be represent-ative of all Frenchmen, but nevertheless intervene between the nation and the living embodiment of its collective will. To build "a political feudal system" around intellectual differences of opinion was simply "to organize the divisions of Frenchmen."[46]

The constitutional side of Gaullism will be dealt with in a later chapter, but, from what has already been said, it is easy to see how naturally de Gaulle's constitutional views coincided with the plebi-scitary democracy which has been endemic in French history from Napoleon onwards and which is perhaps, in some sense, a continuation of the consecration that endowed the kings of France with their mandate to rule. The desire for investiture by the people and not

*Speaking to a journalist, de Gaulle once defined "the feudalities" in terms of French history: "In France's history there have always been feudalities in one form or another. Today they are no longer in castles, but they exist all the same in fiefs. These fiefs are in the parties, in the trade unions, in certain sectors of business . . . of the press and the civil service etc . . ."[45]

merely by the *notables* which brought about the most major constitutional change within the period of the Fifth Republic, the need for the
executive to be directly dependent on the electorate rather than on a
legislative assembly, the insistence on the head of state's right to
address the nation, the use of the referendum to decide questions in
dispute between him and parliament—all these features of de Gaulle's
constitutional theory and practice stemmed from his assurance that his
own incarnation of France implied an uninterrupted communion with
Frenchmen which, in turn, permitted them to communicate with the
transcendent reality, France. This assurance could also have been
described as a personalized version of Rousseau's 'general will,' and it
may have been that the disturbances of May 1968 which decisively
broke the *élan* of Gaullism were due in part to the rigidity consequent
on de Gaulle's implicit hostility to the independent centers of power
found in any 'plural society.'

Much Gaullist ritual can also be traced to this feeling. The visits to
different parts of France, the plunges into crowds, the handshakes, the
speeches, the whole dialectic that de Gaulle always tried to establish
between himself and his audience were nothing less than the creation of
a visible symbol for the dynamic exchange in which the bearer of
France's destiny conveys his own sense of it to his fellow-countrymen
and receives in return—but was this always the case?—the reassurance of
this inspiration called forth by his presence. Despite the witty mockery
of a journalist like Jean-François Revel, these occasions were not
merely the exposure of a somewhat complacent monarch to the
plaudits of his subjects. They were rather the establishment of an
atmosphere in which the communion between the representative of
France and Frenchmen could be carried to a high pitch of creative
dynamism: a national solemnity generative of action.* De Gaulle was
himself exalted by the "great movement of souls" he called forth in
exalting others. If he incarnated France, the crowds that greeted him
'confessed' France through his person.

This relationship between a national leader and those who follow him
is not unusual. It is, in fact, the relationship that most charismatic
leaders have managed to achieve. It is political insofar as politics

---

*It was often noted, during the period of de Gaulle's presidency of the Fifth
Republic, that he would test future policies by references to them in his speeches
throughout France. After this communion with the French people he would
proceed to action.

signifies exemplary public action, though it has nothing in it of the manipulations and strategems of the parliamentary politician or bureaucrat. The style of de Gaulle's political action can best be compared to that of the founding fathers of nations who, by virtue of their historical situation, have also seemed to be the representatives of the whole national community. But his view of his own role was more conscious and more disillusioned than has normally been the case with such national leaders. Despite his romanticism, the realistic element in his conception of politics brought him nearer to Bismarck or Cavour than to Kossuth or Mazzini. And greater self-consciousness introduced the tragic tension which, when the exultation fades and bitter experience comes back to mind, was underlined by the strand of melancholy running through de Gaulle's thought. For if de Gaulle was present to incarnate the national will, to play the part of saviour as others had played it in the past, what would happen when he was gone, and France once again traversed the calamities brought upon it by disunity and the struggle of contending factions? This lucid pessimism, this presentiment of a kind of classical *Götterdämmerung,* conditioned de Gaulle's attitude towards his fellow-countrymen. If France fell again into disunity and confusion, it would be the imperfection of Frenchmen rather than any defect in the transcendent national idea that would be responsible for the disaster. Thus, for de Gaulle, the individual citizen was ambivalent in his virtues and potentially dangerous in his weakness, capable, no doubt, of heroism and sacrifice, but also of weakness and cowardice: "Frenchmen are calves . . . . The whole of France is a country of calves . . . "[47] The same man might respond to the 'appeal' of national unity uttered by the leader who was its symbol or listen to the 'separatists' and 'feudalities' by whom the appeal went unheard and the unity was shattered.

Yet it was to the average citizen that de Gaulle had to appeal against the *notables* of French life, and he usually appeared confident that, providing the worker or peasant was not misled, he would "choose France." It was within the world of politics, finance and administration that he seemed to discern his true adversaries. Much Gaullist polemic adopts the stance of some king of France appealing to the common people over the heads of a recalcitrant and egotistical baronage. Yet it was also true that de Gaulle never sought to exclude any section of Frenchmen from the national community. Unlike the followers of

Maurras and the classical French right, he always saw his task as one of
reconciliation rather than excommunication. Like Péguy he was both
Catholic and Jacobin. As his attitude towards the Communists
constantly showed, the part he has assumed of 'arbitrator' within the
national community was no mere facade. Just as de Gaulle accepted
both the historical tradition of the *ancien régime* and the Revolution
(something which Marc Bloch held to be essential for every patriotic
Frenchman), so, while denouncing Communist 'separatism,' he recognized in his *Mémoires* that the Communist leader, Maurice Thorez, had
performed a service to the public interest.[48] Aloofness guarantees an
icy sense of fair play. All Frenchmen were, in some sense, equal before
de Gaulle and the mission which he incarnated.

V

Some, however, were more equal than others: that is, even greater
demands were made on them in the name of France than on the mass
of Frenchmen. A perceptive witness has described the relationship
between de Gaulle and his immediate subordinates and collaborators:

> He is like a tall, icy prelate whose kingdom is France. He does not
> wish to share this kingdom, and perhaps it is not of this world. We are
> choir boys .... On the chessboard no friendship can arise between
> the knight that is moved and the hand that pushes it. I felt that he
> only realized in us the value which he himself gave us.[49]

And in the same book there is a snapshot of de Gaulle, hands on his
uniform belt, watching the ministers of the provisional government in
Algiers "like a god watching his imperfect creation."[50] Certainly, the
lot of those who worked closely with the General was not an easy one.
The fate of a Debré, whose personal loyalty was ruthlessly exploited to
further an Algerian policy of which he was known to disapprove, or of
a Pompidou, who was dismissed from office after having saved the day
in May and June 1968, is some measure of the lengths to which de
Gaulle's singleness of purpose would go in using the human material at
his disposition. A Soustelle or a Delbecque were dropped and driven
out of political life the moment their path diverged from his and within

two years of having been instrumental in preparing his return to power. The directive which de Gaulle gave to the Oran Committee of Public Safety on June 6, 1958, might in fact be applied to all those who worked for him ('for him' rather than 'with him'):

> What you have to do is to win men's minds to national unity, to the reform of France, to the support of General de Gaulle, moreover without forcing his hand, but within the framework I assign to you.[51]

This peremptory exaction of total and detailed obedience from subordinates was applied discontinuously in practice. French ministers and officials of Free France or the Fifth Republic were left considerable freedom of action within the general lines of a policy laid down by de Gaulle until the moment when the head of state considered that a question had become so crucial that it required his day to day attention. At that point the minutest details were settled at the summit.* These sudden assumptions of responsibility for some particular aspect of policy were frequently and typically motivated by de Gaulle's desire to resist encroachment on France's rights by a foreign power and by his suspicion that, without his personal attention, the attitude of French officials would not be sufficiently firm or rigorous. Allied to this discernment of precisely when a question required his own attention and of the degree of pressure needed to stimulate lagging officials was his ferocious ability to choose the right moment for a show-down with colleagues or opponents. The apology extracted from Fernand Grenier, Communist commissioner for air in the Algiers government, following the latter's accusations of the insufficiency of aid sent to the Vercors *maquis* or the ultimatum given to the leaders of the Communist-inspired "prisoners' movement" in the summer of 1945 show how brutally direct he could be at a moment when his victims least expected it. On an international scale a similarly brusque use of surprise may be perceived in the veto on British entry into the European Economic Community (EEC) in January 1963 or in the

*For example, the Melun conversations with representatives of the Algerian National Liberation Front (FLN) were planned by de Gaulle both with regard to agenda and protocol. Members of the French delegation were forbidden to shake hands with the Algerians.[52]

C

ultimatum of March 1966 summoning France's allies to leave French soil and withdrawing French forces from the unified command system of the North Atlantic Treaty Organization (NATO).

Here again de Gaulle's actions were in accordance with a theory worked out many years before he came to be endowed with supreme authority. In *Le fil de l'épée*, the qualities required of a leader were laid down in passages which read like an attempt at self-portraiture. To begin with, the leader must be a "man of character" recognizable by his readiness to assume independent responsibility:

> When faced with the challenge of events, the man of character has recourse to himself. His instinctive response is to leave his mark on action, to take responsibility for it, to make it *his own business* . . . . The man of character finds an especial attractiveness in difficulty, since it is only by coming to grips with difficulty that he can realize his potentialities . . . . Whatever the cost to himself, he looks for no higher reward than the harsh pleasure of knowing himself to be the man responsible.[53]

While inspiring his subordinates at the moment of action, he will more usually be a strict and demanding chief:

> The man of character incorporates in his own person the severity inherent in his effort. This is felt by his subordinates, and at times they groan under it. In any event, a leader of this quality is inevitably aloof, for there can be no authority without prestige, nor prestige unless he keeps his distance.[54]

Towards superiors he will be liable to fail in that discipline which he demands of others, to show impatience and arrogance in his dealings with mediocrities of the official hierarchy. In moments of crisis, however, he will be carried irresistibly to the foreground of affairs, assigned the hardest tasks, asked for his opinion, provided with the means of action he requires. All this he will accept without recrimination. "He . . . shows a generous temperament and responds whole-heartedly when he is called upon"—a phrase which might have been remembered by those who had to cope with the future General de Gaulle.[55]

The establishment of an ascendancy over those around him will be a function of the leader's prestige—a prestige which stemmed in the first place from the recognition by others of the innate qualities of his own character, but which could also be gained by the use of a deliberate strategy aimed at impressing those around him. The first recipe recommended is that of aloofness and secrecy: "a determination . . . to hold in reserve some piece of secret knowledge which may at any moment intervene, and the more effectively from being in the nature of a surprise."[56] The leader must keep his plans to himself in such a way as to rouse the curiosity and attract the attention of the masses. And this kind of reserve will be accompanied by a similar sobriety in speech and action. Public appearances will be carefully studied to produce the maximum effect; public utterances should usually be laconic, while nothing increases authority so much as silence, "the crowning virtue of the strong, the refuge of the weak, the modesty of the proud, and pride of the humble, the prudence of the wise, and the sense of fools."[57] But all this would be of little use unless it were to be accompanied by a certain grandeur of project and style. This essential strand in de Gaulle's thought has already been discussed above in connection with the collective endeavor that had to be set before the nation state if it were to rise to the height of its own great argument. On the personal level it implied the realization of great things which, since it gave satisfaction to each individual's secret desires, also secured for a leader the devotion of his followers. His avoidance of vulgarity and his scorn for inessentials were exemplary. Even if his plans come to nothing, his prestige would remain.

In *Le fil de l'épée* this discussion of leadership was specifically applied to the soldier, whose attitudes and style of behavior were contrasted with those of the politician. Nevertheless, it was only necessary to read what de Gaulle had to say of leadership and its problems to see that it was intended to be as relevant for the political, as for the military leader. There is a close resemblance between the picture of the ideal leader sketched here and the analysis of de Gaulle's own tactics made by Emmanuel d'Astier:

So, in three days, I saw him use his three weapons in unequal proportions: prestige, secrecy and guile. The guile is mediocre, but secrecy guarded by a natural, icy prestige takes him a long way.[58]

And a note of warning—or self-knowledge—was sounded when de
Gaulle wrote: "Every man of action has a strong dose of egotism, pride,
hardness, and cunning."[59] It was this side of de Gaulle's doctrine of
leadership which provided ammunition for those who, like Jacques
Soustelle, choose to consider him as a prince taken straight from the
pages of Machiavelli, and it is certain that, in the day to day political
exchange he used language as much to conceal his thought as to convey
it. But here again there was a potential conflict within de Gaulle's mind,
or, rather, the union of two disparate elements. On the one hand, there
was a cynical analysis of human nature which appealed to a long
psychological tradition for its knowledge of how men could be
influenced or impressed. On the other, this analysis was placed at the
service of a romantic idea of leadership which was entirely modern in
its inspiration. All the diplomatic finesse of the *ancien régime* became
an instrument to be used in the name of a concept of man wildly out of
tune with the French classical view of human behavior. De Gaulle's
portrait of the leader, the "man of character," would have been almost
a Latin version of the Nietzschean superman—something of a parody in
other words—if he himself had not been there to prove that a style of
leadership not unlike his ideal could in fact be realized.

VI

It is possible to enumerate the oppositions which condition de
Gaulle's thought, emotions and view of the human situation. They are
most conveniently listed in contrasting pairs:

18th century realpolitik	19th century nationalism
the *ancien régime*	the French revolutionary *grande nation*
classical restraint	romantic exultation
the *honnête homme*	the Nietzschean superman
the French tradition of classical moralists	modern vitalism (Malraux, Saint-Exupéry)

It was these conflicting elements which went to create a complex and
continually shifting balance. And if these contradictions were resolved
in "a certain idea of France," the diversity in which that idea expresses
itself stemmed from France's history, political and cultural. As

Professor Alfred Grosser has pointed out, one of the most striking features of Gaullist political doctrine is the large part played in it by history. Nor is this surprising. The elements from which de Gaulle drew his idea of France were necessarily historical elements. "He does not love men: he loves their history, above all, that of France . . . " wrote Emmanuel d'Astier.[60] Indeed, a nationalist who disposes of his fellow-countrymen as cavalierly as did de Gaulle could find an entirely satisfactory object of his veneration only in history. Contemporary France and, above all, contemporary Frenchmen may have proved disappointingly imperfect, but France's past was unchanging and eternally satisfying to the eye of faith.

De Gaulle was, after all, a historian who, in *La discorde chez l'ennemi* and *La France et son armée*, had written two highly intelligent studies.* Even a book like *Vers l'armée de métier* swarms with historical examples—some of them even appearing slightly forced. (The relevance of Varus's or Soubise's difficulties with the terrain beyond the Rhine in a book primarily dealing with the need for modern mechanized and armored forces is not entirely apparent. It looks as though many such instances are there simply because their author could not bear to leave them out.) Every point is driven home with a wealth of illustration ranging over seven hundred years of French history from Bouvines to the Marne. When de Gaulle in his *Mémoires* wishes to emphasize the degradation of Pétain and the Vichy government, it is quite natural for him to adduce the three situations in French history comparable to 1940: "Even the King of Bourges, the Restoration of 1814 and that of 1815, the government and Assembly of Versailles in 1871 had not yielded themselves to this."[61]

The high degree of historical consciousness that exists in all Frenchmen and enables such references to be understood by the average French reader is carried to extreme lengths in examples like this. Vichy is seen to be condemned by the whole of French history. But was de Gaulle's point more than a rhetorical one? Was there any real analogy between the position of Charles VII before the coming of

La discorde chez l'ennemi is a book which has hardly had justice done to it. It is an astonishingly coherent account of the First World War to have been written only six years after 1918. Despite the lack of published documents and memoirs from which de Gaulle must have suffered in writing it, it stands up very well to the passage of time.

Jeanne d'Arc and that of a government which had just been defeated by
Adolf Hitler? An even odder example of de Gaulle's historicism is to be
found in the memorandum he presented to France's military and
political leaders on January 26, 1940, which contains a final plea for
the construction of an adequate armored striking force. Urgent as such
a document might be supposed to have been and busy as were the men
for whom it was intended, it nonetheless begins with a three-page
review of the past from the failure at Crécy to the victories of Foch.[62]

History in such a case is used to establish an atmosphere of myth in
which past events point the simple moral of an *image d'Epinal* rather
than reveal their own indeterminate complexity. If de Gaulle had
derived his own idea of France from history, he had also imposed his
own pattern upon it—a pattern that involved the neglect or obliteration
of certain aspects of the past. He accepted both the Revolution and the
ancien régime, but it was by no means certain that he would accept
Candide's "Après tout, il faut cultiver notre jardin" or Rabelais's "Fay
ce que vouldras." De Gaulle's history, the history of grandeur, excluded
the day to day lives of small men. It was political and military history
rather than social or economic. And if it showed the central role played
by France in world politics, its continued interest for him depended on
France's still being in a position to take the part his passionate
attention assigned to it. For de Gaulle, 1940 was, in a very real sense,
an eclipse of history in which the diminution of France implied the
extinction of a light which alone had given interest or intelligibility to
world events. His struggle between 1940 and 1944 was to reverse the
decision of this slice of history, to render null and void the events of
one fatal summer that had reduced his country to impotence.

But if de Gaulle's wartime experience was that of a successful fight
against the verdict of history, it was also true that his career after the
war was an attempt to reverse a longer-term historical trend: the
gradual dwarfing of European countries in comparison with the
continental states of Russia and America. To preponderance in terms of
population, territory and economic power was also added the possession of weapons which allowed none of the old European nation states
to seriously entertain the idea of opposing such overwhelming military
superiority. This historical situation was confronted by de Gaulle with
the same inflexible political will as brought him success in 1940-44;
but, in this case, he was faced with a deeper movement of history than

the merely contingent catastrophe of France's defeat by Germany.

Thus de Gaulle's relationship to history was also ambivalent. In true Plutarchian style he used it as a source of exemplary instances to aid the birth of the national myth in whose name he rejected the altered position of France in the world, fighting contemporary history with the history of the more distant past for a weapon. A nationalist who draws sustenance from his country's past finds himself in some difficulty when the curve of relative national importance begins to turn downwards. It was this struggle with history which was at the heart of the tragic element in de Gaulle's thought. Beyond the mistrust of future French governments or the pessimism about the behavior of the average Frenchman if deprived of the Gaullist summons to greatness seemed to lie both a realization that the recent diminution of France was in fact irreversible and a nostalgia for the opportunities of leadership that were present even fifty years ago. All the political genius of the most effective French ruler of the twentieth century could not create the conditions necessary to re-establish any kind of concrete French influence throughout the world. What was gained from the confrontation with history was in some sense a cultural achievement rather than a political one, the incarnation of a myth valuable for its exemplary quality and its regenerating effect on the national consciousness. It is not a small thing to restore national pride and self-confidence, however little such a reintegration of the French national personality may affect the facts of world politics.

VII

The mixture of thought and emotion personal to Charles de Gaulle and best expressed by the word "doctrine" had therefore many resemblances with the romantic nationalism of the nineteenth century. The single-minded concentration on France, the appeal for national unity, the use of history to engender myth, the quasi-religious atmosphere and the almost messianic sense of mission that informed de Gaulle's utterances—all these features of Gaullist doctrine have been familiar enough in new nations.* But France was an old nation with a

*This is seen at its most extreme in various passages of the *Mémoires*, for example in the ending of Vol. II: "Now the people and the leader, helping each

political and cultural tradition stretching over hundreds of years. Instead of de Gaulle's nationalism having been revolutionary in the sense of creating a nation state *ab initio* out of the destruction of some older order, it was rather a restoration of the France (or the Frances) of the past, a recreation of a grandeur that had many prototypes. Involved in this restoration was de Gaulle's concept of *raison d'état*: his regard for the ruthless realism of the *ancien régime*. However romantic his nationalism may have been in its aspirations, its style could not have been entirely romantic since it included within itself a classical idea of France as well as a romantic one. It has sometimes been said that a nation state must have existed since the sixteenth century to deserve that title as far as de Gaulle was concerned. Certainly, his form of nationalism was only conceivable in terms of such a nation.

Yet, as has been remarked already, Gaullist doctrine has been very different from the *nationalisme intégral* of *Action française*, the pre-1914 nationalists or the leagues of the thirties. As René Rémond has pointed out, Gaullism has preserved the alliance of a plebiscitary democracy with nationalism which was discarded by the French right after Boulanger.[64] De Gaulle's doctrine cut across the line between right and left which runs through French political thought. Despite the coincidence of his views on a strong presidency with the demands for a strengthened executive periodically put forward by right-wing movements, there were few signs that de Gaulle was much affected by the thought of Maurras or other intellectual leaders of the right from 1900 onwards. If the well-known quotation "Maurras has been so right that he has become mad because of it" expresses a certain admiration, it also implies such strong reservations as to destroy much of the effect.[65] Barrès and Péguy are perhaps the only figures whose influence was discernible in any marked fashion, and this seems to have been exerted rather as part of a general current of vitalist, romantic thought than as a doctrinaire nationalism. The relationship to the mass of Frenchmen in which de Gaulle saw himself was completely foreign to the imperative of *ordre social* which commanded French right-wing thinking since the Revolution. During his career de Gaulle brought the French bourgeoisie not so much social order as a call to action and national greatness. Nor

---

other, were to begin the journey to salvation."[63] The French word *guide* here should be translated by *guide* rather than by *leader*—a change which emphasizes the messianic quality of the passage.

did he show much respect at times either for the Church or *autorités sociales* on which French right-wing parties were usually based. Coming from a devout Catholic family with a father who was a professor in a Jesuit college (but who was also a Dreyfusard), de Gaulle never displayed much religious feeling except insofar as he identified the Church with its creative role in French history: "the Catholic religion is part of the political structure of France," he remarked to Soustelle.[66] The metaphysical side of his own works distilled an atmosphere of lucid pessimism rather than any confidence in the ultimate possibilities of divine providence. *Gesta Dei per Francos* is as far as he went.

De Gaulle's thought had already taken on its definitive form very early in his career. In *Le fil de l'épée*, published in 1932, it received its most concise and striking expression. From that time on it was only concealed through tactical necessity. What de Gaulle learned during the war years and his twelve years exile in the wilderness of Colombey-les-deux-Eglises was rather suppleness in political maneuver and skill in negotiation than anything that changed the structure of his basic beliefs. Behind the necessities of day to day politics was a view of the world which, in the final analysis, determined the attitude of the General toward the major choices presented to him. But, in its application, this view was modified by experience. It was experience that taught de Gaulle to perceive the developments threatening France as well as those likely to serve the cause of its greatness. The categories of good and evil as far as France's destiny was concerned always existed in Gaullist thought. The allocation into those categories of men, nations and historical trends was a matter of experience and, in any case, had to alter with time since there could be no question here of constants. Thus the experience of de Gaulle and his followers—in the first place their experience of the moribund Third Republic—had a profound effect on practical results which, nonetheless, were based on a set of immutable ideas that formed the inner sanctum of Gaullist belief.

C*

CHAPTER II

The Third Republic: Prelude to Failure

Un gouvernement républicain a la vertu pour principe; sinon la terreur. Que veulent ceux qui ne veulent ni vertu ni terreur? . . .

—*Saint-Just*

On June 28, 1919, the day of the signature of the Treaty of Versailles, it might have seemed that the Third French Republic had reached its apotheosis. It had been born out of the defeat of the Franco-Prussian war and the civil strife of the Commune. Despite the loss of the heavy industry of Alsace-Lorraine and a war indemnity of five billion francs, it had recovered from this difficult start. A series of political crises and scandals—Panama, Boulanger, Dreyfus—and the alienation from the régime of a large section of the Catholic right had not prevented the republic taking root ever more deeply throughout a France that was still largely rural. In face of a more heavily populated and more industrialized Germany, France had reformed its army, acquired allies and founded an overseas empire in the teeth of metropolitan opinion. By 1914, when the great powers blundered into war, the durability of the Third Republic and the skill of its political directors seemed established. Whatever might be the failings of pre-1914 French politicians, compared with the leaders of Wilhelmian Germany they and their policies appeared models of common sense. Thus, after the torment of a war largely fought on French soil, Versailles, presided over for France by a Clemenceau, implacably determined to exact the last ounce of advantage from the victory, seemed pre-eminently a success of the Third Republic as well as a promise of French supremacy in Europe for many years to come.

But appearances here were delusive, and the somewhat paranoid style of French nationalism between 1919 and 1939 suggests that this was realized subconsciously while being carefully excluded from the conscious thoughts of politicians and officials. In retrospect, of course, it is easy enough to see the hollowness of the Third Republic's achievement. For de Gaulle and many future Gaullists, who were in their teens or early twenties during this period, the last phase of the Third Republic was to be one in which foreign policy and national defense were to be disastrously mismanaged; in which faulty institutions and factious political parties compounded the disunity of Frenchmen; in which inadequate understanding of economic factors brought about years of industrial stagnation and a failure to equip France with the technology of the twentieth century. All this made a profound impression on the men who were later to manage the affairs of the Fourth and Fifth French Republics. Gaullism in particular was to harp upon the themes of firmness abroad and unity at home and also to make its own a 'productivism' which had already been adopted by the Fourth Republic under the impulsion of Jean Monnet and those economists and statisticians he had gathered around him at the *Commissariat Général du Plan*. The experience of the last twenty years of the Third Republic is therefore highly relevant to the analysis of Gaullism, constituting a sort of negative pole against which the Gaullist movement reacted (even while operating in much of the same basic framework). All these themes—a fumbling foreign policy, disunity and economic stagnation at home—were to be drawn together in the searing experience of 1940 which provided the initial psychological shock needed to create the Gaullist movement.

II

As regards foreign policy and defense, it would have been easy enough for percipient observers of the Third Republic to see what was coming. The changes in the European balance of power brought about by the war—in particular, the total disappearance of Austria-Hungary and the temporary eclipse of Russia—left France face to face with a Germany whose population of sixty million (as against France's forty million) made it by far the strongest continental power. Of the wartime alliance there remained a connection with Britain which was to grow stronger again as Hitler emerged over the horizon, but which rarely resulted in common policies. France and Great Britain went to war together in 1939, as they had in 1914, but, before that, they had only occasionally acted in unison, and, when they did, it was usually to retreat. In any case, for France, Britain could never be a substitute for a strong continental ally with a large conscript army. Just how true this was was proved in 1940.

The object of French foreign policy during the period between the wars was, therefore, to build a security system for France with the aim of holding Germany to the Treaty of Versailles. And, for this purpose, it seemed logical to create alliances with those East European states which owed their very existence to Versailles and Trianon and which might be supposed to provide an 'eastern front' against Germany as Russia had done before 1914. In 1921, France signed a defensive military alliance with Poland; in 1924 with Czechoslovakia which was already linked with Yugoslavia and Rumania in the Little Entente. On the western front a defensive alliance with Belgium was concluded in 1920—an alliance from which Belgium was to withdraw by a reaffirmation of its neutrality after the German reoccupation of the Rhineland in 1936.

But this system of alliances designed to force a war on a resurgent Germany on two fronts if necessary, was combined with a defensive military strategy which, as de Gaulle himself foresaw, doomed it to failure.[1] The fortifications on France's eastern frontier which took their name from André Maginot, minister of war between 1929 and 1932, might have been useful if they had been prolonged to cover the Belgian frontier or masked the maneuvers of the armored striking force for which de Gaulle campaigned throughout the thirties, but all the experience of the French generals during the First World War predisposed them to believe in the superiority of firepower ensconced behind fortifications over any attacker. This, in particular, was the view of Marshal Pétain who had always been a believer in the power of the defensive, whose prescience had been demonstrated by the bloody failure of 'Plan XVII' in 1914 and who had enormous influence over

French defense policy between the wars.* French military orthodoxy was dominated by the memory of the appalling losses suffered between 1914 and 1918. Its point of view was well enough expressed by the Minister of War, General Maurin, who in the mid-thirties, told the chamber: "When we have devoted so many efforts to building up a fortified barrier, is it conceivable that we would be mad enough to go ahead of this barrier, into I know not what adventure?"[3] Here again the result was to be seen in 1940 when, to Churchill's questions as to what was to be done with France's strategic reserve, the only answer that could be given was "There is none."* *

With these inadequate means France's last real attempt to keep Germany to the letter of Versailles was Poincaré's occupation of the Ruhr in January 1923, following the Reparation Commission's condemnation of Germany for falling behind with deliveries. Despite the collapse of German passive resistance, the international isolation of France and the breach created between French and British policies made it quite clear that this kind of operation could not be repeated. Moreover, the French left, which shared the liberal, Wilsonian conceptions of world organization, had been shocked by Poincaré's use of force.

With the arrival in power of the *Cartel des Gauches* on May 11, 1924, the new policy—that associated with the name of Aristide Briand—was put into effect. France accepted the Dawes plan for the modification of reparations in the summer of 1924 and signed the Locarno treaty on December 1, 1925. Locarno, with its system of reciprocal guarantees based on the status quo, might have met France's need for security, and the relationship between Briand and Stresemann prefigured a later and more lasting Franco-German reconciliation. But the positive results of this attempt to construct a solid international security system out of

---

*Holding these views, it is all the odder that he should have opposed the construction of fortifications along the Belgian frontier. In 1932 a proposal by Weygand and Gamelin to cover northern France by a continuation of the Maginot line was turned down by Pétain on the grounds that the French would have to advance into Belgium—precisely what they did in 1940 with disastrous results.[2]

**"On many later occasions during the war, Churchill evoked the scene at the Quai d'Orsay on the afternoon of the 16th . . . above all, Gamelin's shattering, unbelievable answer to his question: 'Where are the reserves, where is the *masse de manoeuvre?* ' 'There is none,' said Gamelin, 'il n'y en a pas . . . ' "[4]

the unpromisingly heterogeneous elements left behind by the war, foundered in the great depression that helped to bring Hitler to power in Germany in 1933. After that, there was nothing for it but to revert to a policy of defensive alliances. In 1935 it fell to Pierre Laval to travel reluctantly and incongruously to Moscow to ratify the Franco-Soviet alliance. The Hoare-Laval agreement of the same year was a desperate attempt to keep Italy as a potential French ally. But in 1936 and 1938 France could neither prevent German military reoccupation of the Rhineland—a breach of the treaties of Versailles and Locarno—nor save its Czechoslovak ally. In 1939 it was Poland's turn, and, this time, France did move, but unwillingly and with forebodings that were to be fully justified.

Meanwhile, the same division that had appeared in French opinion over Poincaré's reparations policy had also made itself felt, with disastrous inappropriateness, over the attitude adopted toward Hitler. Part of the right—a Paul Reynaud or a Louis Marin—took the traditional national line. They wanted to stand up to Germany, modernize the French army (it was Reynaud who provided the political support for de Gaulle's schemes) and keep close to Britain, France's ally. But others on the right saw things very differently. Their view was succinctly expressed by Charles Maurras in *Action française* (January 11, 1937):

Among the readers of the *Action française* not one ignores or can possibly ignore that their country's Enemy No. 1 is Germany ... After Hitler, or, who knows, before him on quite another plane, there is another enemy. It is the democratic Republic, the elective and parliamentary régime legally superimposed like a grotesque and repugnant mask on the true essence of France.[5]

Even if the majority of right-wing politicians still accepted the republican régime, even if the proto-Fascist 'leagues' had little success with the provincial bourgeoisie that made up the mass of conservative France, there were still many whose dislike of the *Front populaire* led them to a grudging admiration of the 'strong' governments in Germany and Italy.

Moreover, the Spanish Civil War had polarized opinion, in France as elsewhere, with an intensity that influenced the general view of international politics held by individuals. But if the right was often scared of communism, the left was impotent in face of national-socialism and all that it represented. Deeply pacifist by instinct, French Socialists were hard put to make the changes in attitude required by a world where the ideas of Briand were no longer relevant, and where the facts of the situation were obscured in a fog of recrimination and ideological bickering.* It was easier for the Communists to make a sudden switch in their opposition to French rearmament when the necessities of Soviet foreign policy demanded it of them. But they, in their turn, were to be thrown into confusion by the Russo-German pact of August 1939—a confusion from which they recovered only after Hitler's attack on the Soviet Union.

Thus the background to the last twenty-one years of the Third Republic was one of fear of a German *revanche* which, when it was finally seen to be justified, was realized in a form that, because of its ideological content, was deeply divisive of French opinion. Between 1919 and 1939 French statesmen failed to find a solution to the problem of living next door to a far stronger Germany increasingly resentful of the Versailles "Diktat." And de Gaulle, observing their failure between 1932 and 1937 from the vantage point of the prime minister's defense secretariat (*Secrétariat général de la défense nationale*), could hardly fail to be reinforced in his opinion that France must rely on its own strength rather than on that of hesitant allies. But that strength, if it were to be built up, needed a continuous and, if it were to be wielded, a firm direction of the state. The reality of the closing years of the Third Republic was the opposite:

Hardly had the Premier taken office when he was at grips with innumerable demands, criticisms and bids for favor, which all his energy was absorbed in warding off without ever contriving to master them. Parliament, far from supporting him, offered him nothing but ambushes and desertions. His ministers were his rivals. Opinion, the Press and sectional interests regarded him as the proper target for all complaints. Everyone, indeed—and he first of all—knew that he was there for only a short time. In fact, after a few months, he had to give place to another.[7]

*The pacifism of the left was well expressed by the member of the *Syndicat national des instituteurs* (SNI) who, at a national congress, cried "Anything rather than war! . . . There is no glory in being a hero for one or another country. In the end there is only one glory: to be alive." The date of the congress was August 1933![6]

Early on the evils of ministerial instability and the need for a strong executive became a part of de Gaulle's personal convictions as they were later to become one of the main political planks in the Gaullist platform.

III

The political history of the declining Third Republic has a certain regularity of pattern about it despite its apparent anarchy. The key to this pattern is contained in André Siegfried's lapidary remark that a Frenchman's heart is on the left, but his pocket on the right.[8] It was because many French deputies, while voting on the left on political or ideological issues, would turn to the right as soon as it came to economic questions, that chambers elected to execute left-wing policies like those of the *Cartel des Gauches* in 1924 or the *Front populaire* in 1936 could end by producing quite an opposite orientation, in the one case supporting Poincaré's *Union nationale* government formed to save the franc, in the other, under the stress of military defeat, voting the Third Republic out of existence and granting full powers to Pétain. This dichotomy between the Frenchman as politician and the Frenchman as taxpayer had, of course, existed before 1914 and can be traced back to a Revolution which firmly established an almost insuperable physical and ideological obstacle to further upheavals: the conservative power of the small peasant holding. But before 1914 the main struggles of political life took place on a number of familar ideological battlefields: the relations between church and state, educational policy, anti-militarism.* After the war these were no longer real issues, but it was only when such themes could be invoked that there was any chance of a left-wing majority appearing either in the country or the chamber. For their part the Catholic, right-wing parties could gain support on their left by the use of economic and financial questions as they had never been able to do before the war when their own rejection of the régime and the 'republican discipline' of the left barred them from governmental office. Now that they had fought for the despised

*As Albert Thibaudet put it, "The normal platform of the Radical party is a spiritual platform or one concerned with the spiritual."[9]

republic, it could no longer be held against them that they refused to accept 'the revolution as a whole.'

French politics, in fact, were changing; property interests were replacing the purity of a deputy's acceptance of the events of 1792 as a decisive determinant of the alliances and alignments that created governments. This, however, did little to diminish the intensity of party warfare. Indeed, it added a new dimension of bitterness to it by giving the left a bewildered sense of betrayal at every defection from their majority. For it was in the interests of the left to conceal even from themselves the new evolution, since, whereas the old ideological war cries united majorities, the new economic struggles divided them. Thus in 1924 Edouard Herriot's government of the *Cartel des Gauches* had as its program the application of anticlerical legislation to Alsace and Lorraine (which were still administered under a concordat with the Vatican), the withdrawal of the French ambassador to the Holy See, the strict application of the law controlling the religious orders and the introduction of free secondary education under the slogan of the 'single school'—a definition which made it look as if the independent Catholic schools were threatened. But the problem which dominated Herriot's eleven months of office was that of stabilizing the franc, and to this ideology provided no answer. In April 1925, his government was brought down by the senate following the revelation that the legal limits of the circulation of banknotes had been exceeded as well as the state's power of borrowing from the Banque de France.

Twelve years later, in June 1937, Léon Blum, head of the *Front populaire* government of 1936, was also overthrown by the senate which refused his request for 'full power' to deal with a worsening economic and financial situation. The immediate cause of his defeat was growing international pressure on the franc, but the flight of capital was merely one symptom of a more general failure of economic policy. No doubt, with the threat of war growing and increasing domestic and international confusion, it was not the moment for a French government to resolve the delicate problem of how to follow a left-wing policy without the means to effectively control the flight of capital. But the *Front populaire* government had little in the way even of information about the economic condition of France and its policies were those of ignorance. In particular, it failed to see the disastrous effect of the introduction of the forty-hour week upon the general level of economic activity. Despite two devaluations, in May 1938, after the second Blum government and the end of the *Front populaire,* the index of industrial production was at 82 as compared with 87 in May 1936, when the first Blum government took office.[10] It is not surprising that a recent historian should write that "Léon Blum did not succeed in changing himself from a skillful leader of the opposition to an energetic head of government."[11] The social intentions of the *Front populaire* did represent a more serious attempt to better the lot of the French industrial worker than had been made under the Third Republic. But however well-intentioned the measures that were carried out—the forty-hour week, holidays with pay, a law on collective agreements, an immediate rise in pay of about twelve percent for all workers—may have been, some of them were ill-conceived economically, and there was no realization on the part of the government that, in order to succeed, it would have to bring about economic expansion. Nor was it helped towards more effectively expansionist economic policies by the workers' occupation of factories and by the general atmosphere of revolutionary rhetoric that immediately accompanied its coming to power.

Thus two governments of the left starting out with vaguely reformist intentions were finally brought down in the upper house on an economic issue. It is not surprising, therefore, that left-wing militants should have chosen to console themselves with the 'wall of money' theory of a conspiracy by financial oligarchies against the popular will. Conspiracies there may have been—certainly there was alarm and dislike directed towards the *Front populaire*—but there was also the simple fact that, while Frenchmen did not want a totally Socialist system of the kind discussed by intellectuals and invoked in the rhetoric of politicians, left-wing reformers did not know enough to make the economic life of France respond to their good intentions. But in 1936 expectations of the coming of a new heaven and a new earth ran high among the French working-class. The disappointment it suffered when the promised land failed to materialize—either because of the presumed machinations of the money power or else the weakness of Blum and his colleagues—was great and left an inheritance of bitterness which neither the Fourth nor the Fifth Republic has been quite able to dispel despite all attempts.

The fact that the French Communist party, while supporting the

Front populaire, did not participate in its government meant that it was able to take advantage of this disillusionment. It is during the thirties that we begin to see a steady rise in the Communist vote and the successful take-over bid for the Socialists' industrial working-class supporters, the results of which were to dominate the political life of the Fourth Republic. As one writer has put it, "The Socialists were taking the part of neo-Girondism to the neo-Jacobinism of the Communists, and such a situation was politically fatal in a country where historical myths are major determinants of current attitudes . . . "[12] The growth of fascism abroad and at home was to the advantage of the Communists, whose opposition to Hitler and Mussolini appeared—delusively enough—more vigorous and less hamstrung by pacifist scruples than that of the Socialists. The communiqué issued after Laval's visit to Moscow in May 1935 contained the phrase "Stalin understands and fully approves the policy of national defense pursued by France in order to maintain its armed forces at a level consistent with its security," and this was to provide a framework in which French Communists could take their place as part of a 'united front' against fascism.[13] The last and most violent of the Third Republic's scandals, the Stavisky case, had produced an explosion of agitation on the part of the right-wing leagues which, after the rioting of February 6, 1934, and the resignation of the Daladier government forced by right-wing demonstrations, made it look as though a *coup d'état* were to be expected from the same direction. It is possible now to see that nothing of the sort was at all likely, but, at the time, the Communists profited from their energy and decision in defense of working-class interests as well as from their newly donned patriotic mantle of resistance to the threat from beyond the Rhine. In the 1936 chamber their representation increased from 10 to 72 deputies.*

The build-up of Communist strength under the Third Republic, the party's implantation of itself in its working-class and rural strongholds, were to prove one of the most unchanging features of French politics after 1945. But on the right too the last years of the Third Republic saw an evolution which was to have its importance later on. It was in the late thirties that the French right proved conclusively that it was

*The percentage of registered voters voting Communist at the elections between the wars was as follows: 1924–7.9; 1928–9.3; 1932–6.8; 1936–12.6.[14]

conservative rather than Fascist, profoundly traditionalist and scared by the prospect of social change, but, for that very reason, unwilling to embark on any totalitarian adventure. The 'leagues' might be able to create disorder in Paris with the help of their student henchmen from the *Quartier latin*, but the provinces remained unmoved. France was perhaps insufficiently industrialized, too untouched by any experience such as the inflation in Germany, its middle-class too deeply rooted in republican traditions for a totalitarian mass movement of the right to be possible.* In this connection the history of Colonel de la Rocque's *Croix de Feu* movement is significant. Starting as a para-military formation with a vague program, it transformed itself into a regular political party, the *Parti social français* (PSF), after Blum's dissolution of the 'leagues' on June 18, 1936. From being a movement existing outside the republican system it became a party like the others and bigger than any of them, claiming in 1938 a membership of three million. Its success in its new role—greater than that which it had enjoyed before—shows conclusively that, while the French right-wing voter was not prepared to take the risk of a change of régime, he was willing to give his support to a mass conservative party of a kind which had previously existed in French politics.[16] In many ways the PSF, although its appeal was never to be tested in legislative elections, foreshadows such political formations of the Fourth Republic and Fifth Republic as the Gaullist *Rassemblement du peuple français* (RPF) and *Union pour la nouvelle république* (UNR) and the non-Gaullist *Centre national des indépendants* (CNI)—all of them loose right-wing coalitions which could muster considerable numbers of members and voters. Between the PSF and the inheritors of its position came the Vichy régime which, despite its authoritarian overtones, also demonstrated the real conservatism of the French right. For the widespread consent which Vichy received in 1940-41 was due, not so much to its ideological connections with *Action française* or its technocratic side, as to the reassuringly paternal personality of the Marshal and its appeal to traditional values. The genuine ideological Fascists (or National-

*The 'leagues' included Georges Valois's *Faisceau*, Pierre Taittinger's *Jeunesses Patriotes*, Marcel Bucard's *Francisme*, Jean Renaud's *Solidarité française*, Colonel de la Rocque's *Croix de Feu* and Jacques Doriot's *Parti populaire français* (PPF). According to Professor Rémond, only Doriot's PPF can be considered as genuinely Fascist in character. Significantly, Doriot had been a prominent figure in the Communist party.[15]

Socialists) of *Gringoire, Je Suis partout* and Radio Paris were never able to attract anything in the way of a following among the right-wing bourgeoisie.

In the last decade of the Third Republic, then, there began to appear the political patterns—including a left split between Communists and the rest, and a right capable of a loose unity—which would dominate postwar France.

IV

Other trends too—social and economic trends this time—would be continued in the years to come or would be reversed as a result of a repudiation of the *damnosa hereditas* of the interwar period. The thirties in France were a time of economic stagnation when production fell under the influence of the world economic recession or was sacrificed to maintain an artificially high value for the franc, and much of the emphasis placed on growth under the Fourth and Fifth Republics sprung from the determination of a number of economists and engineers, who had lived through this depressing decade, that its experience of stagnation should not be repeated. The 'productivism' which has dominated French economic thinking since the war and has also expressed itself in the ethos of the European Economic Community, was founded on the realization of the mistakes made in the thirties.

At the time of the signature at Versailles, France's economic situation had the same mixture of apparent advantages and real weakness as its political position in Europe. At this time it was already clear just how heavy France's losses during the war had been. The worst aspect of this was the diminution of an already shrinking population. 1,310,000 Frenchmen had been killed or had disappeared in the fighting (ten and a half percent of the active male population). But the diminution of population (excluding Alsace-Lorraine) was far greater: 2,900,000 taking into account an increase in civilian deaths and the fall in the birthrate. On the material side, the damage amounted to some 55 billion 1913 francs—a figure which included losses resulting from the German occupation of France's northern provinces as well as from the liquidation of a part of the Banque de France's gold reserves.[17]

Nothing could be done about the human losses which still further weakened France's ability to maintain its position in Europe, but French public opinion confidently expected that the defeated enemy would be forced to meet the material damage. "Germany will pay" was the phrase which was pronounced before the armistice was signed. But the difficulties in the way of its realization were overlooked even by the experts. At first French representatives had spoken of 800 billion gold marks in reparations; finally, after long negotiations, the occupation of the Ruhr and two different plans for settlement (the Dawes plan of 1924 and the Young plan of 1929), France got far less than had been expected: 9,580 million gold marks between 1918 and 1931. During this period France, for its part, was burdened with war debts of $3,991 million to the United States and $3,030 to Great Britain. These were not finally disposed of until their repudiation by the chamber in December 1932 had brought down another Herriot government.[18]

Another legacy of the war was inflation and the depreciation of the franc. This was a problem which had not been present before 1914, and successive governments grappled ineffectually with it. Between 1919 and 1926 the franc fell from 5.45 to the dollar to a low of 40.95 (July 1926). Only with the arrival in power of Poincaré could stabilization of the rate of exchange be achieved at 25.33 francs to the dollar (December 1926). In 1928, a new law established the rate of the franc at 25.53 to the dollar. Poincaré had succeeded where even the presiding genius of prewar French finance, Caillaux, had failed, but the success was due to a rigorously applied deflation which included the raising of bank rate to 7.5 percent and increased taxation (income tax, however, was reduced). The price which had to be paid was a recession during 1927 in industrial production which, however, showed a recovery between 1928 and 1930—only to be hit by the depression from 1931 onwards.[19]

Poincaré's deflation with its accompanying industrial stagnation was to set the tone for a major failure of France's economy during the thirties. Successive governments met the crisis caused by the depression with more deflation and a franc held at an artificially high level. The result was catastrophic for French industry. It was only in 1924 that industrial production had sufficiently got over the effects of the war for its index to pass that of 1913 by a few points. Almost immediately, expansion was again compressed by Poincaré, and, when the deflationary grip was relaxed, the economic crisis overwhelmed France together with most other countries. At first the crisis did not affect France as directly as it did Great Britain, America and Germany; the best figures for industrial production were in the first months of 1930. But by 1931, under the influence of the devaluation of the pound and the Hoover moratorium, the depression was making itself felt. Perhaps its advent had been delayed by André Tardieu's 'policy of prosperity,' the only systematic attempt at an expansionist economic policy made in France between the wars which was, however, doomed to failure both by its timing and the insufficient economic knowledge behind it. Once the depression arrived, stagnation set in. Between 1930 and October 1938 the annual index of industrial production dropped by 21 percent. The devaluation of the franc which might have prevented stagnation was eventually carried out under the *Front populaire,* but its effect was destroyed by an ill-advised attempt to increase employment by shortening the hours of work (the forty-hour week). Only at the very end of the Third Republic, when Paul Reynaud became minister of finance, was a policy instituted with a solid basis in economic fact and theory. But by then it was too late for such a policy to bear fruit.[20]

V

A feeble foreign and defense policy, disunity at home, a stagnant economy—it is no wonder that France should have gone into the Second World War expecting to lose it or that younger men observing the failure of the system should have reacted strongly against it under subsequent French régimes. In May and June 1940 hardly more than a month was required to break the resolution of the leaders of the Third Republic. After the German breakthrough at Sedan, Dunkirk and the renewed battles along the Somme and the Aisne, there only remained the long, painful road to Bordeaux for Reynaud and his ministers, harassed with demands for an armistice from generals who, like Pétain and Weygand, "wished at all costs to stop a game they had ceased to understand."[21] On June 16, 1940, Reynaud was replaced as prime minister by Pétain who announced to the country the next day his determination to ask for an armistice from the Germans. On that same day de Gaulle, who had fought skillfully and persistently at the head of his armored troops near Laon and in the Abbeville bridgehead, before becoming under-secretary for defense in the Reynaud government, flew to England with General Spears. On June 18 he was to launch his famous appeal to his fellow-countrymen and inaugurate Free France (*La France libre*).

The end of the Third Republic, the leaderless confusion and the intriguing of Bordeaux, the total failure of authority rubbed in the lessons drawn from ministerial instability in a way that a new generation of Frenchmen proved able to understand. In particular, the example of the virtual effacement of the President of the republic, Albert Lebrun, was to provide powerful support for Gaullist arguments in favor of a strong presidential executive. This somber climax to the history of the Third Republic underlined the failure of the system as nothing else could have. The consequences of political disunity pointed to the need for a strong executive, and institutions which could resist party warfare. The consequences of economic stagnation pointed to the need for energetically pursued policies of expansion. A new school of technocrats and administrators was to react against the past and in favor of a political system that would enable them to carry out their plans without the delays imposed by politically weak governments. Under the Fourth and Fifth Republics these trends would express themselves in action, and the party system would gradually evolve to a point where the natural majority would be seen to be of the right as it had been of the left before 1914. But to take advantage of this situation required a man endowed with the charisma of national leadership during a supreme crisis and surrounded by followers whose devotion was unshakable. In London and Algiers de Gaulle was to acquire the prestige which made him France's last card in 1958. And Gaullism was to take on a number of the special characteristics which have distinguished it as a political movement.

CHAPTER III

The War Years:
The Founding of Gaullism

*La France a perdu une bataille! Mais la France
n'a pas perdu la guerre!*
—*Charles de Gaulle:
Proclamation to all Frenchmen,
London, July 1940*

*Croyez-vous qu'en 1940 un homme de bon sens
pouvait imaginer autre chose que la victoire de
l'Allemagne?*
—*Pierre Laval at the trial of
Philippe Pétain,
Paris, August 1945*

The history of the Gaullist Free French movement (*La France libre*)
during the Second World War can be divided into three parts. First
came the period from June 1940 to the spring of 1943 when de Gaulle
was established in London. This ended with his arrival in Algiers on
May 30, 1943. During this time Free France—which became Fighting
France (*La France combattante*) from July 29, 1942, onward—
gradually expanded its authority in metropolitan France, in the French

colonies and within the alliance against Germany. Secondly, there was the Algerian period which lasted until de Gaulle's return to Paris on August 25, 1944, and which saw the founding of the *Comité Français de Libération Nationale* (CFLN). On June 3, 1944, this became the *Gouvernement Provisoire de la République française* (GPRF). Finally, after the liberation of France from the German occupier, there was the period when de Gaulle headed the French government. It was his resignation on January 20, 1946, which really marked the transition to the Fourth Republic, whose institutions, however, were only to be decided later.

From the moment of de Gaulle's first appeal to the French people the immediate purpose of the Free French movement was clearly defined. The Vichy régime which had yielded to the 'law of the enemy' was denied the quality of a truly national French government. This being so, a 'new power' would have to assume the responsibility of guiding France through the war.[1] The aim was to restore the independence and the greatness of France; the means to this end would be a growing revulsion on the part of the French people at the shameful conditions of the armistice and an ever increasing measure of resistance to German domination.

The complex task of re-establishing France's position in the world involved giving battle on three fronts. Immediately there was the fight against the German enemy and the creation of a renewed French presence in the field. But there was also de Gaulle's struggle for recognition by the Allies as the custodian of France's rights and interests. Only if he and Free France were regarded as the legitimate representatives of the French state could his inflexible defense of the national patrimony be effective. For this recognition to be forthcoming, however, the Allies had to be shown that the French people were behind de Gaulle and his followers, and before any such demonstration could be achieved, the French people must be convinced of the bankruptcy of Pétain's régime, for which there had existed 'a very broad consensus' in June and July 1940.[2] Thus Free France, as well as following its military struggle against the Germans, undertook a political struggle against Vichy and, secondarily, against its own allies as the champion of France's world position. Without the military effort, which provided an exemplary pledge of the Gaullists' patriotism, all the political moves would have been unavailing, but, in terms of the history of Gaullism, the political direction imparted by de Gaulle was even more significant.

The most immediate effect of his proclamation was to pose the question of *legitimacy*—a word of some importance in the Gaullist vocabulary. As one early follower in metropolitan France was to write many years later:

> No legitimacy ever appeared more blinding than his to us at that moment. That legitimacy called up for us the idea of a law founded on justice, honor and equity; a law infinitely superior to that which all the Vichy lawyers could teach us as being legality.[3]

In the eyes of de Gaulle and his adherents they themselves were the true heirs to France's past—an inheritance forfeited by the Vichy government from the moment of Pétain's demand for an armistice. Total intransigence on the principle of France's rights accompanied a total refusal to compromise with those Frenchmen who had yielded to the invader, though the execution of these policies was often supple in detail.

The Gaullist stance of these war years, which aimed at maintaining France's rights both against enemies and allies, was to be characteristic of the foreign policy of the Fifth Republic. In his difficult search for French autonomy in the field of international relations, de Gaulle never accepted the view that "my enemy's enemy is my friend." The suspicions nourished by himself and his followers during the war of American and British intentions in regard to France were a striking application in practice of his belief in the fundamentally egotistical character of states.* It is small wonder that Jacques Soustelle, writing years later, could entitle his account of Free France *Envers et contre tout.*

---

*Some of these suspicions are still alive in the work of French historians. René Hostache in his book *Le Conseil national de la Résistance*, Paris, 1958 (Presses universitaires de France) asks "Was not the real aim of the English government—an aim more political than military— above all to prevent this unification of the Resistance, and the reconstitution of internal or external institutions which would allow France to make its voice heard among the Allies?" (pp. 22-3) This seems to fall into the realm of myth, and M. R. D. Foot has replied suitably to it in his history of the Special Operations Executive's (SOE) activities in France. But the legend probably satisfies consumer needs too well to be easily contradicted.

II

The most immediate adversary, however, was the Vichy régime installed in power by the law of July 10, 1940, which gave 'full powers' to Marshal Pétain to produce a new constitution for France and a new device for the French state: *Travail, Famille, Patrie* instead of *Liberté, Egalité, Fraternité*. This law was voted by the National Assembly (the chamber and senate sitting together) by 569 votes to 80 with 17 abstentions. It was completed by a number of 'constitutional acts' on July 12. These gave full legislative, executive and judicial powers to Marshal Pétain, abolished the office of president of the republic, and recessed the senate and chamber which, in future, would only be allowed to meet if called together by the head of state. The vice-president of the council of ministers and the Marshal's intended successor was Pierre Laval. The cabinet, which was to be reshuffled some two months later on September 6, contained such right-wing figures as Raphael Alibert, Adrien Marquet (to be eliminated in the reshuffle) and Paul Baudoin as well as technicians such as Yves Bouthillier (Finance) and Pierre Caziot (Agriculture). The main result of the September changes was to get rid of the few remaining politicians and bring in a number of generals and admirals including Admiral Darlan.

The story of the Vichy régime after its foundation has a melancholy monotony about it relieved only by the court intrigues which centered on the person of Marshal Pétain. Otherwise it is a record of ineffective resistance to German pressure followed by concessions made in the vain hope that the Occupation authorities too would concede something, of empty gestures of defiance followed by passive acceptance of *faits accomplis* created by a brutal partner whose demands became more extreme as his hopes of winning the war diminished. The technicians in the government might fight German demands on French agriculture or prevent German control of French companies; the Marshal might evade pressing requests to re-enter the war on the German side. But Vichy could not stop the appointment of *Gauleiters* for Alsace and Lorraine in August 1940, and had to accept every indignity from the German execution of hostages to the application of anti-Jewish laws and the institution of a service of compulsory labor in Germany (*Service obligatoire de travail*) which did more to create active opposition to itself and the occupier than any other single measure during these years.

Even the one political action carried out in defiance of the Germans, the arrest of Laval on December 13, 1940, was soon followed by new capitulations: the departure of Pierre-Etienne Flandin from the ministry of foreign affairs in the following February and the Berchtesgaden conversations between Hitler and Darlan in May 1941, which ended in promises of economic and military collaboration on the latter's part.* In the end the German occupation of the 'free' zone on November 11, 1942, failed to produce any reaction on the part of Vichy—now directed once again by Laval. Even those parts of the 'armistice' army which had planned renewed resistance were unable to react with the exception of a foray by General de Lattre de Tassigny which was soon brought to an end. In terms of the results achieved, the Gaullists' total condemnation of the policies followed by Vichy was amply justified.

In fact, there were several policies followed by the Vichy government corresponding to differences among the supporters of the régime (that they amounted to much the same in the end merely shows that it was the Germans who called the tune throughout). The policy which was most closely associated with the name 'Vichy'—the policy of Laval—was probably the least representative of the ideas of the régime's supporters. As a somewhat dubious political inheritance from the Third Republic, Laval was suspect to the mass of conservative Catholic Frenchmen who gave Vichy its solid backing. Nor was his policy of out-and-out collaboration with the Germans one which others in the governing circle shared, ready though they might be to make concessions under pressure. For Laval it was clear that France must join the winning side—a process more euphemistically described as 'taking its place in the new order in Europe.' At Pétain's trial he made the statement quoted at the head of this chapter. In June 1940, immediately after the armistice, he had defined his policy for the benefit of those French deputies who had managed to follow the government southwards:

since parliamentary democracy insisted on taking up the struggle against Nazism and Fascism, and since it has lost the fight, it must disappear. A new régime must follow it, a régime which will be bold,

*The historian of Vichy, Robert Aron, gives it as his opinion that, for Darlan, "collaboration was a lesser evil"; for Laval it was "an end in itself." In practice this seems to have made little difference.[4]

authoritarian, social and national . . . . We have no other road to
follow than that of loyal collaboration with Germany and Italy.[5]

During his second term of office, when it was beginning to become
obvious that the Axis powers would lose the war, he displayed far more
willingness to resist German demands. In Vichy this kind of peasant
realpolitik was to remain *sui generis.*

Laval's policy, indeed, was more consistent than it was genuinely
realistic. A week or two after he had talked to the migrant deputies
Hitler defined his attitude towards France for the benefit of Count
Ciano, the Italian foreign minister. France, the Führer said, was now
pretending to be the unfortunate and innocent victim of British
enticements. In fact, things were not so, but France would, if it could,
immediately attack and annihilate Germany and Italy. It should
therefore be absolutely considered as an enemy.[6] Hitler never changed
this attitude even when he had demands to make on Vichy. The kind of
collaboration between France and Germany put forward by Laval or by
the Paris group of Nazi sympathizers (Doriot, Déat, Luchaire etc.) was
never a real possibility. The policy of "loyal collaboration" between
Germany and a defeated France at most existed in the aspirations of
Otto Abetz, the German ambassador in Paris, who, according to
Eberhard Jäckel's study of German policy towards occupied France,
was given no encouragement by his superiors in this direction.

Yet Laval was nonetheless the only politician connected with Vichy
to have a policy at all, however insubstantial it may have been. For
others, Vichy represented the 'divine surprise' which Maurras found in
the leadership of the Marshal. The Maurrassians, indeed, with men like
Alibert, Baudoin and Du Moulin de Labarthète, were the major intellectual influence on Vichy's first period, and their ideas influenced
many of the internal measures which were then carried out. In a different category were the technocrats who simply wanted to be rid of the
squabbling among politicians which had hampered so many of their
plans for reform under the Third Republic. Men like Pucheu, Lehideux
and Bichelonne or, with a slightly different emphasis, Marion and
Benoist-Méchin—the so-called synarchy who came in with Darlan in
February 1941—were men of action and ideas who saw in Vichy an
opportunity for carrying out their concepts of how France should be
governed. They do not seem to have been particularly astute politically,

and it was a curious irony that placed the industrial technocrat Pucheu in the position of minister of the interior where he had to decide moral questions which nothing in his past fitted him to judge. His failure to perceive that a French minister ought not even to discuss the execution of Frenchmen with an occupying power was to cost him his life. His career remains as a warning of what is likely to happen to technocrats when they enter politics.[7]

But the mass of Vichy's support came from the normal recruiting ground of the French right: the army, the church, the clerical and conservative country-side. Included were those who had longed for a 'strong' government and saw in Pétain an instrument of national regeneration, and Catholics who regarded the defeat as a punishment for the sins of the heathen Third Republic, to be accepted with penitential resignation. Others saw 1940 as an opportunity for a new start and the reconstruction of French society on a sound moral basis. Among those stunned by France's overthrow were many normally patriotic Frenchmen such as François Valentin, the head of Vichy's 'legion' of ex-servicemen who, in 1943, published clandestinely an appeal for resistance which was also an apology for having been deceived and having helped to deceive others.[8] This type of Vichy supporter was not pro-German nor even a reader of *Action française*, and the antics of the Paris group of collaborators were profoundly antipathetic to them. What they wanted was a safe, paternalistic régime headed by a figure of moral authority. As long as Vichy seemed to offer this, it was assured of widespread support throughout France, and not only among those normally numbered on the right: as late as April 1944 the Marshal was well-received by the people of Paris.[9] But the obvious subservience of Pétain's government, to the Germans, the increasing hardships of war and the mounting tide of atrocity on the part of the occupier alienated larger and larger sections of French public opinion. The transfer to de Gaulle of the *bien-pensant* opinion on which Vichy depended had already started before the German occupation of the 'free zone' in November 1942. And what had been begun by disgust and disappointment with Vichy was completed by fear of the Communists and the justified hope that de Gaulle would act as a protection against them. From the end of 1941 onwards the Gaullist movement constantly gained what Vichy lost in terms of adherents and sympathizers.

D

From one point of view the Vichy régime was the strong, paternal-istic, dynamic government constantly demanded by the antiparliamen-tary right under the Third Republic. Or, to be more accurate, it was at first seen by its partisans as being these things, for in reality few governments have governed more feebly. From another angle, it was a government where civil servants were allowed to administer without too much interference. It has, in fact, been claimed that Vichy was France's officialdom with the political covering removed, and the fact that some useful and lasting reforms—increased family allowances, encouragement of open-air activities for the young, etc.—were carried through, suggests that some officials did indeed take advantage of the situation to get measures passed for which they now felt the atmosphere to be propitious. There was also a genuine idealism in the momentary assent given to Vichy by an Emmanuel Mounier, the personalist philosopher and editor of the review *Esprit,* and many other intellectuals. In France itself, as in Free French circles in London, a desire for the renewal of French institutions and society was present which would manifest itself in the same recurrent plans for postwar reform. Vichy could not be a vehicle for such reform; it was too compromised by its repeated weakness in face of the occupier. But it is not surprising that some should have looked hopefully towards the Marshal during the summer of 1940, desiring to make anew a France broken by military defeat and longing to get rid of a republic which seemed condemned by the disaster that had destroyed it. But they failed to see the brutal facts of Vichy's situation, and, by the end of the first period of Gaullism, their illusions were utterly destroyed.

III

The first weeks of Free France after de Gaulle's broadcast of June 18 were spent in establishing the movement's status with the British government and in launching appeals—largely fruitless—to the various proconsuls of the French empire. Relations between Great Britain and Free France were regulated by a declaration on the part of the British (June 23) in which recognition was granted to a French National Committee, and the British government agreed to deal with it "on all matters relative to the carrying on of the war, as long as the Committee continues to represent the French elements which are resolved to fight against the common enemy."[10] On August 7, an exchange of letters between Churchill and de Gaulle marked the conclusion of an agreement establishing the status of the Free French forces on British soil and providing for supplies of money and equipment to be furnished by the United Kingdom. In Churchill's letter the most significant passage was the pledge to "restore completely the independence and the greatness of France." For his part, de Gaulle undertook to use the Free French forces in the war against Germany.[11]*

For the time being, however, those forces were very small. Out of volunteers from French troops being repatriated from Britain, Frenchmen living abroad and some early escapers from France itself (including the whole male population of military age of the Ile de Sein off the coast of Brittany), the numbers were gradually built up, but, by the end of July, de Gaulle only had 7,000 troops under his command. These were to be the nucleus of the first Free French division. A number of ships, including some seized by the British at Portsmouth and elsewhere, formed the basis of the naval forces, but neither Admiral Godfroy's fleet at Alexandria nor Admiral Robert's ships at Martinique joined de Gaulle. As for the main French fleet, it was to be attacked by the British, following the rejection of an ultimatum, at Mers-el-Kébir on July 3 and largely put out of action with a loss of nearly 1,300 dead and missing. On July 10, the battleship Richelieu was also disabled by depth charges exploded near her propellor at Dakar. "This odious tragedy," as de Gaulle called it in a broadcast from London, naturally embittered relations between British and French on all levels and had the effect of slowing down recruitment to the Free French forces. The spirit prevailing in the French navy is demonstrated by the fact that, in July 1940, only about twenty naval officers joined de Gaulle. In eight months' time about 40 warships were at sea, while the merchant shipping under the Free French flag totaled 170 ships of 700,000 tons in all.

As for the air force, it was not until the spring of 1941 that independent units could be formed, though many French pilots had fought with the Royal Air Force before then.

---

*It is also significant that, in a secret exchange of letters of the same date, Churchill felt himself unable to guarantee France's frontiers—a point which de Gaulle noted with icy resignation.[12]

But already in 1940 some names begin to appear in the ranks of Free France which were later to be well known: Catroux, Leclerc, de Larminat, Muselier, Dewavrin (Colonel Passy), Legentilhomme, Soustelle, Palewski, Cassin, Schumann, d'Argenlieu. Moreover, by the end of 1940 the first French territories had come under de Gaulle's rule. The governor of Tchad, Félix Eboué, an enlightened colonial administrator from the West Indies, had offered to declare for de Gaulle in July, and his decision was proclaimed publicly on August 26. At Douala in the Cameroons and Brazzaville in the French Congo, Gaullist agents—among them Major Leclerc, General de Larminat and René Pleven—organized *coups d'état* on August 27 and 28. With the declaration of Oubangi (now the Central African Republic) for de Gaulle, only Gabon still continued to obey Vichy in French Equatorial Africa. Late in October the attack on it from the Cameroons began, Libreville the capital, falling on November 9. A solid block of territory and resources stretching from the Congo to the Tibesti mountains had been acquired for Free France.

Before that, however, the Gaullist cause had suffered a severe setback in the failure of an Anglo-Free French expedition against Dakar on September 23 and 24. The unexpectedly determined resistance of Vichy troops and the support given to them by three modern French cruisers, which had been allowed to pass the Straits of Gibraltar by the local British naval commander, sufficed to cause the abandonment of the attack. This was a damaging defeat. In the first place, it showed that Gaullist appeals to fellow Frenchmen to come over to their side would not work if the Vichy commanders were sufficiently energetic. Secondly, the circumstances of the Dakar fiasco cast doubts upon Gaullist security, the arrival of the Vichy cruisers being said to have been the result of a leak in London. Whether this was so or not, the effect of such suspicions on the minds of the British was considerable. To their allies the Gaullists appeared as lacking in discretion at the very time when they had shown themselves less capable of attracting others to their side than had previously been thought.* Soustelle was not mistaken when he wrote in his account of Free France:

*The same impression was sustained by American minds. In a draft letter to Churchill before the North African Operation, *Torch,* Roosevelt was to write (September 16, 1942): "I consider it essential that de Gaulle be kept out of the picture and be permitted to have no information whatever . . . "[13]

Dakar marks a turning-point . . . . Henceforward, British policy with
regard to the French Empire was more and more aligned on that of
the United States . . . . Henceforth Dakar will become, in the mouth
of supporters of Vichy and also in that of certain Anglo-Saxons, the
argument made against de Gaulle.[14]

The lesson would not be without its effect at the time of the invasion
of Syria or at that of the Allied landings in North Africa. Meanwhile,
the Gaullist forces that had been assembled to land at Dakar sailed
unwillingly away to take Libreville.

De Gaulle could now organize those territories he controlled which
included the New Hebrides (July 18), Tahiti (September 2), the French
Indian enclaves (September 9) and New Caledonia (September 23). The
Brazzaville manifesto of October 27, 1940—the real charter of the Free
French movement in that it was issued on French soil—was accompanied by two *ordonnances* setting up a Council of Defense for the French
Empire to direct the administration of the territories under Gaullist rule
and pursue the conduct of the war. Significantly, however, its function
was largely to be an advisory one. Decisions would continue to be taken
by de Gaulle himself.* In an "organic declaration" of November 16
which completed the manifesto, the claims of Vichy to be the legal
government of France were rejected and the actions of Free France
justified in terms of the constitutional legislation of the Third Republic.

Thus two divergent tendencies can be discerned quite early on in
wartime Gaullism. On the one hand, it had the characteristics of a
military organization responsible to one leader with whom decisions
rested in the final analysis. On the other, the rebuttal of Vichy by an
appeal to republican institutions was the beginning of a process which
was to accelerate later on and through which Gaullism, to mark its
opposition to Pétain's *Etat français*, was to rely more and more on its
own democratic and representative character, appearing as the heir to
France's republican tradition.

Meanwhile, Free French forces were fighting their first engagements

*"Decisions are taken by the leader of the Free French, after consultation, if
necessary, with the Defense Council."[15] The members of the council were
General Catroux, Vice-Admiral Muselier, General de Larminat, Governor Eboué,
Governor Sautot, Surgeon-General Sicé, Professor Cassin, Father d'Argenlieu,
Colonel Leclerc.

with the enemy. A French batallion took part in the fighting at Sidi Barrani in the western desert in late 1940, while other troops participated in the campaign against the Italians in Eritrea and Abyssinia, a detachment of the Foreign Legion fighting at Keren and being the first to enter the Red Sea port of Massawa. From Tchad, Colonel Leclerc began the series of raids on Italian positions in the south of Libya; by the end of 1942, these raids were to lead his men to Tripoli and the frontier of Tunisia. The first blow in this campaign was struck by Colonel Colonna d'Ornano who successfully raided the post of Mourzouk in the Fezzan in January 1941, but was killed in the course of the fighting. On March 1, Leclerc himself, overcoming enormous logistical problems, received the surrender of the Italian garrison of the oasis of Kufra more than a thousand miles from his base at Fort Lamy. These raids were to continue throughout 1941 and 1942 ending with the occupation of the Fezzan on the southern flank of the British Eighth Army's advance from El Alamein.

A more painful episode was the campaign in Syria, directed this time against Frenchmen who, under the orders of General Dentz, the Vichy commander, offered fierce resistance to the British and Free French who entered Syria on June 8, 1941, for the purpose of expelling the German agents to whom access had been opened by Darlan. The Free French forces consisted of seven batallions, a company of tanks and a battery of artillery—some 6,000 men in all under the command of General Legentilhomme. On June 21, the Free French entered Damascus, and by July 10, Dentz was asking for an armistice. But Gaullist representatives were excluded from the negotiations at Acre, apparently for fear on the British side that their presence might cause Dentz to prolong the fighting, and this was to be a permanent source of trouble between Free France and the British government.

For de Gaulle himself the Syrian affair was the confirmation of suspicions of British intentions which he was only too ready to entertain. "Their game [was] . . . aimed at establishing British 'leadership' in the whole Middle East."[16]* After conversations between de Gaulle and Oliver Lyttleton, the British minister of state in the Middle East, the differences were patched up by the adoption of an agreed

---

*In the light of de Gaulle's concern for Syria, it is interesting to reflect that this was the one overseas post in which he had served as an officer.

interpretation of the Acre armistice and by the recognition of France's historic interests in the Levant. But the suspicions remained, nourished by a "number of clashes between the British occupation authorities, concerned with Arab opinion and the future of British policy in the Middle East, and Free French officials, concerned to show that France was master in its own territories. For the British the failure of the Gaullists to produce immediate defections among Dentz's troops and the fierce resistance of the latter appeared to emphasize the lesson of Dakar: that Gaullists were best excluded from operations in which Vichy-controlled troops were involved. In 1942 the British landing in Madagascar and the Anglo-American landings in North Africa were to be planned on this principle—not without success.

By now the Free French movement was taking on a wider and wider extension. On September 24, 1941, de Gaulle promulgated an *ordonnance* creating a national committee to act as a government for Free France. This replaced the military committee and the administrative conference which had hitherto handled affairs. The members of this committee, the commissioners, however, were named by, and responsible to the leader of the Free French, who also signed its decrees and to whom diplomatic representatives were accredited.* The *ordonnance* also announced the future creation of a consultative assembly and promised to submit the decrees enacted by the committee to a representative legislature as soon as this became possible—another step in that progress toward the left which marks the political history of Free France. Thus the Free French movement now had institutions approximating to a government and which could easily be transformed and broadened by the participation of representative political figures drawn from metropolitan France where the diminished credit of the

*The commissioners were: René Pleven (Economy, Finance and Colonies), Maurice Dejean (Foreign Affairs), General Legentilhomme (War), Admiral Muselier (Navy), René Cassin (Justice and Education), André Diethelm (Interior, Labor and Information), General Valin (Air), Thierry d'Argenlieu (commissioner without portfolio). By the end of 1942 René Massigli had replaced Dejean, whose attitude was insufficiently intransigent for de Gaulle, and Muselier's quarrel with his leader had led to his replacement by Admiral Auboyneau. Other changes included the appointments of General Catroux as a roving commissioner, of André Philip (Interior and Labor), André Diethelm (Finance), and Jacques Soustelle (Information). Pleven remained commissioner for economic affairs.

Vichy government was already producing a change in public opinion.

By the end of 1941 the first signs of the presence of a Resistance movement against the Germans and their Vichy client state were becoming visible, and incidents of resistance followed by German reprisals multiplied throughout 1942. In the unoccupied zone where conditions were at first easier due to the absence of German forces, an army officer, Henri Frenay, had founded *Combat* in the summer of 1940, a movement grouped around the clandestine publication of that name and with Christian-Democratic connections. Another southern movement was Emmanuel Astier de la Vigerie's *Libération*, a left-wing grouping whose executive committee included Socialists and trade unionists from the CGT and CFTC. The third important movement in the south was *Franc-Tireur* to which many intellectuals belonged, university teachers such as Marc Bloch and Albert Bayet and journalists such as Georges Altmann and J-P. Lévy. In the occupied zone a number of small groups, harried and decimated by the German army's *Abwehr* or the S.S.'s *Sicherheitsdienst,* eventually succeeded in organizing themselves for survival. These were: *Libération-Nord,* a movement with Socialist and trade union support, whose leaders included Louis Saillant of the CGT, Christian Pineau and Louis Vallon—later to be the Gaullist movement's expert on industrial and social problems; the *Organisation civile et militaire* (OCM), a group of officers and intellectuals; the *Front national,* an organization created by the Communists after the German attack on Russia in June 1941, but whose membership was recruited as widely as possible, including Radicals, Socialists, Christian-Democrats and figures from the prewar right. Exceptionally, it succeeded in developing in both occupied and unoccupied zones. Its action group was the well-known *Francs-Tireurs et partisans français* (FTPF) who first appeared on the scene in September 1941.[17]

De Gaulle and his advisers were quick to see the reinforcement of strength and authority that the French National Committee could draw from the Resistance movements. Up to the end of 1941 Gaullist activity inside France had been more in the nature of intelligence missions than of attempts to create organized resistance to the occupier. As such they had been directed by the *Deuxième Bureau* or *Service de Renseignements* (SR) headed by Passy. Now something more was required, and de Gaulle's policy was stated in a letter of October 8,

1941, to Hugh Dalton (the minister supervising the British Special
Operations Executive):

> General de Gaulle and the French National Committee think that it is
> for them to take the effective leadership of this resistance in French
> territory occupied by the enemy or controlled by him.[18]

To this end the *Bureau central de Renseignements et d'Action militaires*
was set up under Passy in January 1942 which eventually headed off
possible rivals—principally the commissariat of the interior—and came
to be the instrument through which the National Committee
established contact with, and control over, the clandestine movements
inside France.* Almost simultaneously de Gaulle sent Jean Moulin, a
staunchly patriotic ex-prefect who had arrived in London in September
1941, back to France with the task "of bringing about in the
unoccupied zone the unity of action of all the elements resisting the
enemy and his collaborators."[19] By March 1943 Moulin succeeded in
persuading *Combat, Libération* and *Franc-Tireur* to merge in the
Mouvements Unis de Résistance (MUR). On May 27, 1943, was held
the first meeting of the *Conseil National de la Résistance* (CNR) which
was really Moulin's creation. A month later he was trapped by the
Germans at Caluire near Lyon and later died under torture. Before this,
however, he had connected the Resistance movements and the
renascent political parties with Free France in London. His report of
October 1941, stating firmly that the object of the Resistance
movements was adherence to the cause of General de Gaulle was of
inestimable value to the Gaullist movement, giving, as it did, the
backing of an increasingly representative section of metropolitan
opinion to what had sometimes seemed to be a group of enthusiastic
but isolated exiles in London.[20]

In the months following Moulin's mission to France many Resistance
leaders would make their way to London to request for their
movements the money, arms and technical aid which London alone was
in a position to supply and to give their support to Free France. Their
presence and that of representatives of republican political parties such
as Daniel Mayer, Christian Pineau, Henri Queuille, Pierre Mendès-France
and André Philip gave a renewed impulsion to the natural movement

---

*It was to drop the *"militaires"* and is best known by the initials BCRA.

which was carrying wartime Gaullism to the left, toward a program based on the re-establishment of democratic institutions in a renovated republic. And, by reinforcing his claim to legitimacy, it would also provide de Gaulle with the strength he needed in the struggle for full recognition from his allies which was to culminate in his political contest with General Giraud in Algiers during 1943.

Before the North African landings of the autumn of 1942 relations with Great Britain pursued an up-and-down course without, however, any serious prospect of a break. Churchill might grumble about de Gaulle's displays of temperament and even become seriously angry at his tactlessness in regard to the Americans, but he also recognized his qualities. For his part, de Gaulle might suspect the worst of the " 'Intelligence,' which to the British is a passion quite as much as a service,"[21] Syria and British attempts to interfere over matters like the dismissal of Admiral Muselier might leave an enduring wound in his memory, but he was sufficiently realistic to avoid any rupture and seems to have recognized that, in the final analysis, he could rely on Churchill's support, provided that the latter were not brought into conflict with the Americans. After the change of name of the Free French movement to that of the Fighting French (*La France Combattante*), the British government in a declaration of July 13, 1942, recognized the National Committee as organizing "the participation in the war of French citizens and territories that unite to collaborate with the United Nations in the war against the common enemies . . ."[22]

The attitude of the American government was unfortunately to be very different. American policy towards France in defeat had been to try to influence Vichy in the direction of resistance to German demands, and Admiral Leahy, a personal friend of President Roosevelt, had been dispatched to execute it:

In Washington there was little difference of opinion on this subject. Secretary Hull felt that it was an important function of the State Department to prevent British-French relations from deteriorating and particularly to influence the Pétain government against entering the war against Britain. The Free French movement was looked upon as a strictly British affair. Few Frenchmen of prominence had adhered to de Gaulle, who as yet was himself pretty much an unknown quantity.[23]

This was a feasible policy, though it increasingly broke down as German pressure led to one Vichy surrender after another. What was less reasonable was Washington's intense suspicion of the Gaullist movement. Even when it became apparent that de Gaulle was gathering support, Roosevelt still continued to regard him as an ambitious general, whose natural inclination was antidemocratic, and to maintain, unrealistically enough, that the French people must be given the chance to choose their government freely once they were liberated. This point of view compounded several errors. It assumed that no political developments were taking place under the Occupation and ignored the extent to which the Third Republic and its political personnel had been discredited by defeat. It misunderstood the nature of French politics, neglecting the existence of a strong authoritarian democratic tradition. Above all, it was badly informed about ascertainable French opinion. Admittedly, things were not made easier by de Gaulle's native intransigence--still further exacerbated by rumors of American plans to liquidate the French empire after the war. The occupation of the islands of Saint Pierre and Miquelon by Admiral Muselier on December 24, 1941, which produced an explosion of annoyance from Washington, was really not worth the trouble it caused, and in retrospect American reactions seemed to have been wildly exaggerated at the time. As the event was to prove, American policy toward France during the war was thoroughly misguided and condemned to failure. A first step towards realism was taken by Washington with an agreement between the United States and Free France in July 1942 (Lease-Lend had already been extended to Free French territories), but relations remained distrustful. The Soviet Union, on the other hand, had recognized de Gaulle as leader of the Free French two days after the formation of the National Committee, though the moment was not yet come for de Gaulle to try to bring in the East to redress the balance of the West. (He did, however, from an early stage display a brutal realism over the dispute between Russia and the Polish government in London.)

In the summer of 1942 the Free French movement was well on its way to achieving its aim of gathering behind it an increasing amount of popular support in France. In the two years since the foundation of the movement it had become clear that its first objective of competing successfully with Vichy for the hearts and minds of Frenchmen had been attained. Symbolically, it was at this moment that the defense of Bir Hakeim by General Koenig's troops in the western desert brought Free France its most glorious feat of arms. But the diplomatic struggle, first for recognition, and then to assert the rights of France in the new international system, remained to be won, and de Gaulle also had to prepare to meet the political situation that would face him once France was liberated. These were to be the dominating themes of the second period of wartime Gaullism which began with the Anglo-American landings in North Africa and saw de Gaulle and his followers transfer their incipient government to Algiers.

IV

The North African landings, Operation Torch, brought to a crisis the relations between the Gaullists and their allies and posed in the most acute form the question of recognition. The landings had been preceded by a conspiracy designed to produce a putsch which would immobilize the Vichy command at the decisive moment. Some of the anti-Vichy elements concerned were Gaullists (like René Capitant), but the leading figures who carried on negotiations with American officers were opposed to the Free French movement. De Gaulle and his followers had been kept out of the operation at the request of the Americans who both disliked Free France and believed that its absence would allow the Vichy commanders in North Africa to change sides more easily.* Their candidate for the command of the French forces there was General Henri Giraud, a fighting soldier with a good reputation who had just escaped from a German prison, but who, as events were to prove, was no politician. It was hoped—wrongly—that the Vichy forces would be willing to place themselves under his command.

In fact, the Allied landings at Casablanca, Oran and Algiers were

*The British had taken a similar point of view during their landing in Madagascar in September. However, the administration of the island was subsequently turned over to the Free French.

resisted by the local Vichy commanders, though this resistance was diminished in the last-named town by the partial success of the putsch. In these circumstances the American command (whose political adviser was Robert Murphy) proceeded to negotiate a cease-fire with Admiral Darlan, who happened to be in Algiers at the time, thereby putting themselves in a moral and political dilemma from which they were only extricated by Darlan's assassination on December 24, 1942. This left the way free for Giraud to succeed Darlan as high-commissioner for North Africa at the head of an 'Imperial Council' consisting of three Vichy governors and one ex-Vichy minister. One of the first actions of the new régime was to order the arrest of 'Gaullists' in Algeria.[24]

In London de Gaulle and his followers were stupified and outraged by the agreement with Darlan. On November 16, after an interview with Churchill in which de Gaulle gave a warning of the consequences in terms of advantage to the Communists if Frenchmen became convinced that an Allied liberation meant a régime led by men like Darlan, the French National Committee published a communiqué publicly dissociating itself from what was going on in North Africa. On November 21, de Gaulle spoke on Brazzaville radio (the BBC having refused to transmit his broadcast) and again denounced the continuation of the Vichy régime in North Africa. Meanwhile he had received strong political support in the shape of a statement signed by representatives of the Resistance movements, the political parties and the trade unions demanding that "the new destinies of liberated North Africa be placed, as soon as possible, in the hands of General de Gaulle."[25] The representative character assumed by the Free French movement was already beginning to pay political dividends. De Gaulle's hand was also strengthened by the Free French seizure of Réunion on November 28, their entry into Djibouti (French Somaliland) on December 26, and the British agreement to hand over the administration of Madagascar on December 14. Moreover, as Churchill noted in a letter to Roosevelt, public opinion in Britain and America had been shocked by the Clark-Darlan agreement.*

The sharpest cause of dissension was removed by Darlan's

---

*"I ought to let you know that very deep currents of feeling are stirred here by the arrangements with Darlan . . . . A permanent arrangement with Darlan . . . would not be understood by the great masses of ordinary people, whose simple loyalties are our strength."[26]

assassination. There remained for de Gaulle the task of re-establishing French unity and of extending his own authority and that of the national committee over all Frenchmen fighting on the Allied side. Immediately after the news of Darlan's death he telegraphed to Giraud proposing a meeting. Giraud replied evasively, and the meeting was only to take place under the auspices of Churchill and Roosevelt at their Casablanca conference in January. But the occasion, which de Gaulle had taken some days to agree to attend, was not a success. Giraud would not agree to get rid of the high ex-Vichy officials (Noguès, Boisson, Peyrouton and Bergeret) in the 'Imperial Council,' while de Gaulle would have nothing to do with a committee headed by himself, Giraud and General Georges. All that could be achieved by American and British pressure was a short joint communiqué. It was Giraud that Roosevelt agreed to supply with arms and to regard as the potential unifier of Frenchmen fighting the Germans.*

But de Gaulle's hand was stronger than that of Giraud for all the latter's support in Washington. The Americans, aware of the need to separate Giraud from some of his advisers and to abolish the last vestiges of Vichy in North Africa, had suggested that Jean Monnet should be invited to Algiers. Under Monnet's influence Giraud, on March 14, proclaimed the annulment of Vichy's legislation (including its anti-Jewish laws) and promised a return to the republic. By the end of May, despite many false starts and one postponement due to Eisenhower's reluctance to have him in North Africa on the eve of the last phase of the Tunisian campaign, de Gaulle was ready to leave for Algiers to establish his government on French soil. He arrived there on May 30. After some days of acrimonious discussion, the *Comité français de Libération Nationale* (CFLN) was formed on June 3 with de Gaulle and Giraud as joint chairmen.** Almost immediately it was

---

*"It was agreed between the President of the United States, the Prime Minister of Great Britain and General Giraud that it was to their common interest for all the French fighting against Germany to be reunited under one authority, and that every facility would be given to General Giraud in order to bring about this reunion." Later Churchill induced Roosevelt to insert the phrase "and to the French National Committee under General de Gaulle" after the words "to General Giraud."[27]

**At first it comprised seven members. These were: René Massigli (Foreign Affairs), André Philip (Interior), Jean Monnet (Armament), Generals Georges and Catroux (commissioners of state). Two days later other posts were filled: Maurice Couve de Murville (Finance), René Mayer (Transport and Public Works), Dr. Jules

decided to replace Boisson at Dakar and Noguès at Rabat (Peyrouton having already resigned). Significantly, both were replaced by Gaullist nominees. Having carried one major point, de Gaulle passed to the crucial question of the control of the armed forces. He maintained that Giraud could not be both commander-in-chief and joint chairman of the committee. Cleverly enough, he invoked the principle of civilian control over the military and, in so doing, succeeded in getting the rest of the committee on his side. Eventually, after an attempt at arbitration by Eisenhower which, by making Giraud appear an American puppet, merely served de Gaulle's purposes, a compromise was reached on June 22: there would be two commanders-in-chief, and Giraud would continue to serve as joint chairman.

But Giraud's position was already eroded, and a trip to America during July allowed de Gaulle to outdistance him still further. For months there had been desertions from the Giraudist forces to the Free French troops who had met them in Tunisia. Now it was decided that unification should take place under the auspices of a Committee of National Defense presided over by de Gaulle, Giraud remaining commander-in-chief and "directing military operations." De Gaulle was to "direct the debates and follow the execution of the Committee's decisions in regard to other affairs and the Committee's general policy."[28]

This arrangement, however, did not last long. In September Giraud's independent action in undertaking the liberation of Corsica without informing his colleagues brought about a crisis which led directly to the CFLN deciding that in future it would only have one chairman: de Gaulle. In November the committee was shuffled, and members of the political parties and the Resistance movement were introduced into it as ministers.* Finally, after a complicated struggle for the control of

Abadie (Justice, Education and Health), René Pleven (Colonies), André Diethelm (Economy), Adrien Tixier (Labor), Henri Bonnet (Information). Catroux in addition became Governor-General of Algeria.

*The new appointments included: Henri Queuille (commissioner of state), André Le Trocquer (War and Air), Louis Jacquinot (Navy), Emmanuel Astier de la Vigerie (Interior), René Capitant (Education), Henri Frenay (Prisoners and Deportees). Pierre Mendès-France and François Menthon had respectively been made commissioner for finance and Garde des Sceaux some time previously. Most of these names were to recur as those of prominent politicians under the Fourth Republic.

the 'special services' (vital because of their role as the channel of
communication between the CFLN and metropolitan France), the
office of commander-in-chief was abolished on April 4, 1944, and
Giraud was appointed to the harmless post of inspector-general of the
army.

In retrospect it seems inevitable that de Gaulle should have defeated
Giraud. The latter's lack of political ability and his isolation from
anything other than his own officer caste made him no match for his
opponent and the Gaullist team of experienced and dynamic officials.
By 1943 de Gaulle was clearly in a position to claim a representative
quality for his movement. One of the last acts of Jean Moulin, as noted
earlier, had been to send a message on behalf of the Resistance
movements demanding that de Gaulle should be the president of a
provisional government and asserting that, whatever the outcome, he
would remain the only head of the Resistance.[29] Patriot though he
was, Giraud represented nobody but himself. Without American
support he would never have lasted so long in a political role, but that
very support damaged him in the eyes of other Frenchmen, all too
sensitive to Allied encroachments on their national independence.
Eisenhower in Algiers seems to have realized this better than Roosevelt
or Cordell Hull in Washington, though time was to diminish even their
enthusiasm for Giraud, while doing nothing to increase their warmth
toward de Gaulle.

Having disposed of a potential rival—compromised, in his eyes, by
arriving in the train of an Allied army—the leader of Free France could
now endeavor to reaffirm France's place in the world and assert his own
authority in the metropolitan territory after its approaching liberation.

To achieve these ends the CFLN would have to transform itself into a
government. In November 1943 the consultative assembly so long
promised by the Free French committee met for the first time. It
consisted of forty representatives of the Resistance movements in
France, twelve of Resistance movements in overseas territories, twenty
members of the old senate and Chamber of Deputies and twelve
representatives of the general councils. It embodied, in a more
immediate form, that claim to represent French opinion which the
CNR had already permitted the Gaullist movement to make, and it was
to play a useful part in the discussions around the future organization

of the state in a liberated France. These were to be codified in a series of decrees abolishing Vichy legislation and restoring republican institutions.* In March 1944 de Gaulle further broadened the base of his government by taking two Communists, Fernand Grenier and François Billoux, into it after some hesitation on the part of their party which wished to name its own ministers. On June 3, 1944, three days before the Allied landings in Normandy, the final step was taken and the CFLN transformed into the *Gouvernement provisoire de la République Française* (GPRF).

The struggle to establish Gaullist authority in North Africa and eliminate Giraud undoubtedly speeded this evolution toward a broadly based representative government, which, in any case, was very much in the logic of the Gaullist movement. As Soustelle put it, regretfully, "Darlan in Algiers meant Grenier in London in December 1942 and Thorez in Paris in 1944."[30] The desire for recognition by Allied governments played its part also. In this respect, the CFLN had not done too badly during 1943 and 1944. It had been able to send delegates to various international bodies meeting under the auspices of the United Nations, and, if it had not been informed about the Italian armistice beforehand, Couve de Murville represented France on the consultative commission for Italian affairs.

But this last concession had been made against Roosevelt's will, and the vital question of who was to be regarded by the Allies as the legal government of France during and after its liberation was still not settled.** On November 27, 1943, the American President wrote to Cordell Hull: "The thought that the occupation when it occurs should be wholly military is one to which I am increasingly inclined."[31] Roosevelt was no more disposed to accept the CFLN than he had been to accept the London Gaullists. More recently, indeed, the action of the Gaullist representative in Lebanon in arresting the nationalist government there had added to his distrust of de Gaulle whom he had always viewed as an incorrigible imperialist. The arrest in North Africa of men like Flandin and Boisson whom he regarded as having collaborated with

---

*The most important of these, the decree of April 21, 1944, also established the right of women to vote.

**In a letter to Churchill of December 31, 1943, he wrote: "I cannot see why France is entitled to anybody on the Allied Control Commission for Italy . . . "

the United States was another irritant. Not merely was he averse to recognizing any French government on the grounds that this would be tantamount to depriving the French people of their free choice, but he also seems to have believed that a civil war would break out in France on liberation and that therefore an Allied Military Government (AMGOT) solution was the only one possible.[32] This was the sense of his memorandum to Eisenhower of March 15, 1944, in which he laid down the relationship to be observed between the Allied Supreme Commander and the CFLN. As late as May 13, 1944, the President was writing that he was unable to recognize any French government "until the French people have an opportunity to make a free choice."[33]

De Gaulle's reaction to a proposed Allied Military Government in France was naturally violent. Behind Roosevelt's policy he saw a threat to France's independence, and he was resolved to assert his own authority in face of it.* In a broadcast on April 4, 1944, he specifically laid down that Frenchmen should deal with no other authority than the CFLN:

> National unity requires that all Frenchmen should follow their government. Wherever they may be and whatever may happen, Frenchmen can take no orders except from their government . . . . No authority is valid if it does not act in its name. No French war effort counts for France if it is not accomplished under its authority.[35]

In fact, this attitude on de Gaulle's part had two purposes. If an American-inspired AMGOT was to be resisted, any attempt to set up a Communist-dominated government based on the Resistance forces controlled by the party had also to be crushed. On the *Comité d'Action Militaire* (COMAC) of the CNR two out of its three members were Communists, and there must, at the time, have seemed a serious danger of a de facto revolutionary authority taking power in France once the liberation was completed.

To meet this danger—which had been considerably increased by the fact that a wave of German arrests at the end of 1943 had eliminated a number of leading non-Communists in the Resistance—de Gaulle relied

---

*"the refusal to recognize us as the French national authority masked, in reality, the American President's *idée fixe* of establishing his arbitration in France."[34]

essentially upon the construction of parallel organizations which could bypass the CNR and COMAC.[36] The first instrument he used for this purpose was the *Délégation-Générale* which was reformed in March 1944 with Alexandre Parodi as its chief. The role envisaged for it was defined in a message of July 31:

> You are the representative of the government. That is, your instructions must prevail in the last resort. Naturally, we attach the greatest importance to the *consultative role and the inspiring action of the Council of the Resistance and the local committees of liberation* . . . . I recommend you always to speak very loudly and clearly in the name of the state. The multiple forms and actions of our admirable interior Resistance are means through which the nation is struggling for its salvation. The state is above all these forms and all these actions.[37] [Italics mine.]

A second type of machinery, through which Algiers could control events inside France, was provided by the command of the *Forces françaises de l'Intérieur* (FFI) given to General Koenig in April and exercised through a *délégué militaire national* and numerous *délégués militaires régionaux* (DMR). Through their control of communications and liaison, and of the arms and money dispatched to the Resistance movements from Britain and North Africa, Koenig and his officers were able to direct operations and to limit the autonomy of the general staff founded by COMAC, whose chief of staff was General Malleret-Joinville.[38] Thirdly, in order to insure a firm hold on the liberated regions of France just as soon as they were cleared of the Germans, *commissaires de la République* were created and provided with an administrative framework in decrees of January 10 and April 21, 1944. In addition, consultations had gone on with the Resistance movements concerning the nomination of new prefects. This question (and that of the *commissaires de la République*) was studied first by the Resistance's *Comité Général d'Etudes* (CGE) and then by a special commission presided by Michel Debré.[39] Algiers accepted the names of some hundred new prefects suggested by them and left the job of filling gaps to the commission. Nevertheless, this recruitment of cadres for a future administration allowed de Gaulle to assert the authority of the state within a few days of the liberation. Almost all those named to such posts were men who had experience in the ranks of regular French officialdom and to whom a restoration of habitual administrative mores came easily. In fact, they were to assert their control over the *Comités départementaux de Libération* (CDL) without too much difficulty.[40] The potential conflict which confronted Communists and Gaullists, the state administration and popular committees, the regular army and the *Milices patriotiques* (MP), a Communist paramilitary formation, was therefore stifled at its outset.*

The resolution of this problem demonstrated de Gaulle's ability to play off one adversary against another. On the one hand, talk of the threat of AMGOT rule in France enabled him to claim that orderly control by regularly constituted authorities behind the Allied lines was the only way to avert enforced military government. On the other, the Communist threat and the possibility of a French civil war which so preoccupied Roosevelt allowed de Gaulle to point to himself and the CFLN as the only means of preventing disorder. This point had already been appreciated by Eisenhower who had said to de Gaulle, before leaving Algiers to take up the position of Supreme Allied Commander, that he would have need of his support, of the cooperation of his officials and the backing of French opinion.[42] The authority of the CFLN and its president could be invoked both as preventing revolutionary disorder and as guaranteeing French sovereignty against Anglo-American encroachment.

With the realization that only de Gaulle could carry out this role, even American policy began to change. A draft directive by Roosevelt of March 15, 1944 (dispatched to London for consideration) still only allowed Eisenhower consultation with the CFLN and did not limit him "to dealing exclusively with the said Committee"[43] but, on April 9, a speech by Cordell Hull went much further:

> We are disposed to see the French Committee of National Liberation exercise leadership to establish law and order under the supervision of the Allied Commander-in-Chief.

It is true that the speech also contained the customary reservation that

*It is, of course, too simple to talk of the Communists intending to 'take power.' The 'revolutionary' faction of the Resistance included a number of non-Communists, and the opposition between the old parties and the Resistance movements cut across the Gaullist/Communist polarization. Communist supporters were also subject to the purely national sentiments which made so many Frenchmen desire to maintain the unity of the Resistance movements at all costs.[41]

"The Committee is, of course, not the government of France and we cannot recognize it as such," but the progress was nevertheless considerable.[44] This improvement was, however, soon followed by renewed friction, the result of the discussion of the role to be played by the CFLN (which by now had taken the title of a provisional government) in the liberation of France. There were disputes over Eisenhower's proclamation to the French people on D-day, over the appointment of French liaison officers to the Allied forces, and over the circulation in France of American military currency. Relations between Churchill and de Gaulle suffered one of their periodic deteriorations. It was at this time that Churchill made his famous remark: "Each time we must choose between Europe and the open sea, we shall always choose the open sea. Each time I must choose between you and Roosevelt, I shall always choose Roosevelt."[45]

But on June 14—eight days after the Allied landings in Normandy—de Gaulle was able to visit the Bayeux bridgehead and install a Commissioner of the Republic, François Coulet, as his representative in the liberated territory. The administrative structure planned by the GPRF went into action with astonishingly little difficulty, thereby confounding the gloomy prophecies of de Gaulle's adversaries in Washington. As the Allied invasion went on, it became increasingly clear that the only possible government for France was the one already in existence in Algiers. By the time de Gaulle went to Washington in early July, an agreement had already been negotiated with the British which, while not dealing with the question of recognition directly, accepted its practical consequences as far as the liberated areas of France were concerned. This was accepted by the Americans in talks during which the relations between de Gaulle and Roosevelt improved somewhat, but the agreements were not ratified until August 26, by which time Paris had surrendered to General Leclerc's armored forces. Finally, formal American recognition of the provisional government came on October 23 despite a last attempt by Roosevelt to delay it still further. The same day also brought British and Russian recognition.

V

At the time of the transfer of the provisional government to Paris from Algiers, de Gaulle had managed to assert his own authority and that of his government both against France's allies and inside the

country itself. It was already a major point that Leclerc's troops should
have been the first to reach the capital, and the entry into Paris of the
leader of the Free French on August 25 was accompanied by a series of
actions designed to mark the restoration of the normal authority of the
French state. His refusal to go at once to the Hotel de Ville to meet the
Paris committee of liberation and the CNR, his rebuke to the Communist FFI Colonel Rol-Tanguy for having placed his own name together
with Leclerc's on the German surrender document, his refusal to proclaim the republic at the Hotel de Ville on the grounds that it had never
ceased to exist—all these gestures were symbolic of an inflexible
determination not to concede any of the rights of the state to an
insurrectionary authority. As he wrote in his *Mémoires* of the decision
to go straight to the ministry of war, "Not that I was not eager to make
contact with the leaders of the Parisian insurrection, but I wished to
establish that the state . . . was returning, first of all, quite simply, to
where it belonged."[46] The point was emphasized on August 26 by a
military parade from the Etoile to Notre-Dame arranged without
informing the CNR or the *Comité Parisien de la Libération* (CPL) and
against the advice of the local American commander, General Gerow.
The Resistance committees protested, but power had passed from
them.

The newly reconstituted government (which was reshuffled on
September 9 to put it on a more representative basis) immediately had
to cope with the chaos which occupation and war had left behind.* On
the military front the Allied forces were pushing toward the Rhine.
Lille and Verdun were taken on September 4, Le Havre on the 12th,

---

*The most important appointments were: the replacement of Emmanuel
d'Astier as minister of the interior by Adrien Tixier, who was undoubtedly
thought by de Gaulle to be a firmer and more obedient wielder of the state's
authority in a key post, and the placing of the President of the CNR, Georges
Bidault, at the Quai d'Orsay. There were still two Communists: Francois Billoux
(Health) and Charles Tillon (Air). Other ministers were: Aimé Lepercq
(Finance)—he was soon to be killed and replaced by René Pleven—Pierre
Mendès-France (Economy), Robert Lacoste (Industry), René Pleven (Colonies),
René Capitant (Education), Alexandre Parodi (Labor), René Mayer (Public
Works), General Catroux (North Africa), Pierre-Henri Teitgen (Information),
François de Menthon (Justice), François Tanguy-Prigent (Agriculture), Jules
Jeanneney (State). The last-named had been president of the senate of the Third
Republic.

Epinal on the 15th. In the second half of November it would be the turn of Metz, Strasbourg and other towns of Alsace-Lorraine. Strasbourg was to be threatened by a German counterattack in January 1945, but was saved after de Gaulle's famous order to de Lattre de Tassigny not to retire to conform with the movements of other Allied (American) forces. On the Atlantic coast, however, the Germans hung on at Royan, La Rochelle, Saint-Nazaire and Lorient and, in the Channel, at Dunkirk. None of these enclaves was taken by General de Larminat's Atlantic army before April 1945.

Apart from its military effort France's provisional government had to assure public order—a task closely linked with that of restoring communications, industrial production and the normal mechanism of administration in the liberated areas of France. Abroad, de Gaulle kept up his struggle to maintain France's 'rank' in the world. Both the foreign and colonial policy of the provisional government, while he was at its head, foreshadowed future developments under the Fourth and Fifth Republics.

By and large, the task of getting France back to normal was carried out with remarkable success both before and after the German surrender (May 7, 1945). The key to the avoidance of civil strife and the physical rehabilitation of France was the attitude of the Communist party. Politically the Communists were given satisfaction by de Gaulle's visit to Russia and the pact resulting from it, and by permission given immediately afterwards, on November 27, 1944, to Maurice Thorez, the party's secretary-general, to return to France. Whether under Russian prompting or not, the attitude adopted by Thorez was one of support for the government's suppression, on October 28, of the *Milices patriotiques*—an armed Communist militia—and for the drive to make good war damage. At this moment of French history he and his party did indeed, as de Gaulle wrote subsequently, "serve the public interest."[47] Soon after the Liberation the FFI had been incorporated into newly formed units of the regular army, while the commissioners of the republic, often left on their own by the severance of communications with Paris, were struggling manfully with the restoration of order and the reconstruction of normal administration.

Some things, however, could not be prevented. After the repression carried out by Darnand's militia with the apparent approval of the Vichy authorities it was inevitable that the Liberation should produce a

counter-terror. The number of summary executions at this time may
have amounted to between twenty and thirty thousand. Many of those
executed were undoubtedly the victims of private revenge rather than
political reprisals.* More regular trials had begun in Algiers with that of
Pierre Pucheu, once Vichy's minister of the interior, which ended with
his condemnation and execution in March 1944. They continued in
1945 with that of Pétain, whose sentence of death was commuted to
life imprisonment by de Gaulle—earlier he had tried to avoid bringing
the Marshal to trial at all by warning him to remain in Switzerland.
Laval, Darnand and Brinon were executed together with minor figures
like Luchaire, Brasillach and Bucard (the founder of *Francisme*).
According to official sources, between six and seven thousand death
sentences were pronounced by the courts, two-thirds of them *in
absentia*. But only about eight hundred of these seem to have been
carried out. In addition there were some 60,000 prison sentences and
50,000 cases in which the accused were deprived of their rights as citizens.[49] The justice of these proceedings was to become the subject of
bitter polemics which have never totally died down. But it is hard to
see how the provisional government could have avoided proceeding
against the survivors of Vichy. What is surprising is how many prominent figures managed to disappear altogether.** Certainly the result of
Laval's trial was a foregone conclusion, but he at least had realized the
risks he was running.

At the time of the Liberation France's economy was in a ruinous
condition. Figures give some idea of the problems facing the provisional
government. Only 3,000 railway engines were left out of 17,000 in
1939, only 200,000 goods wagons out of 439,000. About 1,600
railway bridges and viaducts had been destroyed, 3,000 kilometers of
track and 15 large stations. On the canals 300 sluices were not working,
and nearly 3,000 barges had been lost. On the roads only 200,000

---

*The number of those executed summarily remains obscure. An official
estimate gives the figure of 10,000, while partisans of Vichy have suggested that
there were 100,000 victims. Robert Aron has estimated a figure of 30,000 to
40,000, but his evidence has been destructively criticized by Peter Novick. In the
circumstances 25,000 does not seem an unlikely figure, but this is guesswork.[48]

**For instance, Déat, Alibert, Rebatet, Céline. Doriot had been killed in an
Allied air attack in Germany.

trucks were left out of half a million. Industrial production had fallen
to 40 percent of the 1938 level. In the coal industry the daily output in
September 1944 was 67,000 tons compared to 156,000 tons in 1938.
The coal produced in 1945 only amounted to 35,000,000 tons as
compared with 47,000,000 tons in 1938. Steel production too was
down from 500,000 tons a month in 1938 to 12,000 in September
1944. By December 1945 it had only recovered to the extent of
233,000 tons a month. The output of the chemical industry was 17
percent of its prewar production. Agriculture was naturally less badly
hit, but here the problem was a different one: to transport the food to
the towns and to persuade the farmers to part with their produce for
prices which industrial workers could afford.

In financial terms the situation was also catastrophic with a deficit of
300 billion francs in the budget for 1944. The fact that there was four
times as much money in circulation as in 1939 created an inflationary
situation hardly checked by the control of prices. Immediately after the
Liberation, wages had been raised by 50 percent—a concession that was,
no doubt, necessary in political and psychological terms, but which
added to the pressure on the franc. The balance of payments too was
heavily weighted against France with five times as many imports as
exports, though this fact was, to some extent, alleviated by Allied aid
during the period of the war.[50]

For this situation two opposing solutions were put forward. Mendès-
France, the minister of national economy, produced an austerity plan
entailing deflation, control of prices and wages, a capital levy, the issue
of new bank notes and the blocking of bank accounts, cuts in state expenditure and subsidies to producers. Pleven, the minister of finance,
suggested less drastic measures: a moderate rise in wages, state loans to
diminish the money in circulation and some subsidies to producers.
After a period of indecision which saw the launching of the successful
'Liberation loan' de Gaulle chose the Pleven policy of expansion.
Mendès-France resigned on April 6, 1945. Subsequent inflation was to
give him, deservedly enough, the reputation of the man who has been
right all along. In opting for what was not then called 'growth' de
Gaulle undoubtedly made a basically political decision—a fact which is
not altogether surprising given that his natural tendency was always to
see economic policy in a purely political perspective.

The gradual economic recovery of France was to become strikingly apparent after de Gaulle's departure from power in January 1946. But before then there were some signs of recuperation. There were also a number of important economic and social decisions. A group of coal mines (in the Nord and the Pas de Calais) were nationalized before the end of 1944, and the energy industries (coal, gas, electricity) were to follow the same course through measures prepared, if not finally enacted, under de Gaulle's auspices. The Renault motor works and the Gnome et Rhône aeroplane engine company were placed under state control as was the French merchant navy. Works committees were also created as a gesture to the idealism generated in Resistance circles, but proved to be disappointing in their actual results. As for social legislation, family allowances were raised almost immediately after the Liberation, and a new inclusive system of social insurance was brought into effect by decree of October 4, 1945. This decree completed by subsequent laws, created an insurance structure covering family allowances, health, old age pensions, etc. Given the difficulties, this was a considerable effort in this field. The serious gap in the social services was housing which was diminished by war damage and had, in any case, been insufficient in 1939.

For de Gaulle, however, these social and economic problems were, no doubt, secondary. His personal touch must be looked for in the domain of foreign policy, in his incarnation of France's secular interests against external rivals. From August 1944 to January 1946 the foreign policy of France consisted essentially of an attempt to assert French autonomy in the face of what had been until recently de Gaulle's Anglo-Saxon backers. Into this category fall such episodes as the occupation of the Val d'Aosta beyond the 1939 Italian frontier despite American objections, the occupation of Stuttgart during the collapse against the orders of the American General Devers commanding the army group concerned, and the obstinate effort which, in the end, led to the re-entry of French troops into Indochina after the defeat of the Japanese.

In Syria, French policy was to be less successful. In May 1945 a clash between the nationalist Syrian government of Shukry Kuwatli and French forces under General Beynet, the delegate-general in the Levant, led to British intervention to stop fighting (the British version) or to undermine French suzerainty in Syria (the French version). It seems that the same heavy hand on the part of the local French commander as was to produce another armed clash a little later in Indochina was present here, but this does not exclude the possibility that a number of British officials in Cairo and London felt a French presence in the area to be a useless complication. In any case, de Gaulle's own mind was made up: "I had always expected it, for the national ambitions masked by the world conflict included the British plan to dominate the Middle East. How many times I had already confronted this passionate resolve that was prepared to shatter any barrier that stood in its way!"[51] The temperature of Anglo-French relations was once again reduced to zero, and de Gaulle complained bitterly of the lack of support his policy received in France. Both French and British troops were to withdraw from Syria and Lebanon in 1946.[52]

It was, however, in the Syrian crisis that de Gaulle was to make use of a tactic which reflected a more general view of France's position in the world at this time. Churchill had proposed a conference between America, Britain and France. De Gaulle riposted by suggesting one with Russian and Chinese participation—unacceptable, therefore, to the Americans and British. In fact, the major stroke of a foreign policy designed to balance an excessive reliance on the Anglo-Saxon powers was France's treaty of alliance with Russia—"beloved and powerful Russia"[53]—signed on December 10, 1944. On the one hand, this rather short-lived agreement was useful in terms of prestige and as a reminder to America and Britain that a liberated France had its own cards to play in international affairs.* On the other, Russia and France certainly had a common interest in preventing the revival of German nationalism and an irredentism with claims to Silesia, East Prussia or the Saar. At home, the pact served the purpose both of reassuring French opinion about the future by reviving memories of the old Franco-Russian alliance and of keeping the Communists quiet. In fact, it is hard not to believe that the cooperative attitude of Thorez in 1944 and 1945 had not as its main motive an implicit deal between de Gaulle and Stalin. The attitude of the former towards his Anglo-American allies (including the refusal to meet Roosevelt on his way back from Yalta) may have caused

*The fifth article of the agreement reads: "The High Contracting Parties agree not to conclude any alliance or to take part in any coalition directed against one of them." Clearly, the NATO pact was a breach of this clause.

Moscow to believe that France could be played off against the other Western powers. (At Yalta itself, however, the Moscow treaty did not prevent Stalin from opposing the allocation to France of a place on the German control commission.[54] It was Churchill primarily, and then Roosevelt, who secured a French presence among the occupying powers. On the other hand, de Gaulle's visit to Moscow was something of an *ersatz* satisfaction for the French Communists, a substitute for the positions of real power which he so steadfastly refused them.)*

A policy of balance between East and West, while serving de Gaulle's international prestige, did not produce any very solid returns in terms of diplomatic advantage. Its main repercussions were on the French internal situation, favoring, as it did, national unity and the participation of the French Communist party in the task of reconstruction. It was paradoxical that, at this point, Gaullist diplomacy should have borne its principal fruits on the domestic scene which its author regarded as less important for France than the international. But, while the country was still in ruins after its liberation and dependent on its allies for food and raw materials, no diplomacy, however skillful, could add much to its real power and influence. Only recovery could do that.

France did, however, end up as a permanent member of the Security Council of the United Nations and an occupying power in Germany and Austria. At this time de Gaulle's German policy consisted in the division of Germany into a federation of autonomous states—a plan which, in his view, corresponded to German historical traditions.** The internationalization of the Ruhr and an economic union between France and the Saar completed a picture which was envisaged as one of German subjugation. De Gaulle also refused to join the French zone of Germany (essentially the Palatinate on the left bank of the Rhine and parts of Baden-Wurtemburg on the right) to the administration of the Anglo-American zones which had been merged after the London conference of autumn 1945.

In the whole field of diplomacy, he did his best to impart his own

---

*In the *Mémoires*, de Gaulle recounts how he refused to grant Thorez a Communist foreign minister, defense minister or minister of the interior—"the essential levers of command of the state."[55]

**"There are Germans, there are even Germanies. But where today is Germany?"[56]

style of intransigence to France's representatives. The principles on which this style was based are summed up in a letter to Georges Bidault written on the eve of the San Francisco conference in April 1945:

> You will have to defend yourself, not only against the pressure . . . of the powers . . . but also against the natural inclination of our own negotiators. This inclination, in fact, is to agree with their partners and, as they say, to reach a conclusion. I insist on the fact that such a disposition risks working to our detriment in the present period. That is to say that we must not yield even if an orchestrated storm from foreign and even French press and radio should be unleashed to carry you away. *Since our misfortunes our most fruitful actions have been at the same time those which provoked the most violent storms.*[57] [Italics mine.]

Whether this manner of negotiating was more successful than a less rigid attitude would have been is doubtful. But it provided a foretaste of the brutally dramatic diplomacy of the Fifth Republic.*

In colonial affairs a somewhat mixed inheritance was bequeathed to the Fourth Republic by the provisional government. The Brazzaville conference of January and February 1944, a meeting in which Pleven, the commissioner for colonies, and the governors of the French African colonies and Madagascar took part, decided on a series of reforms ranging from the rationalization of the French administration to measures designed to further economic and social development. Politically speaking, however, there was no question of any break in the connection between France and its colonies. The most that Brazzaville promised was the representation of overseas territories in the Paris parliament, universal suffrage, decentralization and the establishment of local 'autonomous' assemblies. This was, in many respects, a generous program, but it was not one directed in any sense toward independence for France's colonial possessions, nor is it easy to see how it would have been psychologically possible to initiate a real 'decolonization' while the war was still on, and France not yet liberated. In his opening speech

---

*The real criticism of this total unreadiness to make concessions was made by Jacques Dumaine who, in a conversation with Etienne Burin des Roziers, where the latter maintained that the General would never have yielded on a centralized German administration, asked: " 'And what would he have done?' The reply was: 'He would have opposed it'–'And then?'–No reply."[58]

to the conference de Gaulle was still ready to talk of the 'guiding' role to be played by France with regard to the sixty-two million people associated with it. Later he was to pronounce in favor of a federal system for the French empire.*

Brazzaville, nevertheless was a positive achievement which stands to the credit of wartime Gaullism, as does the decree of March 7, 1944, extending French citizenship to certain categories of Algerian Moslem. The system of two electoral colleges for the Algerian assemblies was maintained, but the second (Moslem) college had its representation brought up to an equal number with the first (composed of French and Moslems with French citizenship). It would, in fact, have been easy enough for the CFLN and the provisional government to leave such problems on one side until the war was over. The fact that they did not do so bears witness to a genuine desire for reform which, in terms of previous French colonial policy, was revolutionary enough.

Unfortunately, the evolution of the relations between France and its colonial territories did not always correspond to these good intentions. In May 1943 the Bey of Tunis had been deposed by the French authorities (at the time General Giraud) apparently in breach of the Treaty of Bardo under which the French protectorate had originally been established. It was this deposition that was to set a precedent for that of the Sultan of Morocco under the Fourth Republic. On VE Day (May 8, 1945) there was an abortive Moslem revolt at Sétif in Algeria which was cruelly repressed by the authorities and the local French *colons*. The number of Moslem dead was estimated by an official inquiry at 15,000, and the affair was to provide Algerian nationalism with martyrs and a myth. But it was in Indochina that France was to find itself most immediately facing colonial problems of a dramatic nature.

In 1940 Japanese troops had been stationed in Indochina after an ultimatum which the French governor-general could do nothing but accept. Throughout the war the Japanese gradually extended their hold over the country's administration. On·March 9, 1945, they disarmed or killed the French troops stationed there and, two days later,

*In a press conference at Washington on July 10, 1944: "I believe that each territory over which the French flag waves must be represented inside a system of federal form in which metropolitan France will be one part and where the interests of all will be able to make themselves heard."[59]

proclaimed the independence of Annam under the emperor Bao-Dai. On the collapse of Japan, Indochina north of the 16th parallel was occupied by the Chinese Kuomingtang armies, to the south by the British.

These events, and the evident discomfiture of the French had stirred up a ferment of Vietnamese nationalism which was exploited to full advantage by the Viet Minh nationalist party and its able, Moscow-trained leader Ho Chi Minh.* In these circumstances the re-establishment of French rule would clearly be a difficult operation. But de Gaulle had no doubt that it must be attempted. On the defeat of Japan the Viet Minh, after negotiation with other local nationalist groups in Saigon and Cochin China, had assumed power directly in Hanoi and the northern province of Tonking. It was not until October 3 that elements of General Leclerc's expeditionary force arrived in Saigon. Before that there had already been a massacre of French civilians following an abortive attempt by French prisoners of the Japanese, who had been rearmed by the British, to seize the public buildings of the city. Leclerc was able to pacify the area around Saigon and the Mekong Delta fairly rapidly and then to turn his attention towards Tonking from which the Chinese were to withdraw under an agreement signed in Chunking on February 28, 1946.

This was as far as de Gaulle's provisional government carried its solution to the Indochinese problem, and it is only fair to say that it did much to set France on a course which furnished one of the more disastrous episodes of the Fourth Republic. It seems that Leclerc realized the strength of Vietnamese nationalism and the fact that France would have to come to terms with it. But the appointment by de Gaulle of the Carmelite monk, Admiral Thierry d'Argenlieu, as high commissioner in Indochina brought on the scene a French representative totally unready to compromise, and marked a stage on the road to the hostilities of the autumn of 1946, the French bombardment of Haiphong on November 24 and the Viet Minh attack against French positions in Hanoi on December 19. A policy of strength in Indochina was doomed to failure,

*The full name of the party was Viet Nam Doc Lap Dong Minh Hoi (the League for the Independence of Vietnam), and it was the result of a coalition in May 1941 between the Indochinese Communist party and some small nationalist groups.[60]

and it is possible that, had de Gaulle himself continued in office, he might have acted in accordance with this fact as he was later to do in Algeria. But, during his period of campaigning against the governments of the Fourth Republic, he was to continue to demand a strong hand in Indochina.* Gaullism, therefore, cannot be acquitted of a considerable share in the responsibility for one of the major errors of French policy during the late forties and early fifties.

But de Gaulle was not to continue to direct French policy for long after the end of the war. The Algiers decree of April 21, 1944, had promised that a Constituent Assembly would be called together as soon as possible after the end of the war. Inevitably there would be a return to party politics and the parliamentary atmosphere of which the General had little experience and in which, as time was to show, he felt himself ill at ease. His distaste for the maneuvers of politicians and their regard for party considerations (as opposed to what he considered to be the national interest) dominates the last volume of his *Mémoires*. The depth of his disillusionment is shown in his bitingly scornful remarks about Herriot:

> Edouard Herriot declined my invitation to join the government. I asked him to help in the reconstruction of France; he declared he would devote himself to rebuilding the Radical party.[62]

Léon Blum and Louis Marin also refused to join the government. Moreover, de Gaulle had no party of his own— only great prestige and a handful of loyal followers. The new Christian-Democratic party, the *Mouvement républicain populaire* (MRP), while manifesting a particular attachment to de Gaulle (not without an eye to the coming elections), was to show, after January 1946, that this 'fidelity' had its limits. The bad relations between its leader, Georges Bidault, and de Gaulle also removed it from the latter's orbit.

In the establishment of a new constitution for France it was in

*His statement to a journalist on July 10, 1950, that "the fight carried on for four years in Indochina by France and the French Union is part of this same struggle [against Communist domination]. The ill-disposed people who accuse France of colonialism, while it fights Ho Chi-Minh, will do well to keep silent" looks somewhat odd in the light of the later evolution of his policies.[61]

accordance with de Gaulle's deepest convictions that the provisional government should have decided to bypass the parties and consult the country directly by referendum. On August 17, 1945, a decree was passed setting out the form of the questions to be submitted to the electorate. These were "Do you wish that the Assembly elected this day should be a Constituent Assmbly? " and "If there is an affirmative majority for the first question, do you approve the provisional organization of the public powers set out in the plan submitted to you? " In other words, the voters were to decide whether they wished to change the constitution at all (rather than revert simply to that of the Third Republic), and then whether they were in favor of the provisional government's view of the powers of a Constituent Assembly and the suggested electoral system.

What was at stake here was essentially whether the Constituent Assembly should be able to decide a new constitution without further consultation of the electorate. At the time there appeared to be a considerable danger that any such totally sovereign assembly, with a majority of Socialists and Communists, might be the means of bringing the latter to power via a coalition in much the same way as was proving to be the case in Eastern Europe. The provisional government was to counter this threat by providing that the assembly should sit for only seven months and that the constitution resulting from its deliberations must be submitted to the country in another referendum. It would elect the head of the government, but could only overthrow him by a vote of censure passed by an absolute majority. The voting system was to be one of proportional representation applied at the departmental level.*

These proposals went against a number of cherished republican traditions. By limiting the powers of the assembly, they seemed to be attacking the sovereignty of parliament. By introducing a constitu-

*Without going into technical detail, it can be said that this electoral system had the effect of advantaging the larger parties, thereby corresponding to a fairly general feeling that the 'scrutin d'arrondissement' of the Third Republic had given individual deputies too much independence and contributed to the instability of governments. Since the voters now voted for a party 'list,' the parties could exercise some discipline over their members. It was also felt that proportional representation would give the Communists less seats than they might gain under a simple majority system.

E

tional referendum, they recalled the 'plebiscitary democracy' of the Second Empire which had always been a bug-bear of the French left. The Communists were naturally opposed to a plan directed in the first place against their possible ambitions. The Radicals under Herriot wanted a return to the Constitution of 1875. The MRP and the Socialists eventually decided to answer *Yes* to both questions. But in the consultative assembly on July 29 the government's proposals were rejected by 210 votes to 19. Since, however, the assembly had no direct powers, de Gaulle was able to ignore their opinion. A little later he was to refuse to receive a delegation of protest against the electoral law headed by Léon Jouhaux, secretary-general of the CGT, on the grounds that a trade union official was not empowered to discuss political affairs on the same footing as the representatives of the political parties.[63]

The referendum took place on October 21 and was a success for de Gaulle's view that there should be a Constituent Assembly with limited powers. With only 20.1 percent abstentions, 96.4 percent of those voting answered yes to the first question, 66.3 percent yes to the second one. The 33.7 percent negative reply to the second question represented the Communist vote plus a certain number of traditional republicans shocked by the limitation of the assembly's powers. The Communists also emerged as the largest party from the elections held the same day. They received 26.2 percent of the votes cast as against 23.9 percent for the MRP and 23.4 percent for the Socialists. The Radicals and their allies fell heavily from their prewar eminence with only 10.5 percent, and the right-wing Moderates, many of whose supporters had preferred to vote MRP, did little better with 15.6 percent. Out of the 586 seats in the assembly the Communists gained 151, the Socialists 139, the MRP 150, the Moderates 53 and the Radicals only 29. There were also a number of deputies representing small parties and splinter groups.[64]

De Gaulle was to be unanimously elected as head of the government by the assembly, but immediately found himself faced by the Communists' demands for one at least of the three most important ministries (foreign affairs, defense or interior). Finally after eight days of negotiations, he succeeded in forming a government in which the Communists were given the ministries of labor, national economy and armaments, while Maurice Thorez became a minister of state together with other representatives of the major political parties. Other ministers remained where they were: Pleven at the ministry of finance, Bidault at the Quai d'Orsay and Tixier at the ministry of the interior. With André Malraux as minister of information, a Gaullist entered the cabinet who was to become one of the closest associates of the General.

The immediate problem of cabinet forming was solved. What was not to find any solution was the problem of de Gaulle's relationship to the assembly. The constitutional commission refused to allow him to put to it his own point of view, since he was not a member of the assembly, and, lacking organized party support of his own, he was unable to exercise a controlling influence over deputies only too inclined to the irresponsibility of the *frondeur* and impatient of any check on their powers. The crisis came when, in a debate on national defense credits at the end of the year, the Socialists demanded a 20 percent reduction despite their own participation in the government. After uttering his famous warning that, if the assembly did not heed the necessity for the government to possess authority, dignity and responsibility, they would one day regret it bitterly, de Gaulle decided to resign despite a vote which, in the end, was favorable: "I realized that the matter was already decided, that it would be vain and even unworthy to presume to govern when the parties, their power restored, had resumed their old tricks; in short, that I must now prepare my own departure from the scene."[65] After a week's holiday at Antibes, de Gaulle returned to Paris and, on January 20, 1946, announced to his ministers his intention of resigning, and that he would send a letter to this effect to the president of the National Assembly. The most generous reaction came from Thorez who remarked that this was a departure not lacking in grandeur.[66]* The MRP prepared itself for the 'heavy responsibility' of succeeding the General. The Socialists felt that the assembly, which had been stifled by de Gaulle, could now "freely reveal itself."

It seems probable that de Gaulle's departure at this point had its tactical side. He may well have thought of himself as sufficiently indispensable to France's political stability for his recall to power not to be long delayed. In that case, his position would have been strengthened vis-à-vis the parties, and he would have returned to occupy the position which, in fact, he achieved in 1958: the only resource left

*Another view of the matter was taken by Jacques Dumaine who wrote in his diary for March 11, 1946: "The result is that the General departed one fine Sunday in January, leaving us all flabbergasted."[67]

to France in its greatest need. But that call was not to come for twelve years, and, immediately, as far as public opinion was concerned, there was little reaction to de Gaulle's resignation. The parties and the politicians were relieved by his disappearance from the scene. The man in the street appeared for the moment to be indifferent. Both de Gaulle and the minister of the interior (Tixier) had expected popular demonstrations, but these did not materialize.[68] But he himself at least had little doubt as to the significance of the event: "Gone was that atmosphere of exaltation, that hope of success, that ambition for France, which supported the national soul."[69] In this fact, however, was contained a promise for the future: "In the sidetracked leader, men persisted in seeing a kind of capital of sovereignty, a last resort selected in advance. They supposed such legitimacy could remain latent in a period without anxiety. But they knew it could be invoked by common consent as soon as a new laceration threatened the nation."[70] It was this assurance that was to infuriate the leaders of the political parties. It was this claim that was to provide the basis for political Gaullism under the Fourth Republic. It was this promise that was to be fulfilled in May 1958.

VI

The circumstances of the creation of the Gaullist movement during the years of the Second World War were to have a strong influence on its nature and on the direction of the policies it was to pursue. In the first place, the wartime struggle of de Gaulle created around him a myth, skillfully propagated in the *Mémoires,* which was to become the main driving force of the movement which first produced the *Rassemblement du Peuple francais* (RPF) and then the return to power in 1958. Isolated in London and moving in an atmosphere of military discipline, the men who had chosen to join Free France naturally tended towards a leadership cult, of which the isolated administration of oaths of loyalty to de Gaulle in person was only one instance:

while waiting for France to recognize itself in them, unable to remain loyal to a nationally representative régime which for them no longer existed, they directed towards the Man who had assembled them their sense of patriotic duty and their sense of discipline. They were naturally inclined to magnify their Leader.[71]

It was at this time that the conception of those 'loyal' to de Gaulle (*les fidèles*) and of his companions (*compagnons*) arose. Originally the Gaullist movement in London was authoritarian, given to a military conception of obedience and all the more distrustful of parliamentary institutions for having seen their failure under the Third Republic. Among his immediate associates de Gaulle acquired a charisma that was to prove lasting and that spread to ever wider circles of Frenchmen as the war continued—principally by way of the BBC's French service.

On the other hand, these tendencies of the Gaullist movement were checked by the need for it to appear as the legitimate heir of the republic in contrast to the Vichy government. In its search for legitimacy and recognition wartime Gaullism was led to broaden its basis and to take on a left-wing tinge which never faded and which gave it that appeal to left and right that so strongly resembles the attraction exercised by Bonapartism. This resemblance was accentuated by de Gaulle's own evident predilection for a form of plebiscitary democracy which would allow him to appeal directly to the country over the heads of such 'intermediary powers' as parties and politicians. This trend, always present in his thinking, can only have been accentuated by his experience of party politics during the period of the provisional government. The idea that strong government must be based on direct consultation of the country by a leader placed above the party battle has been the basic constitutional program of Gaullism throughout its existence.

During the war Gaullism also took on a style of intransigent nationalism in its dealings with other countries, whether they were France's enemies or allies. Much of de Gaulle's diplomacy during the war had a character of symbolic action, producing no immediate effect and often appearing counter-productive in terms of the reactions it excited. But, here again, American refusal to recognize the Free French movement and British actions in Syria and elsewhere confirmed the General in his belief in the fundamental egotism of states and made him even more aware of the threat to French interests that could arise from those who were theoretically friends and partners. The tone of Gaullist foreign policy thus became one of desperate resistance to 'usurpation' which, "things being what they are," could hardly fail to be attempted from one quarter or another. In the years between 1940 and 1946 this was felt all the more sharply in that there was little that could be done to counter such encroachments. For five years Gaullists lived a sort of perpetual twilight of France, a continual battle against overwhelming odds, and the movement was marked by this experience—sometimes extending its defensive attitudes as far as paranoia.

Two types of Gaullist emerge during the years of exile. On the one hand, there were the high officials and administrators who did their best to bring order into a chaotic situation: Couve de Murville, Massigli, Cassin. There were also brilliant generals: a Leclerc, a Koenig or a De Lattre de Tassigny, and colonial governors such as Félix Eboué. On the other hand, there were what might be called the 'adventurers' whose wartime experience led them into the ways of intelligence and clandestine action: the Soustelles and the Passys. A figure such as Jean Moulin united the two types, but this was rare. One result of the conditions under which Gaullism was born was that it could appeal to a number of men experienced in political organization, secret intrigue, propaganda and, if necessary, the techniques of the *coup d'état*. In this, as in other respects, the experience of the wartime struggle was decisive.

By 1946 it can be said that the main elements of what Gaullism was later to be under the Fifth Republic had been assembled, though the proportions in which they were to be present at any one time were to change considerably over the years. Moreover, the 'second' Gaullism of the Fourth Republic, the RPF, was to fail—perhaps more because of the ability of the republican régime in the early fifties to pull itself together than because of any inherent inferiority of the *Rassemblement* to the *Union pour la nouvelle République* (UNR). It can now be seen that de Gaulle's position in face of his fellow-countrymen in 1946 was such that any dramatic failure of the Fourth Republic would lead to an appeal to one whose potential as a saviour had not been damaged by compromise with a discredited system. The 'guide' might seem to have been forgotten by the mass of Frenchmen. He was certainly somewhat written down by foreign diplomats and French parliamentary politicians. But de Gaulle, from 1946 onwards, always represented an option which the bankruptcy of the Fourth Republic could quickly turn into a reality. In France, in the late forties and early fifties, saviours were rare—only Pinay and Mendès-France exercised any hold on the country's imagination—but occasions for salvation were to be all too frequent.

CHAPTER IV

The Fourth Republic and the RPF

*Les Ministères de conjonction des
centres ... sont difficiles à faire vivre dans tous
les temps. Leur formation répond souvent à un
besoin. Elle est souvent souhaitée par l'opinion
silencieuse du pays. Pourtant harcelés sur leurs
flancs, les hommes qui les composent emploient
le meilleur de leur temps à disputer à la gauche
comme à la droite une existence que leurs amis
du centre s'empressent mollement à affermir.*
—*Joseph Caillaux*

During the Fourth Republic (1946-1958) Gaullism was an opposition
force on the right of the political spectrum, at first seeming to threaten
the régime with destruction, but later being painlessly absorbed into the
parliamentary game and eventually disowned by its founder. For the
last four years of the régime, de Gaulle himself appeared to be in a kind
of spiritual exile. His last major statement at this time, in which he
declared his intention of making no further intervention in public
affairs, was made at a press conference on June 30, 1955. In the course
of his replies he was to predict the downfall of the régime as he had
done many times before, but he could hardly have believed that it
would come so soon.*

In fact, the Fourth Republic had survived many shocks during the

*"Without being able yet to foresee what factor or what events will bring about
the change of régime, one can believe that the shock will come."[1]

course of its twelve-year existence, and it was hard to foresee that the Algerian rebellion would deal it a fatal blow. Economic crisis, the internal threat from the Communist party or the RPF, the war in Indochina, German rearmament, crises in Tunisia and Morocco—all these factors of political disturbance had been overcome, and the Fourth Republic had certain quiet, but definite successes to be put to its credit. Economic expansion had begun, and the policy of European integration initiated under the auspices of Robert Schuman (and the inspiration of Jean Monnet) was beginning to pay tangible dividends in terms of increased trade and greater prestige. Between 1949 and 1958 the average real hourly wage in France rose by about 40 percent. The damage of the war had been largely repaired and the economic stagnation of the thirties dissipated. It is ironic that political stability, generally held to be the result of economic well-being on the part of the population of modern democracies, should not have accompanied this achievement.

But the Algerian war proved to be the last straw that broke the back of a sorely burdened régime. For, even when resolved, each succeeding crisis brought in its train a legacy of division and dissension, of personal and party enmities which was to make it impossible to find any majority government possessing the authority to cope with a problem behind which loomed the threat of civil war. As time went on, discipline within the parties became harder and harder to maintain, and a parliamentary system, to which it had been hoped that more strongly organized political groupings would give greater stability, was no more able to produce lasting governments than its predecessor under the Third Republic. From January 20, 1946, to the end of the Fourth Republic there were twenty-four governments. And this political kaleidoscope brought with it a frightful wastage of political talent and personal authority. The heads of government under the Fourth Republic were often men of ability, many of whom had fought courageously in the Resistance during the war. But the best of them, through their very success in solving problems, exhausted their own power to make headway against the inertia of the system. At every step new issues were brought into play which, in turn, became factors of division. With the *Loi Barangé* of 1951, which granted subsidies to church schools, the ghost of anticlericalism, laid by the events of the war, was raised again, and the immediate result was to separate the

Socialists from the MRP with whom they had been allied during the Third Force period of the régime. The public debate on the European Defense Community (EDC) split the Socialists down the middle. The MRP were unwilling to pardon Mendès-France his failure to take a 'European' line on this issue or his reversal of an Indochinese policy that had largely been carried out by MRP ministers.[2] To this confused scene were added the action of pressure groups (such as the powerful beet-growers' and vine-growers' lobbies) and the emergence of grass-roots movements such as the Poujadists who owed their existence to discontent in the more backward areas of France with the results of economic change. It is small wonder that only Antoine Pinay emerged from these twelve years with any accumulation of political capital. In 1958 it was to be true that the only 'recourse' was de Gaulle. Other possible leaders had spent what credit they had by virtue of a law which seemed to dictate that, as bees can only sting once, so politicians under the Fourth Republic were only able to solve one or two problems before meeting their political deaths.

In all this de Gaulle and his followers played a negative role, and Gaullism only altered its position—in so far as it had one—to change from being an active threat to the régime to being merely a symbolic condemnation of it. Politicians who had given their support to the RPF might be tempted to participate in the "delights and poisons of the system," but de Gaulle himself never varied from his opposition, though he was prepared to show some sympathy towards the efforts of an energetic prime minister such as Mendès-France.* The Fourth Republic was condemned for him by the indecisiveness of its leadership and the inadequacy of its institutions, which allowed parties and politicians to act as feudal powers intervening between the French people and the genuine exercise of sovereignty.

II

The establishment of institutions for the republic was, indeed, the first problem which de Gaulle's successors at the head of the French

---

*On his investiture on June 18, 1954, Mendès-France at once sent a telegram to de Gaulle. On October 13 they met for discussions and, in a speech on December 4, de Gaulle praised the Prime Minister's "enthusiasm, worth and vigor."[3]

E*

state had to solve and the first occasion of his openly expressed opposition to the régime. In early 1946, under the Gouin government, the Constituent Assembly had produced a draft constitution which corresponded to the ideas of its Communist-Socialist majority and provided for a single-chamber National Assembly electing both the president of the republic and the prime minister, and with practically no checks on its power except dissolution. In that case, the government which had recourse to this weapon would have had to hand over power to the assembly's president. The president of the republic was a shadowy figure forbidden even to designate the prime minister. This was a constitution which followed closely the old left-wing tradition of an entirely sovereign elected body (on the model of the Convention of 1792) accompanied by a merely residual executive. As such it was bitterly opposed by the MRP, the Radicals and, in general, by all those who feared a 'Marxist dictatorship.' At a referendum on May 5, 1946, it was rejected by 53 percent of those voting.

Elections now had to be held on June 2, and the MRP were able to consolidate their success in getting the constitution rejected by becoming the largest party in the new Constituent Assembly The Communists gained 25.9 percent of the votes (153 seats); the Socialsts 21.1 percent (128 seats); the MRP 28.2 percent (166 seats); the Radicals and their allies 11.6 percent (52 seats); and the Moderates on the right 12.8 percent (67 seats). There was, therefore, a distinct gain for the MRP and a distinct loss for the Socialists, while the Radicals too seemed to have done something to restore their traditional positions of strength. Fear of a Communist-dominated 'popular front' was increasingly carrying voters away from the left—a lesson that would soon be learned by the Socialists—and the MRP, with its respectable record of resistance, provided a party on which anti-Communists could concentrate their votes. This change was a decisive one in French political life after the Liberation; it meant the end of the 'Marxist coalition' and the beginnings of that gradual movement to the right which was one of the most constant trends of the Fourth Republic.*

It still remained to find a constitution, and, under the Bidault government, *tripartisme* between the three major parties continued to

*As Professor Chapsal has put it, "The change was a decisive one; it must be realized how important this stage was in the political life of post-Liberation France."4

be the order of the day as a compromise was painfully worked out. There would now be a second chamber, the *Conseil de la République*, and the president of the republic (elected by both chambers in a secret ballot) had restored to him the powers he possessed under the Third Republic. He was to preside over cabinet meetings and could nominate prime ministers. In fact, under the first president of the Fourth Republic, Vincent Auriol, the powers of the office were extended considerably by the vigor of the incumbent and the continuity of his acquaintance with public affairs.* The second draft constitution, like the first, established an Assembly of the French Union which, in practice, was to have little influence on events.

If this constitution (which was to be adopted on October 13, 1946, by 53.5 percent of the vote) contained some strengthening of the executive and some limitation of the powers of the National Assembly, it failed completely to correspond to de Gaulle's idea of what was necessary to insure the existence of a firm and stable executive. At Bayeux, on June 16, he gave a definitive version of his constitutional ideas which was to be put into effect under the Fifth Republic. He demanded two chambers, the second of which would be elected by the *Conseils généraux* and *Conseils municipaux*. He suggested a federal organization of the French Union, whose assembly would be presided by the president of the republic.[6] Above all, he claimed that the executive power should proceed from the head of state, whose wide functions and discretionary powers would correspond to this situation. The passage is worth quoting in full, since it contains the essence of Gaullist constitutional doctrine:

It is therefore from the Head of State, placed above the parties, elected by a college including Parliament, but much wider and composed in such a way as to make of him the President of the French Union at the same time as that of the Republic—it is from him that executive power must proceed. The Head of State has the task of reconciling the general interest as regards the choice of men with the

*Here is Dumaine's judgment: "Auriol is prudently building a presidential function which has never existed before. The President of the Republic no longer confines himself to pointing out objectively the measures that should be taken to insure national well-being; he clearly asserts the necessity of following a certain policy and invites his fellow-countrymen to follow it with him. The Third Republic would never have tolerated such a departure from his position of arbitrator on the part of the first magistrate."[5]

direction shown by Parliament. His is the mission of naming the ministers and first, naturally, the Prime Minister who will have to direct the government's policy and work. It is the Head of State's function to promulgate laws and to make decrees, for both of these bind the citizen in respect of the state as a whole. It is his task to preside cabinet meetings and to exert there the influence of that continuity which a nation cannot do without. It is his province to serve as arbitrator above political contingencies, either normally through the cabinet, or else, at moments of serious confusion, by asking the country to make known its sovereign decision through elections. If it should happen that the country is in danger, it is his duty to guarantee national independence and the treaties concluded by France.[7]

As the final sentence indicates, de Gaulle's view of the powers and duties of a head of state was not uninfluenced by his experience of the French collapse in 1940 when it was hard to find a central figure around whom patriots could unite. In its essence his view of the presidential power appeared to resemble the 'strong' conception of the head of state so often voiced during the Third Republic (by a Millerand, for example). However, it went a good deal further in that de Gaulle's own personal prestige would have enabled him (and nobody imagined that he was speaking of another head of state) to use such a constitution irresistibly even against the opposition of a National Assembly. In the Bayeux speech there is no mention of the referendum as an instrument of government, but de Gaulle had used it before, and his words left little doubt about his opinion that a future president should support himself on a popular plebiscite as against the intermediary powers of parties and politicians. On August 27, 1946, in a statement criticizing the second constitutional draft, de Gaulle was to lay special stress on the president of the republic's inability to communicate directly with the people, and it is clear that, for him, such popular support against the party 'feudalities' was an essential source of strength for the head of state.[8] It is not necessary to see in all this Maurrassian ideas of what the structure of the French state should be. The need for a strong executive had been felt on the French right—and not only on the right—since before 1914. The famous pamphlet of the Socialist Marcel Sembat *Faites un roi, sinon faites la paix* made the same point in 1912.

Such ideas, however, ran counter to republican orthodoxy, as Léon

Blum was not slow to point out after the Bayeux speech. Memories of MacMahon and Boulanger, of Casimir-Périer and Millerand were invoked by proposals which implied essentially the institution of a presidential system. Yet the left was not wrong to perceive in de Gaulle the Bonapartist tradition that runs through French nineteenth and twentieth century history. In practice, a Gaullist constitution, so far from providing for 'countervailing powers,' has meant that all initiatives come from the top and are carried through by the executive. Under the Fifth Republic, until May 1968, the President's wishes were not seriously thwarted by parliament or a public opinion which, on the whole, accepted what was put before it. This is perhaps a democratic form of government, not lacking in public consultation, but it is certainly not a 'republican' one in the traditional French sense of the word. To men reared under the Third Republic in the anarchic conception of the state propagated by Alain it was shocking. To the Communists it was also shocking, but for different reasons: they saw in a strong presidency held by a non-Communist a threat to their own position.

De Gaulle, however, despite his failure to carry the day at the referendum of October 13 and to prevent the adoption of the new constitution, was to come back time and time again to the defects of the system actually adopted by the Fourth Republic. The reform of institutions was to occupy a special place in the RPF's program, and de Gaulle himself was to affirm repeatedly that nothing could be done without a change being made which would provide for a strong French state.*

Immediately after the referendum of October 13 came elections (November 10) to the new National Assembly, the sixth consultation of the electorate within little over a year. On this occasion the Communists improved their June position, getting 28.2 percent of the votes cast and becoming once again the largest single party in the

---

*"Nothing is more necessary for our country than to organize the State in such a way that it disposes of enough strength in its structure; of enough efficiency in its working; of enough credit in its men to direct the nation and insure its salvation whatever happens."[9] The whole of the first section of *La France sera la France,* a collection of de Gaulle's writings and speeches issued by the RPF and edited by Georges Pompidou, is devoted to institutions. On May 15, 1958, commenting on the Algerian crisis, de Gaulle's first words were to be "The degradation of the State . . . " It was from this fact that all the rest followed.[10]

assembly (182 seats). The MRP received 25.9 percent (173 seats); the
Socialists 17.8 percent (102 seats); the Radicals and their allies 11.1
percent (69 seats—a loss of votes, but an improvement in seats); the
right-wing Moderates 12.9 percent (67 seats). The main feature of the
election was the continued decline of the Socialists, partly due to
internal quarrels and partly to the attraction exercised on their voters
by the Communists. A small *Union Gaulliste* founded by René Capitant
without any support from the General had little success, obtaining only
3 percent of the votes cast.[11] With the election of the council of the
republic and of Vincent Auriol as president of the republic in January
1947, the structure of the régime was completed in a form that was to
last, with some slight modifications, until the crisis of May 1958.

III

However, a new constitution did little to solve the problems that were
to bedevil the political life of the Fourth Republic. In part, these
problems sprang from the nature of the French political system and
from its all too accurate reflection of national differences of opinion. In
part, they were the ordinary difficulties with which any French régime
would have had to deal: the economy, foreign policy, the liquidation of
the French colonial empire. Before looking closer at Gaullism under the
Fourth Republic, a clear portrait must be drawn of the régime and, in
part to correct some common misconceptions, of its successes and
failures.

Basically, the political situation under the Fourth Republic was a
simple one: a steady movement to the right.

On May 5, 1947, Paul Ramadier, the Socialist prime minister,
dismissed his Communist ministers and brought 'tripartism' to an end.
Thereafter, the Communists were to exist in the opposition into which
the facts of the international situation and the deepening Cold War had
thrown them. In fact, they were excluded from possible political
combinations just as the right-wing Catholics had been before 1914.
This meant that there could be no left-wing majority in the assembly.
At best, there would be governments headed by Socialists or with
Socialist participation, but these always required support on the right,
and there was bound to be a tendency for political power to slip in that

direction. The dilemma of the Socialists was, therefore, whether to participate in such coalitions (and risk compromising their principles) or whether to abstain from participation (and see their own policies increasingly repudiated or neglected).

Up to 1951 this dilemma was concealed to some extent by the emergence of the Gaullist RPF on the right, and in total opposition to the régime. It looked as if, by helping to maintain the center coalition of the Third Force, the Socialists were defending parliamentary democracy itself. After the elections of June 1951, however, the question of Catholic schools and the voting of the *Loi Barangé* separated the Socialists irrevocably from their MRP partners of the Third Force and pushed the governmental majority still further to the right—a success for the parliamentary tactics of the RPF.* The latter process was also hastened by the gradual absorption of the RPF deputies into the parliamentary game contrary to the orders of de Gaulle himself. After the elections of January 1956, when the Socialists returned to power under the pressure of the Algerian war, it was too late to pursue specifically left-wing policies.

The basic stability of this political trend to the right did not, however, prevent great changes in terms of party politics from taking place under the Fourth Republic. During its twelve years of existence there were two general elections and one attempt (the 1954-55 Mendès-France government) to introduce a new style of politics and impart fresh impetus to a régime that seemed to have slowed down to a halt. From 1947 to 1951 the parties of the center were battling on both their right and left flanks against the Communists and Gaullists, the latter gaining in strength as the former appeared more threatening. It was in October 1947, after the reconstitution of a Communist International in the shape of the Cominform and an outbreak of strikes of an insurrectionary character in France itself, that the RPF won its sweeping successes in the municipal elections, which allowed de Gaulle to claim that the Third Force no longer had the support of public opinion. But, as public order was successfully maintained, and economic conditions began to improve under the influence of the

---

*The *Loi Barangé* provided for a subsidy of 3,000 old francs per year per child at primary school paid directly to the families. Thus it also benefited those families who had their children in private (religious) schools as well as those much greater number who sent their children to the lay state schools.

Marshall Plan, the danger of an actual *coup d'état* from either right or left seemed to have been removed. By April 1949 Jacques Dumaine could write in his diary of "euphoria reigning in France."[12] Not that economic questions had been taken out of politics. Up to 1951 the governments of the Fourth Republic had all fallen on social or economic issues, which were those that separated the Socialists from their partners in the coalition. By 1950 it had become clear that there was a growing gulf between them and the MRP which might make the National Assembly ungovernable.

The Socialists had left the Bidault government early that year, and more and more issues (Indochina, economic policy, education) revealed profound disagreements between them and their partners. Under these circumstances there seemed nothing for it but to advance the elections, and, before holding them, the leaders of the majority intended to introduce a new electoral law. This was eventually passed on May 9, 1951, and provided for alliances between different parties (*apparentements*). If such an alliance received more than half the votes cast in a district, it would get all the seats to the exclusion of other, nonallied parties. If it did not, the seats were divided proportionally between the lists, alliances being treated as one list for the purposes of the division.[13] This, writes one authority, was a "*system fundamentally conceived against the Communist party.*"[14] By allowing the center coalition the advantages of a single party, it averted the danger of the Third Force parties being crushed between the Communists and the RPF and promised to reduce the heavy Communist representation which had at times made the orderly conduct of parliamentary business almost impossible during the previous assembly. The results corresponded to this expectation. The Communists, while receiving 26.9 percent of the total of the averages of the lists—a slight fall from 1946—only got 103 seats. The Socialists with 14.6 percent had 107 seats; the MRP got 12.6 percent and 95 seats; the Radicals and their allies 10 percent and 90 seats; the Moderates 14.1 percent and 96 seats; and the RPF 21.6 percent and 121 seats.*

Thus the parties of the Third Force emerged from the 1951 elections with their immediate objective of defeating both Communists

---

*The departments of the Seine and Seine-et-Oise were excluded from this system. Since incomplete voting papers were accepted, it has been necessary to take the percentage gained by each party of the general average of the lists.[15]

and RPF achieved. Indeed, the RPF under the old electoral system would only have had 144 deputies, and its relatively disappointing result was therefore due to a fall in its support as much as to the *apparentements.* What was, however, a long-term threat to the position of parties other than Communist or RPF has been succinctly described by François Goguel in his analysis of these elections:

> The two opposition parties, the RPF and the Communist party, received together the votes of 42.2 percent of the registered voters in the seventeen industrial departments, compared with 35.3 percent received by the Center parties. In the rest of France, the opposition won the votes of only 34.7 percent of the registered voters, compared with 40.6 percent won by the government parties. In other words, the parties of the Center have a majority in the country as a whole because of the votes they received in those parts of France which are least dynamic economically and least modernized.[16] *

This distinction between 'active' and 'static' France, roughly divided by a line drawn between Le Havre and Marseille, was to give some substance to Gaullist claims to a modernity superior to that of the governmental parties. It also pointed to a future in which the positions of the traditional political parties would be progressively eroded by the social change brought about by French economic growth.

Meanwhile, the result of the elections produced a National Assembly divided into six almost equal groups, "the hexagon" as an ex-prime minister called it. With Socialist participation in, or support of, a government there would have been a fairly substantial center-right or center-left majority. But the Socialists had been cut off from their previous allies by the *Loi Barangé* and felt the freer to indulge the prejudices of their party-members in that any immediate threat to the régime seemed to have been removed. Without them, MRP, Radicals and Moderates did not possess a majority. This dilemma was resolved by the gradual absorption of the RPF deputies into the coalition which now became definitely right-wing in character. The occasion for the first breach in the RPF's total opposition to the régime was the investiture of Pinay in March 1952 when 27 Gaullists voted for him to the displeasure of de Gaulle who described them as soldiers who did not

*Another calculation based on the productivity index for different departments produces the same results.

wish to fight but had gone to draw their rations.[17] This group formed
itself into the *Action Républicaine et Sociale* (ARS), but, in January
1953, after the failure of Soustelle to form a government, the RPF
deputies as a whole voted for the investiture of René Mayer. On May
26, 1953, the group changed its name to the *Union des Républicains
d'Action Sociale* (URAS) after a statement by de Gaulle calling a halt
to the *Rassemblement's* electoral and parliamentary activity. In June
1953 Gaullists were for the first time to participate in a government of
the Fourth Republic, that of Joseph Laniel.*

Thus a center-right majority existed in the assembly. But the entry of
the Gaullists into the complicated game of coalition politics did nothing
to simplify it. For not merely were the old causes of disunity present
within the majority, but the new ones had been added to them—in
particular, the issue of the European Defense Community (EDC). This
not only opposed the 'European' MRP to the Gaullists, but also split all
the other parties with the exception of the Communists. And the years
between 1951 and 1958 also saw other divisive issues of foreign policy:
Indochina, Tunisia, Morocco and, finally, Algeria. In fact, the entry of
the Gaullists into the political system of the Fourth Republic—in itself
a natural enough result of their election as deputies—partly coincided
with, and was partly responsible for, a shift in French political
preoccupations. From Pinay onwards, with only one exception,
governments would fall on questions of foreign, rather than domestic,
policy.**

The obvious weakness of a régime based on a deeply divided public
opinion and the growing crisis abroad (primarily in Indochina, but also
in North Africa) were to lead at this period of the Fourth Republic to
two attempts to govern, which, although very different in style, both
succeeded in gaining wide support among ordinary Frenchmen, but, for
that very reason, were unwelcome to members of the National
Assembly. The first of these was the Pinay government which lasted
from March to December 1952. Its nature was described by André
Siegfried as a "new attempt at expression on the part of the right,

---

*The internal contradictions in the RPF, which brought about this decision, will
be discussed later.

**Pinay's fall was apparently on the issue of family allowances. Behind the
immediate question, however, lurked MRP doubts of his European orthodoxy and
loyalty to EDC.

under the as yet untried form of a liberal Conservatism, to find whose equivalent one would doubtless have to go back to the Third Republic."[18] Pinay, in fact, was a figure in the most constant traditions of French politics, and his program of restoration of economic confidence, deflation and the lowering of prices was supported by public opinion which kept him in power despite the reservations of the deputies. Some of the remedies such as the cuts in capital investment may have been dubious, but the family doctor approach adopted by Pinay himself was highly successful.

Abroad, however, the problems continued to pile up. If Pinay signed the Bonn agreements by which Germany became a sovereign state again and the Treaty of Paris establishing the EDC, he did not get it ratified by the assembly. Nor did he succeed in mastering the mounting agitation in North Africa where, in Tunisia, the appointment of a strong Resident, de Hautecloque, had marked the beginning of a repression including brutal reprisals in the Cap Bon area and the arrest of the prime minister and four other members of the Chenik government. In Morocco there had also been riots and reprisals in Casablanca after demonstrations to protest against the murder by French counter-terrorists of Ferhat Hached, the secretary-general of the *Union générale des Travailleurs Tunisiens* (December 5, 1952). With this type of problem neither Pinay nor his majority were well fitted to cope. Nor could he do anything to disengage France from the war in Indochina where, after the death of de Lattre de Tassigny in January 1952, the military situation was again deteriorating.

The Pinay 'experiment' succeeded in combatting the immediate crisis of inflation and a deficit in the balance of payments, but it left to its successor all too many problems in other fields. Moreover, Pinay had not imparted any new style to French politics. Certainly, he had gained the confidence of the average Frenchman, but this success was more in the nature of a return to the father-figures of the Third Republic than a signpost of the future. Pinay was probably more modern than he seemed or than was indicated by his choice of Jacques Rueff (who had already been one of Poincaré's advisers in 1926) as his principle financial expert. In fact, his government can perhaps be considered as the zenith of the Fourth Republic, the point at which the system appeared to be at its most efficient. But, just for that reason, Pinay's policies were not precisely a clarion call to those who believed that

France was changing and that French institutions needed reforming in consequence. Perhaps, after all, his major achievement is to be found in the area of pure parliamentary politics: his successful bid for the support of some Gaullist deputies which signified the beginning of the end for the RPF.*

It was left to Mendès-France to introduce a new style of vigorous government. In a government lasting from June 1954 to February 1955 he made an effort to produce a sort of French 'New Deal' in which problems would be faced and solved. His phrase "to govern is to choose" had already been pronounced in 1953 when he failed to secure the investiture of the assembly, and his intention of living up to his assertion had been widely diffused by an adulatory band of journalists centered on the weekly paper *L'Express*. Around Mendès-France were grouped a number of advisers who were deemed to represent the dynamic elements in French life, the 'new wave' of young people now growing up and the technocrats who had been responsible for expanding French productivity and ending the economic Malthusianism of prewar days. Immediately, Mendès-France had to deal with Indochina; the fall of Dien Bien Phu and the apparent deadlock at the Geneva conference placed it first upon the agenda. After having announced that if a solution were not found by July 20, he would resign, he succeeded in getting an agreement at Geneva by that date. In Tunisia he calmed the nationalist agitation by flying to Tunis and promising "internal autonomy" to the protectorate. The EDC treaty was allowed to be defeated in the National Assembly without the government committing itself in its support and after a vain effort by Mendès-France to get its terms modified.** "His attitude," wrote André Siegfried, "is that of a liquidator: a liquidator first of all of the Asian war, of the Tunisian question, of EDC . . . . The year 1954 will therefore correspond to a rapid succession of spectacular liquidations, giving the impression at the time that they are really solutions. The effect is great, even sensational, but afterwards it appears that the

*De Gaulle's own opinion of Pinay at this time was contained in the remark: "I did not save France to give it to a tanner."[19]

**His adversaries were to maintain that this attitude on the part of Mendès-France's government was part of the price paid for assistance from Molotov during the Geneva negotiations. Bidault, on the other hand, regards the defeat of EDC as the counterpart of Gaullist votes.[20]

problem remains all the same and that the root of the difficulties has not been extracted."[21]

That, indeed, was the trouble. Mendès-France could let EDC drop, but he had to agree to a scheme for German rearmament and entry into NATO far less advantageous for France than the original supranational one. In North Africa, Tunisia might momentarily be settled, but the Algerian rebellion was to begin on November 1, 1954, and, in Morocco, the crisis created by the deposition of the Sultan Sidi Mohammed ben Youssef on August 20, 1953, had not been resolved.* Meanwhile Mendès-France and his government were accumulating implacable enemies: 'European' deputies outraged by his attitude towards EDC, right-wingers alarmed by his policy in North Africa and his withdrawal from Indochina, deputies representing the rural alcohol distillers (whose privileges he had attacked), deputies hostile to the *scrutin d'arrondissement* to which he wished to return, rivals in the Radical party and those politicians who were suspicious of a new style that implied addressing oneself to the country over the heads of the assembly. All these forces were soon to combine for the government's defeat. The immediate occasion was Algeria, and the action which gave rise to it, ironically enough in view of subsequent events, was the appointment of Soustelle as governor-general of the province. After his defeat Mendès-France committed a political error by returning to the rostrum to defend himself and denounce the result of the vote, thereby justifying those who had always claimed that he had little respect for the assembly.

Mendès-France's had been an attempt to change French political habits by a head-on collision with them, and it is probable that such an enterprise was doomed to failure unless carried out by a leader enjoying even more prestige in circumstances even more desperate than those prevailing after the fall of Dien Bien Phu. It may be that he would have been more at ease in a presidential-type régime, but, in the absence of a change of constitution, his policy of dynamic movement was bound to become bogged down in the morass of conflicting interests and opinions that formed the 1951 assembly. "In so right-wing an Assembly

*Mendès-France reacted vigorously to the Algerian rebellion declaring: "Do not expect from us any consideration for the sedition, any compromise with it. One does not compromise when it is a question of defending the internal peace of the nation and the integrity of the Republic. The departments of Algeria form part of the Republic, they have been French for many years . . . " The Minister of the Interior, Mitterrand, also said: "Algeria is France."[22]

a liberal leader had little chance, and that little was denied him by the Allies' insistent demand for German rearmament."[23] EDC was certainly the biggest factor in bringing about Mendès-France's downfall, but, by falling when he did, he, at any rate, avoided becoming too committed to a policy towards the Algerian rebellion which he had started off on a note of intransigence. Meanwhile he had disposed of some problems and had shown that a government based on the traditional parties (and the Radical party was the most traditional of them all) could also be dynamic. In the 1956 election this was to serve his party well with that section of the electorate which welcomed strong leadership and which had, therefore, voted RPF in 1947 and 1951. The intellectual cult of Mendès-France had, indeed, more than a whiff of Bonapartism about it, and it was this that brought into play against him something of the same suspicions as had been held against de Gaulle.* The Mendès-France 'experiment' can also be viewed as a sort of aborted Gaullism, a preview of what was to be more successfully carried through under the Fifth Republic. It was certainly a demonstration that de Gaulle's opinion that institutional change must precede other reform had some reason on its side. The ultimate failure of Mendès-France was an example of the limits set to the action of an intelligent and forceful political leader under the constitution of 1946.

After the Mendès-France episode, France returned during the government of Edgar Faure (also a member of the Radical party) to a more classical conception of the duties of a prime minister of the Fourth Republic. This skillful politician was prepared to maneuver rather than to attack problems directly. The difference in style from Mendès-France is suggested in Faure's investiture statement to the assembly which proposed the exact opposite of his predecessor's "to govern is to choose":

The true choice is not between ideals, it is the choice between means;

---

*"These voters for a reformed radicalism seem to come to it for the most part from milieux which had voted MRP in 1945 and 1946, RPF in 1947 and 1951. That is, more than any other category of non-Communist voters they are particularly conscious of the necessity for a profound renewal of French political life .... But experience proves that these voters (especially responsive to the prestige of an individual: it is in this sense that the Mendèsist wave of the Paris area in 1956 evokes, not only the Gaullist wave of 1947-51, but even the Boulangist wave of 1889) are particularly unstable."[24]

the bad choice between means is the only real choice as against the ideal. Is not to choose the means precisely to govern? [25]

This method brought Faure his successes, and they were not negligible. Under his auspices, although the position in Algeria continued to get worse, France's economy was healthy, and the Sultan of Morocco returned to his throne. But Mendès-France's attempt to assert his control over the Radical party threatened Faure's position directly, and he decided to go to the country before his opponents were fully prepared for the elections. A defeat on a vote of confidence in November 1955 gave him his chance to dissolve the assembly*–a step which aroused bitter enmity among the opposition and caused him to be expelled from the Radical party along with other right-wing Radicals who retired into the *Rassemblement des gauches républicaines* (RGR).**

The elections of January 2, 1956, took place in a great deal of confusion, and the results showed that Edgar Faure's gamble had failed. The governmental coalition which he headed, and whose supporters were essentially the MRP, the Moderates, the dissident Radicals (RGR) and some ex-Gaullists (*Républicains-Sociaux*), had hoped that the ex-Gaullist vote would fall to them. But this calculation was undermined by the intervention of an unexpected factor: the Poujadists or the *Union de Défense des Commerçants et Artisans* (UDCA). This movement, at first an apparently spontaneous protest on the part of 'static' France against economic change and a tax burden which were combining to make the occupations of small shopkeeper, farmer or businessman increasingly hard to pursue, ended by being submerged in the nationalist tide that was beginning to sweep France under the impulsion of the Algerian war.*** Meanwhile the movement was

---

*The constitutional revision of 1954 had abolished the 1946 provision by which the president of the assembly became head of government in the event of a dissolution. Faure could therefore continue in office until the election. This made dissolution possible.

**Bitterness between the factions went very far. In December 1955 *L'Express* spoke of "Faure-Laval" and published a cartoon showing Laval's head on Faure's shoulders.[26]

***Pierre Poujade, the movement's founder, was to express these feelings in a way that recalls *Action française*: "The French people has had enough of compromises, scandals, treasons and desertions. It has had enough of seeing 'the rigadoon danced on its belly' by a stateless Mafia of traffickers and pederasts."[27]

characterized by familiar anti-parliamentary sentiments and the suspicions of Parisian politicians commonly held in the provinces. In the election it was to win nearly two and a half million votes (11.6 percent of the total of the average of the lists) and elect 52 deputies. This was enough to ruin the chances of the right-center coalition led by Faure. Its MRP supporters only got 11.1 percent (73 seats); the Moderates (Independents and Peasants) 15.3 percent (95 seats); the RGR 3.9 percent (14 seats). On the left, the Communists maintained their position with 25.9 percent of the vote but improved it in the assembly by occupying 150 seats. The components of the "Republican Front" alliance led by Mendès-France, Mollet, Mitterrand and Chaban-Delmas also did well. The Socialists had 15.2 percent of the vote and 94 seats; the "Republican Front" Radicals and their allies 11.3 percent and about 75 seats, though it is difficult to estimate the exact political orientation of some Radicals elected. As for the Gaullists they received 3.9 percent and elected 21 deputies, of whom about a third were to support the "Republican Front."

If the right-center's hope of a clear majority had been destroyed by the emergence of the Poujadist right-wing opposition, there was also no majority for the Republican Front which was called on to govern under the prime ministership of Guy Mollet by the President of the Republic, René Coty.* At first it was supported by the Communists and the MRP as well as the Socialists and Radicals. But, after Mollet's road to Damascus conversion to the pursuit of the Algerian war on his visit to Algiers of February 6, 1956, the Communists gradually withdrew their support, although they voted the special powers requested by the government in March 1956 for the more effective prosecution of the war. Mendès-France also resigned from his post as minister of state in May 1956; the left wing of the Socialist party sympathized with him, but was unable to assert itself against Mollet's grip on the party machine. On the contrary, the right-center welcomed Mollet's conversion, while right-wing extremism was making itself more and more felt both in the assembly and in the country at large as nationalist feelings were exacerbated by the Algerian war and the failure of the Suez expedition in the autumn of 1956. Despite the worsening climate of opinion, the Mollet government had three achievements to its credit which were to have a profound and beneficial influence on France's

*He had been elected on December 23, 1953, after thirteen votes—a record number.

future: the Defferre law which prepared the independence of France's African colonies; the Treaty of Luxembourg which resolved the Franco-German dispute over the Saar and returned that territory to Germany; and the signature of the treaty of Rome (March 25, 1957) which established the European Economic Community (EEC). But, by 1957, it was too dependent on right-wing votes in the assembly to be able to pursue a left-of-center economic policy. It was therefore normal that the desertion of a number of the moderates should bring it down on a financial issue in May 1957.

Between then and the crisis of May 1958 there were two governments, both of them led by Radicals and both of them brought down on the Algerian issue, which by now dominated the whole of French political life. This domination was expressed in the assembly by a quadrumvirate of Soustelle, Morice, Bidault and Duchet (the last-named being the creator of the *Centre national des Indépendants et Paysans* which had endowed the anarchic moderates with an organization), the founders of the *Union pour le Salut et le Renouveau de l'Algérie Française* (USRAF). In an atmosphere of bitterness and violence, of conspiracy and demogogy, which atomized and dissolved the cohesion of political groupings, the Fourth Republic dragged to its end. The crisis of May 13, 1958, was to find it without a government after nearly a month during which it had been impossible to build a majority in the National Assembly.

IV

But the Fourth Republic, despite its political decline, was not without achievements to its credit, though this credit is often not allowed it.

In terms of internal policy, the régime's economic record in particular was largely a success story, though marked by a constant fight against inflation, a deficitary balance of payments and a deficitary budget— problems which reached a catastrophic level between 1956 and 1958.* It is typical of the less than justice that has been done to the leaders of

---

*The budgetary deficit for 1956 was 1002 billion francs; for 1957, 1042 billion; for 1958, 690 billion. The balance of payments deficit was: 1956, $1405 million; 1957, $1715 million; 1958, $1855 million. The retail price index rose from 148 in 1956 to 175 in 1958.[28]

the Fourth Republic on this score that the improvement of the situation in 1958 should have been due to measures taken in the summer of 1957 by Gaillard, then minister of finance, rather than to the plan put into operation by de Gaulle's first government. Similarly, the improvement in France's housing situation—often put down to the credit of the Fifth Republic—really began in 1955, though it only reached the figure of over 300,000 dwellings a year in 1959.[29] The foundations for an essential element of the political stability of the Fifth Republic had been laid under the Fourth which, however, has received little thanks from those who have benefited by its inheritance.

The basis for the economic achievement of the years from 1945 to 1958 was the reversal of the drop in the French birthrate which by the end of the Third Republic had created a catastrophic situation. In 1901 France had 40.6 million inhabitants; in 1936 only 41.9 million which fell back due to wartime losses to 40.5 million in 1946. France's population grew only 15 percent in the hundred years before 1946, whereas those of Great Britain, Italy and Germany doubled. Moreover, the structure of the population showed a menacing increase in the number of old people as compared with children and adolescents. In 1932 an attempt had already been made to reverse this trend by giving family allowances to wage-earners, and this had been extended to the whole population by the Family Code of 1938-39. Vichy, with its insistence on the family as the basis of society, had reinforced this policy, and, despite wartime conditions, the birthrate had begun to rise. In September 1944 the provisional government raised family allowances by 50 percent, and a law of August 22, 1946, added still more benefits and once again raised existing ones. The results of this policy were immediate. By 1958 the birthrate, which had been 14.6 per thousand in 1938 had risen to 18.2—a figure which was to be steadily maintained throughout the years of the Fourth Republic and even exceeded in the immediate postwar period. In 1958, France's population was estimated to be 44.5 million. Between 1945 and 1965 the increase was to be more than that between 1830 and 1945.[30]

Accompanying this demographic expansion went an increase in productivity which again reversed the stagnation of the prewar period. At the end of 1945 the provisional government then established the *Commissariat général au Plan* which was headed by its originator Jean Monnet. His first plan, the *Plan de Modernisation et d'Equipe-*

ment, covered a period of four years (1947-1950), and its aim was to reach a national income 25 percent higher than in 1929, the best previous year. This aim was not to be realized. Despite Marshall aid and an investment of 2,250 billion francs, the 1929 level was only just passed in 1950 and was still not exceeded by 25 percent in 1952.* But a serious effort had been made to modernize the infrastructure of French economic life: communications, electricity, coal, steel, cement, the mechanization of agriculture and the construction of plants to manufacture nitrate fertilizers. The increase of production in these essential fields was considerable and provided a firm basis on which to build economic expansion.** During this period progress had been hampered by inflation and by a shortage of labor despite immigration (principally from North Africa) and the exodus from country to town, which has lowered the proportion of France's working population engaged in agriculture from 37 percent in 1938 to 27 percent in 1954 and 20 percent in 1962.*** During an episode like the Pinay 'experiment' production and capital investment were cut back for the sake of monetary stability. But the Monnet plan has its lasting monuments in the shape of the great dams on the Rhône at Génisslat and Donzère-Mondragon, the electrification of the French railway system, the reconstruction of ports like Dunkerque and Marseille, the re-equipment of the iron and steel industry in Lorraine and the discovery and exploitation of the natural gas deposits at Lacq. It provided an impetus and an example without which France's recovery from the war and subsequent economic expansion would have been inconceivable.

The second plan (1954-1957) was to place more emphasis on consumer goods—perhaps too much emphasis, for, although a rise of 30 percent in national production was achieved by the time it came to an end, its failure to strike a balance between capital investment and consumer goods, and a considerable rise in wages which stimulated

*Taking an index of 100 in 1938, the figures were as follows: 1929/119; 1945/54; 1946/83; 1950/123; 1952/129.[31]

**In 1952 the increases compared with 1946 were as follows: coal +16.5%; electricity as a whole +77%; hydro-electricity +98%; motor-fuels +668%; steel +148%; cement +153%; tractors +1230%. Agricultural production also rose by 23%.[32]

***The absolute number of departures per year now seems to be running at the figure of 135,000.[33]

demand still further had an inflationary effect and also led to a deficit in the balance of payments. In the last stage of the Fourth Republic the third plan (1958-61) was elaborated, but could not be executed because of the need for retrenchment and the balancing of exterior accounts. But, nonetheless, by 1958 productivity had risen to double that of 1938, and throughout the period of the Fourth Republic the standard of living of the average Frenchman continued to rise except during phases of deflation such as 1952 and 1958. Between 1949 and 1958 the purchasing power of the wages of an industrial worker had risen by about 50 percent.[34]

The reverse side of the medal was agriculture—a problem that would continue to haunt the Fifth Republic—where both productivity and income lagged behind that of other sectors of the economy. Since 1950 agricultural incomes have remained at considerably less than the national average. "For the standard of living of Frenchmen living from agriculture to reach that of urban wage-earners, which itself should rise, it would be necessary for it to be improved in ten years or so from now [1956] by at least 75 percent."[35] This has not happened, and by 1962 the total of French peasants was already down to the minimum figure which the authority just quoted considered desirable and looked as though it were falling farther.*

The Fifth Republic was also to continue the Fourth in its alternating of inflationary periods of expansion with 'stabilization plans.' Between December 1945 and December 1958 five devaluations carried the franc from the February 1940 figure of 43.80 to the dollar to 493.70 to the dollar (=176.40 and 1375 francs to the pound). After the inflationary policies of the immediate postwar period, in which rises in wages and in social benefits were not balanced by a sufficient increase in production, in January 1947 the Blum experiment of a general 5 percent cut in prices was the first of many attempts at deflation. It was a failure, since to lower prices at that time of scarcity proved to be impossible, while France's apparent lack of political stability did not provide the basis of

*There seems to be a strong irrational element in judgments like that of Jeanneney: "A people's equilibrium is the better for the presence of a considerable number of peasants."[36] In fact, France seems to be evolving in another direction from that implied by such moral criteria. The widespread purchase of country houses by the French professional classes points to an attitude towards the countryside resembling that of the English nineteenth century: a recreation-ground as much as a profit-making investment.

confidence needed for such an operation. A year later René Mayer was to try another series of measures including the blocking of 5,000 franc notes, devaluation, the creation of a free market in gold, the reduction of state spending and a loan. This policy was successful in stabilizing prices and eliminating the wartime black market, but produced a slight recession which acted as a brake on production. In 1950-51 there was a new wave of inflation produced partly by the beginning of the Korean war in June 1950, and partly by the freeing of wages from control in early 1950, though the *Salaire minimum interprofessionel garanti* (SMIG) was still fixed by the state. This was the situation faced by the Pinay experiment of 1952. The experiment took the form of a loan tied to the price of gold, a cut in prices controlled by the state, and a cut of 110 billion francs in state spending including 90 billion taken from the program of capital investment. Here again a slowing up of economic expansion followed stabilization, and the refusal to devalue left the prices of French exports too high.

From July 1953 to the end of 1955 Edgar Faure, first as minister of finance and then as prime minister, was to exert a considerable influence on France's economy. Throughout 1954 and 1955 he was to try, with some success, to get expansion started once again, but without an inflationary race between prices and wages. Rather than an overall increase of the minimum wage (SMIG) he had recourse to 'bonuses' added to it for lower-paid workers, but this tended to diminish the differential between different categories of worker and, therefore, in the long run to lead to further wage demands. He lowered the bank rate and made tax concessions to encourage capital investment by companies. Important reforms in taxation were also carried out at this time, including the introduction of the famous added value tax (TVA). But Faure did not succeed in getting rid of the budgetary deficit, which, in 1955, rose to 714 billion francs covered essentially by short-term borrowing. By 1955 there was only a small deficit of $20 million in the balance of payments.

In 1956 and 1957, however, the situation suddenly worsened. The growing expense of the Algerian war, a bad harvest in 1956 and increased imports due to economic expansion at home carried the balance of payments deficit to $1,715 million in 1957, while that of the budget rose to 1,042 billion francs in the same year. By the beginning of 1958, despite the new Gaillard 'stabilization plan' carried out in 1957, France appeared to have exhausted its credit both at home and abroad. Between 1956 and 1958 it had used up its reserves to the tune of $1,200 million and contracted foreign debts of $1,300 million. Inflation therefore dogged the Fourth Republic to the end. Its political system and its external problems were not such as would have allowed its very real achievements in the economic sphere without this price being paid. The difficulties of its last two years were undoubtedly due in part to lack of confidence in the stability of the régime, and the effects of the Treaty of Rome had not yet begun to make themselves felt sufficiently to counteract fears for France's economic future. But equally the loss of confidence in the régime itself was due in some measure to its inability to arrest the decline in the value of money. This appeared to be another flagrant demonstration of the inadequacy of political institutions and of a lack of political will power in those running them. Against this background the real achievement was neglected.[37]

V

With the Fourth Republic's foreign policy, the positive side has similarly tended to be lost in the reverberations of the régime's failure in Indochina and Algeria. But in Europe, having inherited a policy from de Gaulle's provisional government which could plainly not be executed, France's diplomacy was skillfully adapted and, through espousing the'European' cause, by the end of the Fourth Republic had notably enlarged the country's possible action within Europe.

The main area of change was French policy towards Germany. France, as an occupying power, had its word to say on the future of Germany, and under the Fourth Republic the French government remained for some time totally opposed to any reconstruction of a central German government. Its policy was the old French nationalist one of a Germany of separate states united only by a weak federal bond. The Rhineland, the Ruhr and the Saar were to be separated from Germany altogether.

But, whatever complaints de Gaulle and his followers might make about the weakness of the régime, such a policy would hardly have been possible even if a perfect understanding had continued between the three participants in the Yalta and Potsdam conferences.* It was

*For de Gaulle's attitude, see, for example, his remarks on Germany in a speech at Vincennes on May 22, 1949: "for three years, alas! there has been the chronic failure of our official policy--the policy which our representatives vaguely claim to be defending .... This weakness has been one of the elements which

clearly doomed from the moment that the world became divided into two blocs of powers and Germany became the most immediate object of rivalry between them.

At first French policy conducted by Bidault tried to struggle against the facts. When the Anglo-American 'bi-zone' was created at the end of 1946 France refused to add its own zone to it. At this time the Saar was separated from Germany, as was France itself, by a customs barrier. There were constant squabbles between France and Britain about coal deliveries from the Ruhr. The Moscow conference of March-April 1947 showed clearly enough France's dilemma:

> The only thing which France did get was more coal from Germany; but this was not recorded in the agreement, although Molotov seemed well-disposed on that issue. But he refused to let us decide anything about the Ruhr unless Russia was included in its administration and control. In other words, he wanted a share in the parts of Germany that were under Western occupation . . . . Although France had the support of the English and the Americans over the Saar, it was not able to get what it wanted from the Moscow conference.[39]

Meanwhile, the growing tension in Europe, the Marshall Plan, the dismissal of the Communists from the French government and the Czech Communist *coup d'état* of February 1948 were rapidly changing the scene. In March 1948 General Sokolovsky, the Soviet representative, left the Allied Control Council in Berlin. The need to resuscitate Germany economically, if it were not to be an actual burden to the occupying powers, led to the gradual abolition of restrictions on German production and to the ending of the dismantling of German factories. In June 1948 the London agreements between America, Britain and France proclaimed the necessity for the integration of 'bi-zonia' and the French zone of Germany into the Western European economy. The agreements also recognized the necessity "of giving the German people the possibility of arriving, within the framework of a free and democratic form of government, at the ultimate re-establishment of its unity, at the moment destroyed." This was, in effect, the end of France's attempt to put forward its own policy for Germany. On October 8, 1948, the French zone was joined to the other Western

---

have caused the French, the European, the human solution of the great German problem to be set aside. We have therefore arrived at what is called the Bonn solution. Do not let us have any illusions, it is the reconstitution of the Reich! "[38]

zones for economic purposes. On April 8, 1949, an agreement signed in Washington settled the future status of West Germany and set up a tripartite High Commission sitting in Bonn. The way was cleared for the emergence of a West German state. France had reluctantly and slowly bowed to the inevitable.[40]*

This forced change in French policy had been accompanied by an increasing integration of France into a Western alliance system. Beginning with the Treaty of Dunkirk between Britain and France in March 1947, a series of economic and political agreements were signed which were to form the basis of French foreign policy and European security during the decade to come. On March 17, 1948, a treaty of mutual assistance was signed between Britain, France and the Benelux at Brussels. Then on April 16 a convention set up the Organization for European Economic Cooperation (OEEC), establishing the machinery through which the Marshall Plan, proposed by the American Secretary of State in June 1947, could operate. In June a bilateral agreement between France and the United States on economic aid within the framework of OEEC was concluded. On April 4, 1949, the signing of the North Atlantic pact, a military alliance which added Canada, Denmark, Iceland, Italy, Norway, Portugal and the United States to the Brussels Five, marked the completion of a program for European economic recovery and military defense, whose construction had certainly been hastened by Russian policy in Eastern and Central Europe and the Communist shift to a posture of violent opposition in the West, particularly in France and Italy.

If those directing French foreign policy had as their main objective to obtain an American commitment to the defense of Europe, French public opinion was by no means so favorable to integration within the Atlantic system. Criticism of the Atlantic pact on the grounds that, by its signature, France had lost the possibility of an independent policy came not from Gaullists but from left-wing intellectuals and politicians, who were also concerned about the rejection of the Communists from the national community which seemed to follow logically upon France's ranging itself within the Western camp. A French nationalist reaction against American leadership in Europe began to manifest itself

*When de Gaulle returned to power in May 1958 he called together three high officials of the Quai d'Orsay to brief him on France's foreign policy. One of the first questions he then asked was "What remains of my German policy?" To which the unanimous reply was "Nothing, mon général!"

on the left.* Later it was to spread to the right, but for the moment "the Gaullists were uncompromising in their denunciation of neutralism."[42]

The construction of an integrated Europe was to strike deeper roots in French opinion than the Atlantic connection. The European movement had met with a considerable response, and the French proposals for the formation of the Council of Europe had been strongly oriented towards integration, though the final solution adopted in January 1949 had been watered down in accordance with British views. The leap forward was to come with Robert Schuman's proposal of May 9, 1950, that a Franco-German Coal and Steel Community, open to other European countries, should be created under a common High Authority. The idea, inspired by Monnet, had as its basis a concept of European collaboration founded on Franco-German reconciliation, in the framework of which, it was hoped, economic advantage could be used to bring about political integration. Schuman's offer was immediately accepted by Konrad Adenauer, the German chancellor, but rejected by the British government with momentous and unfortunate consequences, and the treaty was to be signed on April 18, 1951. In its political aspects it represented an irreversible integration of Germany into Western Europe, but also a potential substitution of Germany for Great Britain as France's natural partner in world affairs.**

The subsequent battle over the European Defense Community (EDC) was, at least in part, a reaction by those who were not especially enthusiastic about the new position of Germany and the possible consequences for the relations between France and Great Britain. The EDC issue, in fact, allowed Frenchmen who were cool about European integration to make an appeal to public opinion on an issue which

*As an American scholar puts it, "During the first years of the Fourth Republic once again the left took over the symbols of an ardent national sentiment. This was the tendency, the mood, which reappeared in the neutralist criticism of the Western alliance as a limitation of the independence of France."[41]

**A number of French policymakers were unhappy about the divergence between France and Britain. Dumaine in his diary writes of "the necessity" of British participation and "the complex dangers" of a bilateral negotiation with Bonn. But there is no need to exaggerate this. France and Britain were still to act in concert at Geneva in 1954 and—for the worse—at Suez in 1956. The German orientation of French foreign policy probably depended (1) on the continuance of political Catholicism as a force in both countries, and (2) the continuance of Germany's somewhat *schwärmerisch* attitude toward France. Both these factors became weaker in the late sixties.[43]

F

aroused far wider and profounder emotions: that of German rearmament. If the original "Pleven" plan of October 1950 was designed in the
mind of its author and his colleagues to get round the issue of German
rearmament (already decided on by France's allies) by providing for a
European army into which German units could safely be integrated,
anti-Europeans could turn it the other way round by maintaining that
the movement towards a federal Europe was not only endangering
French sovereignty, but also leading to the creation of a German army.
"The European idea was popular. Its popularity could bring about the
acceptance of the obviously unpopular remilitarization of Germany.
But it was obvious, too, that this possibility was marked by the risk of
the opposite result; the unpopularity of German rearmament might be
carried over to the European idea."[44] The Gaullists had already
denounced the Coal and Steel Community—"shams like the coal and
steel pool and the plan for a European army"[45]—and were now to join
the Communists and the left in a bitter struggle against EDC which left
few political alliances unbroken or parties unsplit. Undoubtedly, as the
result was to show, the "Europeans" in the French government had
overestimated their strength in the country when they chose this
particular issue as the next step in European policy.*

The agreements of Bonn and Paris of the 26th and 27th of May 1952,
established an organization for a European army modelled on that of
the Coal and Steel Community and restored full sovereignty to the
Federal Republic of Germany. These treaties were immediately
attacked by de Gaulle as "protocols of surrender" through which
France "must pour its men, its arms and its money into an un-national
hotch-potch."[47] But they were not to be submitted to the National
Assembly until early the following year, and, after the fall of René
Mayer's government in May 1953—due principally in fact to Gaullist
opposition to the ratification of EDC—the whole question was shelved
for more than a year. When it arose again Mendès-France was to try in
vain to obtain alterations of the treaties at a meeting of the Six in
Brussels (August 19, 1954) and then to allow them to be quietly buried
in the National Assembly on August 30 without the government staking
its existence on their passage—an action which the "Europeans" (and
notably the MRP) were never to pardon him.

*Even Auriol, the president of the republic, was opposed to EDC and used his
not inconsiderable influence against it.[46]

In fact, another solution was rapidly found to the German problem as a result of some rapid and skillful diplomacy on the part of the British Foreign Secretary, Anthony Eden. The solution found and embodied in the Paris agreements of October 23, 1954, was to allow Germany to join the Western European Union (WEU) which had arisen out of the Brussels Treaty. Germany would regain its full sovereignty and enter NATO, while giving a number of guarantees to restrict its manufacture of armaments (especially nuclear armaments) and placing its armed forces under the Supreme Allied Commander Europe (SACEUR). Great Britain had already helped Mendès-France by undertaking to keep a minimum of four divisions on the continent during the duration of the Brussels Treaty—that is, made certain that a majority of NATO forces could not be German. At the end of December the agreements were ratified by the National Assembly after one negative vote and a demand for a vote of confidence on the part of the government.

Thus the net result of the long dispute over the status of Germany in the Western alliance was German rearmament in a much more definite form than would have been the case had EDC been carried through. "The French deputies finally preferred the *Pentagon* to the *State Department* solution, and this choice was approved by the European Left."[48] This was a fitting conclusion to a French policy on Germany in which, as Professor Alfred Grosser has written:

> By keeping on saying what one does not want, by holding on to untenable positions, one does not say what one does want or, more precisely, one lessens the value of French positions on Europe, defense, East-West relations and even Germany's future by maintaining the claims of another era.[49]

The last stage in the *débâcle* of a French policy towards Germany based on purely national interests was to be the reunion of the Saar with Germany under the Treaty of Luxembourg, October 27, 1956, after a massive vote in the territory itself against the previously agreed Statute of the Saar—in fact, against the French connection.

This surrender of a national objective, however, was to clear the way for a step towards European integration far more important for France and for Western Europe as a whole than anything that had gone before. In 1955 the Messina conference had seen the foreign ministers of the

Benelux countries suggest an advance towards general European economic integration and collaboration in the nuclear field. The conference resulted in agreement by the Six that the formation of a European common market should be their next economic objective and that they should study the creation of a European nuclear authority. The advent of the Mollet government of 1956 allowed detailed negotiations to start, and, after a series of conferences and arduous technical discussions (in which France through the technical skill of its officials got more than its share of concessions), the Treaty of Rome was finally signed on March 25, 1957, and ratified by the National Assembly on July 10 by 342 votes to 239. It provided for the systematic abolition of tariff barriers, the creation of common economic, agricultural and monetary policies and the establishment of an executive commission in Brussels to carry out these measures. It also created a European Atomic Energy Authority (EURATOM). Among the opponents of ratification were the remnants of the Gaullists, the Communists and isolated critics who included Mendès-France.* As for de Gaulle, he had by this time withdrawn from public affairs, but his attitude towards EDC and the utterances of his close associates left no doubt as to his views.**

Given the political divisions in France and the multitude of problems besetting the rulers of the Fourth Republic, its European policy was a remarkable achievement. It was brought about by a small body of men devoted to the European idea and filled with a vision of the benefits for France and for the world if it were realized. In France the Europeans had to struggle against difficulties far greater than those in other countries, against a nationalist backlash and against the fears of small industrialists and shopkeepers that they would be swamped in any general freeing of trade. By their action the French Europeans laid the foundations for a continuation of France's economic expansion and an increase in the standard of living of Frenchmen which, ironically enough, was to aid the Gaullist opponents of the Treaty of Rome. It

*His criticism seemed mainly directed at the risks to French democracy of subordinating the decisions of the government to a body outside France.

**Debré wrote at the time: "Europe is not a nation. It is an assembly of nations . . . . To wish to constrain nature and, through supranational authorities, to create a new nation . . . is to launch Europe into an adventure from which it might not recover; it is being led to anarchy, to the arbitration of a nation outside itself or to the domination of one nation over the others."50

was too late for the Fourth Republic itself to reap what it had sown. Its involvement in the Algerian morass was to rob it of all but the credit for a far-sighted policy, the full effects of which have yet to be seen.

VI

Even if one leaves aside the relations with Algeria, the history of colonial problems under the Fourth Republic can be summed up in the phrase "too little, too late." The one exception was the *loi-cadre* of June 23, 1956, introduced by the Socialist minister for overseas territories, Gaston Defferre, which provided for the election of local assemblies by universal suffrage, setting up local councils of government and restricting the power of colonial governors. The framework was thus provided for a peaceful evolution of France's colonies (that is, everything except Algeria) towards autonomy and independence. The process was to be speeded up by the territorial elections of March 1957 and to reach its conclusion under the Fifth Republic, at first in the form of autonomous African states within the French community and finally, in 1960, in that of complete independence. This was a considerable step forward from Brazzaville. Defferre must undoubtedly be given the credit for initiating the one peaceful 'decolonization' carried out by France and for the relative success since then of French policies in Africa south of the Sahara. The severe repression of the revolt in Madagascar in 1947 and the subsequent trial and imprisonment of three Malgache nationalist deputies in the French Assembly had given little grounds for hope that such an end to the story might be possible.*

In Indochina the beginning of the Fourth Republic saw France already embarked on a long and exhausting effort at pacification which was to last until 1954. The breakdown of the Fontainebleau conference with representatives of the Viet Minh was soon followed by fighting in Tonking where Haiphong was bombarded by the French at the end of November on the order of the local commander and by a surprise Viet

*The 1947 revolt in Madagascar also showed the casualness with which the men on the spot disregarded orders from Paris. In July 1948 a witness at the trial of the deputies was executed despite an order from the president of the republic staying the sentence.[51]

Minh attack on French positions in Hanoi on December 19, which was
beaten off. The Viet Minh forces retired into the jungles, swamps and
mountains from which they were to carry on guerrilla warfare, while
the French commanders hastened to reoccupy towns and strategic
positions throughout the country. "The French occupied only the cities
and a few fortified posts in the hinterland (including, since the summer
of 1947, frontier posts along the Chinese border), and they depended
for food on regions controlled by the Viet Minh. Saigon and
Hanoi . . . were honeycombed with supporters of the resistance who
collected taxes from the Vietnamese and Chinese inhabitants."[52] In
these conditions it was not surprising that the military situation soon
began to deteriorate. In 1950 the disaster of Cao Bang and the
evacuation of the important garrison town of Lang Son in north
Tonking showed what was to come. In December 1949 the arrival of
Chinese Communist forces on the Tonkinese border had practically
ended any chance of finishing the war with a defeat of the Viet Minh.
Henceforward the military side of the story was to be a series of
disasters ending with the capitulation of the fortified perimeter of Dien
Bien Phu on May 7, 1954, and only punctuated by de Lattre de
Tassigny's energetic defense of the Red River delta in 1951.*

During this period successive French governments and their representatives in Indochina were gradually led to realize that they must
offer political concessions calculated to win support among Vietnamese
nationalists hostile to Communism. By the Ha Long Bay agreement of
June 1948 France recognized the independence of Vietnam as an
associated state within the French union as well as the unity of the
country (that is, a Vietnam including Cochin China which had
previously been governed under a different régime from the rest of
Vietnam). The interlocutors chosen by the French government were the
Emperor of Annam, Bao Dai, and General Xuan, head of the
provisional central government of Vietnam. However, opposition to this
policy within French political and administrative circles was strong, and
it required a formal exchange of letters in March 1949 between Bao Dai

*Some of those in power saw the military situation in Indochina without
illusions. By the spring of 1953 Pierre de Chevigné, then occupying a post in the
ministry of war, could say to a fellow MRP deputy: "Don't let's be children; we
haven't the shadow of a chance of ending the Indochinese operation decently.
Since completion of the victory of Mao over Chiang Kai-Chek our fate is sealed
there. The problem is only one of how long it will take."[53]

and Vincent Auriol before any real steps towards giving independence to a Vietnamese government were taken. Even then the state of mind of French officials on the spot was illustrated by the Commander-in-Chief, General Carpentier, who stated in March 1950 when the question of American military aid came up: "I will never accept that this equipment should be given directly to the Vietnamese."[54]

But even an increasing amount of American aid from 1950 onwards could not make a success of French policy.* The Saigon government struggled in a chaos of warring sects, corruption, banditry and periodic French interference. Currency trafficking made fortunes for dubious figures, while, in France itself, the discovery (in the briefcase of a Vietnamese arrested on a Paris bus) of a report on the military situation in Tonking after the Chinese arrival on the frontier, drawn up by the Chief of Staff, General Revers, led to the scandalous "affaire des généraux" which ended with the forced retirement of both Revers and General Mast. American aid, however, implied a possible 'internationalization' of the war in Vietnam, and ultimately it was this fact which was to force the partition of the country at Geneva in 1954. But the question for the French government was for how long France was to continue a war which now appeared as an indefinite containment of Communist expansion in Southeast Asia, a task which most Frenchmen felt themselves both unfitted and unwilling to undertake. It was expressed by General Navarre, the unfortunate loser of Dien Bien Phu: "Another possible war aim for France was simply to take part in the American policy of 'containment' of Communism in Southeast Asia. It would have renounced any national advantage in Indochina and agreed to withdraw at the end of the war . . . . While continuing to fight alone, we would be pulling the chestnuts out of the fire for others . . . "[56] It was French reluctance to assume this role that led to the Geneva agreements of July 1954. It was the danger that France might be forced to take that path, if no acceptable compromise could be reached, that produced an unexpected moderation on the part of Molotov and Chou En-Lai. Vietnam was partitioned at the 17th parallel, whereas the military victory of the Viet Minh might reasonably have led them to hope that the whole country would now fall into their hands. The

*The most massive slices of American aid were actually received after the Indochinese war was over: $350 million in 1954 and $400 million in 1955. They did not help the French war effort, but they did help the French economy.[55]

result of the Geneva conference was a success for Mèndes-France, but
the whole story of the Indochinese war is one that does little credit to
those directing French policy.

In fact, after Chinese Communist arrival on the border, there were
two choices open to the French government: either withdrawal or a
conscious attempt to produce an American intervention, including the
presence of American troops. But, to choose either, the French
government would have had to make up its mind to an independent
Vietnam far more quickly than it actually did. Alternatively, agreement
with Ho Chi Minh on his own terms would also have been possible at an
early stage, but this policy was never seriously considered. In fact, a
collaboration between France and America to stabilize the situation
might have been the most feasible course, except that it did not seem to
correspond to any very obvious French interest. The actual policy
followed was a mixture between the maintenance of narrow, French
interests, habit, and internationalization of the war. But for China's
military strength being tied up in Korea until the armistice agreement at
Panmunjom in July 1953, it would have come to grief far sooner. After
the Geneva agreements there was little left for the French to do but
withdraw from the north, often leaving their partisans there to be
massacred by the Viet Minh.[57] In the south their influence was soon to
be replaced by that of the United States, whose protégé Ngo Dinh Diem
first became prime minister and later president of the Republic of
Vietnam after the deposition of Bao Dai in October 1955. American
suzerainty replaced French—a fact that was not to be forgotten in
France during the massive American involvement in Vietnam during the
middle sixties.*

During his tenure of office Mendès-France also managed to settle one
other overseas problem which had been allowed to go from bad to
worse: the problem of the French protectorate of Tunisia. Immediately
after the war a liberal policy had been executed under the Resident-
General Jean Mons, who, in 1949, authorized the return to Tunis of
Habib Bourguiba, the nationalist leader of the Néo-Destour party. But
the latter's demands led to protests on the part of the powerful French

---

*In November 1954 it was announced that American military aid was to be
given directly to South Vietnam, Cambodia and Laos rather than channelled
through France. "It was clear enough that, economically as well as politically,
leadership in southern Viet Nam had passed from Paris to Washington."[58]

community in the protectorate, and Mons was replaced in the summer of 1950. Yet in June of the same year, Robert Schuman, then foreign minister, was to speak of "leading Tunisia towards independence which is the final objective of all the territories within the French Union"[59] – but a year and a half later he was to reply to a *démarche* from the Chenik government demanding internal autonomy by a note whose main motif was the idea of associating the French colony in Tunisia with the exercise of the country's sovereignty. Immediately, there were protest strikes, and a complaint was made to the UN by the Tunisian government. The French reply was to send a tough resident, Jean de Hautecloque, who underlined the nature of his task by arriving in Tunis on a warship (January 13, 1952). He ordered the arrest of Bourguiba and other leaders of the Néo-Destour, and in March four of Chenik's ministers were arrested—apparently without Schuman being informed beforehand. In reply to the terrorist attacks of the 'fellaghas' French counter-terrorists assassinated the Secretary-General of the *Union Générale des Travailleurs Tunisiens* (UGTT), Ferhat Hached (December 5, 1952), while in the UN General Assembly a motion hostile to French policy was voted.

In 1954 Mendès-France, as already described, cut this particular Gordian knot by flying to Tunis and solemnly recognizing the internal autonomy of Tunisia in an audience with the Bey at the Palace of Carthage. By taking with him Marshal Juin, whose resistance to North African nationalist claims had until then been impeccable, he forestalled criticism from the right at home. In August a new Tunisian government was formed which included members of the Néo-Destour, and later in the year an amnesty was granted to the 'fellaghas' provided that they laid down their arms, while negotiations proceeded between the French and Tunisian governments. In the middle of 1955 a series of agreements were signed granting the protectorate "internal autonomy"–agreements which, within a year, were to evolve into full independence. In 1957 Tunisia became a republic with Bourguiba as its first president.

In Morocco a similar evolution had taken place, though with worse examples of defiance of Paris on the part of local French officials. In December 1950 General Juin, then resident-general of Morocco, had presented an ultimatum to the Sultan demanding that he should either disavow the Istiqlal nationalist party or else abdicate. The Sultan

F*

yielded on this occasion, but this did not prevent him from asking for the raising of the state of siege nor inhibit a small band of French officials and French Moroccan *colons* from intriguing to get rid of a monarch whom they regarded as a danger to French influence in the protectorate. The weapon they used was the Sultan's old enemy, the Pasha of Marrakesh, El Glaoui. In February 1951, during the troubles following Juin's ultimatum, it had been the threat of Berber tribesmen marching on Rabat that had caused Sultan Sidi Mohammed ben Youssef to give way to French demands. In 1953 the same pressure was exercised with more efficacity and ended by placing on the throne the aged Ben Arafa. On August 11, Bidault had cabled to Rabat that "the government will not accept being placed before a *fait accompli* by whoever it may be."[60] But the cabinet decided to replace the Sultan on August 20, and the Resident-General, General Guillaume, arrested him in person. Since then Bidault has claimed responsibility for a policy which he pretended at the time to forbid. Much of the tragedy of France's relations with its overseas territories under the Fourth Republic resides in this fact.* One minister, Mitterrand, resigned in protest against the decision to depose the Sultan in what was certainly a violation of the Treaty of Fez (1912) which established the French protectorate.

As with the arrest of the ministers of the Chenik government in Tunisia, the exile of the Sultan led to a political impasse between France and Morocco and a mounting tide of terrorism and counter-terrorism. Mendès-France was given no time to find a solution to this problem. It was left to his successor, Edgar Faure, to send to Morocco a Gaullist strongman, Gilbert Grandval, who had been a daring leader of the Resistance and a tough French High Commissioner in the Saar. Arriving in Rabat after the assassination by counter-terrorists of the liberal businessman (and wartime American agent) Jacques Lemaigre-Dubreuil, Grandval got rid of a number of the more conservative officials in the Residency. His policy was to obtain the abdication of Ben Arafa and Ben Youssef and to form a representative government. On realizing that Faure was moving towards a simple restoration of Ben Youssef he resigned, but not before there had been a massacre of Europeans at Oued-Zem on August 20, 1955. He left behind him a

*"In 1953, I suggested to the Laniel government that Sultan Sidi Mohammed ben Youssef . . . should be deposed."[61]

durable judgment on colonial rule which bears quoting in this context as it is probably representative of the views of those close to de Gaulle at this time:

> One does not possess almost absolute power with impunity, above all in a backward country. The facilities one disposes of to use it, themselves add to the too human temptation to abuse it, and, in any case, to reserve it for oneself. In order not to yield to this, it would be necessary to have rare personal virtues or the constant, imperious impulsion of a far-sighted policy.[62]

After this Faure moved fast. In August there were conversations at Aix-les-Bains with Moroccan politicians. In September Catroux was deputed to visit the exiled Sultan in Madagascar. On September 20 the new Resident was given the order to get rid of Ben Arafa. In November the declaration of La Celle-Saint-Cloud on the part of Pinay, the foreign minister, and the Sultan Ben Youssef announced France's intention to grant Morocco independence. This declaration was to be completed in detail by agreements signed in March and May of the following year. The Moroccan crisis had lasted a shorter time than the Indochinese war, but there had been little necessity for it apart from the intrigues of a small number of men to whom the idea of an independent Maghreb was anathema. The harm that their policies could do was to be seen in Algeria.

VII

The Algerian rebellion had broken out on November 1, 1954, with a series of terrorist attacks in the department of Constantine and the Aurès area of Kabylia. Almost immediately it was to appear that these had been organized by a nationalist body composed of extremist elements from earlier Algerian Moslem parties and to be known as the *Front de libération nationale* (FLN).* In the mountainous villages of Algeria which had never been effectively administered by the French there now began a savage guerrilla war in which the FLN took the

*This had emerged from the *Organisation de Sécurité* (OS) of the party founded by the veteran Algerian nationalist Messali Hadj, the *Mouvement pour le triomphe des libertés démocratiques* (MTLD). In the OS appear such names as Ahmed ben Bella, Hocine Ait Ahmed and Mohammed Khider.

opportunity to settle scores with political opponents as well as with the
French. From April 1955 onwards a state of siege was proclaimed in
Algeria, and 400,000 French troops were gradually accumulated in the
area a number which still proved insufficient to suppress the fellaghas.
In September 1955 sixty-one Moslem members of the Algerian
Assembly or the Paris parliament men who had been passed through
the sieve of the French administration's control of the elections—
affirmed the existence of a separate Algerian nation and called for an
end to the repressive measures of the French police and military.
Among them was Ferhat Abbas, until this moment a moderate partisan
of integration between France and Algeria, who was shortly to take the
prime ministership of the *Gouvernement provisioire de la république
algérienne* (GPRA).

Increasingly, from 1956 onwards, the FLN received support and
sympathy from Tunisia and Morocco where Algerian armies of national
liberation (ALN) were formed and along whose frontiers there were
constantly incidents with French troops. Inside Algeria itself the
rebellion had taken on something of the characteristics of a civil war.
The FLN was at loggerheads with the followers of Messali Hadj and his
Mouvement national algérien (MNA). Both in Algeria and among the
numerous Algerian workers in France there were savage reprisals
culminating in the Melouza massacre of the spring of 1957 when FLN
forces slaughtered nearly three hundred political opponents in circumstances of great atrocity. For their part, the French security forces also
reacted with brutality, using torture and indiscriminate reprisals against
the population in their struggle against the fellaghas.

The attitude of the French government to all this might have been to
find a way to independence as one had already been found in Morocco
and Tunisia. But Algeria was different, containing nearly a million
Frenchmen, many of whom had lived there for generations, united to
metropolitan France by Algeria's status as several French departments.
Above all, it was the last ditch of a French nationalism which had been
on the defensive since the war. Algeria was the strongest citadel of a
colonial achievement in the Roman style, all the bastions of which
seemed to be crumbling one by one. For the army the war was a
testing-point as to whether it would always be required to undertake
hopeless campaigns ending in withdrawal and a dishonorable abandonment of local allies to the wrath of the victors. For the young French

officers in the Algerian *bled* there was little point in their presence at all, if they were not there to win the struggle against the enemy. Convinced that they could develop counter-insurgency tactics to meet the terrorism of the FLN, asked to carry out dirty tasks such as General Massu's breaking of the FLN networks in Algiers in 1957, often vilified in the metropolitan French press, fresh from a humiliation in Indochina which they were determined not to undergo again, condemned if they left Algeria to the *ennui* of French garrison towns, it is small wonder that the officers of the French army in Algeria began to feel themselves more and more separated from the nation as a whole. As the war went from bad to worse, as successive governments vacillated, this gap increased. The army had already blamed the existing régime for its defeat in Indochina.* And it had before it the example of de Gaulle himself in 1940, of a revolt against a legal government by an officer in the name of a true patriotism which was later to condemn those who had exercised the old military virtue of blind obedience to constituted authority.** The events of 1940-45 had perforce involved the French army in politics, and they had not been forgotten by those fighting in Algeria. After de Gaulle's return to power an officer was to explain his adherence to the *Organisation Armée Secrète* (OAS) in the following terms: "We think that a savagely determined group of men can influence the course of events. The chief of state [de Gaulle] showed it in 1940. A certain former commander-in-chief in Algeria, today *in revolt in his turn*, shows it at present."[65]

The last years of the Fourth Republic were marked by the threat of military conspiracy (for example, the case of General Faure at the end of 1956) and arbitrary military action including the diversion to Algiers of a Moroccan plane carrying Ben Bella and other FLN leaders and the torture and murder by means of which the army carried on its successful campaign against the FLN network in the Algerian cities. In Algeria itself the European population was united in its determination

---

*The defeated Supreme Commander at Dien Bien Phu, General Navarre, was to write "The accumulated delays, errors and cowardice of eight years . . . are the fruit of the régime. They proceed from the very nature of the French political system."[63]

**At the trial after the war of General Dentz for having resisted the Allied invasion of Syria, the public prosecutor replied to the accused's plea of obedience to orders: "At the grade you hold and in the functions you fulfill, one is judge of the orders one receives." Dentz was sentenced to death.[64]

to resist the FLN and to compel the metropolitan government to do so too. In this they were not unsuccessful. When Guy Mollet became prime minister in early 1956 with a mandate to pursue a more liberal policy in Algeria, his attempt to install General Catroux as governor-general was received with unanimous hostility on the part of the European population. His visit to Algiers on February 6, 1956 (an ominous date!), impressed upon him the burning feeling of the *petite bourgeoisie* and working-class. The demonstrations which he encountered there effectively changed the policy of the Mollet government. Catroux resigned, and, under his successor Robert Lacoste, there was no further talk of concessions to the Moslems. Only after the fall of the Mollet government, under its successor, that of Bourgès-Maunoury, was a new law (the *loi-cadre*) worked out which placed Moslems on the same list in elections as Europeans. By then, of course, it was too late. After Bourgès-Maunoury had fallen on the Algerian issue, Gaillard's short-lived government was to follow suit when America and Britain offered their 'good offices' after a French reprisal bombardment of the Tunisian village of Sakiet (February 8, 1958). The Gaillard government was defeated in the assembly on April 15, 1958, after a philippic by Soustelle, and for a month no majority could be found. Then, on May 13, it was the turn of the MRP leader Pierre Pflimlin to present for investiture the last government of the Fourth Republic.

After Indochina, after Morocco and Tunisia, Algeria faced the Fourth Republic with a problem too great to be solved by any *tour-de-force* in the Mendès-France style. Coming on top of other divisive factors in French life the war made France progressively more difficult to govern in the prevailing parliamentary terms. Also it brought with it into metropolitan France censorship, political assassination and police brutality which resulted in the growing alienation of intellectuals and the idealistic young. Weakened on the left by its inability to end the war, weakened on the right by its inability to win it, the régime was utterly unable to resist what many observers had seen for months as an approaching military revolt. When the blow came the hollow structure of state authority caved in at once. The collapse came as de Gaulle had predicted:

If there is no government, the army will take power in Algiers. And I myself, concluding that there is no longer a state, will take power in Paris to save the Republic.*

As this diagnosis implies, the Fourth Republic was not so much murdered as pronounced dead on arrival.

VIII

The part played by Gaullism in the Fourth Republic was, as has been shown, one of opposition. The formal beginning of that opposition dates from the foundation of the *Rassemblement du Peuple français* (RPF) announced by de Gaulle at Strasbourg on April 6, 1947, although his own hostility to the régime was implicit in the Bayeux speech of June 1946 and already overt in his remarks at Bruneval on March 30, which in fact caused the Prime Minister, Ramadier, to visit Colombey-les-Deux-Eglises to inform the General that, on political occasions, he would not receive the official honors paid to him on ceremonial ones. In the previous year René Capitant's *Union Gaulliste*, formed to fight for the ideas put forward at Bayeux, but without the General's authority, had had little success at the November elections. The RPF, on the contrary, was to be the medium of de Gaulle's political career until May 6, 1953, when he withdrew it from electoral and parliamentary action. It was to have considerable political success, make the Fourth Republic even more difficult to govern coherently, and exercise a decisive influence on at least one major political issue. Its withdrawal from practical politics was soon to be followed by the withdrawal of its founder from all political activity (July 2, 1955). Henceforward until May 13, 1958, Gaullism would consist of small bands of faithful followers loosely connected and working for the Gaullist cause by means ranging from study groups to conspiracy.

As a French political party the RPF had a number of special features which bore clearly enough the mark of its founder. In the first place, was it a political party at all? De Gaulle himself in his founding statement claimed for it another and a wider base:

*In a conversation with André Philip in March 1958.[66]

> The *Rassemblement du Peuple Français* has as its object to promote above the parties, in economic, social, imperial and foreign affairs, the solutions I have indicated, and to support the policy which would aim at realizing them in the framework of a state made capable of applying them.[67]

This conception of the RPF was in accordance with de Gaulle's view of his own unifying mission, but left its relationship to other political groupings ambiguous. For the political parties this approach looked like an attempt to win away their own followers under cover of de Gaulle's authority. The MRP, whose clientele was the most immediately threatened by the emergence of the RPF, promptly passed a resolution forbidding its members to belong to any other political party. If the founders of the RPF had ever seriously expected to appeal to members of other parties, this hope was to be disappointed, but the *Rassemblement* was to bear the imprint of its 'supra-party' origins throughout its existence. For, once established as de facto another party, the question of political tactics that dominated and divided its leadership was whether or not it should act like one in circumstances where playing a party game implied a certain degree of collaboration with the other parties and hence some recognition of the detested régime of the Fourth Republic.

On this issue the lines of division were quite clear. De Gaulle and his *fidèles* were unalterably opposed to any kind of participation in the political life of the Fourth Republic. The parliamentary representatives of the party, on the other hand, saw lost opportunities of carrying through policies or gaining positions of power in the mosaic of government-making which took up so much political time and energy. In a letter addressed to de Gaulle, Gaullist 'dissidents' complained that it was hard to subordinate everything to a "fatalistic conception of history, when every day we are facing concrete realities . . . . In short we think that the way to power will only be opened for you by a political evolution brought about by our conditional entry into the majority, since it seems to us unthinkable to modify the system while remaining outside it."[68] This letter was written on May 29, 1952, and the subject in dispute was the support given by RPF deputies to the Pinay government. The dissidents were soon to leave the RPF and form the *Groupe d'action républicaine et sociale* (ARS).

To such arguments in favor of participation de Gaulle himself answered with an intransigence revelatory of the real aims of his *politique du pire*. In a discussion among the leadership of the RPF over the attitude to be adopted towards Pinay's investiture he argued that, at a time when the Fourth Republic was in crisis, it would be folly for the RPF to save it:

> As long as the French masses can live on their own substance, or else from international mendicancy, they will not feel the need of having recourse to us. But when they feel things becoming dramatic, when they are on the verge of catastrophe, they will appeal to the man who has already saved France in even more dramatic circumstances. Régimes collapse at moments of drama.*

In the long run this was to prove an accurate view of the situation, but it held out little that was attractive to the RPF's parliamentarians. If the party's policy was to be purely one of expecting the collapse of the régime, then why have deputies and senators taking part in its institutions? The contradiction was finally to dissolve the RPF as a political party. De Gaulle's decision to put an end to the political action of the *Rassemblement* was the logical conclusion of an attitude which he had held all along.

Another feature of the RPF which set it apart from other political parties was its constitution. As Christian Purtschet has pointed out, the party's constitution reproduced in terms of a party the conceptions of presidential power expressed in the Bayeux speech and realized under the Fifth Republic. At the top of the pyramid is an all-powerful president. His task is to lead the *Rassemblement*, and his powers include that of forming the executive committee and the general secretariat. He can also decide disputes within the movement and depute members of the executive committee to special tasks. He is elected by the national congress of the *Rassemblement* much as the president of the Fifth Republic is elected by universal suffrage. The National Council of the RPF was also elected by the congress, but had no right of control over the leadership of the movement. Its function was to plan policy in the long term and along the lines laid down by the leadership which fixed its

---

*In terms of immediate political tactics he also said "We must systematically overturn governments. It is the only way for us to come to power."[69]

agenda in advance. Thus it assumed a role analogous to that of a Gaullist parliament. Both congress and council could only be called into session by the president. All power in the movement, therefore, really stemmed from de Gaulle himself. Not merely did he choose its directing bodies, but, at the grassroots, a series of delegates appointed by the leadership were in fact the real directors of the RPF's local groups. It is true that the president was theoretically elected by the congress of the movement, but, in the circumstances, it was impossible that there should be any other candidate than de Gaulle. From his unchallenged position in the RPF its whole centralized organization followed.*

The RPF was also constructed on a more lavish scale than other French political parties. Immediately after its foundation the movement was to open at least one center (and sometimes three) in each *arrondissement* of Paris.[71] Meetings, at which the General himself spoke to audiences in Paris or the provinces, were of impressive dimensions like the one at the Hippodrome of Vincennes on October 5, 1947, which was attended by half a million people and policed by 5,000 stewards. Rows of masts with banners inscribed with the Cross of Lorraine surrounded the enclosure, and rows of Resistance members, old soldiers and war wounded were there to recall the heroic days of London and Algiers. The "Assizes" (*Assises Nationales*) of the RPF—the name by which the yearly national congresses of the movement soon came to be known— were also an occasion for symbolic pagentry.[72]** The propaganda services of the movement were active as was shown by the appearance on the walls of French cities of innumerable posters bearing the picture of the lady—half Liberty on the barricades, half Niké of Samothrace—adopted as the symbol of a resurgent France. The movement did not really have a press of its own (with the exception of a weekly bulletin *Le Rassemblement*). There was, however, a party school installed in Saint-Germain-en-Laye where members could follow courses of lectures and take part in discussions. The ideas on which the RPF based its campaign were to be found in the extracts from de Gaulle's writings, which appeared under the title of *La France sera la France*, edited by Georges Pompidou and carefully revised by de Gaulle himself.

*The organization of the RPF is contained in its statutes (May 29, 1947) and an *Instruction sur l'Organisation du Rassemblement du Peuple français* (November 13, 1947).[70]

**The Assizes were held, in the course of the RPF's existence, at Marseille, Lille, Paris (twice) and Nancy.

The scale of the RPF's effort required money. The normal public devices of French political fund-raising—subscription, the buying of stamps or postcards—were plainly insufficient, and many allegations have been made as to where the funds originated. Many Gaullists had contacts with industry or banking—the best known of such connections is that of Pompidou with the Banque Rothschild, of which he was a director—and there also seems to be evidence that the RPF received subsidies from the *Comité national du Patronat français* (CNPF) until after the 1951 elections. At this stage of the Fourth Republic the *patronat* was prepared to subsidize any anti-Communist candidate, and the RPF cannot be said to be especially representative of big business except insofar as its greater modernity made it more *en rapport* with industry than parties like the Radicals whose connections were with small-scale business.[73]*

Once founded, the RPF got off to a flying electoral start in the municipal elections of October 1947. The results of these showed the Gaullists capturing control of the municipal council of Paris with 52 of the 90 seats and also coming in at Bordeaux, Rennes, Strasbourg and Marseille (where violence marked the takeover from a Communist mayor). The RPF had received some six million votes (about 40 percent of the total) and taken power in the thirteen largest towns of France.[75] The measure of this success was probably delusive; the RPF had often put forward coalitions, and municipal elections are very different from national ones. But nevertheless if this was not a total vote of confidence in de Gaulle, it was a considerable expression of no confidence in the Third Force, whose main pillars, the Socialists and MRP, only received 25 percent of the vote. The RPF, however, was left in the not very satisfactory position of feeling that it had a majority in the country, but being unable to bring about the dissolution of the National Assembly which would have allowed the *Rassemblement* to realize its assets. All it could do for the next four years was to protest loudly that the Third Force did not really represent France.

The 1948 elections to the *Conseil de la République* gave the Gaullists 54 seats out of 246 for metropolitan France together with 117 members of their 'inter-group' (the non-RPF were drawn from the *Rassemblement des Gauches* [RGR] and the right). But in the National Assembly the Gaullists and their allies only comprised some 40 deputies. Gaullist means of pressure within the parliamentary system

*The CNPF's paymaster was Senator Boutemy.[74]

were therefore insufficient. Meanwhile, France's general return to
normal economic conditions as a result of the Marshall Plan diminished
the unrest which might have led to an overturning of the régime.

Gaullist hopes were pinned to the 1951 elections, but, when these
came, the electoral law permitting *apparentements* caused the RPF to
pay dearly for its isolation. In the first place the four million votes it
polled were somewhat less than had been hoped. Secondly, its 121
deputies were fewer than it had the right to expect had the seats been
allotted proportionally to the vote. Under the 1946 electoral system
the RPF would have had 144 deputies. (But it still suffered less than
the Communists who would have had 180 deputies instead of their
actual 101.)[76]

Once installed in the assembly the Gaullist parliamentary leadership
had a considerable tactical success: by helping to raise the issue of
subsidies to religious schools and to elaborate the *loi Barangé* they
succeeded in throwing the Socialists into opposition. The way was now
open for an extension of the center coalition towards the right with
Gaullist participation at a price. It was this obvious move which was
rejected by de Gaulle, and it is easy to understand the annoyance of
Gaullist tacticians in the assembly who had put themselves in a
commanding political position only to find their leader unwilling to
exploit its possibilities.

The attraction towards the majority, however, proved too strong. In
March 1952, 27 Gaullists had voted for the investiture of Pinay against
the decision of their party. In the summer of the same year it was these
27 who formed the main body of those expelled from the RPF and
assembled in the ARS. They included such well-known right-wing
figures as Edmond Barrachin and Edouard Frédéric-Dupont. Meanwhile
in a by-election in Paris the RPF had seen its candidate, Edmond
Michelet, beaten, and its share of the vote fall to 13.8 percent from
24.2 percent a year earlier. In January 1953 the RPF voted the
investiture of René Mayer after Soustelle had failed in his soundings to
form a government himself.* In April the municipal elections were a
disaster for the RPF; the movement only won 10.6 percent of the seats

---

*It seems that de Gaulle was furious at Soustelle's acceptance of the request
from the Elysée to undertake soundings. The growing rift between himself and
the RPF parliamentary leader would appear to have dated from this example of
the latter's 'compromise' with the system.[77]

contested as against 25.8 percent in 1947. On May 6, de Gaulle made his declaration releasing RPF deputies and senators from their allegiance and ending the movement's political and electoral activity. "Before everything, [the *Rassemblement*] must draw away from a régime which is sterile and which it cannot, for the moment, change."[78] On September 14, 1955, two and a half months after his own withdrawal from public life, de Gaulle put the RPF into cold storage. The parliamentary party, become the *Union des Républicains d'action sociale* (URAS), had gone on to participate in the Laniel government and those that followed it. In the 1956 elections, Gaullists without de Gaulle, they were only to receive 842,000 votes (as against four million in 1951) and elect 21 deputies.

What was the RPF and who voted for it? For it is clear that its rapid decline is only explicable in terms of the heterogeneity of its support. In the first place, it represented an attempt to carry the spirit of wartime Gaullism into postwar political life. The 1949 *Conseil de Direction* of the movement reads like a roll-call of London Gaullists and Resistance members: Guillain de Benouville, Capitant, Diethelm, Malraux, Michelet, Palewski, Soustelle, Rémy . . . . The atmosphere was established from the start amongst other things, by the use of the term *compagnon* to describe members and a considerable effort was made to bring in Resistance organizations and the various associations assembling those who had belonged to Free France. In particular the support given to the RPF by a number of those who had been Gaullist secret agents during the war placed at its disposition men accustomed to clandestine organization and the techniques of political warfare.*

The RPF was also a party of the right despite its evocation of wartime Gaullism and despite the presence among its leaders of a Capitant, a Vallon or a Malraux all of whom had pronounced left-wing sympathies.** But a glance at the electoral map is sufficient to reveal that it found its right-wing support in totally different places from, for instance, the Poujadists later on. The only area where heavy Gaullist

*This support could be double-edged. The RPF's security services did not improve the image of the movement when they opened fire on hostile demonstrators in September 1949, killing a Communist.

**Roger Frey, then secretary-general of the *Union pour la Nouvelle République* (UNR), when asked to define the difference between the present Gaullist party and the RPF replied that "the old RPF had above all grouped different elements of the French right."[79]

and Poujadist support overlaps is in the traditionally Catholic region of the west. Otherwise Poujadism is mainly confined to the industrially backward departments south of the Loire, while the RPF found its votes in the 1951 election in the more advanced areas of the northeast, Normandy and the Paris region. South of the Loire (that is, in the unoccupied zone governed by Vichy until 1942) the RPF was to remain weak, and there is perhaps some significance in this historical background to a division in voting habits between north and south. The old Vichy right, in any case, remained intransigently hostile to de Gaulle despite the latter's plea for better conditions of imprisonment for Pétain.

Apart from this group, the RPF seems to have attracted two very different types of right-wing vote. On the one hand there were those who were drawn by the dynamism and modernity which the movement seemed to promise. Among its members were many technocrats and businessmen. It had more voters between the ages of 18 and 34 than any other party except the Communists, and some 20 percent of its support came from the industrial working-class.[80] The picture is of a modern type of conservatism finding adherents in areas and in sections of the population where the postwar transformation of French society was making itself felt and affected by the ideas which had been developed during the war in London and among Resistance groups in France. On the other hand, a more traditional kind of conservatism attached itself to the RPF as a means of combatting Communism. Before 1947 this body of opinion had given its support to the MRP; after the success of the Pinay experiment it was to find a more congenial political vehicle in the Independents. The moment at which it took this decision was marked by the departure of those RPF deputies who were to compose the ARS, all of whom (with the exception of General Pierre Billotte) can be described as traditional conservatives, more at home in the ranks of the Moderates or Independents.*

The policies of the RPF frequently foreshadow developments under the Fifth Republic. At home its key policy was one of association between capital and labor, an old idea of de Gaulle's and one which was

---

*The number of RPF members was considerable in French party terms. In 1948 it reached a peak of about 1,200,000 only to decline to 300,000 by mid-1949. By the end of 1950 it was up again to half a million, but thereafter tailed off. The ups and downs seem to be related to the international situation. At moments of crisis Frenchmen felt the need of de Gaulle.[81]

emphasized in *La France sera la France* as "one of the major themes" of the RPF and "an essential point of its doctrine."[82] What it implied was more fully spelled out in a law placed before the National Assembly by Soustelle and Vallon after the 1951 elections. This envisaged "contracts of association" negotiated in each firm between management, shareholders and workers. This would not in any way have weakened the authority of the management, and had, therefore, nothing in common with plans for *co-gestion,* that is, the participation of workers in the actual running of a plant or business. The contracts would have meant the sharing of profits and also of savings resulting from increased productivity or cuts in expenditure. In all this there was a strong emphasis on incentives to greater productivity: "The worker must feel the connection between the collective effort produced and the results obtained."[83] It is hardly surprising that trade unions and left-wing French parties should have denounced the scheme as a fraud designed to give a progressive veneer to what was, in fact, a form of paternalism, though this view of it hardly did justice to de Gaulle's own conviction that association was the only alternative to class war.

Another important aspect of the RPF's domestic policy (and one which situates it politically to the right) was its espousal of the cause of religious schools which ended in its parliamentary representatives sponsoring the *loi Barangé.*

It was, however, in foreign policy and defense that the movement was to make its most characteristic contribution to French political life and itself undergo an evolution of some significance. The *Rassemblement* had been created at a time when it seemed as though Europe was exposed to a serious threat from the East. This view de Gaulle fully shared. "The Cossack advance-guards . . . are encamped at 158 kilometres from the Rhine."[84] For him the *raison d'être* of the *Rassemblement* was to provide Frenchmen with an organization around which they could assemble in the crisis whose advent in 1947-48 seemed all too probable. Hence his insistence on the necessity of the Atlantic alliance ("The United States must henceforward be bound to Europe."[85]) and of an adequate capacity for self-defense on the part of France. Hence his admiration for General MacArthur during the Korean war, and his tendency to see the Indochinese war as part of a world struggle against "Communist domination." Thus during the years when the Russian threat seemed the most vital political reality in the countries of Western Europe the RPF was unswerving in its support for the Atlantic pact and its denunciations of the Communist danger inside, as well as outside, France. On July 27, 1947, in a speech at Rennes, de Gaulle had referred for the first time to the French Communist party as "separatists," and this was to be a constant theme of RPF orators.[86] Moreover, the Gaullists:

> were uncompromising in their denunciation of neutralism. One of their charges against the governments of the Third Force was that these governments were actually motivated by secret neutralist tendencies.[87]

By and large, therefore, it can be said that de Gaulle and, with him, the RPF supported the construction of the American alliance system in Western Europe as a defensive barrier against the Soviet Union.

Early on, however, discordant notes were being struck. De Gaulle was soon protesting against an American strategy which seemed to envisage the defense only of "some moles: England, Spain, Africa, the Breton redoubt."[88] Marshall aid would not be a good thing if it were used to exert pressure on France's foreign policy. The military dispositions of the Atlantic pact gave too much weight to England, not enough to France. The defense of Europe must be centered on France.[89] Naturally the blame for France's failure to assert itself and gain more favorable conditions from its allies rested upon the weak governments of the Fourth Republic.

De Gaulle's suspicions that France's interests were being neglected within the Atlantic alliance system were turned into a certainty by the proposal for a European Defense Community (EDC) put forward as the Pleven plan in October 1950. His attacks against the treaties of Bonn and Paris as "protocoles d'abandon" were to grow sharper and sharper as the battle over ratification raged and, with them, his criticisms of the Atlantic pact which now seemed to him to have assigned to France the role of "a kind of protectorate."[90] His opposition to the treaty establishing the European Coal and Steel Community was no less decided, even if the community could be dismissed more contemptuously than the European army.

The battle of EDC was to be a battle which the Gaullists won. The remark of André Diethelm when RPF deputies, just before their metamorphosis into the URAS, helped to defeat the René Mayer government on the European issue—"So we are not dead, since we can still destroy! "—in some sense serves as an epitaph on the *Rassemblement*. The defeat of EDC and the revival of French nationalism which went along with the bitter debate were its most lasting achievement. A future Gaullism would be anti-American. EDC marked the moment at which de Gaulle began to regard the hegemony of an American ally as more threatening than the possible actions of a Russian enemy.*

With the fading away of the RPF and de Gaulle's own retirement from public life in July 1955 Gaullism became an affair of small groups, of gatherings where men assembled whose fidelity to the General was unquestioned and who, moreover, knew one another intimately. There were lunches on Wednesdays at which Debré, Chaban-Delmas, Soustelle, Michelet, Pompidou, Guichard, Frey, Foccart, Malraux and Terrenoire were often to be found. The left-wing Gaullists—Grandval, Buron, Hamon and others—had their own meetings. Other, more clandestine reunions were conspiratorial in character. All of those who maintained their loyalty to de Gaulle at this time, however, shared one characteristic: they were not opportunists. "With the RPF, and its reduced successors, disintegrating as a political force, Gaullism was transformed increasingly back again into a mystique."[91] This fact was to have its influence on the nature of Gaullism under the Fifth Republic. Among the prominent Gaullists who stuck to their allegiance during the three years from 1955 to 1958 only one, Soustelle, was subsequently to break with de Gaulle. This low point of Gaullism at least had the advantage of separating the faithful from the time-serving.

*Another aspect of the RPF's policies is its attitude towards colonialism and colonies. This, however, will be better discussed in connection with de Gaulle's evolving position on Algeria. (See chapter V.)

CHAPTER V

The Founding of the Fifth Republic:
Gaullism and Algeria

La conduite de la France appartient à ceux qu'elle en a chargés. Elle appartient donc par excellence à moi-même.
—*Charles de Gaulle*

Vous verrez, après la musique de chambre, ce sera la musique militaire.
—*Georges Bidault*

On May 13, 1958, a crowd of young French 'activists' and students headed by Pierre Lagaillarde, a student leader wearing camouflaged parachutist's overalls, forced their way into the building of the *Gouvernement-Général* in Algiers, the seat of the Resident Minister, scattering archives and throwing furniture out of the windows to cries of "Algérie française!" Not only did these demonstrations go unopposed by the French army, but the Commander-in-Chief in Algeria, General Raoul Salan, did not prevent the local commander, General Jacques Massu, from presiding over a Committee of Public Safety—whose name evoked the period of the French Revolution—set up

immediately after the sack of the administrative building.* The aim of
the committee was to take over civil powers under the authority of the
army. When the news reached Paris, the reaction of the retiring Prime
Minister, Félix Gaillard, was to grant Salan "full military and civil
powers."

Shortly afterwards, the National Assembly voted the investiture of
Pflimlin's new government by 274 to 129 votes with 137 abstentions
(among these last the Communists). But the Pflimlin government,
which had been brought to power by a reaction of "republican
defense," immediately found itself unable to affect the situation in
Algeria one way or the other a state of impotence later mordantly
summarized by René Pleven:

> The Minister of Defense: the army no longer obeys him.
> The Minister of the Interior: he no longer has any police.
> The Minister of Air: he no longer controls the military aircraft.
> The Minister for Algeria: he cannot go to Algeria.
> The Minister for the Sahara: he can no longer go to the Sahara.
> The Minister of Information: he can only exercise a censorship. [2]

Gaillard's granting of full powers to the commander-in-chief was in
practical terms irrelevant. In fact, the 13th of May was, as André
Siegfried put it, "a successful 6th of February"—successful because of
the geographical position of Algeria, the sympathy of the French army
and the bankruptcy of the Fourth Republic. [3]

Behind these public events, however, there was a background of plot
and counter-plot that went back some way. It is hard to disentangle the
diverse groups who, in Paris or Algiers, were conspiring against the
régime, much more so to estimate their actual influence on events. A
number of the conspirators were Gaullists. Some of them, including
important personalities of the future Fifth Republic such as Debré,
Foccard, Frey, Guichard, Soustelle, had been in the habit, as noted, of
holding meetings where various possibilities were discussed (one
project apparently being the creation in Algiers of a Committee of
Public Safety). Another Gaullist, Jacques Chaban-Delmas, minister of

*Salan's first reaction to the insurrection seems to have been hostile. In a
telephone conversation with the chief of staff of the French army, General Ely, at
eight o'clock in the evening of May 13, he described the rioters as "ruffians and
swine." [1]

defense in the Gaillard government, had sent an emissary, Léon Delbecque, to Algeria ostensibly on an official mission, but really to see how the situation could be turned to de Gaulle's advantage.* There he organized a Committee of Vigilance, composed of both Gaullists and French Algerian "ultras," which was responsible for demonstrations in Algiers on April 26 against a possible Pleven government. It seemed clear to Delbecque, who had been a commando officer during the war and an effective party worker for the RPF in the Nord later on, that a successful coup in Algeria would bring about the collapse of the régime and offer de Gaulle an opportunity to return to power. His aim and that of the prominent Gaullists mentioned above was to steer any such movement in the direction of an appeal to the General and, meanwhile, to raise the temperature of Algerian politics.[5] His and their actions at this time demonstrate clearly enough that the adventurous habits acquired in the service of Free France or the Resistance had persisted down the years.

What is not at all clear is how far de Gaulle himself approved of what was being plotted in his name. That he knew of it seems almost certain since he saw Delbecque twice in April.[6] But rather than overt approval, his attitude towards the shadowy doings that led to May 13th was one of wary expectancy. By 1962 the movement had become for him "an enterprise of usurpation."[7] For the time being, he was willing to profit by it, hiding his own reservations about its nature beneath an enigmatic silence which all were free to interpret as they chose. Later, in his *Mémoires d'Espoir*, he was to disavow Delbecque and his fellows completely, albeit in veiled terms:

It is true that two or three active persons, who had taken part in my action at the time when I had one, were living in Algeria to spread the idea that, one day, it would be necessary to place the public weal in my hands. But they did it without my endorsement and without having even consulted me.[8]

Not all the plotters that brought about May 13th were Gaullists. The leaders of the Algerian "ultra" committees who controlled the students and the *lycéens* that made up the bulk of Lagaillarde's shock troops—a

*Delbecque's account of his instructions shows the tentative nature of his mission: "I was not sent to bring about May 13th, but to help to win this war, to put things in order, to mobilize what remained of Gaullist energies."[4]

Robert Martel, Joseph Ortiz or a Dr. Bernard Lefèvre—had never been Gaullists. Nor had powerful and rich *colons* such as Alain de Sérigny, proprietor of the influential newspaper *Echo d'Alger*—he, indeed, had been a strong supporter of Vichy. What these men had in mind was a 'strong' government constructed around the four pillars of French Algeria: Bidault, Duchet, Morice and Soustelle.

A 'strong' government was also the aim of many army officers, whose views had been stated in a telegram by an admiral and the four top-ranking generals in Algeria, which they sent on May 9 to General Ely, the chief of staff, for communication to the president of the republic. After stating that the French army was troubled by its responsibility toward those who might be fighting in vain (that is, the soldiers)—and toward the Algerian population, both French and Moslem—if the "national representation" did not decide to maintain French Algeria the telegram ended:

> The French army would unanimously feel as an outrage the abandonment of this national heritage. Its reaction of despair would not be calculable.
> I ask you to call the President's attention to our anguish which can only be removed by a government firmly decided to maintain our flag in Algeria.[9]

On the other hand, the army, especially at its junior level, was no particular friend of the Algerian *colons,* whose policy toward the Moslem population it considered selfish and stupid.* In addition, General Salan in particular might have been supposed to be hostile to the Algerian activists who had tried to assassinate him in 1957.

This complex situation was further embroiled by other groups of plotters such as, for instance, those of the so-called Grand O, a conspiratorial organization in metropolitan France having at its head two retired generals, Paul Cherrière and Lionel Chassin, and possessing connections with the Algerian activists and also with some officers serving in Algeria (notably Colonel Thomazo, organizer of the locally

---

*As one example, contrast Colonel Roger Trinquier's sympathy for the mass of the French population of Algeria ("With all my heart I was on the side of these good people") with his objections to the admission of the wealthy Sérigny to the Committee of Public Safety on the grounds of the latter's attitude towards the Moslems.[10]

raised *Unités Territoriales* which were to become hot-beds of activism).
Nonetheless, the basic elements of conspiracy consisted of (1) the
Algerian activists whose intention it was to carry out some coup that
would bring down the régime and produce one with a firmer
commitment to French Algeria and (2) the Gaullists who were prepared
to encourage them in this direction in the hope of being able to exploit
the resulting crisis for their own purposes.[11]

It was, in fact, the activists who engineered the demonstration of May
13th, and the subsequent intrigues in Algiers were due, on the one
hand, to the army's attempts to control the movement by going along
with the coup, and, on the other, to the Gaullist bid to take it over
altogether. The immediate cause of the coup was the fear that the
incoming Pflimlin would be able to form a government which would
then proceed to negotiate with the Algerian nationalists. The retiring
Resident Minister in Algiers, Robert Lacoste, by expressing his belief
that a "diplomatic Dien-Bien-Phu" was imminent, had given the
impression that a crisis was near in which decisive action on behalf of
French Algeria must be taken. Once the Rubicon was crossed, and the
Gouvernement-Général occupied, ultras, army and Gaullists remained
on the Algerian scene the latter two parties to events seriously
embarrassed.

Whatever student activists like the Lagaillardes and Martels (and even
some colonels) might think, the senior officers commanding in Algeria
realized that they had been put in the difficult position of appearing to
be in rebellion against the legal government. Both Salan and Massu had
been unaware of any plot and, for all their implicit support of the
takeover, wished to avoid a break with Paris. The Pflimlin government,
for its part, was also intent upon keeping the wires open to Algiers–but
took some precautionary measures: the proclamation of a state of
emergency and the surveillance of some officers including General
Maurice Challe, deputy defense chief of staff (thereby bringing about
the resignation of General Ely on May 16). But neither side was sure of
what it wanted, and neither side knew what to do next or how to find a
way out of the immediate stalemate.[12]

From this dilemma they were rescued by the Gaullists who were quite
sure of what they wanted (de Gaulle's return to power) and also of how
to get it (the exploitation of the Algerian coup to put pressure on
politicians and public opinion in metropolitan France). Delbecque and

his friends had been outdistanced by the Algerian ultras on May 13, but on May 15, the former was able to induce Salan to cry "Vive de Gaulle" at the end of a speech to the crowd in the Forum of Algiers. The Commander-in-Chief may not have taken too much persuading. He would have a natural preference for de Gaulle over the plotters of Algiers, and, according to General Ely, had already said, in a telephone conversation on the night of May 13, "Only de Gaulle can save the situation."[13] On May 17, Jacques Soustelle, having escaped from protective custody, arrived in Algiers somewhat to Salan's displeasure where he was able to reinforce Gaullist influence and, in particular, use his past connections to gain a number of influential Algerian French for an appeal to the General.[14] Such an appeal now offered a way out for everybody concerned: for the army which would otherwise have had to answer the vexed question of what to do with its power, and for the government in Paris, whose lack of that commodity would otherwise have been demonstrated. Even the Committees of Public Safety, which by now had spread all over Algeria, if they were not enthusiastic, were willing to take Soustelle's word that a Gaullist régime would safeguard French Algeria.

From May 13 onward, therefore, strong natural forces were working for the return of de Gaulle to power. He was a national symbol, the 'final recourse' in moments of emergency. He was an alternative both to the crumbling Fourth Republic and to army rule, the latter of which practically no one in metropolitan France would have welcomed. De Gaulle himself desired his return, but he desired it by the way of legality, in a framework of national unity and legitimacy "the national legitimacy which I have incarnated for twenty years."[15] But the fact was that the only chance of such a return lay in a sufficient intimidation of the politicians in Paris by the threat from Algiers. It was the prospect of civil war which would overcome the last hesitations of the parties and their leaders, and, for this to be present, there had to be enough pressure to convince them that there was a real chance of a putsch in metropolitan France.

In Algiers plans were laid for the seizure of power with the help of General Miquel commanding the southwestern military region and Colonel Gribius commanding an armored group near Rambouillet, the police, and the *Compagnies républicaines de sécurité* (CRS). On May 24 the capture of Corsica by a mission from Algiers headed by a deputy,

Pascal Arrighi, showed how near collapse the authority of the French state was. After hearing the news the Christian-Democrat Robert Buron noted that de Gaulle, who, twelve days earlier, had appeared as a threat to the régime, now took on the aspect of the only possible protector of the republic.[16] Meanwhile, a flood of mysterious messages over Algiers radio served the same end of convincing Paris that no time should be lost in recalling de Gaulle.

In fact, the threat of civil war—the plan for which was called "Operation Resurrection"—was real (and not merely an operation of political warfare). Once unleashed "Operation Resurrection" might well have led to fighting, though this could hardly have lasted long. As de Gaulle himself said, it would have been "an adventure leading to civil war in the presence, and soon with the participation on different sides, of foreign powers."[17] It would also have meant his return to power as the nominee of a mutinous army—a role he would certainly not have relished. While some Gaullists, therefore, were encouraging the preparation of a military *coup d'état* de Gaulle himself was concerned to stave it off until he had won acceptance from the National Assembly.* Only it was a race against time, since he could not be sure that he would be obeyed even by the conspirators who were working in his name, let alone by the army.

II

The steps of de Gaulle's return to power were marked, therefore, by repeated attempts to establish his democratic credentials, but also by frequent glances over his shoulder in the direction of Algiers. He could not let himself be carried to power by the army and the activists, but neither could he denounce them, since this would mean surrendering the only lever he possessed to use upon the politicians in Paris.

The first move was to place on record his own willingness to take power. In a communiqué of May 15, which, characteristically enough, began with a condemnation of the weakness of the state, he made his availability clear:

*De Gaulle was informed of the details of "Operation Resurrection" on May 28 at Colombey by General Dulac, Salan's *chef de cabinet*. He asked for information about the numbers of troops in the first assault and remarked that they were too few.[18]

G

Not long since the country, in its depths, put its faith in me to lead the whole of it to its salvation. Today, in face of the trials which it is once again approaching, let it know that I am ready to assume the powers of the Republic.[19]

But this way of announcing his candidature was too reminiscent of the style of a Louis-Napoléon or a Boulanger not to arouse disquiet in the Palais Bourbon. It was this anxiety which Guy Mollet expressed when he remarked the next day that de Gaulle should answer three questions: (1) Do you recognize the present government as the only legitimate one? (2) Do you disavow the promotors of the Committees of Public Safety? (3) Are you ready, if you are called to form the government, to come before the assembly and, if you are not invested, to withdraw?[20]

In the minds of parliamentarians (and particularly in those of the Socialists) the obstacle to a government headed by de Gaulle was the fear that he might prove hostile to parliamentary and republican institutions. On May 19, in a press conference, de Gaulle did his best to calm these apprehensions. He denied that the phrase "assume the powers of the Republic" contained any hint of a possible *coup d'état*. He had flattering words for Mollet, while evading a direct answer to his questions. Above all he tried to dispel any idea that he might install a dictatorship or destroy the "public liberties." "Have I ever done so . . . . Do you think that, at the age of sixty-seven, I am going to begin a career as a dictator? "[21]

Mollet was already convinced that only a government headed by de Gaulle could avoid a military coup or a Communist-dominated *Front populaire,* but he had to convince others. Events were to help him. The Corsican expedition of May 24 revealed the impotence of a government which could not rely on its army, navy, air force or police. Letters were now exchanged between de Gaulle and Mollet and Vincent Auriol, in which the latter tried to obtain assurances from him which would satisfy the Socialists, on whom the vote in the National Assembly would depend.[22]

A secret meeting was arranged between de Gaulle and Pflimlin at the Château de Saint-Cloud on the night of the 26-27 of May. The Prime Minister seems now to have become convinced that he must resign, but wished to sound out de Gaulle before recommending him as a successor. The meeting was not an unqualified success. Though Pflimlin was convinced that de Gaulle would not take power by force, the latter refused to condemn publicly the capture of Corsica, on the reasonable grounds that to do so would rob him of all control over the situation.[23] Instead, the next morning, the 27th, a new statement issued by de Gaulle came as a total surprise to the government:

> Yesterday I began the regular process necessary for the establishment of a republican government capable of ensuring the unity and independence of the country .... In these conditions, any action, from whatever side it may come, which threatens public order, runs the risk of having serious consequences. Even taking into consideration the circumstances, I could not approve it.[24]

The communiqué concluded with an appeal to the armed forces in Algeria to remain 'exemplary' under the orders of their commanding officers.

This statement, which proved to be the decisive step on de Gaulle's somewhat tortuous road to power, had two immediate results. "Operation Resurrection," apparently planned for the night of the 27th was postponed, and the Pflimlin government resigned the same night despite its continued possession of a majority in the National Assembly.[25] It was clear to everyone that the only possible successor was a government headed by de Gaulle. What was uncertain was how a majority of deputies could be induced to vote for him, if he continued to maintain his refusal to appear before the assembly.

On the night of May 28-29, de Gaulle once more went to Saint-Cloud to meet the presidents of the Council of the Republic and the National Assembly and discuss with them, at the suggestion of the President of the Republic, René Coty, the forms of his return to power. André Le Troquer, the Socialist president of the National Assembly, showed himself bitterly hostile to de Gaulle's return to power, rejecting his demand for the adjournment of parliament and for full powers and a new constitution, and insisting that de Gaulle must appear before the assembly. The interview ended with de Gaulle telling him that "If Parliament follows you, I shall have nothing else to do than to leave you to have it out with the parachutists and return to the seclusion of my home to shut myself up with my grief."[26] An impasse had been reached, and de Gaulle returned to Colombey-les-Deux-Eglises in the early morning.

On the morning of the 29th, however, the deadlock was broken. Coty sent a special message to the two chambers in which he said that he had decided to call upon "the most illustrious of Frenchmen" and that, if the assembly rejected his choice, he himself would resign. This placed the deputies before a choice which they could not avoid, and, moreover, put the responsibility for what might happen later squarely on their shoulders. Under this compulsion even the Socialists began to waver, coaxed as they were by Mollet who, on the following day, was able to bring back from Colombey two concessions on de Gaulle's part: responsibility of the government before parliament and his readiness to appear in person before the assembly. Auriol's disclosure of the General's conciliatory reply to his own letter of several days earlier also had its effect, and, finally, the Socialists agreed by a majority of three to vote for the investiture. It is hard to see what else they could have done. Attempts at a strike and calls to demonstrate republican solidarity had shown that the French working-class was quite unwilling to make sacrifices for the continuance of the régime.[27]

On June 1, de Gaulle appeared before the National Assembly, and the investiture of his government was voted by 329 votes to 224. About half the Socialists had voted against. Among them were Mendès-France and Mitterrand, who adopted the attitude of opposition to which they were to adhere throughout de Gaulle's eleven years of office.

The government that de Gaulle then formed was a surprise. It contained none of the leaders of "French Algeria" and few of de Gaulle's personal associates: only André Malraux as minister-delegate in the prime minister's office and Michel Debré as minister of justice. At the key ministries of defense, foreign affairs and the interior were three technicians, one of whom, however, Couve de Murville had already served in the CFLN in Algiers. Apart from these, there were the traditional party leaders Mollet, Pflimlin and Jacquinot as ministers of state, and Antoine Pinay, a guarantee of financial orthodoxy, at the ministry of finance. All in all, it was for most observers a reassuring government, though not to the supporters of French Algeria who were not even given the sop of the presence of Soustelle.* Even faithful Gaullists were shocked at the idea of finding themselves seated in the same cabinet as the old party leaders.** But the composition of the

---

*De Gaulle apparently told Vincent Auriol on May 30 that Soustelle would not be minister for Algeria. He became minister of information in July.[28]

**"On the eve of his promotion to ministerial rank Michel Debré exploded at the thought of finding himself in the government beside so-and-so."[29]

government corresponded to the atmosphere of *union sacrée* around the person of Charles de Gaulle—always one of the basic concepts of Gaullism.

On June 2-3, the National Assembly voted two laws at the request of the government. The first gave the government full powers for six months. The second gave it the power to revise the constitution after consulting the constitutional consultative committee and submitting the proposals to a national referendum. The passage of the second law needed the presence of de Gaulle himself, displaying a new parliamentary skill, and was carried by 350 votes to 161—a larger majority than that of the investiture. After this the National Assembly was adjourned on June 3. It was never to meet again, and the Fourth Republic was, in fact, if not legally, at an end. Its last action had been to give de Gaulle the freedom he wanted to establish new institutions and deal with Algeria.

III

"Frenchmen wanted before everything else the solution of the Algerian problem, only very incidentally the reform of the state. For de Gaulle the order was the opposite . . . " writes Professor Jacques Chapsal.[30] It might be added that it was the existence of the Algerian problem which enabled de Gaulle to undertake the reform of the state. Throughout the first period of the Fifth Republic until mid-1962 when Algeria was disposed of, the continuing threat from this problem, with its overtones of military putsch and domestic terrorism, ensured for de Gaulle the overwhelming support of public opinion, demonstrated in three referendums. Only after the Evian agreements were ratified in 1962 and had begun to be executed could opposition to the Gaullist régime begin to develop.

But de Gaulle was hampered as well as helped by the existence of Algeria. Until the threat of subversion was lifted, he needed all the political support he could get both at home and abroad to carry through his policies. This meant that the full unfolding of Gaullist intentions on the international, as well as the domestic, scene could only take place after the Algerian settlement. Indeed, it might be said that the four years spent in dealing with Algeria, from 1958 to 1962, were never completely regained, and that other Gaullist policies never wholly got off the ground after the traumatic first years of the Fifth

Republic even though immediately upon the ending of the war, the
pursuit of de Gaulle's policies was made easier both by the new prestige
the General had acquired, and by the institutions he had been able to
introduce under the pressure of the crisis in a referendum on September
28, 1958. The electors who voted *Yes* in the referendum were not so
much approving a complex set of proposals, which most of them had
probably not read, as expressing the view that de Gaulle was the only
man to handle Algeria.*

The development of the Algerian crisis was therefore to dominate
even the creation of new political institutions for France. Thus, before
recounting the course of that tragic drama, it is well to look at the
institutions which were offered to France for acceptance in the
September referendum. The main architect of the changes was Debré,
although their contents corresponded to the ideas expressed by de
Gaulle himself in his Bayeux speech (June 1946). The principal features
were as follows:

The President of the Republic is elected by an electoral college. He
"sees to it that the Constitution is respected. By his arbitration he
insures the regular functioning of the public authorities as well as the
continuity of the State. He is the guarantor of the nation's
independence, of its territorial integrity, of respect for Community
agreements and treaties." [art. 5] He appoints the Prime Minister and
other ministers on the proposal of the Prime Minister. [art. 8] He
presides over the Council of Ministers. [art. 9] He may "submit to a
referendum any government bill dealing with the organization of
public authorities, carrying approval of a Community Agreement or
proposing to authorize the ratification of a treaty which . . . would
affect the functioning of institutions." [art. 11] He may dissolve the
National Assembly. [art. 12] He signs *ordonnances* and decrees,
appoints to civil and military posts, accredits ambassadors, is chief of
the armed forces and presides over the councils and committees of
national defense. [arts. 13-15] "When the institutions of the
Republic, the independence of the nation, the integrity of its
territory or the execution of its international commitments are

*This view emerges clearly from the discussions within the Socialist party on
whether to vote for the new constitution or not. Gaston Defferre, whose powerful
federation of Les-Bouches-du-Rhône was to swing his party towards an
affirmative vote, recommended his followers to vote *Yes* "so that, in a renovated
democracy, a strong and stable power may apply a liberal policy in the overseas
territories and in Algeria."[31]

gravely and immediately threatened and the regular functioning of the constitutional public authorities is interrupted, the President of the Republic takes the measures required by these circumstances after official consultation with the Prime Minister and the Presidents of the Assemblies as well as with the Constitutional Council. He informs the nation of these measures by a message." [art. 16] He can communicate with Parliament by messages. [art. 18] He negotiates and ratifies treaties. [art. 52]

"The Government determines and guides the policy of the nation . . . . It is responsible to Parliament . . . " [art. 20] The *Prime Minister* directs the action of the government. [art. 21] A member of the government cannot exercise a parliamentary mandate. [art. 23]

Parliament comprises the National Assembly and Senate. [art. 24] Laws are voted by Parliament. [art. 34] The government can only be overthrown by a vote of censure which must be voted by a majority of members of the National Assembly. [art. 49]

The Constitutional Council consists of nine nominees chosen by the President of the Republic, and the Presidents of the two Assemblies, plus ex-Presidents of the Republic. [art. 56] It examines elections and decides as to the constitutionality of both ordinary and organic laws. [arts. 58-61]

In *the French Community* "the States enjoy autonomy; they administer themselves and manage their own affairs democratically and freely." [art. 77] The Community deals with foreign affairs, defense, currency, common economic and financial policy. [art. 78] The President of the Republic "presides over and represents the Community." [art. 80] He also presides over the Executive Council of the Community. [art. 82] [32]

In a press conference on April 11, 1961, de Gaulle himself was to comment on the somewhat mixed character of the 1958 Constitution. After criticizing those who complained that the Constitution was neither parliamentary nor presidential in character he commented:

Let us say, if you like, that our Constitution is both parliamentary and presidential, consistent with the requirements of our equilibrium and the traits of our national character. [33]

The intention of the new Constitution was clearly to provide for a strong executive whose supreme power of decision and whose principle of continuity were embodied in the presidency. "The result," write Williams and Harrison, "is a Hanoverian monarch masquerading as a republican president . . ." adding that "the president's fresh prerogatives are few."[34] But those fresh prerogatives included at least two means of appealing to the public at large over the head of parties and parliamentarians: the power to call a referendum and the presidential right to dissolve parliament. In fact, the application of the Constitution was to work out very differently from what discussion of it at the time of its promulgation might have led prophets to suppose. The much-contested article that granted the president emergency powers (Article 16) was not misused during de Gaulle's tenure of office. On the other hand, the Constitutional Council, from the outset, has had little effect as a safeguard or anything else. Further, the so-called community, with all its institutions, was dead almost as soon as born. And despite the fact that, constitutionally, a referendum could only be initiated by the government or the assemblies, de Gaulle was able to turn this institution into an instrument for obtaining a plebiscitary approval of his policies. In fact, the issue in the five referendums held under the Fifth Republic has never been so much the particular law submitted for approval as the whole political content of Gaullism, opposition to which was beaten back by a mass expression of public approval.

During the Algerian crisis, de Gaulle was able to do what he wanted with the powers provided by the Constitution (though he was later to mold it still nearer to his own ideal) largely because of his personal prestige, the exceptional status he possessed in terms of recent French history. When that prestige diminished from May 1968 onwards, the technique of the referendum worked against its author, but until then, the Constitution proved an effective vehicle for the political expression of de Gaulle's personal appeal to Frenchmen.

Theoretically, an insoluble conflict could have arisen between the president and the prime minister with the latter receiving the support of parliament. In that case the president would have had to try to impose on parliament a prime minister of his choice and would have been led eventually to dissolve it. (This would have been precisely the situation which led to the downfall of France's President, MacMahon in 1876.) But this impasse has never so far been reached by the Fifth Republic, despite the disagreement in May and June 1968 between de Gaulle and George Pompidou. Moreover, since 1962, the election of the president by direct universal suffrage has greatly strengthened the president's position. (This later modification of the Constitution poses the question of why this provision was not included in 1958. It may already have been in de Gaulle's mind at that time, but, as François Goguel has pointed out, the fact that, in 1958, the presidential electors had to include representatives of French overseas territories and of Algeria was a sufficient reason to make direct election impossible. By 1962 this situation was changed, and, a separate point, de Gaulle, as we shall see, was also less concerned to pay attention to the susceptibilities of the parties.[35])

Another factor contributed to the strength of the presidential office. The standing of parliament vis-à-vis a government chosen by the president was weaker than would appear from Article 20 of the Constitution, which formally made the government responsible to the parliament. In the first place, the senate and assembly normally only sit for just under six months of the year. The government possesses constitutional powers to fix the parliamentary time-table, to have its own text of a law discussed (and not a text hostilely amended), to prevent proposals to reduce taxation or increase expenditure, to impose the budget by decree if it is not passed within seventy days. To thwart ambition among deputies there was the rule that anyone becoming a minister must give up his seat in the senate or assembly. The procedure for votes of confidence, whereby only positive votes of censure were counted at all (making the assumption that abstainers favored the government), was calculated to produce the maximum governmental stability. Finally, a constitutional distinction between 'laws' and administrative 'rules' has deprived parliament of its power to legislate on the details of governmental policy over a wide range of subjects.

Debré's Constitution, therefore, envisaged a high degree of governmental control over parliamentary business with an eye to the British model, but without that respect for the sovereignty of parliament which puts life into the House of Commons. It is not surprising that he rejected as "dangerous to put into operation at the moment" a presidential régime with a real separation of the powers and an independent legislature.[36] The executive and the legislative are united in the Fifth Republic, but with the balance heavily in favor of the former.

Further, under de Gaulle, the moving force of the executive was firmly situated at the Elysée. In the very first year of his presidency, at the 'national assizes' of the Gaullist *Union pour la nouvelle République* (UNR) at Bordeaux, Jacques Chaban-Delmas, president of the National Assembly, put forward an interpretation of the Constitution which radically altered the role of the responsibility of the government to parliament as envisaged in Article 20. This is the theory of the so-called *domaine reservé*:

> The presidential sector includes Algeria, without forgetting the Sahara, the Franco-African Community, foreign affairs, defense. The open sector comes down to the remainder—a remainder which is, moreover, considerable since it comprises . . . the very elements of the human condition. In the first sector, the government executes; in the second, it originates.[37]

In practice, throughout his tenure of the presidency, de Gaulle reserved for himself the questions he considered important, releasing them to be dealt with by ministers in the normal way when he considered that they had lost their urgency. And these questions usually (but not invariably) concerned the *partie noble* of government—the war and diplomacy which interested the General most.* Partly under the influence of de Gaulle's own dominant character, partly under that of the Algerian war, there was throughout his term of office a gradual concentration of power in the Elysée.

Other parts of the Constitution too have been susceptible of presidential interpretation. Both de Gaulle's refusal, in March 1960, to call a special session of parliament to discuss agricultural problems and his decision, in August 1961, that when meeting in special session, parliament could not vote laws, limited the powers of the legislature in a way that could not easily have been deduced from the 1958 Constitution.** The fact that this could be done without arousing public protest shows the strength of de Gaulle's position and the weakness of

*It is significant that when de Gaulle included France's monetary policy among the subjects reserved for himself, it was to use it as a weapon in the struggle against American 'hegemony.'[38]

**According to the Constitution, parliament could hold a special session at the request of a majority of members of the National Assembly (Article 29), and there was no mention of any limitation on what might be done in such a session. On the other hand, the president of the republic was charged with seeing that the Constitution was respected and implicitly endowed with a right of interpretation.

that of the parliamentary politicians who were, in any case, unwilling to move into total opposition as long as the Algerian war remained unsettled.

In the referendum of September 28, 1958, the new Constitution was approved by the electorate by 17,668,790 votes to 4,624,511 (79.2 percent as against 20.7 percent of those voting) with the lowest figure of abstentions since the *Front populaire* elections of 1936. Those voting *Yes* have been estimated to include some two million Communist voters who disobeyed the orders of their party—a phenomenon which was to recur subsequently.

Indeed, the elections of November 23 confirmed the dissidence in the Communist ranks. At the first ballot the party only received 3,907,763 votes (19.2 percent of those voting) as against 5,514,403 in 1956. The Radicals also dropped nearly two million votes, being hopelessly split by Mendès-France's attempts to bring new life into the party. The MRP and the Socialists, on the other hand, kept their 1956 positions, but the MRP was now confined to strongly Catholic areas of France, and the Socialists seemed more and more to be becoming what the Radicals had once been—a party implanted in the backward rural areas of the country. The successful parties were the Conservative Moderates who increased their vote from 3,259,782 in 1956 to 4,502,449 (22.1 percent) and the Gaullists (the UNR and other labels) who had 4,165,453 votes (20.4 percent) compared with less than a million in 1956. As the elections of 1962 were to show, the Moderates owed their success to their identification with de Gaulle rather than to their support for French Algeria; they were also helped in 1958 by the disappearance of Poujadism. Despite the General's refusal to allow his name to be associated with any one party, the UNR too owed its success to its claim to represent a pure and faithful brand of Gaullism.

The upshot of the election was that in the National Assembly the Communists had 10 seats, the Socialists 44, the Radicals 23, the MRP 57, the UNR 198, the Moderates 133.* Moreover, many important

*The system of voting adopted for these elections (majority voting in individual constituencies with two ballots) was (and was intended to be) particularly unfavorable to the Communists. Professor Duverger points out that with 18.8 percent of the vote (leaving out its allies) the Communist party only received 2 percent of the seats in the National Assembly—a bigger discrepancy even than that existing under the Third Republic. But he also concludes that "the isolation of the C.P. is a profound sociological phenomenon." Other results in terms of seats also showed big discrepancies.[39]

figures of the Fourth Republic were beaten: Mendès-France, Faure, Defferre, Bourgès-Manoury, Laniel, Lacoste. It was as if the electorate had wished to make a clean sweep of the old leadership.

At the beginning of the new year René Coty retired from the presidency of the republic, and the construction of the new régime was completed by the election of de Gaulle with 78.5 percent of the votes of the electoral college. Debré was called upon to form a new government in which the Socialists were conspicuous by their absence. Soustelle was still in the government with no clearly defined functions, de Gaulle having refused to give him the ministry of the interior. Seven important ministries, including defense and foreign affairs, were occupied by technicians, Pinay was still at the ministry of finance, and a Radical, Jean Berthouin, was at the ministry of the interior (he was to be replaced later in the year by Pierre Chatenet, another high official). It was a less political government than its predecessor. A trend on the part of de Gaulle's governments towards isolation from political parties other than the UNR—one of the major themes in the political life of the Fifth Republic—had already made its appearance with the dropping of the Socialists.

IV

With the political institutions of the Fifth Republic established, and the structure of the French state transformed in the direction which de Gaulle had been advocating for fifteen years, the new régime could turn its attention to the Algerian crisis, though it should also be noted that de Gaulle made a tour of France's African territories.* Here de Gaulle, first as prime minister and then as president, was the object of widely differing expectations. On the one hand, partisans of a liberal approach to Algeria and a speedy end to the war believed that his point of view was close to theirs. Had he not said to Christian Pineau, the Socialist ex-foreign minister, "the only solution is independence."[40] On the other, the Gaullists who appeared to be closest to him, such as Debré, Frey and Soustelle, were apparently convinced that their support of *Algérie française* represented their leader's views. In the

*Gaullist African policy is discussed in the chapter dealing with the foreign policy of the Fifth Republic.

summer of 1958 Debré was still writing "There is no chance for France if it does not remain sovereign in Algiers."[41]* Moreover, de Gaulle's attitude towards colonial problems at an earlier period of his career may have been liberal in terms of granting better material conditions and a greater degree of representation to the associated peoples, but had remained inflexible when France's predominant role was called in question. Syria and Lebanon, the story of France's re-entry into Indochina under the provisional government—all these seemed to show that de Gaulle could be expected to stand up for French rights in Algeria, rights which the colonels and the *colons* of May 13th interpreted in the sense of integration between France and Algeria. During the heyday of the RPF some of de Gaulle's statements about Algeria could be quoted in support of this thesis. The nuances—for instance, his admission that the Algerian territories were not exactly comparable to French departments—were missed.[43]

In fact, de Gaulle's thinking on colonial problems seems to have undergone a considerable evolution during his years out of power. In 1955, in a conversation with Louis Terrenoire on the future of Algeria he had spoken of "a wave carrying all the peoples towards emancipation. There are fools who will not understand it; it is not worth talking to them about it."[44] To anyone who had followed the development of de Gaulle's political doctrine and observed the importance he attached to the concept of the nation state, it ought to have appeared highly unlikely that the integration into France of the Moslem population of Algeria would have appealed to him as a solution: "It is impossible to receive one hundred and twenty Algerian deputies at the Palais Bourbon."** De Gaulle's attitude toward Algeria before May 13th was most accurately represented by a conversation with André Philip in March 1958 (referred to in the previous chapter), in which he expressed his conviction that France would only get out of the Algerian impasse through the independence of Algeria (to be achieved in stages, if possible in association with France).[46] To this extent a Debré, a Soustelle, a Delbecque were self-deceivers, but de Gaulle cannot be acquitted of a careful ambiguity in his treatment of the Algerian theme or of using a

---

*One of the most intimate members of de Gaulle's entourage at this time, Olivier Guichard, has since given it as his opinion that the majority of Gaullists were favorable to "French Algeria" before de Gaulle's return to power.[42]

**In a conversation with Raymond Schmittlein.[45]

different language according to the attitude of the person addressed.* It was, indeed, to his interest not to disillusion the adepts of "French Algeria." If he were to return to power, it could only be with the support of those who wanted a strong régime to win the Algerian war as well as of those who saw in him the one man who might bring about a negotiated solution. But the misunderstandings thus created were to weigh heavily on the future Algerian solution and, more especially, on the manner of its reception by the French army.

For all the ambiguity, de Gaulle on assuming power had a general view of what his Algerian policy was to be. In the *Mémoires d'Espoir* this is described perhaps as more of a logical whole than it actually was. "In the first place, I excluded from the domain of possibilities any idea of the assimilation of the Moslems to the French people."[48] Integration, desired so intensely by the colonels and the *colons*, he held to be an impossible policy, "a clever, empty formula." But the status quo was also untenable: "That would mean keeping France bogged down politically, financially and militarily in a bottomless swamp . . ."[49] And the exclusion of these two alternatives led to the conclusion that only Algerian self-determination would serve to end the war and resolve the political dilemma:

> Whatever may have been dreamed formerly or might be regretted today, whatever I myself, certainly, may have hoped at other periods, there was no longer any way out in my eyes except Algeria's right to dispose of itself.[50]

This, however, was subject to a number of conditions. In the first place, self-determination would be granted by France, not extorted by force or by the pressure of foreign countries. Secondly, the French community in Algeria should be free to choose either to remain there or return to France. Thirdly, treaties should lay down "privileged relationships" between France and Algeria. "The Algeria of the future,

---

*Writing to Soustelle on December 4, 1956, to thank him for a copy of his book *Aimée et souffrante Algérie,* de Gaulle gave it as his opinion that a success for France in Algeria would require "une très grande politique." The lack of this was due to "the régime," and the general impression that a reader would gather from the letter was that, should de Gaulle return to power, things would be different. The letter, though ambiguous if read carefully, could only encourage a partisan of "French Algeria" to believe that de Gaulle was of the same opinion.[47]

by virtue of a certain imprint it has received and would wish to keep, would remain, in many respects, French."[5][1]

This was de Gaulle's strategy, but, significantly, he added, "as to the tactics, I had to make the march in stages and cautiously."[5][2] The *Mémoires d'Espoir* give the impression that, having decided the end to be attained, he moved steadily towards it with no detours or changes of course along the way. This, however, is hardly the impression given by his Algerian policy in the years between 1958 and 1962. The general aim of an independent Algeria somehow or other associated with France might be maintained, but, when it came to what sort of association this would be, there was a wide range of better or worse possibilities. De Gaulle is said to have once described the destiny of Algeria as "at best Houphouët-Boigny, at worst Sékou-Touré."* Between these two alternatives lay all the difference for a French government, between the success and failure of a policy. In other words, as well as a question of *whether* Algeria became independent, there was also a question of *how* it became independent. The future would depend on the answers found to both.

De Gaulle was determined to bring the war to an end under conditions that would preserve as many as possible of the links between France and Algeria and safeguard French interests (investments, military bases, Saharan oil) in so far as this could still be achieved. But the immediate necessity was to restore the authority of the French state over its army and over the French population of Algeria. Without this nothing could be done. Faced by the aftermath of a successful military putsch, he could not reveal his long-term intentions too rapidly before the restoration of authority had gone sufficiently far to enable him to cope with a possible repetition of May 13th. Immobility on the political front was, however, impossible for domestic reasons. What remained was advance by inches; the slow exploration of possible solutions combined with a steady sapping of the positions held in political life and held within the army by the men of May 13th.

On his first visit to Algeria, on June 4, immediately after his investiture, de Gaulle confined himself to careful ambiguities. In the light of later events his "I have understood you" to the crowds on the

---

*By Alain de Sérigny – a suspect witness.[5][3]

Forum of Algiers appears full of irony, but at the time it drew frantic applause from his hearers. At Mostaganem he even allowed himself a "Vive l'Algérie française!"—the only time he was to pronounce these words.[54] But there were also signs of some significance for the future. Recognizing that the struggle of the FLN was courageous, he called upon its members to take part in the political life of an Algeria where Moslems would be "Frenchmen with full rights" (*français à part entière*).[55] At Oran he was visibly irritated by cries of "Soustelle, Soustelle" from the crowd, and did not hesitate when addressing the local Committee of Public Safety to remind them sharply that they had no governmental function. On his return to Paris he sent a telegram to Salan denouncing the presumption of the *Comité d'Algérie-Sahara* in transmitting to him a sort of ultimatum and recalling that its only function was to express the opinion of its members under Salan's authority. On his next visit to Algiers at the beginning of July he was to refuse to receive a delegation of the local CSP.[56]

Over the next three years de Gaulle's Algerian policy was to evolve by fits and starts, interrupted in its development by upheavals in Algeria which sometimes forced a tactical retreat. Its stages are marked by a series of statements which, while frequently sibylline, show clearly enough the main lines of his policy and its gradual evolution.

In the autumn of 1958, France's Algerian policy was defined in three major statements. Opening the campaign for the September referendum (in a speech in Algiers on August 29) de Gaulle emphasized that this would give Algerians the chance to decide their own future. An affirmative vote would mean that "you wish to conduct yourselves like Frenchmen with full rights and believe that the necessary evolution of Algeria must be accomplished in a French framework."[57] After the referendum, which produced nearly 80 percent *Yes* in Algeria, on October 3, in a speech at Constantine, de Gaulle announced the so-called Constantine plan for the economic and social development of the country. This was quickly followed in a press conference of October 23 by the offer of "the peace of the brave":

I have spoken of the peace of the brave. What does this mean? Simply this: let those who opened fire cease fire, and let them return without humiliation to their families and their work.[58]

This was an offer of a military armistice with the FLN rather than a political negotiation, and it was immediately rejected by the leaders of the movement who were soon to set up the *Gouvernement provisoire de la République Algérienne* (GPRA).

At this point Gaullist policy was a combination of economic development, military pacification and the hope that there would emerge among Algerian Moslems some political force other than the FLN which would be ready to govern an Algeria enjoying a large measure of independence, but nonetheless associated with France. In fact, the elections of November 30 were to produce forty-eight Moslem deputies largely favorable to integration.[59] But this was certainly not what de Gaulle wanted. The election of men too close to the Algerian French population and therefore compromised in the eyes of the mass of Algerian Moslems, appeared to mark the failure of his policy inasmuch as it aimed at discovering emergent political forces in the Moslem community. Moreover, an earlier attempt in June to make Abderrahmane Farès, a Moslem political personality with close links to the FLN, minister of state for Algeria, had met with Farès's refusal—no doubt because his friends were not prepared to consent to his participation in the French government.*

Nearly ten months were to pass before there was a further public evolution in de Gaulle's Algerian policy. Since it soon became clear that attempts to conjure up a negotiating partner outside the FLN were doomed to failure, it might be asked why de Gaulle chose to wait so long before travelling a farther stage on the road which was now unavoidable. To this question there is perhaps a double answer. In the first place, de Gaulle no doubt genuinely wished to make sure that his first combination of policies was not going to succeed before passing on to something else. Secondly, he wanted more time to strengthen the government's position in Algeria itself. At the end of 1958 Salan was removed to more or less honorific functions, and control in Algeria was divided between a civilian Resident-General, Paul Delouvrier, and a military commander, General Maurice Challe. Jouhaud, the air force commander in Algeria, retired at his own request after Salan's departure, and other officers involved in the events of May 13th were

*It would seem as if Farès's opinion that a cease-fire could be discussed with the FLN without the prior recognition of Algerian independence may well have been responsible for the first form assumed by de Gaulle's Algerian policy. Unfortunately, Farès turned out to be wrong—or to have less influence on the councils of the FLN than de Gaulle had thought.[60]

moved. Nonetheless the state of mind of the French army in Algeria was still far from satisfactory from the point of view of the home government, as was to become clear later on. The army's attitude provided an imperative reason for caution in announcing the reversal of a policy dear to its heart.*

This reversal was publicly announced on September 16, 1959, in a broadcast by de Gaulle, but it had been preceded, as was de Gaulle's wont, by a warning shot in the direction of those favoring integration. In April, in an interview with the deputy for Oran, Robert Laffont, de Gaulle had remarked that those who cried integration most loudly were the very people who had previously been against it, adding in another famous phrase: "What they want is to be given back daddy's Algeria, but daddy's Algeria is dead, and if they do not understand this, they will die with it."[62] In his speech of September 16 he was to bury integration forever, while apparently preserving it as a choice. Declaring that the time had now come to proclaim the recourse to self-determination (*autodétermination*) for Algeria, he went on to offer Algerian Moslems three alternatives. First came complete independence described in the most forbidding terms:

> secession, where some believe independence would be found .... I am convinced personally that such an outcome would be incredible and disastrous. Algeria being what it is at the present time, and the world what we know it to be, secession would carry in its wake the most appalling poverty, frightful political chaos, widespread slaughter and, soon after, the warlike dictatorship of the Communists.[63]

The second alternative was integration revealed in an equally disenchanting light for metropolitan Frenchmen by the enumeration of all the rights and privileges which Algerians would enjoy within France itself. Thirdly came what was clearly de Gaulle's own preference—the mean between the two extremes—"the government of Algerians by Algerians, backed up by French help and in close relationship with France, as regards the economy, education, defense and foreign relations."[64]

Thus, while association with France was still seen as a preferable

*Among officers shifted by the end of 1959 were General Allard, and Colonels Vaudrey, Lacheroy, Goussault, Crazafor and Trinquier. Lacheroy and Trinquier were both leading experts in counter-revolutionary war.[61]

solution by the French President, he had for the first time envisaged complete independence as an alternative and placed the decision between the two in the hands of the Algerian Moslems themselves. Even the psychological warfare officers in Algeria, who sought a French Algeria, can hardly have thought that at this stage in such a consultation the Moslems would choose integration. Moreover, this was precisely the moment when France's African territories were acceding to the practical independence offered them during de Gaulle's lightning tour of August 1958. It did not seem likely that what had been granted to the Senegalese and Malagasy could be denied indefinitely to Algerian Moslems.* As the French community gradually dissolved into a series of independent states, its evolution was bound to weigh on the destinies of Algeria.

In a press conference of November 10 de Gaulle reinforced his speech of September 16 by another appeal to the FLN to negotiate the conditions of a cease-fire. Meanwhile reactions to this shift in policy were not slow in making themselves felt. Self-determination for Algeria was denounced by Marshal Juin as "arousing hope in the camp of rebellion," and nine UNR deputies, including some of those who, like Delbecque, Arrighi, Biaggi and Thomazo, had been most closely associated with the events of May 13th, resigned from the party in protest.** In Algeria itself the reaction of the new Commander-in-Chief, General Challe, was to call together representatives of the various units and, at the instance of Colonel Gardes, head of the *Vème Bureau* (psychological warfare), to tell them that the army would still campaign for a French Algeria—that is, for integration.[66]

In January 1960 the real crisis was set off by an interview given by General Massu to a correspondent of the *Süddeutsche Zeitung* in which his disagreement with de Gaulle's policy was made tactlessly clear. He was recalled to Paris, but his dismissal was the signal for activist demonstrations under the leadership of Lagaillarde, Ortiz and the

*Only a week before the speech of September 16, Senegal and Mali (the components of the short-lived Federation of Mali) had made it known that they were asking for complete independence.

**This was a consequence of the episode, in October 1959, known as the "francisation vote" within the parliamentary group of the UNR. It says something about that state of mind of the party at this point that apparently both Delbecque and a liberal like Terrenoire still believe that, on the evening of October 13, the UNR very nearly swung to the *Algérie française* side.[65]

French Algerian student leader, Jean-Marie Susini. On January 24 began what became known as *les journées des barricades*, which lasted until February 1.

In an atmosphere heavy with plotting and intrigue, the immediate impetus for the demonstrations seems to have come from Colonel Argoud, Massu's chief of staff, who gathered from a telephone conversation with his commander after the latter's interview with de Gaulle that Massu had withdrawn his previous orders to prevent activist demonstrations.[67] Colonel Gardes also actively collaborated with Ortiz and his para-military *Front national français* (FNF).[68] The demonstrators were, therefore, assured of the sympathy or, at least, the neutrality of the army in Algiers, most of whom were parachutists. Barricades were set up around the buildings of Algiers University and the FNF command post, and the activists prepared to stand a siege. These tactics were intended to demonstrate publicly the unwillingness of the army to take action against the supporters of 'French Algeria,' and their success was soon evident. On January 24 attempts by the gendarmerie to clear the streets ended in their being fired on and suffering heavy casualties. The parachutists who should have assisted them did nothing.

De Gaulle's immediate reaction to the crisis had been to telephone the Delegate-General in Algiers, Delouvrier, and to tell him that the affair must be settled by next morning. Next morning it was still not settled despite a broadcast by the President himself in which he spoke of "an ill blow struck at France."[69] Within the government there were differences of opinion as to whether or not the barricades should be stormed. Left-wing Gaullists like Malraux and Michelet, a Christian-Democrat like Buron, a high official like Sudreau thought that force should be used if necessary. Soustelle believed that some gesture should be made towards the European population (something that was to be urged on de Gaulle by the army in the person of the Chief of Staff, General Ely, who had been reappointed by de Gaulle on his coming to power),[70] while the Minister of Defense, Guillaumat underlined the moral disarray of the army, and another minister, Bernard Cornut-Gentille expressed his doubts about firm action.[71] As for de Gaulle, there was no possible doubt as to his choice. On January 29, he appeared in uniform on television and, among other things, appealed to the Algerian French to end their quasi-rebellion, but also ordered the army to restore order. In the council of ministers he is reported to have expressed himself more brutally still:

Those who have taken up arms against the State cannot be pardoned. The military don't want to cause bloodshed, as if they were not there for that! All the same the Army is not made to be afraid of blood. The Army is made to obey.[72]

Ordinary infantry troops were brought into Algiers to replace the parachutists. On February 1, Lagaillarde and Ortiz surrendered, the latter making his escape to Spain, the former being brought to Paris for trial. The mass of the army had not moved as the activists had hoped. Still, the danger had been considerable enough to deflect de Gaulle's immediate policy.

For the speech of January 29 had contained more than orders. De Gaulle had spoken of the refusal of the FLN to agree to a cease-fire without a previous negotiation on the political destiny of Algeria "which would be tantamount to building it up as the only valid representative and to elevating it in advance to being the government of the country. *That I will not do.*"[73] [Italics mine.] And, as Alfred Grosser has pointed out, there was also the evocation of a theme dear to the French army: the idea that the loss of Algeria would be a disaster for the West. The General appealed to the Algerian French not to believe those who told them that France and de Gaulle wanted to abandon them, withdraw from Algeria and surrender it to the rebellion. He proclaimed his own preference for "the most French solution." All these phrases were verbal concessions to both the Algerian French and the army of the kind that had been urged upon de Gaulle from all sides throughout the 'barricades'—the pledge not to negotiate with the FLN was by far the most important—and all the implied promises they contained were to be broken. That de Gaulle found it necessary to utter them at all suggests that this new revelation of the state of mind of the French army in Algeria had once more forced him to slow down the pace of his search for a political solution. (Since the FLN had rejected self-determination and a cease-fire as a formula, there was in any case no hurry.)

This interpretation of the reasoning behind the shift in de Gaulle's attitude is confirmed by his March 1960 tour of officers' messes in Algeria (*la tournée des popotes*) during which he devoted himself to reassuring his hearers with phrases like "There will be no Dien-Bien-Phu in Algeria" or "France must not depart. She has the right to remain in

Algeria. She will stay there."* It is small wonder that, on March 10, a minister, Robert Buron, should have written in his journal the anguished question: "Where, then, is the prince of equivocation leading us?"[75]

Some inkling of de Gaulle's true intentions, however, might have been gathered from the government's assumption on February 25 of special powers for a year, its formation of a committee of Algerian affairs on February 14, and the dismissal from the government of Soustelle and Cornut-Gentille, the two ministers who had argued in favor of a gesture to the Algerian French.** Guillaumat was replaced by Pierre Messmer as minister of defense—apparently because he was felt to have been insufficiently firm with the military—but was retained in the government. In Algeria colonels like Argoud, Broizat and Godard who had shown sympathy to, or complicity with, the insurgents were removed, and one of the most deeply implicated, Gardes, put on trial. (He was acquitted.) Challe himself was transferred to another command in April, and the *Vème Bureaux*, formerly headed by Gardes, was dismantled in May.[78]

On March 7, Soustelle's successor as minister of information, Louis Terrenoire, gave a press conference in which he repeated that three choices were open to Algerians: "secession" which would lead to chaos and might require "a vast regrouping of populations on portions of territory" (a threat of possible partition); "an Algerian Algeria connected to France"; or a return to "the direct domination practiced by metropolitan France since the conquest."[79] The press conference

---

*This version of "la tournée des popotes" is contrary to the official Gaullist one to be found, first, in Terrenoire and then in de Gaulle's own account of the incident. According to the official version the impression given by reports of the General's remarks to officers was the result of "the faculty of invention and interpretation of the press" (de Gaulle) if not of actual falsification by the military (Terrenoire). But the whole incident is so much in line with the verbal concessions of the speech of January 29 that it seems more probable that de Gaulle was executing a slight tactical withdrawal which he wished to disavow later.[74]

**'Dismissal' appears to be the *mot juste* in describing the departure of ministers under the Fifth Republic. In January Pinay had been replaced as minister of finance following his expression of disagreement with certain aspects of government policy. The communiqué breaking the news read "M. Pinay ceases to exercise the functions of minister of Finance."[76] Soustelle, in his final interview with de Gaulle, was greeted by "I am going to ask you to leave the government."[77]

was intended to allay the fears aroused by de Gaulle's statements during *la tournée des popotes*, and, as Soustelle subsequently pointed out, it contained one significant difference from the 'self-determination' offer of the previous September. Integration or 'complete francisation' was no longer mentioned. Instead there was a reversion to direct French rule.[80]

De Gaulle's tactics at this point, in fact, appear peculiarly tortuous. With one hand he was reassuring the army, though the partisans of a 'French Algeria' were not deceived, being by now thoroughly aroused. With the other he was pursuing the chances of contacts with the FLN. And between March and June there was also the hope of dissension in the FLN camp led by the commander of Willaya IV (a guerrilla military district), Si Salah. This attempt to conclude a cease-fire with a faction of the FLN seemed at one time so promising that de Gaulle himself received the dissidents on June 10, in the hope of finding in them the interlocutors he needed. The plan was not to succeed, but, on June 14, the President of the republic made yet another appeal to the FLN to discuss the conditions of an end to the fighting and, this time, elicited a response. After much bickering over protocol two emissaries of the GPRA—the provisional government established by the FLN—arrived to hold conversations with French representatives in the prefecture at Melun. These talks which aroused excessive hopes in France were to break down after four days (June 25-29). On the FLN side the aim of the Melun meeting seems to have been to demonstrate that the GPRA was as interested in peace as the French government. On the French side the object of negotiations was still a cease-fire, since it was felt—not unreasonably—that the direct conversations between de Gaulle and Ferhat Abbas, which the Algerians wanted, could hardly take place while fighting was still going on and Frenchmen being killed in Algeria.[81] The French government was not yet ready to recognize the GPRA as a representative government, but it was only such recognition that interested the Algerians.

The failure of the talks increased left-wing pressure in France for an end to the war. Intellectual dissent was demonstrated both by the trial of the 'Jeanson network'—a group of intellectuals accused of helping the FLN—and the 'manifesto of the 121' which, signed by intellectuals (among them Jean-Paul Sartre) and university teachers, proclaimed the right of the individual to resist the demands of the state. De Gaulle was to stop a prosecution against Sartre which had been started at the instance of the prime minister.[82]

Soon de Gaulle was to take another step on the road to a settlement. While letting it be understood that FLN terrorism would not help the start of a negotiation ("All [France] asks is that, before entering the room, one should leave one's dagger behind"[83]), on November 4, in a televised speech, he spoke for the first time of "the government of the Algerian Republic, a Republic which will one day exist . . ."[84] This was practically to admit that an independent Algeria was the only solution, and it is not surprising that General Ely, taking part in the Algerian committee next morning, should have noticed the tense faces of the President and Prime Minister, Debré having read a text to which the phrase "Algerian Republic" had subsequently been added.[85] The speech contained a hint that a referendum would soon be held, and, on November 16, it was announced that, on January 8, 1961, Frenchmen would be called upon to vote on a law organizing the conditions of Algerian self-determination and allowing the government the right to negotiate with the GPRA.* A little later a new and tougher Delegate-General in Algeria, Jean Morin, was apointed to replace Delouvrier, and Louis Joxe, an ex-secretary-general of the Quai d'Orsay and an old Gaullist, was made minister of state in charge of Algerian affairs.

During the second week of December, de Gaulle made his last visit to Algeria in an atmosphere of increasing turmoil. Everywhere there were demonstrations against him by the Europeans. In Algiers and Oran there were bloody clashes between *pieds-noirs* and the security service and between Moslems and Europeans. The official figure of dead for Algiers was ninety-six. More important, during the rioting, FLN flags had appeared over the Casbah of Algiers, and the Moslem crowds had shouted "Algérie-FLN." The myth that there existed other political forces among the Algerian Moslems than the FLN had finally been shattered. "Never was an inspection in Algeria more sad . . . " wrote one observer.[87] The twilight of French rule had begun.

*The question posed to the electorate was whether they approved the draft law "concerning the self-determination of the Algerian population and the organization of the public powers in Algeria before self-determination." The law empowered the government to establish the conditions of the consultation by decree and also to make the changes it deemed necessary in public organization in Algeria in order to give greater responsibility for its own affairs to the Algerian population, assure the cooperation of the different communities and create institutions competent to handle matters common to France and Algeria.[86]

The results of the referendum of January 8, 1961 were overwhelmingly favorable to de Gaulle's policy. The voters answering *Yes* exceeded those answering *No* by over ten million.* Those who had exhorted the electors to vote *No* included partisans of a 'French Algeria' united either in the *Comité National pour la Défense de l'Intégrité du Territoire* (among whose leaders were to be found names like Bidault, Bourgès-Maunoury, Lacoste, Morice and Poujade) or in Soustelle's *Regroupement National pour l'Unité de la République* (which principally included ex-members of the UNR and men associated with May 13th). In their publications, emotional and patriotic exhortation alternated with appeals to self-interest: "Holland used to eat butter; today she eats margarine .... Because she lost Indonesia and its petrol."[89] There was also strong military support for a negative vote ranging from statements by Juin and Salan to an open letter from sixteen retired generals who had commanded in North Africa. Among the political parties the Communists advised their supporters to vote *No* "while demanding immediate negotiations with the GPRA." Some Radicals were also shocked at the plebiscitary character of the whole proceeding. The MRP and the Socialists, on the contrary, came out for the answer *Yes*, and, despite the attitude of the Communist party, the left seems to have been responsible for about 40 percent of the *Yes* vote.[90]

It was clear that the French people supported de Gaulle in his moves to end the war. The support was, in fact, even greater than was indicated by the results since much of the *No* vote consisted of left-wing voters who disapproved of giving the government full powers and distrusted de Gaulle's intentions. Before the vote, the President's political authority had been shaken by the apparent lack of direction of Algerian policy and the growing public disorder--a loss of prestige symbolized by the senate's rejection of the law establishing France's nuclear striking force and by the successful flight of Lagaillarde and his accomplices who had been provisionally freed by the court before which they were appearing. After January 8, de Gaulle was once more in a position to dominate events. But there were also ominous signs of what was to come. On January 22, Challe, who had been transferred from Algeria the previous April, retired from the army, and during the winter there began to appear in Algeria the first pamphlets of what was

*The percentages were: Yes: 55.9. No: 18.3. Abstentions: 23.5. Spoiled voting papers, etc.: 2.1. The figure of abstentions was high, but not noticeably higher than usual in a French election.[88]

later to become the *Organisation Armée Secrète* (OAS). The new appointments in Algeria had done something to whittle away still further the powers of the army, but it was uncertain how far the situation could be held during the approaching negotiations with the GPRA. In February, contact with the FLN was made in Switzerland by an emissary of the French government (Georges Pompidou) whose closeness to the General underlined the importance of the occasion. By the end of March arrangements had been made for a conference at Evian on April 7, but a phrase of Joxe's as to the possibility of bringing Messali Hadj's *Mouvement National Algérien* (MNA) into the discussions caused the FLN to postpone the meeting.[91]

At this point the sequence of events was interrupted by the 'generals' putsch' of April 22, 1961. All de Gaulle's precautions, all his ambivalence had not prevented the French army in Algeria from making an irretrievable error. Of the four generals involved none could be described in terms of the traditional military obscurantist, and one at least—Challe—was among the brightest minds of the French army. Of the others, two—Jouhaud and Salan—had been deeply involved in the Algerian war, and the last—Zeller—had been the hope of the activists in the months before the week of the barricades. Supported by some battalions of parachutists and the inevitable colonels, most of whom had been involved in the events of January 1960, the generals managed to seize Algiers and imprison the Delegate-General and a minister— Buron—who happened to be there at the time.* In Paris itself the *coup d'état*, badly prepared as it turned out, was accompanied by detonations of plastic explosive which caused some casualties.

De Gaulle's first reaction to the putsch was one of cold fury ("Ils ont osé!" "They have dared!"[93]), a reaction which resounds in the words with which he denounced the rebels in his broadcast of April 23:

> Now the State is flouted, the nation defied, our power degraded, our international prestige lowered, our role and our place in Africa jeopardized. And by whom? Alas! Alas! By men whose duty, honor and reason for being was to serve and obey.[94]

But, in Paris and within the government, the disarray was considerable despite the President's assumption of special powers (under Article 16

*The colonels included Argoud, Broizat, Gardes, Godard and Lacheroy.[92]

of the Constitution). In another broadcast on the night of the 23rd, which betrayed a certain loss of nerve, Debré appealed to the population to go out to the aerodromes to prevent an airborne landing. De Gaulle had emphasized that every means must be used to stop the insurgents, and arms were distributed to faithful Gaullists in the courtyard of the ministry of the interior.

Meanwhile, in Algeria itself, the generals had not had the success they had hoped in winning over army units outside Algiers. Most of the generals commanding in the areas of Constantine and Oran remained loyal. Only General Gouraud, the commander of the Constantine army corps, hesitated. Moreover, among army conscripts and, even more, within the air force, resistance to the putsch was becoming evident. Transistor radios and television had enabled most of the troops to become acquainted with de Gaulle's broadcast. As he said himself to his minister of education, Pierre Sudreau, "During the war I won with the microphone. Now I am winning with the radio-television."[95] This was to be no 13th of May. The government's assumption of special powers under Article 16 and de Gaulle's own inflexible will-power nailed to their posts those civil and military authorities who might otherwise have been tempted to throw in their lot with the insurrection. On April 24 a general strike of an hour bore witness to the solidarity of the trade unions against the rebellion. Earlier Joxe, minister of state of Algerian affairs, and Ely's successor as chief of staff, General Olié, had been dispatched to Algeria to stiffen the backbones of hesitant officers and officials. On April 25 the coup was already over. Challe and, a little later, Zeller surrendered, and their colleagues faded away into the half-world of the clandestine activities of the OAS.

In retrospect it is easy to see that the generals had misjudged their moment. After the January referendum had clearly shown the state of mind of the French people, they could hardly hope for a convincing show of support in metropolitan France. The time for that would have been earlier on. Moreover, none of them appeared to have any idea of what they should do after they had captured Algeria (which, in fact, they failed to accomplish). They had also neglected to take into account the impact of a firm will and a historic personality in the Elysée. In that sense de Gaulle's summing up to Buron, quoted in chapter one ("There is a fact which they [the generals] have not decided to take into account, an essential fact, however—one which destroys all their calculations. That fact is de Gaulle."), was accurate. It was certainly his leadership that saved the day. Without it, it is not hard to recognize in the situation after the coup the elements of panic and reinsurance with the supposedly stronger side which had brought down the Fourth Republic. De Gaulle's personal preponderance had never been so clearly demonstrated.

The story of the next year was to be one of intermittent negotiation with the GPRA in an atmosphere of terror and counter-terror, of OAS assassinations and (in Algeria itself) of FLN reprisals. The negotiations themselves largely consisted of gradual retreat on the French side and were rendered still more difficult by the ever-present possibility that the Algerian delegation might be disowned by the GPRA itself. As a counter to this possibility and the use made of it as a bargaining point by the Algerians, the French possessed only the somewhat remote threat of partitioning the country and protecting a bridge-head which would contain the European community. In a press conference held just before the attempted *coup d'état* de Gaulle had made it quite clear that France had no interest in ruling territories and peoples that did not want to be ruled by her. If Algerians were intent on a complete break with France, then France would naturally cease to pour money into the country and would both repatriate its own nationals and send home Algerians working in France. Moreover, "certain populations" which would probably express the wish to belong to France might be regrouped and protected.[96] This appeared to be another reference to the possibility of partition and perhaps also to a possible separation of the Sahara from a future Algerian state. In fact, however, the state of public opinion in France itself, and the necessity of removing the army from the corrosive atmosphere of Algeria (especially after the generals' putsch) made any solution involving a permanent French military presence on the other side of the Mediterranean highly unlikely. In the negotiations the GPRA had most of the cards in its hand.

The negotiations began on May 20 at Evian, whose mayor had been killed by an OAS bomb some days before, presumably for having allowed his town to be used for the consummation of a "policy of abandonment." Simultaneously Ben Bella and his fellow prisoners were transferred from their island jail to house arrest in a château on the French mainland, and the French government declared a unilateral truc in Algeria itself. But the talks were to be prolonged for nearly a year generally by the suspicions of the FLN:

> in every subject under discussion it saw, on our side, the intention of keeping a direct hold on Algeria or, at least, pretexts for intervention when, on the contrary, it was of this that we wanted to rid ourselves.[97]

However, at Evian between May 20 and June 13 and then at Lugrin from July 20 to 28, it was the French desire to maintain some grip on the Sahara which led to deadlock. The Algerians wanted assurances that the area would form part of a future Algeria and were even unwilling to discuss the status of the European population before this was agreed, while the French wished the desert's petrol and natural gas (not to mention its possibilities for nuclear weapon testing sites)' to remain under French sovereignty or, at least, to be ruled by an international body composed of France and the Saharan states. At the end of July no progress had been made, and some members of the government seem to have pressed de Gaulle either to proceed with the partition of Algeria or else to go ahead and set up the institutions of an independent country without waiting for an agreement of the GPRA. De Gaulle himself, however, was by now firmly decided not to accept this kind of compromise solution which would have only prolonged France's proximity to the Algerian hornet's nest and rendered permanent the deep cleavages in French political life which had been brought about by the war.[98]

The consequences of not reaching agreement were underlined at this time by two further incidents. Around the French base of Bizerta in Tunisia heavy fighting followed Tunisian pressure on French forces with the object of hastening their withdrawal from the base. It was to take place later, but meanwhile, Franco-Tunisian relations entered into a state of crisis. The second incident occurred on August 27, when Ben Khedda replaced Ferhat Abbas as president of the GPRA—a change, it was (wrongly) believed at the time, in the direction of intransigence.

De Gaulle now realized that it was time to make another concession. No independent Algerian government would abandon its claim to the

Sahara, and there was therefore little point in refusing to accept this fact. In a press conference on September 5, he announced a change of direction:

> With regard to the Sahara, our line of conduct is that which safeguards our interests and which takes realities into account. Our interests consist in the following: free exploitation of the oil and gas ... disposal of airfields and traffic rights for our communications with Black Africa. The realities are that there is not one Algerian—I know this—who does not believe that the Sahara should be a part of Algeria ... [99]

In the same conference, he also spoke of "the institution of an Algerian state," and this combination of concession and recognition was to bring a response from the GPRA. It was also to bring a response from the OAS: on the night of September 8-9, the first attempt was made to assassinate de Gaulle while he was travelling on the road to Colombey-les-Deux-Eglises.*

The OAS now began to intensify its bombings and murders in metropolitan France as well as in Algeria. August saw the first pirate broadcast of the OAS. Throughout the autumn and winter of 1961-62 the number of incidents increased steadily. On October 30 there were seventy 'plastic' explosions in Algiers. In Paris on the night of January 17-18, 1962, there were eighteen. In November the *Comité de Vincennes,* which sought a French Algeria, was dissolved by the government. Soustelle and Bidault were already in exile. While secret contacts went on with the representatives of the GPRA, the atmosphere in France itself steadily deteriorated. Apart from the wrecking of the flats of well-known opponents of 'French Algeria,' there were acts of terror such as the mined car of Issy-les-Moulineaux which killed three people and wounded forty-seven or the bomb intended for André Malraux which blinded a little girl. On February 8 a demonstration organized by the trade unions to protest against the OAS and banned by the police, resulted in clashes which left eight demonstrators dead. On the 13th, the victims were buried at Père-Lachaise before a crowd of half a million. This type of police action combined with the inability of

---

*There is some evidence to the effect that this attempt was made without the knowledge of the main leaders of the OAS. See the deposition of Maurice Gingembre.[100]

the authorities to track down the OAS *plastiqueurs* created an atmosphere of suspicion and malaise.

In retrospect the handful of activists and officers who followed the banner of Salan and Jouhaud (though their discipline and cohesion apparently left a good deal to be desired) seems insignificant enough. Their hope of bringing about a new putsch in Algeria—not to speak of metropolitan France—was quite illusory. As one of them was later to put it, in a letter from prison, "the OAS officers bluffed themselves."[101] For all their success in *coups de main* (in Algeria from the putsch to April 1962 they killed 12,000 Moslems),[102] they had no program which could conceivably have won them support within France, were unable even to organize the Algerian Europeans effectively, and remained divided among themselves until the end. The OAS was never an army with a single commander and a defined strategy. It was always a series of small groups of different views and different allegiances directed intermittently from Algiers, Madrid and Paris or simply acting on their own when communication with the leaders became too difficult.

But in the winter of 1961-62 the OAS seemed much stronger than it was, and its activities served to strain the over-taxed national nerve to the breaking-point. The government was to do its best to destroy the organization, but—no doubt because of the complicity of a number of officials—its efforts were not to be rewarded until the spring. Meanwhile talks between French and Algerian experts were going steadily on near the Swiss border. On December 29, de Gaulle announced the impending withdrawal of two French divisions from Algeria in accordance with the army's program of modernization, which was to provide for its officers an alternative attraction to the Algerian mirage. In February there took place, at Les Rousses in the Jura, a secret and decisive meeting between the French negotiators, Joxe, Buron and De Broglie (a Gaullist, a member of the MRP, and an Independent respectively). From March 7 to 18 a public conference was once again held at Evian. This time it was successful in reaching agreement.

The Evian agreements provided for a cease-fire, an Algerian referendum to be held on July 1 and the setting up of transitional institutions with a French High Commissioner, Christian Fouchet, and a provisional executive consisting of three Frenchmen and nine Algerians, six of them representatives of the FLN. The head of this executive was to be the Moslem, Abderrahmane Farès, then in prison in France. There were also provisions for the safeguard of French interests and of those of the Algerian Europeans. The French army was to stay for three years, the base at Mers-el-Kébir was to be leased for fifteen, and France was to be allowed the use of other bases—principally those necessary for nuclear tests. Algerian oil was to be exploited by a Franco-Algerian organization, and royalty rights were assured. As for the Algerian Europeans, for three years they could exercise Algerian civic rights and would then have the option of choosing to be Algerian or French nationals. A series of clauses guaranteed their personal and property rights.[103]

It was an agreement which, though the words "independence" and "cooperation" were associated in it, meant in reality that the FLN were to get all they had asked for: an independent Algeria with the Sahara and no special status for the Europeans. France maintained certain rights, but de Gaulle himself had no illusions about their value. "That the agreements are hazardous in their application is certain," he remarked at the somber cabinet meeting in which the Evian agreements were discussed.[104] Even if an instant split in the ranks of the FLN had not led to Ben Bella's arrival in power, supported by the *Armée de Libération Nationale* (ALN) from Morocco and Tunisia against the candidates of the Willayas inside the country, it was not probable that any sort of *modus vivendi* could have been found between Europeans and Moslems. Soon streams of *pieds-noirs* were crossing the Mediterranean (700,000 by the end of August), stories of the massacre of the *harkis* (French auxiliary Moslem troops) were seeping back to Paris, and constant incidents were embittering relations between France and the new Algerian régime.[105]

Still, as Paul Reynaud was to remark, "the war has not ended in good conditions, but they were the only conditions possible." This judgment was fully shared by the French people who were called to approve the Evian agreements in a referendum on April 9, 1962. This time even the Communist party campaigned for a *Yes*, and the results—17.5 million voters said *Yes* as against only 1.75 million *Nos*—were far more conclusive than in January 1961. The abstentions, however, did increase to over 6.5 million.*

*The percentages were: Yes: 64.8. No: 6.6. Abstentions: 24.4. Spoiled voting papers etc.: 4.[106]

The only forces campaigning for the rejection of the agreements were the hard-core adherents of a 'French Algeria.' Salan had established a *Comité National de Résistance,* according to the wartime model, on March 30. However, despite the continuance of violent incidents in Algiers between security forces and Europeans (on March 26 the former had opened fire on a *pied-noir* procession in the Rue d'Isly killing forty-nine and wounding one hundred and twenty-one), the latter could now count on little sympathy in metropolitan France. The *Yes* vote "translates a general *yes* to peace."* As if to symbolize this defeat, Salan was to be arrested in Algiers on April 20, about one month after the capture of Jouhaud.

Four years of maneuvers to end the war in confusion and bloodshed—no account of de Gaulle's Algerian policy can avoid at least posing the question of whether the price that was paid for the eventual disengagement was not excessive or whether (which comes to the same thing) other methods might have cost less. The impression given by the French President's actions during these years is, it must be confessed, one of the iron Machiavellian Prince rather than that of a statesman concerned to explain his actions to his fellow-countrymen. His were the tactics and equivocations of a Richelieu, the secrecy of the *raison d'état* of the *ancien régime.* Perhaps the situation could have been resolved in no other way, and it would certainly seem that much of the impression gained from observing the succession of his actions was, in fact, due to genuine, if unadmitted, changes of policy. At the start he had hoped for a better solution than was finally achieved. From an Algeria in association with France he fell back to an independent Algeria, to the 'secession' and the political negotiation with the FLN which he had excluded as late as January 1960—just as during the final negotiations he was to fall back to the recognition of Algerian sovereignty over the Sahara and its resources. But by January 1960, however, it is hard to think that he did not foresee what was to come, and that the speech which ended the barricades and the phrases subsequently uttered during *la tournée des popotes* were not expedients to appease the mounting wrath of the army. If they had been successful in doing this, the *raison d'état* would have been worthwhile. As it was, they added to the sense of betrayal which drove men like Challe to their suicidal putsch.

Yet those liberals who would have liked de Gaulle, once in power, to

*It is interesting to note that the *No* vote was some 700,000 less than the Poujadists received in 1956.[107]

H

come straight out with a negotiation on independence with the FLN failed to take into account the state of feeling of the army as well as the elementary fact that a restoration of the authority of the state was necessary before any decisive action could be undertaken. That authority lay in ruins in May 1958. It was de Gaulle's unflinching and, at times, ruthless purpose that was the instrument of its recreation.

Nor should it be assumed that the events leading to the Algerian solution created no conflict for de Gaulle himself. In his *Mémoires d'Espoir,* speaking of his resolve to disengage France from its empire, he was to write:

> It can be imagined that I would not do it, as they say, easily. For a man of my age and my formation, it was really cruel to become, on one's own initiative, the architect of such a change.[108]

It cannot have been easy for him of all men to break the spirit of the French army, if only temporarily. He struggled to keep something of France's presence in Algeria and failed. He tried to hold back the army from irreparable actions and failed. The Evian agreements were a considerable political feat—an essential one even for the future of France—but for a man who was basically a French nationalist, the path to them was strewn with wreckage.

V

The Algerian inheritance weighed heavily on the Fifth Republic and on the Gaullist movement. Indeed, it might be true to say that neither fully recovered from it. In the short run, of course, the danger in which the régime stood during the four years until April 1962 caused many Frenchmen and political parties such as the MRP and the Socialists to see in de Gaulle the only barrier to a coup by activists and army. Thus, even if they disliked the General's peremptory ways and plebiscitary appeals to the people over the head of the assembly, their opposition could only be limited. The only out and out opponents of de Gaulle during these years were the right-wing extremists. Even the Communists were restricted by circumstances.

But the Gaullist party itself, the UNR, was to be profoundly changed by the Algerian crisis. In the course of the years between 1958 and 1962 the party was to shed some of its more conspiratorial and

Bonapartist members and to exchange their support for that of the left-wing Gaullists grouped in the *Union démocratique du travail* (UDT). The Soustelles and the Delbecques, the Biaggis and the Arrighis, many of the secret agents and conspirators who had helped bring the General to power on the Algerian issue were gone, and, in their place, were high officials like Joxe or Messmer or left-wing Gaullists like Terrenoire or Michelet. For others, such as Chaban-Delmas, Debré, the prime minister, or Frey who, in their day, had been partisans of *Algérie française*, either loyalty to de Gaulle, a change in convictions, or simple opportunism overcame their previous emotions and views. In particular, the fact that the Prime Minister had had to reverse his own previous views on Algeria (though not without one or two moments of rebellion)* eliminated him as a possible competitor for the succession to de Gaulle and, therefore, had a considerable influence on the evolution of the Fifth Republic. The final result was a somewhat chastened Gaullism. Compared to the earlier RPF, it seemed less of a party of the radical right, but the dangerous crisis through which it had passed had made it more dependent than ever on its aging leader.

The structure of the institutions of the Fifth Republic had also changed in a similar way under the pressure of the Algerian crisis. The conception of the presidency which had prevailed at the time of the constitutional discussions in the summer of 1958 had been that of an arbitrator: "The President of the Republic, I emphasize, is essentially an arbitrator," de Gaulle himself had said before the consultative constitutional committee.[110] But this view of a president above the battle and acting mostly as a mediator and director of other political powers could hardly survive a period of four years during which the President of the republic had personally taken all the most important decisions and where his personal interventions had been the turning points of political life. It was true that the president of the 1958 Constitution was assigned the function of "taking the measures" required when régime or nation were threatened. The Algerian crisis fell, no doubt, into this category, but the nature of the presidential power could not fail to be changed by so long a period of emergency which, amongst other things, prevented any challenge to the role played

---

*According to Albin Chalandon, Debré went so far as to restore activists to positions from which he, as secretary-general of the UNR, had removed them.[109]

by de Gaulle. There had been clashes with the National Assembly—notably when, in March 1960, de Gaulle had refused to call a special session, even though the required number of signatures had been attached to the request, and when, in August 1961, he denied the right of passing laws to parliament, then meeting in special session during the application of Article 16 of the Constitution—but, until the end of the Algerian war, while politicians might grumble, they were precluded from taking any more decisive action by their awareness that the President of the republic could not be replaced.[111]

After April 1962, however, the leaders of the political parties expected that the President would revert to his mediatory role, and that there would be a return to normal politics. As Raymond Aron put it, there was no longer an Algerian war to take the place of a parliamentary majority. Debré, the prime minister, believed that the best way to deal with this situation was to hold elections. This would give the Gaullists the necessary parliamentary support and start the 1958 Constitution working as had originally been intended. De Gaulle disagreed. The results of the April 8 referendum seemed to him too ambiguous to promise well for elections where the left would be able to cash in on the popularity of the Evian agreements. Also he wished at this time to make a new approach to the political parties and was not enamored of the UNR to the extent of wishing to rely totally on its support. He therefore accepted the Prime Minister's resignation (April 13) and asked Georges Pompidou, his former *directeur de cabinet,* to form a government.

As it turned out, however, any new approach to the parties, if one had been intended, was to be abortive. It was true that the new government included four members of the MRP, among them Pflimlin. But de Gaulle had failed with the Socialists, arousing intense hostility on the part of Mollet by his exercise of personal power in replacing Debré by Pompidou.[112] Moreover, defense and foreign affairs were still run by ex-officials, Messmer and Couve de Murville; at the ministry of finance was Giscard d'Estaing, where he had been since January. In May an attack by the General on European integration led to the resignation of the MRP ministers.

De Gaulle's decision to change the government rather than hold elections in reality represented an intention of strengthening the power of the president. The new Prime Minister had no personal political base and depended entirely on de Gaulle's support. On June 8 in a broadcast the General hinted for the first time at another referendum which would deal with constitutional change.[113] All these factors added up to what Professor Chapsal has called "the opposition of points of view between de Gaulle and what might be called 'the political class.' "[114] A trial of strength was approaching between the Gaullists and the other political parties.[115]

The results of such a battle would clearly be more favorable to the Gaullists if the chosen ground were that of de Gaulle's own position and powers as the head of state rather than a mere competition between political parties. The refusal to hold elections in April was undoubtedly sound tactics, though it might also be maintained that, by perpetuating the constitutional position established during the Algerian years, it kept the Fifth Republic in a position which eventually led to the extra-political outburst of May 1968. Immediately, however, a constitutional reform instituting the election of the president of the republic by direct vote was the kind of issue that would be most advantageous for the Gaullists. It was a measure, whose plebiscitary overtones would be violently offensive to the political parties and the National Assembly, but which could hardly be attacked as undemocratic.

But de Gaulle had other reasons than tactical ones for proposing such a change. It corresponded to his personal conception of his own position as the direct representative of France without intermediaries in the shape of political parties or *notables.* His was a national mandate, and what could be more logical than that it should proceed from universal suffrage? Moreover, he himself had felt the hostility of parties and politicians—at the moment they were engaged in attacking his European policy—and he wished to make sure that any successor not enjoying his own personal prestige would have behind him the strength that comes from a popular election:

the President needs the direct confidence of the nation. Instead of having this confidence implicitly, as I had it in 1958 for a historic and exceptional reason . . . it is necessary that the President henceforth be elected by universal suffrage.[116]

Undoubtedly, the exact timing of the reform was also influenced by another event: on August 22 the presidential car was riddled with machine-gun fire at the crossroads of Petit-Clamart near Paris. De Gaulle escaped miraculously, but at the first cabinet meeting after the attempt, the subsequent communiqué was to underline the necessity of insuring "the continuity of the State and the maintenance of Republican institutions.[117]* The urgency of constitutional reform seemed to have been increased by events, and, after the cabinet meeting, on September 19, during which only one minister (the minister of education, Pierre Sudreau) had shown himself opposed to it, the communiqué announced that a law had been adopted which would submit to the country in a referendum the proposal for the election of the president by universal suffrage.

For the members of parliament not only the substance, but also the form in which the change was proposed was objectionable. Under the 1958 Constitution (Article 89), constitutional change could only be carried out by a procedure which involved agreement between senate and National Assembly. Against this the Gaullists invoked Article 11 which permitted "the organization of the public authorities" to be put to a referendum. This interpretation was, however, to be disallowed by the *Conseil d'Etat* just then in a somewhat anti-Gaullist frame of mind.**

Whatever the rights and wrongs of the legal position, it was to be expected that de Gaulle's political opponents should see the referendum as an attempt to evade the provisions of the Constitution. Gaston Monnerville, the president of the senate (and the successor of the President of the republic in case of his death) was to speak of "a deliberate, voluntary, premeditated and outrageous violation of the Constitution."[120] The lead in opposing the reform was taken by the aged Paul Reynaud, whose protégé de Gaulle had once been. On

*The author of the conspiracy was Colonel Bastien-Thiry, a guided missile expert of the French army. He was executed in March 1963. The state of mind of the conspirators can be judged from a statement by one of them (Alain Bougrenet de la Tocnaye) in court: "We reject capitalism and Marxism and, therefore, Gaullism which first leads us to a mixture of the two in order to deliver us to Bolshevism . . . "[118]

**In September it had annulled the *ordonnance* by which the *Haut Tribunal Militaire* had been replaced by the *Cour Militaire de Justice* following the former's sentence of life imprisonment on Salan (Jouhaud, his subordinate, having earlier been condemned to death) and the recognition of his right to 'extenuating circumstances.'[119]

October 5 a motion of censure was voted by the National Assembly by 280 votes out of 480—a figure which implied the unanimity of deputies other than those of the UNR. This was a coalition of traditional political forces which saw in the constitutional issue a good occasion to end Gaullist rule now that the Algerian war no longer required its continuance. The National Assembly was thereupon dissolved by de Gaulle.

The high hopes of the opposition were to be disappointed. The referendum of October 28 was to produce a majority of nearly five million votes for those voting *Yes*.* The only satisfaction for the opposition was to be the fact that the proposal had not obtained an absolute majority of the electorate (46.44 percent of those eligible to vote). In a broadcast on October 18, de Gaulle had hinted that he might retire if the *Yes* vote were "Weak, mediocre, uncertain"—a phrase interpreted at the time to mean if it were not an absolute majority.[122] But, of course, he did nothing of the sort.

The succeeding elections for the National Assembly on November 18 and 25, were perhaps even more of a disappointment for the opposition. In the first round, with over eight million abstentions, the UNR (and UDT which had fused with it under pressure from de Gaulle) received 31 percent of the votes cast—the highest percentage ever won by any party since the Liberation. The Socialists, MRP and Independents all lost ground. In the second round the UNR's share rose to 42 percent, and its number of deputies from 175 to 233. The allies of the Gaullists, Giscard d'Estaing's Independent Republicans, had 35 seats— enough to give the government a majority. The Communists and Socialists also slightly increased their representation. The Center and MRP grouped in the *Centre démocratique* had 55 deputies and the *Rassemblement démocratique* (mostly made up of Radicals) had 39.**

Thus the November elections resulted in an apparent triumph for the Gaullists. It was, in fact, only at this point that it can be said that Gaullism fully established itself as a permanent force in French politics.

*The percentages were: Yes: 46.4. No: 28.7. Abstentions: 22.7. Spoiled voting papers etc.: 2.[121]

**The percentages of votes on the first round were: Communists: 14.4; extreme left: 1.6; Socialists: 8.4; Radicals: 5; MRP: 5.9; UNR-UDT: 21.2; Independent Republicans: 2.8; Moderates: 6.3; extreme right: 0.5. There were 31.3 abstentions and 2.1 spoiled voting papers. (These are, of course, percentages of eligible voters.)[122]

This was its first peacetime victory. To the final shape of the Fifth Republic's institutions so far achieved, there now corresponded the emergence of its dominating political conjuncture: a loose right-wing coalition gathering within it many shades of opinion, but secure beneath the shelter of de Gaulle's charisma and, ultimately, an instrument which he was to use to put into effect those policies which he had long meditated upon and was now, in the aftermath of the Algerian war, free to initiate.

The trial of strength desired by the parties and their leaders had turned disastrously against them. Henceforward they were to have few illusions and to strive pertinaciously, but without too much success, to reform themselves and to create a new political force able to resist the victorious wave of Gaullism. The purely political history of the Fifth Republic up to May 1968 focuses on these maneuvers—Byzantine in character and constantly interrupted by real events scattering and disordering what had already been assembled.

The Gaullists, on the other hand, in the exultation of victory failed to note one or two facts which might have modified their self-congratulatory interpretation of events. In the four referendums so far held, the percentage of *Yes* votes had been as follows: September 28, 1958: 66.41 percent; January 8, 1961: 55.01 percent; April 9, 1962: 64.86 percent; October 28, 1962: 46.44 percent. These figures showed, to say the least, that, in any other than exceptional circumstances, the referendum might be a double-edged political instrument. Similarly the complete dependence of the Gaullists on de Gaulle's own personal prestige would make it hard for them, in the long run, to exercise that capacity for political maneuver which alone assures the survival of political parties. The time would come when the Gaullist party (within which those whose main loyalty was to the person of de Gaulle were by now a minority) would look for leadership from a more politically pliable chief.

As for the General himself, he now relied for backing in parliament and country on a party with which he had never totally identified himself. Willy-nilly he was no longer an 'arbitrator,' but the head of a party—a position carrying with it the necessity of satisfying the demands of the party for electoral victory. When, in 1968-69, de Gaulle no longer appeared able to guarantee success there would be a transfer of loyalty to what, by that time, was the welcome alternative of

Georges Pompidou, a politician's politician. In 1962, however, the latter was only at the beginning of the process of building up his own political clientele. And de Gaulle was free to give his attention to the matters that really interested him: the strategy of defense and a foreign policy devoted to the pursuit of France's grandeur.*

*The view taken in this chapter of de Gaulle's Algerian policy has recently been confirmed by Malraux who has written: "Louis Martin-Chauffier has told me that the general said to him in '58: 'We shall leave Algeria.' To me he only said: 'Algeria will remain French as France has remained Roman. But be prudent!' Like him I believed then in the 'peace of the brave.' He wanted agreement at any price and held it for certain that he would get it. An Error." [123]

CHAPTER VI

Gaullism Abroad:
The Foreign Policy of the Fifth Republic

D'autre part, si aucune nation ne se trouve plus isolée dans un monde de plus en plus réduit, la France, géographiquement, intellectuellement, moralement, est et demeurera la moins isolée de toutes. C'est dire que, de l'attitude qu'elle prendra vis-à-vis des autres et de celle que les autres prendront à son égard, dépendent, non seulement son propre avenir, mais aussi, dans une large mesure, l'avenir de l'humanité.
                                                —*Charles de Gaulle*

Peuples d'Europe réduits et exténués, nous sommes entre ces deux masses: Amérique et Russie; ces deux moitiés immenses d'un horizon d'airain.
                                                —*Pierre Drieu La Rochelle*

To describe the foreign policy of the Fifth Republic as Gaullist is to apply to it an adjective which, in this context, becomes more evocative than when it is used simply to qualify a régime or a political party. For the phrase "a Gaullist foreign policy" immediately evokes a *style* of international behavior as well as the various objectives which de Gaulle assigned to France's policies (total national independence, freedom from the 'hegemony' of one or the other of the two world blocs, etc.). The style and the objectives were, indeed, separable; the so-called German and British Gaullists could hardly have existed otherwise. De Gaulle's French nationalism dictated the ends of his policies, and it is impossible to conceive of an international of nationalisms. But objectives aside, admirers of a firm hand in foreign affairs could still envy the not infrequent brutality of de Gaulle's policy, while its deviousness and secrecy could appeal as strongly to those who distrusted diplomacy conducted in terms of public relations.

Under de Gaulle, France undoubtedly gained at times from both his unwillingness to envisage any compromise and the functional efficiency and coordination which he imposed upon the Quai d'Orsay. Instances of intransigence such as the total neglect of the opinion of the United Nations or of rebukes from the tabernacles of the Third World when either opinion or rebukes were considered contrary to France's interests (for instance, on the occasion of testing various French nuclear weapons) were undoubtedly effective in silencing outside criticism and also invigorating to a normally nationalist French public opinion. Moreover, the resolution of the Algerian war had forced Gaullism to inflict wounds on French nationalism. Under such conditions, even if de Gaulle himself had not been so disposed, it was all the more important to give an impression of unyielding devotion to the national interest in the conduct of foreign policy. France was to be cured by homeopathy of the enflamed feelings left over from the Algerian episode.

From the beginning of the Fifth Republic it was clear that foreign policy would be conducted by de Gaulle himself. Not only had he always considered that it, together with defense, should be given priority over other national needs, but also these two areas formed essentially the *domaine réservé* of the president of the republic as defined by Chaban-Delmas (discussed in chapter five). In practice, during his presidency de Gaulle was always the director of the Fifth Republic's action abroad, and its various stages were marked by his press conferences. For much of this period (from 1958 to 1968) Maurice Couve de Murville was foreign minister, a loyal executor of

Gaullist policies which he himself approved in substance, if not invariably in style.

As noted earlier, from his experience in 1944-45 as head of the provisional government, de Gaulle had acquired a distrust of the Quai d'Orsay's tendency to compromise—"this desire to agree with their partners and, as they say, to reach a result."* His own brusque diplomatic style was well designed to impose a literal obedience upon the executants of his policies and to exclude the possibility of unwelcome concessions. Officials critical of the Gaullist line were ruthlessly relegated to unimportant posts. Only rarely can the Foreign Office in the Quai d'Orsay be observed taking a different position from the presidential office of the Elysée.

The main lines of French foreign policy under the Fifth Republic were not to be clearly drawn for the outside world until the Evian agreements freed France from the Algerian tangle. It was not until then that Gaullist diplomacy could develop policies which were conditional upon France's recovery of a certain independence of action and freedom from commitments. But while the Algerian war was still continuing, a number of steps were taken to prepare for the role which de Gaulle wished to see France play on the international scene. It will be convenient to examine several of these developments before discussing the central themes of French foreign policy revealed after 1962.

II

The most important of the decisions during the period before 1962 concerned nuclear weapons. Regarding military power as the very basis of national sovereignty, it was inevitable that de Gaulle should wish to push ahead as rapidly as possible with the nuclear weapons program started at the end of the Fourth Republic and to develop adequate means of delivery for the warheads produced. The formal decision to construct a bomb had been taken by the Gaillard government in April 1958, the last month of the Fourth Republic.** De Gaulle set out his

*The phrase is taken from a letter of instructions to the foreign minister, Georges Bidault, on the eve of the San Francisco Conference in April 1945.[1]

**This decision had been foreshadowed and implied by the establishment of a

reasons for this policy in an address to the pupils of the various *Ecoles de Guerre* and the *Centre des Hautes Etudes Militaires* on November 3, 1959. After speaking of the defense of France, which must be a "French defense," he continued:

> The consequence is that clearly we must be able to provide ourselves . . . with a force capable of acting on our account, with what we have agreed to call "a striking force" liable to be deployed at any moment and in any place. It goes without saying that, as the basis of this force, there will be an atomic armament—whether we make it or whether we buy it—which must belong to us: and since France can possibly be destroyed from any point in the world, our force must be made to act anywhere on earth.[3]

This major statement of strategy clearly implied the intention of producing French intercontinental ballistic missiles (ICBMs) as well as the "all azimuths" targeting of them to be recommended in 1967 by General Charles Ailleret, France's chief of staff.[4]

Three months after de Gaulle's statement, on February 13, 1960, the first French atomic device was exploded at Reggane in the Sahara, eliciting from de Gaulle a message beginning "Hurrah for France!"[5] Since then there have been many French nuclear weapons tests including the explosion of thermonuclear devices (1968), though their site had to be moved to French Polynesia after Algerian independence brought to an end the use of the Saharan bases for this purpose.

A short account of the French nuclear striking force (*force de frappe*), created under two *lois-programmes*—five year plans (1960-65 and 1965-70)—is in order here. The first generation consisted of the production of ordinary atomic bombs carried by Mirage IVA strike aircraft, sixty-two of which—all that France had—were in service by 1967. These had a range of some 2,000 miles, but could be refueled in the air by KC-135F tankers purchased from the United States. The second generation, now in progress, is concerned with solid-fuel intermediate-range ballistic missiles (IRBMs) installed in silos (in

---

nuclear weapons planning bureau in the Commissariat of Atomic Energy (1954) and by the decision to build the Pierrelatte plant for the production of enriched uranium, the main use of which was military (1957). It is difficult to resist the conclusion that French military planners had always intended to have their own bomb.[2]

Haute-Provence) and using a more powerful nuclear charge as a warhead. These are to have a range of about 1,800 miles, and the first squadron of nine missiles is expected to become operational during 1971. Finally, the third stage of the *force de frappe*, also in progress, involves the building of a number of nuclear-powered submarines armed with a battery of sixteen underwater IRBMs each. The first of these, the *Redoubtable*, was launched in 1967 and should become operational during 1971. Two others are expected to be added to the force by 1976, of which one, the *Terrible*, is now under construction.[6]

The *force de frappe* has not been created without difficulties and delays (the atomic bombs for the Mirage IVA were apparently delivered two years late, the IRBMs in Haute-Provence were held up even longer, etc.), and, after the events of May 1968 and the crisis of the franc in the following November, budget cuts have forced a drastic revision of the whole program.[7] In early 1968, before the May events, the Minister of Defense, Messmer, was writing in the *Révue de défense nationale* about the alternatives open to France for the 1970s: a much enlarged fleet of missile-firing submarines or the development of an intercontinental ballistic missile (ICBM). But there have been no such noises since.[8]

The *force de frappe* does represent a considerable technological achievement. The question is, however, whether it is worth what it has cost and whether it represents a credible strategy. As to the first question, the cost must be regarded as very high. The second *loi-programme* (1965-70) provided for an expenditure of nearly $11 billion, of which $5.4 billion were to have been spent on the *force de frappe*.[9] * In fact, the already high proportion has proved to be even higher since funds have been diverted to the program from conventional forces. In France, as previously in Great Britain, the arguments have been made that a nuclear striking force is a good deal cheaper than conventional military forces of comparable strength and that the

*The amounts spent on defense in France, reckoned as a percentage of the gross national product (GNP), are: 1966: 5.0. 1967: 5.0. 1968: 4.8. 1969: 4.4. Since, however, a certain amount of military expenditure is concealed in other budgets, it has been estimated that the real percentage may be higher. It is certainly remarkable that this level of cost has not aroused more criticism in France. It would seem that, at a time of rapid expansion for the French economy, the heavy military budget could be absorbed and presented as decreasing as a percentage, while growing in absolute terms. Also France is a country where pacifist attitudes have traditionally found little support.[10]

'spin-off' from research carried out for military purposes benefits industry and science. But this last argument has been turned inside out by the opponents of the force who have claimed that there is no reason why research into the peaceful uses of atomic energy should not be carried on directly and that scarce resources of scientific manpower have been diverted from other uses by the military nuclear program.[11]*

As to the second question, the effectiveness of the *force de frappe* has often been called in question. The Mirage IVAs, for instance, with their range of 2,000 miles could just about reach the western areas of the Soviet Union, but it is very doubtful if they could get back, while the silos in Haute-Provence which contain France's IRBMs have been criticized as being insufficiently armored. The weapons of both the first and second generations of the *force de frappe* are 'first-strike' systems, liable to draw down pre-emptive attacks from an opponent. Only with the entry of the nuclear submarines on the scene will France have a 'second-strike' capability, and the development in the 1970s of anti-ballistic missile systems (ABMs) will make it increasingly hard for countries with relatively unsophisticated nuclear weapons systems, such as France's, to regard them as a reliable deterrent against a super-power. The 'all-azimuths' strategy was always incredible and must be considered rather as an ideal assertion of national independence than as providing the guidelines for a real course of action.

At any rate the *force de frappe* remains a striking and expensive symbol of the Gaullist will to national autonomy. As such its political consequences were important. Not only did the American refusal to impart nuclear technology to France under the 1958 amendment to the 1954 Atomic Energy Act embitter relations between the two governments and underline the favored position enjoyed by Britain (which did receive such aid), but France's refusal to sign the Nuclear Test Ban Treaty (1963), to take part in the U.N. disarmament conference, or to adhere to the Nuclear non-Proliferation Treaty (NPT) marked its dissent from a world political system in which stability was assured within the framework of Russo-American agreement. As will be discussed later,

*Another argument which has sometimes been put forward for the *force de frappe* is that it was necessary to give the French armed forces nuclear weapons in order to console them for events in Algeria. This may have played a minor part in Gaullist thinking, though there is not much evidence that French officers were particularly keen on the idea. It was certainly not a major factor in de Gaulle's mind.[12]

the *force de frappe* was thought in Paris to have a role to play in France's European policy. It could insure France's superiority over Germany or offer an inducement to Bonn to collaborate closely with Paris. It could also, in the more euphoric moments of Gaullist foreign policy, be considered as the core of a European nuclear force which would, of course, remain strictly under French control.

Another aspect of Gaullist foreign policy before 1962 which was to prepare the way for the future was the "decolonization" of Africa which took place very rapidly after de Gaulle's return to power. A start on this had been made in 1956 under the Mollet government with the *loi-cadre* (introduced by Defferre), which had produced territorial councils that included African ministers elected by assemblies and were presided over by French governors. (The introduction of the *loi-cadre* is discussed in chapter four.) Subsequently, disputes over the future shape of *Afrique francophone* and rivalries between African leaders (principally Félix Houphouët-Boigny of the Ivory Coast and Léopold Senghor of Senegal) were to slow down progress. By the end of the Fourth Republic it looked as though the *loi-cadre* was already outdated, but it was uncertain what could take its place.[13]

De Gaulle's solution was a radical one. The Constitution of 1958 contained provisions for a "French Community" whose member states would manage their own internal affairs, while the community itself would deal with foreign affairs, defense, monetary questions and common economic and financial policy. The community was to have an executive council and a senate, the former composed of the prime minister of France and the heads of government of the other member states as well as ministers responsible for common affairs on behalf of the community, and the latter made up of parliamentarians and largely confined to an advisory function. The whole would be presided over by the president of the French Republic "who represents the Community."[14]

It was this package which de Gaulle offered to the various African territories in the course of a week's tour between August 20 and 27, 1958. African politicians and their followers were in effect asked to choose at the then forthcoming referendum between accepting the French Community and an independence which would imply the severing of all links with France. The point was rubbed in in a speech by de Gaulle at Abidjan:

Each Territory, if it sees fit . . . has the right to reply "no" to the question which will be asked by the referendum. If it replies "no," if it refuses on its own behalf to form part of the Community with Metropolitan France and its African brothers, well, it will take its fate into its own hands, it will follow its path in isolation. Of course . . . Metropolitan France and the other African Territories would draw all the consequences from such a choice.[15]

In the event, the only territory to vote *No* was Guinée under the leadership of Sékou Touré–an exception which was immediately punished by the withdrawal of French administrators and the cutting off of all aid.*

But the success of de Gaulle's offer had no lasting results. The French community contained too many internal contradictions to be viable for the African territories except as a step on the road to complete independence. As Grosser has written, the one method of insuring its survival would have been to make its institutions more egalitarian as between French and African members. But this would have meant giving the latter a voice in French policy–an impossible idea both for de Gaulle and for the majority of Frenchmen.[17] By the end of 1959 the French government was prepared to accept the opening of negotiations for complete independence between France and the Federation of Mali (this Federation included what is now Mali plus Senegal, but fell apart during 1960). The executive council of the community had its last meeting on March 21, 1960, and that year saw *Afrique francophone* take on its present form of fifteen independent countries linked to France by bilateral agreements of cooperation (and sometimes to each other by a variety of regional pacts).[18]

In relations with Morocco and Tunisia de Gaulle also pursued a policy which followed logically from the recognition of the independence of those countries under the Fourth Republic. In June 1958 agreements were signed accepting the withdrawal of French troops from the greater part of both countries, and by 1963 the last French base on their territories was evacuated. President Bourguiba of Tunisia and the King of Morocco, Mohammed V, were even able to exercise a certain influence on events in Algeria, counseling moderation to the FLN and urging the necessity of a quick settlement on Paris. However, despite

*The 'example' made of Guinée went as far as the destruction of archives and the tearing of telephone wires out of the walls in government offices.[16]

the visit of Bourguiba to Rambouillet in the previous February, the Bizerta fighting in July 1961 cooled relations between France and Tunisia for some time, though it hardly delayed French withdrawal from the bases in Tunisia, which were evacuated in October 1963.*

What was to be the characteristic style of Gaullist diplomacy showed itself during this period in Africa in several ways. Protests against French nuclear tests at Reggane from states around the borders of the Sahara were sharply rebuffed or ignored, and attempts through the United Nations to put pressure on France to stop the tests were repulsed. American abstention on the Afro-Asian resolution condemning France's Algerian policy and support for the entry of Guinée into the U.N. were the subject of reproaches on the part of de Gaulle to Dulles when they met in December 1958. France also refused to take part in the U.N.'s Congo operation in 1960-61 or to pay its share of the costs. French-serving officers seem to have taken part in the resistance to U.N. forces in Katanga, and U.N. transport aircraft were refused the right to fly over Francophone African countries. From de Gaulle's point of view the U.N. intervention was, of course, a striking infringement of national sovereignty. Nor did the confusion and inefficiency of the U.N.'s administration of the Congo improve matters. It is perhaps hardly surprising that he reserved some of his most dismissive phrases for the organization and its secretary-general: "now the meetings of the United Nations are no more than riotous and scandalous sessions . . ."[20]

Later on, in the sixties, French policy was to show more regard for the U.N. as a forum in which France's new role as the best friend of the countries of Asia and Africa could be shown to advantage. Here, as in other areas of foreign policy, the end of the Algerian war opened new possibilities. From the moment that hostile resolutions were directed against the United States the General Assembly could be seen in a different light—not for its own sake, but for the use that could be made of it by a skillful diplomacy.

Beyond 1962—briefly—French 'cooperation' (an important feature of much of Gaullist foreign policy) in Africa has meant not just economic aid but also military assistance and even military intervention, as in Gabon in 1964 or the Central African Republic in 1967—in

---

*De Gaulle claimed that the reason for the Bizerta incident on the Tunisian side was his refusal at Rambouillet of a demand for the cession to Tunisia of the oil-bearing region of Edjelé in the Algerian Sahara.[19]

both cases with the object of keeping existing régimes in place. More recently French troops have been fighting a small war in Tchad to contain the "dissidence" of that country's northern, Arabic-speaking nomads. French forces to the number of some 12,500 in all are still stationed in the Ivory Coast, Niger, Tchad, Gabon, Senegal and the Malagasy Republic. More important are the two or three brigades (the so-called *forces de manoeuvre*) stationed in metropolitan France and earmarked for intervention in Africa, if France's defense agreements with its African clients require it.[21] There are also French military missions in many African countries, and French intelligence and security experts play an obscure, but definite role there under the direction of the Secretary-General for African and Malagasy Affairs in the Elysée, Jacques Foccart. By and large, French political influence in Africa has been exerted in the direction of good sense and political stability. Nor has it been the case that France always acceded to requests for intervention--witness the abandonment of the President of Congo-Brazzaville, the Abbé Youlou, in 1963. But the French presence in Africa has not prevented a rash of *coups d'état,* and the business of preserving French influence and the continuity of government in these poor and often barely viable states is becoming visibly more and more difficult.[22]

French aid to French-speaking African countries has been severely criticized both on the grounds that the money would be better spent at home (what has been called "Cartierisme" after Raymond Cartier of *Paris-Match*) and for its wastefulness and bad administration. The Jeanneney report of 1963 recommended that aid to Africa should be gradually cut down and that France's efforts in this field be diversified to other underdeveloped countries. In 1968 the budget for cooperation with *Afrique francophone* was running at about $240 million—still a considerable sum—and France, under the 1964 Yaoundé convention, has succeeded in getting some of the cost of its influence in Africa born by the development fund of the European Economic Community (France's participation in which will be discussed later).* Nonetheless, the franc zone which includes these African countries is still closely controlled by France, and the fact that foreign exchange earnings have to be kept in Paris restricts the independence of their financial policy

*French official figures give a much higher sum: $347.1 million. But this includes not only private investment, but such items as the cost of running the secretariat of state for foreign affairs and aid and cooperation missions.[23]

and their accessibility to commercial investment from other countries. Another important aspect of cooperation in this area is to be found in the 10,500 French technicians (most of them teachers) at present working in Black Africa.[24]

Gaullist policy in Africa has been, therefore, a policy of prestige modified by a determination to keep down costs. Critics may have attacked it as economically unprofitable, but that is not the point. As will be seen, Gaullist policy in the Third World was largely a cultural policy. The *présence française* in African countries, poor in resources and unstable in their politics, really rested on the assumption that France has something special to offer the peoples of those countries— French culture and civilization—and that in offering them France is fulfilling its own mission in the world. It was precisely this assumption which, as we saw, lay at the heart of de Gaulle's own view of France.

Although he himself did not care sufficiently about Africa to repeat his visit of 1958, the long succession of state visits to Paris by African presidents was very much part of the ceremonial apparatus of the Fifth Republic. To what extent the present heirs to Gaullism will be willing to pay a high economic price for this kind of prestige is still an open question. However, it does not seem very likely that the present structure of a belt of subsidized French client states extending from the Sahara to the Congo will last very long, although any change will probably not be to the benefit of the inhabitants of those territories, however much it may satisfy the nationalism of the elites.*

In Tunisia in 1964, French economic reprisals followed Tunisian expropriations of French lands. With Morocco similar measures led to the cutting off of French aid, which, however, was resumed after an agreement was reached in July 1964 for compensation to be paid to French citizens. Another incident, much more serious, had a lasting effect on Franco-Moroccan relations. A Moroccan opposition leader, Mehdi Ben Barka, was kidnapped in Paris in October 1965, apparently at the instigation of the Moroccan Minister of the Interior, General Oufkir, and with the active assistance of the French 'special services.' Ben Barka was never seen again, and, in the subsequent investigation, much lurid light was cast on the scant respect for legality of the Paris police and organizations like the *Section de Documentation Extérieure*

*Towards the end of de Gaulle's term of office, French policy in West Africa branched out to support the Biafran secession from Nigeria. This will be discussed at the end of the chapter.

et de Contre-Espionage (SDECE). De Gaulle himself was furious at the scandal and tried unsuccessfully to get Hassan II, the new King of Morocco, to dismiss his minister who was condemned in absentia by a French court to life imprisonment. The resulting breach between Paris and Rabat lasted as long as de Gaulle was at the Elysée.[25]

Relations with Algeria after 1962 were to France the most important of its connections with the Maghreb. As might have been expected these relations proved stormy. During 1963, a series of expropriations both of lands and of businesses violated the Evian agreements and were followed by another round in 1967-68. In the meanwhile, Frenchmen who had opted for Algerian nationality were subjected to various disadvantages. In military matters, by June 1964 French troops had been withdrawn from Algerian territory; the base of Mers-el-Kébir was abandoned in 1968. Nor was France much more successful in establishing its relations with the new régime on the issue of developing the Saharan deposits of oil and natural gas. An agreement signed in Algiers in July 1965 (just after the overthrow of Ben Bella by Colonel Boumedienne) provided for joint development of these resources and was designed to remain in force for fifteen years. But since then France has been constantly under Algerian pressure to improve its terms and to pay more for Algerian oil, of which it consumed 65 percent in 1964. These demands were to lead to a crisis of Franco-Algerian relations in the early seventies.[26] *

But the most important part of Gaullist foreign policy was to be centered on Europe, and it was here and in relations with the United States that, prior to 1962, a general stance was taken that was of great significance in marking the future course. De Gaulle returned to power convinced that it was necessary to disengage France from the 'hegemony' exercised by the United States over its European allies. Although he had at first been favorable both to the Marshall Plan and to the Atlantic alliance as a means of resisting the Russian military threat in the late forties and early fifties, his attitude quickly changed to hostility when he judged the integrated command structure of NATO to have robbed France of any power of independent decision. The successful struggle against the European Defense Community

*Aid to the Maghreb countries in 1968 was as follows: Algeria: $89.3 million. Tunisia: $14 million. Morocco: $16.1 million. This is all so-called public aid.[27]

(EDC) intensified this feeling, while also demonstrating that, in terms of French domestic politics, nationalist attitudes brought ample rewards (see chapter four). But, if one facet of his policy was to free France from its unwilling symbiosis with the world power of the United States, another would require him, by making the most of France's diplomatic assets, to substitute some other political system in Western Europe for the present Atlantic constellation.

For this purpose, it was necessary for France to assume the moral and political leadership of such other continental European states as would consent to it, in the first place the nations of Western Europe and then perhaps (and this is the significance of the much quoted phrase "Europe from the Atlantic to the Urals") some of those countries of Eastern Europe which might emerge, in the future, from the 'hegemony' of the other super-power.[28] These perspectives are described in the third volume of the *Mémoires de Guerre* (published in 1959):

> to persuade the states along the Rhine, the Alps, and the Pyrenees to form a political, economic, and strategic bloc; to establish this organization as one of the three world powers and, should it become necessary, as the arbiter between the Soviet and Anglo-American camps. Since 1940, my every word and act had been dedicated to establishing these possibilities ... [29]

In the *Mémoires d'Espoir* (published in 1970) they appear more modestly—possibly in the light of bitter experience:

> My policy therefore aimed at the institution of the concert of European states, in order to increase their solidarity by developing links of all kinds between them.[30]

This "concert of European states" would not come about of its own accord. De Gaulle was perhaps not unrealistic in thinking that, if such an association could be formed, France would come to lead it. The quality of French diplomacy as demonstrated in the initial years of de Gaulle's reign by negotiations within the European Economic Community (EEC), the prestige of French culture and of the French language as a vehicle of international communication, above all his own will-power and his position as a world statesman—all these factors might reasonably lead him to expect that France would take first place in

.European councils. The only possible rivals were Great Britain and Germany. But Great Britain formed part of the "Anglo-American camp" and must be excluded from a system in which it would otherwise play the part of "a Trojan horse," while Germany's postwar inferiority complex and strategic and diplomatic vulnerability could be exploited to intimidate its leaders into playing second fiddle to France.

De Gaulle, in fact, possessed two fulcrums by means of which he might exert leverage to make good France's claim to European leadership. The first of these was possession of the only nuclear striking force—hence the political importance of the *force de frappe*—within the Europe he envisaged. As one leading Gaullist wrote in 1964:

> Is an integrated European strategic nuclear force possible today? No. Does Europe need to obtain its nuclear independence? Yes. Which country can bring Europe its strategic independence? France.[31]

France within a European concert would be the sole nuclear power—a position which would naturally be one of primacy.*

The second means by which it was hoped to bring about a French-dominated "concert of Europe" was a special relationship with the Federal Republic of Germany. However, the phrase "special relationship," with its whiff of Anglo-American mythopoeia, does not completely convey the complexities and ambiguities of Franco-German relations. Gaullist policy chose Germany as a working partner in Europe. The choice may have been inevitable, since Germany was the only possible rival to France within the existing Western European grouping of the Six (the six country members of the EEC). But the Federal Republic was also chosen because its vulnerable position with regard to the Soviet Union and its interest in a continued Western presence in Berlin made it peculiarly sensitive to pressure from any of the powers participating in the postwar occupation of Germany and

---

*It was, no doubt, with the intention of excluding all other European countries from participation in France's nuclear advantage that one of de Gaulle's first actions on returning to power was to cancel the so-called Strauss-Chaban-Delmas agreements of early 1958. Under these, Germany and Italy would have contributed to the cost of the Pierrelatte isotope-separation plant in return for technical information, some of it with military implications. De Gaulle cancelled the agreement in September 1958. It should be added that the existence of this arrangement has been contested on the French side, but its reality seems to be in little doubt.[32]

still maintaining a Berlin garrison. It would have been possible and perhaps more sensible for de Gaulle to try to align British policies on his side, but Great Britian would have been a more equal partner and, therefore, a less satisfactory one. The Federal Republic, so it seemed, could always be cajoled by firm French support over Berlin or browbeaten by threats to reach separate arrangements with Russia or break up the Common Market. French policy towards Western Germany during de Gaulle's tenure of office was a judicious mixture of the carrot and the stick, the former being offered to Adenauer, always disposed to put the best interpretation on French actions, and the latter being applied to Erhard when he fell away from the line followed by his predecessor. And a corollary of this policy was an increased degree of contact with the Soviet Union either as the advocate of German interests, if Germany behaved in accordance with Gaullist ideas, or else as a potential threat to them, if it did not.

In all this there was, of course, a strong element of fantasy. Looking back, it is possible to see with some clarity what was dimly perceived even in France at the time: that de Gaulle's policy of a concert of Europe reposed on a fundamental overestimate of France's attractiveness for other European countries. A leading German Social Democrat, Fritz Erler, once expressed the position of these countries courteously, but succinctly: "No Europe without France, no European security without the United States."[33] Professor Grosser has pointed out this definition implied a choice—and not the choice of France.

No Western European country could possibly have afforded to abandon the protection given by the United States for any Gaullist 'Third Force.' On any occasion when such an alternative was sharply placed before them, they would be bound to opt for Washington rather than for Paris. The *force de frappe* for geographical reasons alone (not to speak of its technical deficiencies) could never reassure them. And even had it been an effective protection for Western Europe, why should other European countries trust to the good will of a government whose head was the major contemporary theoretician of the sanctity of purely national interests? The United States, at least, had given proofs in the past of its desire to aid and defend Western Europe.

To these doubts the Gaullist answer was the one given in an article published in 1965 in *Politique Etrangère* under the signature XXX (apparently the somewhat transparent veil of an official source):

the presence of American troops has, after all, only a symbolic value. It is not this, but the American deterrent which is the guarantee of European security, and the use of this deterrent itself will only depend, in the final analysis, on the importance America attaches, *for its own security,* to keeping Europe out of the Soviet sphere of influence.[34]

Yet if this were the case—that the American deterrent would in fact be used to protect Europe for the sake of American security—then what was the point of the *force de frappe*? No doubt, it played its part as a symbol of de Gaulle's declaration of independence from the Atlantic system. But if its value was merely symbolic, it was an exceedingly costly gesture. In fact, Gaullist apologists have tended to adopt both attitudes simultaneously: to maintain that France's *force de frappe* had some value in securing European security, but that American protection would be available in any case.

At the beginning of de Gaulle's eleven-year reign the contradictions in his European policy were not yet in evidence. As in other areas, the direction of that policy was to some extent concealed by the existence of the Algerian drama. Also the Gaullist tendency to practice diplomacy on several different levels enveloped the real content in clouds of ambiguous verbiage.

The first major move in French foreign policy after de Gaulle's return to power was not devoid of this ambivalence. In a note sent to Eisenhower and Macmillan on September 24, 1958, the French government suggested the creation, within the Atlantic alliance, of a tripartite directorate consisting of France, Great Britain and the United States. "This body should have the responsibility of taking joint decisions on all political matters affecting world security, and of drawing up and, if necessary, putting into action strategic plans, especially those involving the use of nuclear weapons."[35] * In case this plan were not accepted France would not participate in any development of NATO and reserved the right, by virtue of Article 12 of the NATO treaty, either to ask for the organization's reform or else to withdraw from it.[37]

---

*The text of this note has never been published officially, but has been leaked in a number of versions with slight verbal differences. De Gaulle's own account in *Mémoires d'Espoir* leaves it unclear whether or not the scheme implied a right of veto over American use of nuclear weapons.[36]

From the first, the interpretation of what de Gaulle was actually asking in the note of September 24 was doubtful. Did it imply a right of veto by the other members of the directorate on American use of nuclear weapons anywhere in the world? Some French official sources said that it did; others claimed that it merely meant closer consultative arrangements between the three Western 'global' powers. It has also been stated that de Gaulle confirmed the first interpretation to Dulles at their meeting of December 15, 1958. In fact, though the question may have fluttered the diplomatic dovecotes at the time, it is not one of very great importance. The implied diminution of Germany, the effects on the Afro-Asian countries of a global association of America and Britain with France at the height of the Algerian war, worry about French domestic stability four months after the events of May 13, an all too human desire not to have to take into account complicating factors such as France's residual interest in the Lebanon these were reasons enough not all of them good ones for America and Britain not to wish to set up this kind of directorate. With or without the veto on America's use of nuclear weapons, there was more than enough contained in the proposal to insure its rejection. And, as de Gaulle wrote subsequently in his *Mémoires d'Espoir*, it was precisely in this expectation that the proposal had been made.[38] The note was, in fact, a sort of diplomatic clearing of the decks for action, designed to put its recipients in the wrong in the eyes of French opinion as well as to confirm de Gaulle's own preconceptions about American and British determination to deny to France its 'rank' in the world. Once the three-power directorate had been tacitly rejected by his allies, de Gaulle was free to go ahead and fire a warning shot across the bows of NATO.* This he did on March 7, 1959, by withdrawing the French Mediterranean fleet from NATO command.**

Meanwhile, steps had also been taken towards bringing about closer

---

*One controversy has now been laid to rest. In the *Mémoires d'Espoir* de Gaulle has admitted that Eisenhower and Macmillan did reply "evasively" to his note. Many French writers, however, still claim that it was ignored. Of course, it might have been better for the recipients to accept a negotiation on the proposal, given the fact that the whole episode was something of an exercise in political warfare.[39]

**De Gaulle's own explanation of this that NATO's scope did not extend to the southern shore of the Mediterranean and that, therefore, France had to have the free use of its own fleet—does not stand up, since, in fact, Algeria was within the area covered by the pact, and the fleet was already under French command in peacetime.[40]

relations between France and the Federal Republic of Germany. On September 14, 1958, de Gaulle received the German Chancellor at Colombey and found Adenauer disposed to accept the conditions for Franco-German understanding that he offered:

> the acceptance of *faits accomplis* as far as frontiers were concerned, an attitude of good will in relations with the East, a total renunciation of atomic armaments, a patience to withstand every trial in the matter of reunification.[41]

For his part de Gaulle said that France would execute the Treaty of Rome (that is, support the European Economic Community), adding that agriculture and also the question of Great Britain's relationship with the EEC were points on which he would require German support.* This Adenauer, either then or at a later meeting, seems to have agreed to provide.

It was, indeed, easy for him to be persuaded by de Gaulle. Strongly though he felt the need of American protection, Franco-German reconciliation remained the cause dearest to his heart. As a Rhinelander he looked West both politically and culturally. The primary objective of his policy was to integrate Germany into a Western European community rather than to seek German reunification or pursue adventurous policies in the East.[43] Adenauer's immobilism in his relations with Eastern Europe was based more on a feeling that the whole question was best left alone than on any irredentism. And this attitude in turn fitted in neatly with de Gaulle's determination that, in any future European negotiation with Russia, France should take the lead.

The only hint of future difficulties at the Colombey meeting was Adenauer's insistence on the danger for Germany of having Russia as a direct neighbor and on the importance of the American alliance, though he also drew attention to the possibility of American withdrawal from Europe and, consequently, the necessity of "making Europe independent from the United States."[44] Despite de Gaulle's indication of his

*In the *Mémoires d'Espoir* de Gaulle talks of "the English candidature" in his description of this conversation. But, in 1958, there was no question of Great Britain being a candidate to enter the Common Market. Here, as elsewhere, the *Mémoires d'Espoir* show a chronological confusion which makes the book an untrustworthy source.[42]

understanding of Adenauer's position as chancellor "of a Germany conquered, divided and threatened,"[45] even in this opening conversation there were present the first signs of a divergence between the views of Bonn and Paris which would grow into a yawning gap as Gaullist policies increasingly rode roughshod over the German need for security. For the moment, these clouds were only on the horizon, and relations between the two countries were to pass through the stage of a kind of Carolingian honeymoon. Adenauer, indeed, had been captivated by de Gaulle: "I was happy," he wrote later, "to have found quite another person than I had feared. I was sure that de Gaulle and I would have a good collaboration in a spirit of mutual trust."[46]

For the next four years the special relationship between France and West Germany continued to flourish, powerfully aided by two factors: first, France's execution of the Treaty of Rome and its consequent apparent devotion to the idea of European unity and, second, de Gaulle's support of Germany on the Berlin issue raised in an acute form by the Russian note of November 17, 1958, demanding the negotiation of a new status for West Berlin.

De Gaulle's willingness to allow the European Economic Community to come into existence had been a pleasant surprise for his German partner. De Gaulle's past views on the Coal and Steel Community and the European Defense Community might have led anyone to suppose that a Gaullist France would repudiate the Treaty of Rome. However, de Gaulle, partly under the influence of anguished special pleading from the Quai d'Orsay, was prepared to see in EEC a possible instrument of French power. To destroy it would have deprived France of the hold it possessed over its five partners. In the autumn of 1958, therefore, France took the lead in defeating Britain's attempt, in the so-called Maudling negotiation, to create a European free-trade area. On this occasion, unskillful British diplomacy (apparently supervised by Macmillan himself) gave de Gaulle the opportunity of using his determination to exclude England from European arrangements as an instance of France's devotion to the spirit of the community.

For the first four years of the Fifth Republic, therefore, it seemed as if Gaullist attitudes towards European unity were far more favorable than could possibly have been hoped beforehand. Divergences between de Gaulle's concert of Europe and the community ideal would only appear later on when there were serious issues for the Six to settle. For

the time being everyone hoped for the best, and the sincere devotion of
Adenauer (and, indeed, of most German statesmen) to the emergence
of an economic and, eventually, a political Europe could easily be
reconciled with an increasingly close relationship with Gaullist France.*

That there developed a Russian offensive against West Berlin at the
same time that a Gaullist régime took power in France was a coincidence,
but it provided an occasion for France to show its friendship to
Germany. For some three years, Khrushchev brandished the threat of
signing a separate peace treaty with East Germany, though the Russians
were finally to choose the 'more moderate' solution of the construction
of the Berlin Wall in August 1961. On various occasions during this
period France appeared in German eyes as the firmest of Bonn's allies.
In a press conference of March 25, 1959, de Gaulle was to set the
uncompromising tone which, in Adenauer's ears, contrasted so favor-
ably with the more uncertain utterances of Macmillan and even
American leaders: "We would not allow West Berlin to be given up to
the Pankow régime."[48] Nearly three years later his point of view was
the same:

[refuse] to negotiate on Berlin or Germany so long as the Soviet
Union does not put a stop to its threats and its injunctions . . . [49]

Naturally, this firmness was reflected in the Paris-Bonn axis—particularly in the emotional atmosphere following the construction of the
Berlin Wall when suspicions of President Kennedy's intentions combined with the all too apparent fact of the West's inability to make any
effective counter-move to produce friction between Bonn and Washington. With the death of Dulles, Adenauer had lost his most trusted
American interlocutor, and he regarded with misgiving the new figures
at work in Washington. From this, de Gaulle was the gainer, and the
high point of relations between Gaullist France and Germany was
reached during his state visit to the Federal Republic in September
1962. But the same correspondent of the *Neue Zürcher Zeitung* who
noted the extraordinary burst of applause with which the Munich
crowd greeted de Gaulle's call for Franco-German unity[50]—made in

*This was all the easier in that Adenauer was willing to sacrifice the
supranational principle represented by Hallstein, president of EEC's commission,
in favor of a more gradual European evolution towards unity which would not
pose problems in his own dealings with de Gaulle.[47]

German—saw in his success "an enthusiastic acceptance of the reconciliation of both peoples," but observed, behind the scenes, "manifold resistance against a Franco-German bilateralism . . . "[51]

But, whatever the future might hold, the personal relationship between the French President and Adenauer, and the latter's increasing estrangement from the new men in Washington, whom he suspected of being willing to arrive at an agreement with Russia at the expense of German interests, meant that French diplomacy could exert influence in Bonn of crucial importance when, in the early sixties, it came to beating back Great Britain's belated attempt to enter the EEC.

At the same time that France was strengthening its relations in Europe, there was a gradual worsening of relations with the United States. Given de Gaulle's views on European politics and his intention of disengaging French forces from the command structure of NATO, this was probably inevitable, but matters were certainly not helped by the waverings of American policy at this time. It would have been hard enough to cope with a Gaullist France in any event. A change of administration, the internecine rivalries of the various departments connected with American foreign policy, and the brooding presence of such bodies as the Joint Congressional Committee on Atomic Energy made the task an impossible one.

The development of the *force de frappe* had alarmed Washington, raising, as it did, the specter of nuclear proliferation. But there was also a strong faction in American government circles which thought that, since France would possess nuclear weapons in any case, the United States might as well help its ally with material and information. The visible effect of these opposing forces was one of vacillation. In July 1958 Dulles promised de Gaulle a propulsion system for nuclear submarines, but in early 1959 the offer was withdrawn—only to be revived and again abandoned in May 1960.* France did get 440 kilograms of Uranium 235 from America and (rather surprisingly) KC-135F tanker aircraft—necessary to prolong the range of the Mirage IVAs sufficiently to make them an effective delivery system. On the other hand, in 1959 the State Department prohibited cooperation between an American firm

*There is some conflict of evidence as to whether this cancellation caused the withdrawal of the French Mediterranean fleet from NATO command or was caused by it. De Gaulle would, no doubt, have taken this step anyway, but the fact that he did it at precisely that moment suggests that there was a connection.[52]

and two French ones for the production of solid fuel missiles—just as, later in 1964, there was to be a ban on the sale to France of very large computers. Thus the United States can hardly be said to have pursued a consistent policy towards France's nuclear force. America, in fact, got the worst of both worlds, helping the *force de frappe* along in important and possibly decisive ways, while, at the same time, arousing French resentment.*

Gaullist complaints about American behavior were given more plausibility both in the eyes of French opinion and of other Europeans by the fact that this period saw the promulgation of the McNamara doctrine of "flexible response"—a change in American military policy which looked to many Europeans like an attempt to restrict them to a non-nuclear role, while depriving them of the assurance that the United States would instantly retaliate with nuclear weapons against any attack on its Western European allies. De Gaulle could also make out a very good case for his insistence, in 1959-60, that American strategic and tactical nuclear weapons should be withdrawn from French soil. His aim was to insure that all forces on French territory should be under France's control, and he had in his favor the instinctive dislike felt by most Frenchmen for the presence of nuclear warheads on their soil. Here, as so often in Gaullist actions, there was a shrewdly calculated appeal to opinion at home.

By April 1962, then, the main lines of Gaullist policy abroad were already laid down, though it was not always clear to observers just how far they could be extrapolated.

During this time, the prestigious side of foreign policy—so much a part of de Gaulle's personal style—had not been neglected. There had been presidential state visits to Great Britain, the United States, and Canada (where de Gaulle had been able to observe "the deep realities which make of the Canadian Federation a state perpetually ill at ease, ambiguous and artificial").[54] There had been the visit of Kennedy to Paris in the summer of 1961, an occasion on which, according to the *Mémoires d'Espoir,* de Gaulle warned him against further American involvement in the Vietnam imbroglio.[55] Above all, in March 1960, there had been Khrushchev's visit, and de Gaulle's first opportunity to appear as the Western interlocutor of a Russian leader.

*France had also been helped by information gathered by French soldiers and scientists from their American opposite numbers prior to de Gaulle's return to power.[53]

The main discussion concerned Berlin. Khrushchev once again threatened to sign a separate peace treaty with the German Democratic Republic (GDR), causing de Gaulle to retort that "If it leads to war, it will certainly be through your fault."[56] Then, as later on, Russian insistence on raising the German problem in the course of contacts with the French government—Khrushchev could hardly have appreciated de Gaulle's prediction of eventual German reunification in his press conference of the previous year, on March 25, 1959[57]—was inhibiting to the development of any real dialogue. Moreover, 1960 was the year when de Gaulle, irritated by Russian support of the Algerian rebellion, made a series of particularly harsh attacks on the Soviet Union. (It was clear that Algeria still had something to say about the limits of French foreign policy.)

De Gaulle's attitude in the autumn of 1960 corresponded to the worsening climate of international relations which had followed the U-2 incident and the break-down of the Paris summit conference in May 1960. During this meeting de Gaulle seems to have exerted himself as chairman to try to prevent Khrushchev's demand for a public apology for the U-2 incident from rendering the conference useless. He also took his customary firm line on Berlin—the more so in that Adenauer had come to Paris to see that German interests were respected.[58]

But it is probable that the French President was not sorry to see that "the spirit of Camp David" no longer reigned in Russo-American relations. Gaullist policy inevitably enjoyed its greatest freedom of action when the dialogue between the United States and the Soviet Union was interrupted, but the relations between the super-powers were not in so dangerous a state as to imply a serious threat of war, which would have meant a reinforced solidarity between Washington and its European allies. Bad relations between Russia and America, but not so bad as to drive the other countries of Western Europe to strengthen their ties with Washington—these were the ideal conditions for Gaullism—as, indeed, for any political movement seeking to establish itself outside the confrontation of the two opposing world blocs.

III

The period from the summer of 1962 to February 1963 was to be a decisive one for Gaullist foreign policy, for it put to the test de Gaulle's ability to achieve a 'concert of Europe.' During this space of time, not only was de Gaulle himself set free from the burden of the Algerian war and political preoccupations at home, but the United States and France's European allies began to perceive the full consequences of his conception of a European security system led by France. Also the British demand for entry into EEC required some decisive action on France's part. Its response was to veto that entry in January 1963.

Before then, in early 1962, another important episode of European politics was played out. This was the inability of the Six to agree on a treaty drawn up by the so-called Fouchet Commission which put forward proposals for political cooperation between the countries concerned and for the development of the existing European communities. The commission, with an old Gaullist, Christian Fouchet, as its chairman, had been established after a meeting of the six heads of state or government in Paris on February 10-11, 1961. It had reported to another summit meeting held in Bonn during July and was then given the task of preparing a draft treaty which would create the structure for political cooperation. The declaration after the Bonn meeting reaffirmed the importance of the alliance with the United States and stated that the six governments would continue to apply the Rome and Paris treaties.[59]

De Gaulle's conception of what form political cooperation within the EEC should take was quite clear. It should consist of intergovernmental consultations and the creation of intergovernmental commissions to study specific questions. It should not include Great Britain which, on August 10, 1961, made its formal request to enter the Common Market.

The importance which de Gaulle attached to the discussions of the Fouchet Commission is shown by the place they occupy in *Mémoires d'Espoir* and also by the fact that it was French pressure for political cooperation between states which had led to the commission being set up in the first place. In late 1959 the foreign ministers of the Six had accepted a proposal put forward by France and Italy for regular consultations on international affairs. During the first half of September 1960 de Gaulle had pressed his view of Europe on the prime ministers and foreign ministers of Italy and the Benelux countries. From Adenauer he had extracted a somewhat uneasy assent during their meeting at Rambouillet in July (sharper differences, however, had begun to appear between the French and German points of view about NATO).[60] De Gaulle expressed his own idea of Europe at a press conference on September 5. Resolutely opposed to any supranational body, he chose this moment to utter the famous panegyric of the states quoted in chapter one: "To imagine that something can be built, efficient in action and approved by peoples, above and beyond States is a delusion."[61] What remained was "a regularly organized concert of responsible governments and then, too, the work of specialized bodies in each of the common areas, bodies subordinate to governments . . . "[62] Nor had his opinion changed when it came to writing his *Mémoires*.

Having clearly indicated his own views, it is little wonder that de Gaulle ran into opposition from the supranationalists among the Six. The Dutch, for instance, were suspicious of the whole idea of further political cooperation unless Britain were brought into it, and they were to be encouraged by British acceptance of the Bonn declaration following the report of the Fouchet Commission. Later they received support from Belgium where Paul-Henri Spaak had just become foreign minister.

When the draft of the commission's treaty began to be discussed in the autumn of 1961 both Holland and Belgium objected to its patently Gaullist character: it spoke of a "Union of states," and, contrary to the Bonn declaration, made no reference to NATO or the American alliance.[63] To meet these objections Fouchet and the Quai d'Orsay produced a compromise draft which went some way to meet the demands of those who wished to safeguard supranational institutions and were concerned to keep the door of any political union open for Great Britain.

On January 18, 1962, however, Fouchet arrived late at a meeting of the commission with yet another draft agreement. This had been drawn up in the Elysée on the orders of de Gaulle himself and clearly reflected his disapproval of the Quai d'Orsay's readiness to compromise. It represented an even more decidedly Gaullist point of view than the original draft. "The Atlantic alliance was not mentioned. Both defense and economic policy were again listed as being within the purview of the Union of States. The guarantees to the communities had disappeared. And finally, it was specified, contrary to the compromise arrived at by the Council of Ministers on December 15, 1961, that admission to the Union of States would not automatically result from membership in the communities."[64] The reception of this by France's five partners was glacial, and, despite an Italian compromise proposal and attempts to keep discussions going, negotiations broke down at a Paris meeting of the Council of Ministers on April 17. The reason chosen by the Belgians and the Dutch was their unwillingness to sign any treaty for a union of states before Great Britain had entered the community; they were joined by Italy in their objections to the French draft.[65]

The intervention from the Elysée had killed any chance of getting a union of states, and it seems improbable that de Gaulle either expected or desired this outcome. Indeed, it is difficult to exaggerate its significance. By rejecting the compromise treaty France lost its chance of luring the Five into institutionalized consultations between governments where it could largely have had its own way through the superior quality of French diplomacy, Adenauer's support, and a constant threat of withdrawal held over its partners. The Quai d'Orsay's negotiators might well have been able to use their professional skill to as good effect as they had within EEC. De Gaulle's *Mémoires d'Espoir* betray his bitterness over this failure. The villains of the piece are Luns, the Dutch foreign minister, and Spaak, "the spokesman of every negation,"[66] but it was de Gaulle's own intervention that had given them their chance. (It is possible that German support had produced a mood of overconfidence which induced de Gaulle to treat Belgian and Dutch objections as negligible.)

The French President expressed his irritation in a violent outburst against "integrated 'esperanto' or 'volapük' " which caused the resignation of the MRP ministers from the government (see chapter five).[67] But the fate of the Fouchet Commission had finally demonstrated the difficulty, if not impossibility, of lining up France's partners in EEC for a Gaullist 'concert of Europe.' Even with France and Germany in agreement (a state of affairs that would not survive Adenauer's chancellorship), it was not possible to persuade the other states to fall into line. Fears of a "little Europe" dominated by the Carolingian monarchs of Bonn and Paris, and the desire not to be led away from the American alliance were too strong.

Thus, the occasions on which France could successfully influence the Five were those on which it could threaten to break up an established European institution. Even before France's veto of Britain in January

1963 fully revealed the nature of de Gaulle's European policy, it had been made clear that its positive aims could not be achieved.

At the time of the suspension of the Fouchet Commission's work, the negotiations with Great Britain had only just begun to reach their decisive stage. The Macmillan government's decision to apply for entry had been taken slowly—too slowly as it turned out. The two or three years after the termination of the Maudling negotiation (which, in opposition to EEC, sought a free-trade area)—years during which de Gaulle's freedom of action was severely restricted by Algeria—were allowed to pass by as the British government made up its collective mind. After de Gaulle's return to power, Macmillan had hoped that the French leader might be favorable to a wider free-trade area and seems even to have proposed the dissolution of EEC to de Gaulle at their first meeting on June 29, 1958.* If so, he was soon to be disillusioned by the abrupt breaking-off of the Maudling negotiation and the *rapprochement* between Bonn and Paris.

The result of Britain's hesitation in the years to follow was not only that a favorable political conjuncture was missed in Europe but also that the talks at which Britain sought entry into the EEC, the Brussels talks, which started in November 1961 and lasted until January 1963, took place far too near to the approaching British elections to give Edward Heath and his fellow-negotiators any freedom to maneuver. Their best course would have been to accept as much as possible as quickly as possible and ask for alleviations of hardship once inside the community, but this was not deemed to be politically feasible.** Instead there was protracted discussion over details ranging from the notorious Pakistani kips (goatskins) to New Zealand butter and Hong Kong textiles. Some major points were settled when the talks adjourned at the beginning of August, but the haggling kept alive suspicions of British intentions. These suspicions, indeed, were present not only among Gaullists. Large sections of French opinion were hostile to British entry, and still more thought that Britain should be made to pay the full price for joining the community. Even in the Brussels

*No doubt, Macmillan's remarks as reported by de Gaulle should be treated with some caution until their full context becomes known.[68]

**It was Monnet's opinion that speed was essential and that everything that could be signed rapidly should be.[69]

Commission itself there were those who had doubts as to the desirability of British entry.

On June 2, 1962, Macmillan and de Gaulle had a meeting at the Château de Champs near Paris. During their conversations Macmillan seems to have raised the question of collaboration between Britain and France in the making of nuclear weapons. The allusion was made in a somewhat veiled form and received no very clear answer. De Gaulle in his turn dropped a hint to the effect that, in case of a reversal of alliances in Western Europe, Great Britain might prove a more acceptable partner for France than the Federal Republic of Germany. There was perhaps here a Bismarkian policy of reinsurance. If so, it did not come to anything.

Still the meeting was greeted by optimistic commentaries on all sides, both from official sources and in the press. The fact that de Gaulle had not pronounced a veto at this point was taken as a good omen. That he was under attack on account of his European policy (on May 13, 293 deputies had signed a document condemning it) attracted less notice. It was widely thought that France, as Couve de Murville put it to a journalist earlier in the year, "could not do otherwise" than accept British entry.[70]

By the time de Gaulle and Macmillan met again at Rambouillet on December 15, a successful referendum and elections had freed the former from his political restraints, while the British Prime Minister found himself in the midst of a crisis. It had been brought about by the decision of the United States Department of Defense to cancel production of the air-to-ground missile *Skybolt* which happened to be the one chosen by the British government to prolong the life of its V-bomber nuclear striking force. The Secretary for Defense, Robert McNamara, had acted in apparent ignorance of the political consequences for Macmillan of such a decision. The very existence of a British nuclear force was at that time a hotly contested issue in British domestic politics, but neither McNamara nor anyone else in American governing circles seems to have realized the implications of this fact or to have seen how unfortunate the spectacle of the United States phasing out an ally's nuclear weapons might be.*

The situation led to a meeting in Nassau, which took place immediately after Macmillan's Rambouillet meeting with de Gaulle.

---

*Looking back on this episode, it is difficult not to agree with Henry Kissinger's verdict on the disastrous diplomatic effects of McNamara.[71]

The Nassau conference was marked by some uncertainty on the part of the Americans. There was the desire to rescue Macmillan, but there was also the desire (on the part of certain officials in the State Department) to assert some control over "third-power" nuclear forces. In the end, there was a compromise. Great Britain was to receive the Polaris missile and the technology to make the nuclear-powered submarines from which to fire it, but these were to be assigned to NATO except when "supreme national interests" demanded otherwise (a promise which clearly meant nothing very much). Moreover, there now appeared on the scene the famous "multilateral force" (MLF) into which, it was hoped by the State Department, independent deterrents could eventually be absorbed. For the moment it was unclear what this reference to a concept gestated in the Policy Planning Council of the State Department meant. Later the MLF was to be unveiled as a force of surface vessels armed with nuclear weapons and manned by mixed crews from various NATO countries. Such a force would be integrated into the NATO command, and from this there followed the conclusion that Germany could be a participant. Thus from being a device to absorb "third-power" nuclear weapons into the integrated military structure of the North Atlantic alliance, the MLF became a lever to prize the Federal Republic of Germany away from a Gaullist France and, simultaneously, a satisfaction of Bonn's desire for equality within the alliance.

De Gaulle had been offered the same terms as Macmillan—Polaris and technological aid—in return for committing the *force de frappe* to NATO (once again, such an undertaking would have meant very little). But it was clear from the start how the Nassau agreements would be interpreted in Paris. In the words of a commentator (Jacques Vernant) who often expressed official opinion:

> Consequently, the British armament industry, in its nuclear section, will be still more integrated into the American armament industry than was the case before, and the British nuclear force will be integrated into the NATO force.[72]

The substantial offer (substantial in terms of technology) made by Kennedy could only be rejected. The military value of the *force de frappe* could not be improved at the expense of its symbolic value. In de Gaulle's eyes, its total independence was worth more than its effectiveness.

The refusal of the American offer was to be one of the themes of the famous press conference of January 14, 1963–perhaps the climax of the Fifth Republic's foreign policy, certainly its most dramatic episode up to that point. A second was de Gaulle's other major negative–his veto of the British entry into the Common Market. Already, at Rambouillet, he had let Macmillan see that he was determined to refuse. The Nassau agreement allowed him to accompany the refusal with some specious remarks to French deputies about Great Britain choosing America rather than Europe.[73] But the agreement had not effected a change in Gaullist policy. To say that, if Great Britain entered EEC, "there would appear a colossal Atlantic Community under American dependence and leadership . . ."[74] was simply another way of putting the fact that British membership would render impossible France's use of the European community and a preferential relationship with Germany to increase its own power.

The statement of January 14, 1963, marked yet another declaration of independence vis-à-vis the United States. It brought to a sudden halt all the plans produced by the Kennedy Administration to place its relations with its European allies on a more substantial political base–"Atlantic community," "equal partnership" and the rest.

The British government, of course, was both deeply angered and damaged politically by de Gaulle's veto. Although negotiations had reached an impasse on the question of the common agricultural policy and the British desire for a special period of transition, it had looked in January 1963 as though a solution could be found.[75] Even so, perhaps the veto itself might have been accepted, but the humiliating brutality with which it was conveyed and what was seen as the duplicity of French diplomacy roused deep feelings in the British politicians and officials concerned.* For the moment they could do nothing, but later on, when de Gaulle appeared intent on a switch of policy, his action in 1963 would be remembered.

IV

The veto on Britain finally restricted France's freedom of diplomatic

*On January 11, Heath had asked Couve de Murville whether France would oppose British entry if the technical problems were settled and had been told it would not. Pompidou had also said the same.[76]

maneuver by excluding arrangements between Paris and London, it did not insure the achievement of de Gaulle's aims in Europe. Relations between France and its five partners were considerably shaken. Although Adenauer had already agreed to German participation in the MLF, he remained loyal to de Gaulle. Despite pressure from the United States and an outcry in some German political circles, the Franco-German Treaty of Friendship was signed in Paris on January 22. It was a kind of bilateral Fouchet plan, providing for meetings between heads of state and government and between other ministers (of foreign affairs, defense, education, etc.). The two governments undertook to consult each other about any important decisions in foreign policy and to try to harmonize their ideas in the field of defense. There were also provisions for educational and cultural exchanges, technological cooperation, etc.

The agreement was placed under the auspices of European unity, but its conclusion was anything but reassuring for the other members of the EEC. In fact, it looked very like an attempt to establish a Franco-German hegemony whose dictates would have to be followed by the smaller partners.[77]

They need not have worried. The signature of the treaty was in a sense the last hurrah of relations between Germany and Gaullist France. By the end of 1963, François Seydoux, a French ambassador in Bonn, was writing of it:

> From the start the Federal Republic has been impressed by the wave of discontent and concern which the event produced practically everywhere, especially in the United States . . . in Bonn eyes were kept fixed on Washington.[78]

The ratification of the treaty by the German Bundestag on May 10, 1963, showed how far distrust of Gaullist intentions had gone. For the German parliament insisted on voting a preamble in which the country's attachment to the connection with the United States, the Atlantic alliance, European unification (including Great Britain) and the elimination of trade barriers was reaffirmed.[79] In the course of the summer of 1963 Kennedy's visit to Germany matched the reception received by de Gaulle the year before. It is not surprising that doubts should have been felt in Paris about the usefulness of the treaty. In July, two days before a visit to Bonn, de Gaulle expressed the doubts in a famous phrase: "Treaties ... are like young girls and roses: they last as long as they last."[80]

This summer 1963 meeting with Adenauer did not produce any further convergence of French and German policies. In the next six months two major foreign policy decisions were taken by France without any attempt to consult Bonn: the refusal to sign the nuclear test-ban treaty in August 1963 and the recognition of the People's Republic of China in January 1964. Meanwhile Adenauer had been replaced as chancellor by Ludwig Erhard who (like his foreign minister Gerhard Schröder) was strongly in favor of an "Atlantic direction" for Germany.

Throughout Erhard's chancellorship Franco-German relations remained tense. In 1964 a principal cause of that tension was German support for the MLF then winding its way through a tortuous series of negotiations. In July 1964, de Gaulle's visit to Bonn was marked by visible coldness between him and Erhard as well as by French attempts to mobilize the "German Gaullists" against the Chancellor and Schröder.[81] On his return to Paris de Gaulle noted in a press conference (July 23, 1964) that "a common line of conduct has not emerged" from the Franco-German treaty and hinted that France might be led to "change her direction" by "major external changes" (presumably the coming into being of the MLF).[82] But even the abandonment of that complex scheme by President Johnson in December 1964 did not improve matters. The German government's commitment to NATO led it to disapprove strongly such acts as France's withdrawal of its Altantic fleet from the integrated command (June 1963.) And its devotion to the principles underlying EEC was soon to embroil it in a fresh dispute with Paris.

The European community had survived the emotions consequent upon France's veto on British entry better than expected. "Everyone," said Hallstein, the president of the European Commission, "is agreed the existence of the Community must not be jeopardized."[83] The general instinct was to try to achieve what could be achieved, and, by April, a "working program" had been produced which enabled the community to push ahead with outstanding business. The main items on the agenda were the implementation of the "common agricultural policy," association agreements for some (Francophone) African states and agreement on the community's position in the coming 'Kennedy round' of tariff negotiations. The fact that France was keenly interested in reaching agreement on the first two points meant that progress could be made.

The French government, indeed, had constantly tried to speed up the adoption of the agricultural regulations. In January 1962 agreement had been reached on the general shape of an agricultural Europe—an agreement which was regarded by France's partners as an essential preliminary to British entry into the community. After the French veto there was a pause, but, in December 1963, a 'package deal' was negotiated in which arrangements were made for dairy produce, beef and veal, and rice, and the commission was given authority to continue the Kennedy round negotiations. An issue left unsettled was the price level of cereals. The Germans were reluctant to set these before their elections in 1965. Meanwhile, the Yaoundé convention of association with the Francophone African states had been signed on July 20, 1963.

During 1964, the vexed question of the price level of cereals produced a warning from Pairs that failure to proceed with the common agricultural policy as had been agreed might lead to France's withdrawal from the community. Finally, in one of the community's exhausting marathon negotiations (December 10-15, 1964) the Germans gave way, and another 'package' was successfully completed.[84]

This success, however, led directly to the serious crisis of 1965. The European (Brussels) Commission, in its understandable euphoria at the resolution of the immediate difficulty, seems to have concluded that the community could now begin once again to advance more rapidly and also that the common agricultural policy now gave France too great an interest in its continuance for any Gaullist attempt to break it up to be possible. It therefore presented a new 'package' to the Council of Ministers which, in addition to the regulation for financing the common agricultural fund, contained proposals for endowing the Common Market with its own financial resources, giving the European parliament some control over its budget, and marginally increasing the commission's own budgetary powers as against the Council of Ministers. In other words, the proposals represented a small, but significant advance in the development of supranational institutions. As such they were bound to be unwelcome to de Gaulle. Moreover, they came at a moment when Gaullist hopes for a concert of Europe realized through

Franco-German collaboration had waned to a point where France's membership of the community no longer seemed to have its pristine political value.[85]

At a meeting of the EEC Council of Ministers, held at the end of June 1965, Couve de Murville, who was presiding at a late session on the night of June 30, declared that it was obvious that no agreement could be reached and refused to continue. After a French cabinet meeting the following day an announcement read by the Minister of Information, Peyrefitte, stated that the French government "has decided to draw . . . the economic, political and legal consequences of the situation which has just been created in this way."[86] There followed a boycott by France of the community's institutions.

This "policy of the empty chair" lasted until January 1966 when, in two meetings in Luxembourg, an agreement was patched up between France and the Five. Couve de Murville presented a series of ten demands designed to limit the role of the Brussels Commission and to oblige it to consult with governments before putting forward any important proposals. France also wanted the abolition of decisions by majority vote—that is, a practical right of veto. On this latter point France and its partners agreed to differ. A somewhat watered-down version of the French ten points was accepted, but the significance of this was largely symbolic. De Gaulle had not succeeded in getting rid of the supranational content of the community.[87]

French policy during this episode was somewhat puzzling. Before the night of June 30, it had not seemed as though anyone wanted a crisis, and, as Miriam Camps has written, "it is generally agreed that the French could have achieved at least the substance of the Luxembourg agreement—probably rather more—without having provoked the crisis."[88] As it was, the French deliberately brought about a collision and walked out—only to return six months later without having made any very noticeable gains.

No doubt, part of the explanation lies in the different attitudes towards the community of de Gaulle on the one hand and his ministers and officials on the other. He himself disliked the whole idea of EEC and had only been persuaded to continue French participation in it on the grounds that it would be a useful lever for the realization of his own concert of Europe under French leadership. However, the Five had proved disappointing in this respect, as the failure of the Fouchet

Commission had shown.* From de Gaulle's point of view, therefore, there was a lot to be said for bringing the Brussels Commission to heel—the more so in that he must have been conscious of the danger of France abandoning itself once again to supranational institutions after his own disappearance. And it may be that, in forcing a crisis, he had hopes of being able to destroy the European community in its present form. His ministers and officials, however, took a different attitude. They too were prepared to use the maximum toughness in imposing French wishes on France's partners, but they were too conscious of the consequences, both political and economic, to desire the dissolution of the community.

It rather looks as though it were de Gaulle who forced the issue, and the Quai d'Orsay which settled for the Luxembourg agreement. Why did the French President not go to the bitter end of the crisis he had created? Two factors may have influenced him. First, the split was forcing the Five into a cohesive bloc ably headed by Schröder. It might, therefore, have seemed counter-productive to carry the battle further. Second, France's presidential elections of December 1965 had revealed a considerable amount of "European" sentiment which carried with it political implications. Jean Lecanuet, the centrist candidate, had gained a number of "European" votes, mostly those of farmers who believed that France's boycott of the community was hurting them financially.[90] Whatever the reasons, it looks very much as though de Gaulle had been forced to retreat from an original intention of settling accounts once and for all with a supranational Europe.

Such an explanation would also be consistent with other aspects of France's European policy in 1965. For, by the end of 1964, de Gaulle had apparently resigned himself to the failure of his European policy and to the consequences of France's inability to offer a sufficiently attractive "special relationship" to the Federal Republic of Germany. In a press conference of February 4, 1965, he devoted a long exposé to the German problem and the conditions of its resolution. These he saw

*It is significant that Couve de Murville, speaking before the National Assembly of the Common Market crisis caused by the French boycott, could say: "Perhaps the situation would have been different if, as France has suggested for five years, it had been possible to institute the beginnings of regular political cooperation between the Six." (October 20, 1965.) As it was, the utility of EEC to Gaullist plans was much diminished.[89]

coming about through the evolution of Russian attitudes and through a reknitting of the ties between Eastern and Western Europe. It is, of course, a truism to say that German reunification can only be realized under such circumstances and there was nothing very surprising in de Gaulle's arriving at this conclusion. But the tone adopted marked a change of direction. To say that one of the objectives of French policy was so to arrange matters that "Germany henceforth becomes a definite element of progress and peace ... " was very far from the conviction, expressed in a statement two years previously, that "the new policy of French-German relations is based on an incomparable popular basis."[9][1] The new position was a return to immediate postwar Gaullist attempts to keep Germany subordinate, the *corpus vile* of a European security system. Since the Federal Republic had proved an unsatisfactory partner for France, it must be contained by arrangements which would sharply limit its freedom of action.

It was, naturally enough, also at this time that de Gaulle's conception of a reunited Europe began to be given practical expression through contacts with the Soviet Union which could also serve the purpose of somewhat broad hints to recalcitrant German statesmen of what they might expect if they did not accompany France on the road to "a European Europe." In his 1965 New Year's Eve message to the French people de Gaulle said: "lastly, we are multiplying our relations with the Eastern European States as their internal development guides them toward peace."[9][2] Later in the year there were two meetings between Couve de Murville and the Russian foreign minister. Gromyko's April visit to Paris irritated the Germans, but, otherwise, the main result of the talks was to clear the way for a ceremonial visit by de Gaulle to Russia. This took place between June 20 and July 1, 1966, and was the occasion for a further development of Gaullist views on the future of Europe. The essential elements of these were set out in a speech by de Gaulle on June 20:

> for France, without her disregarding in any way the essential role that the United States has to play in the pacification and transformation of the world, it is the restoration of Europe as a productive whole, instead of its being paralyzed by a sterile division, that is the primary condition. Also, an entente between hitherto antagonistic States is above all, to the French, a European problem .... This holds true for

the settlement that will one day have to determine the destiny of all Germany and the security of our continent.[93]

Implied in this was a program for *détente* between Europeans which would give France the opportunity of negotiating on behalf of the Western states, while the Soviet Union would be the representative of the East. The program required both the exclusion of the United States from Europe and the taking of decisions about the future of Germany without much reference to Bonn.

However, this policy did not strike de Gaulle's Russian hosts as either practicable or, in some of its aspects, especially desirable.* Despite the exceptional honors accorded to the French President—his occupancy of a suite in the Kremlin and his visit to secret nuclear and space-launching installations—there was no political meeting of minds. What interested the Soviet leadership was the effect of Gaullism in weakening NATO, its critique of America's global policies, and also the possibility of extracting from France recognition of East Germany. De Gaulle's desire to dissolve the European blocs and find a solution to the German problem was in opposition to the Russian interest in keeping a tight hold on Eastern Europe and, above all, on East Germany. It must also have seemed to the Russian leaders hopeless to try to exclude the United States from Europe, while, as for Germany, as has since become clear, they preferred to negotiate directly with Bonn on the future of Central Europe.

For his part, de Gaulle was restrained in his criticism of America (the final communiqué contained a reference to the worsening of the situation in Vietnam, but did not go further than agreement on the necessity of a settlement on the basis of the Geneva agreements of 1954) and could hardly have recognized East Germany, even had this been consistent with the rest of his policy. The communiqué contained the phrase "the two Governments are agreed in thinking that the problems of Europe must be considered firstly in a European context," but was not more specific. A direct telephone line was to be established between Moscow and Paris, agreements for scientific and technological cooperation were signed, the Franco-Soviet agreement of March 1965

*As one expert has written: "Such grandiose concepts as de Gaulle's vision of a united Europe 'from the Atlantic to the Urals' are hardly relevant to the actual problems facing Soviet policy-makers."[94]

concerning the joint use of a French system of color television was to be put into operation and a consular convention was negotiated. Political consultations between the two countries were promised—an intention reiterated after Kosygin's return visit to Paris in December 1966. But the harvest was meager enough in any terms except those of prestige.[95] In his final broadcast over Russian television de Gaulle had said that "it is also a matter of implementing successively *détente*, entente and cooperation throughout all of Europe."[96] The Moscow visit did not go very far in that direction, and, in the event, little in the way of concrete results was to come from it.

VI

De Gaulle's foreign policy in the last two or three years of his presidency gives an impression of precipitancy, of a race against time little suited to the requirements of successful diplomacy. There was something of this haste in an announcement which preceded the Moscow trip and, for France's allies and the United States, cast a somewhat sinister light upon it. On February 21, 1966, de Gaulle had spoken of France's intention of continuing "to modify successively the measures currently practiced" within the Atlantic alliance.[97] Then, on March 7, he sent a letter to Johnson declaring that France would withdraw its forces from the integrated NATO command and demanding that all NATO forces on French soil should be placed under French orders. Since this condition was unacceptable, the demand meant the withdrawal of Allied forces from France. In future the armies of NATO's central front (from the north German coast to neutral Austria) would have only a very limited zone of maneuver, their communications through France would have to be redesigned, their headquarters moved, and they might not be able to use French airspace or the oil pipeline from the French Atlantic coast. France, however, was also dependent on the NATO Air Defense Ground Environment (NADGE) structure—an early warning radar system without which the *force de frappe* would have found it difficult to operate. Some sort of modus vivendi could therefore be worked out: the two French NATO divisions in Germany remained following agreement with the German government, and NATO aircraft were allowed to fly over France, provided that notification of the flights had been given.*

De Gaulle had always intended to withdraw from NATO. His disapproval of the integration of French forces into an Allied military command reposed too solidly on the deepest levels of his belief for any change to be possible.** And though his compromise still left France theoretically within the alliance, it seemed questionable whether it remained there for any other purpose than to maintain a residual (and potentially irritating) presence. Moreover, despite claims by Gaullist spokesmen that the effectiveness of the defense of Western Europe was not diminished by France's action, it was clear that the outbreak of war under late twentieth-century conditions would leave no time to harmonize France's strategy with that of its allies.*** Thus, NATO was seriously damaged by France's withdrawal from its command structure.

Uncertainty about French intentions in various contingencies made life more difficult still for NATO officers. An article published by General Ailleret, the French chief of staff, in the *Revue de Défense nationale* (December 1967) seemed to announce a new French strategy of "defense in all directions" (*défense 'tous azimuths'*). The conception behind this was that France, instead of targeting its nuclear weapons in accordance with the requirements of an alliance formed against one particular country, should be prepared to shift its aim with a shifting international system. The article advocated the acquisition of ICBMs and was approved by de Gaulle himself in an obvious reference to it in January 1968.[101] The defect in the argument—quite apart from the consequences for France's population—was the long delay that must ensue before ICBMs could be manufactured and the development in the meantime of ABM systems by America and Russia. Though Ailleret was willing to contemplate the deployment of nuclear weapons in space and

*French forces in Germany comprised the 2nd Corps of NATO consisting of the 1st Armored and the 2nd Infantry division. But a serious gap was created by the loss to NATO of the *Ier Commandement Aérien tactique* (ICATAC), a powerful, well-equipped and well-trained force of 450 aircraft and 23,000 men.[98]

**Couve de Murville told a journalist during the 1967 election campaign that he had known of de Gaulle's intention since 1958. But little discernment was needed to divine it.[99]

***See Couve de Murville's statement before the National Assembly (April 14, 1966): "it is both absurd and insulting to say that an alliance without organization automatically loses all its value."[100]

did not rule out France's entering into alliances, his strategy was impracticable and demanded resources far beyond France's capacity. In the aftermath of May 1968 it was to be abandoned by his successor, General Fourquet. Meanwhile, it added to the uncertainties surrounding the relationship between French strategy and that of the Atlantic alliance.

After France's withdrawal from the NATO command structure, de Gaulle's European policy continued along its usual lines. Links with Eastern Europe were further developed by state visits to Poland (September 1967) and Rumania (May 1968) where the themes that had marked the Moscow visit were once again deployed. Meanwhile, in Western Europe, France's relations with Germany had somewhat improved following Erhard's resignation, and the formation of the 'great coalition' between Christian Democrats and Socialists. The new Chancellor was Georg Kiesinger—a politician from Baden-Württemberg in south Germany with a more Francophil bent than his predecessor—and the foreign minister was the Socialist leader Willy Brandt. The new government wished to mend its bridges with Paris. It was American intransigence over the support costs of American troops in Germany which had helped to overthrow Erhard, and negotiations on the nuclear nonproliferation treaty (NPT) were causing increasing tension between Bonn and Washington.[102]

In Brussels the European Economic Community had been able to agree to the financial arrangements for its agricultural policy, most price levels and the elimination, by July 1968, of trade restrictions on agricultural products and tariffs on manufactures. However, Gaullist diplomacy now had to combat once again a familiar adversary. The conversion of the Labor Prime Minister, Harold Wilson, to seeking British entry into the Common Market meant that, for a second time, after a round of exploratory talks with the governments of the Six, the British candidature to the EEC was posed (May 10, 1967).

On May 16, in a press conference, de Gaulle discussed the problem in discouraging terms. For him there were three alternatives: (1) the entry of Great Britain and its European Free Trade Association (EFTA) partners, which would be equivalent to "the creation of a free-trade area of Western Europe, pending that of the Atlantic area, which would deprive our continent of any real personality"; (2) an association agreement between Britain and the Six; (3) waiting for "a certain internal and external evolution on the part of Great Britain which, at some future date, would fit it to join the Community."[103] These alternatives were probably intended to nip the British candidature in the bud, but Wilson persevered, and, by November, de Gaulle was constrained to refuse the opening of negotiations between Britain and the Six.

It was easy enough for him to point to British economic difficulties (the pound had just been devalued), but that was not the main reason for his decision. His desire to exclude Great Britain from Europe remained unchanged, and de Gaulle still seems to have hoped that he might realize the 'concert of Europe' which had so often eluded his grasp. With Kiesinger at the helm in Bonn there was some chance of reviving the idea of a Franco-German Europe within which France could take the initiative in improving relations with Eastern Europe. This turned out to be a delusion, but the changed situation in Germany clearly meant that to refuse the British no longer implied the same dangers as it would have if Erhard had been chancellor and Schröder foreign minister.

When the new chancellor had come to Paris at the beginning of 1967, he had been told that support for Great Britain would mean the end of Franco-German collaboration.[104] It was this factor which prevented a serious crisis at the meeting of the Six in December 1967—France against all the others.* Once again it had been proved that, within the community, de Gaulle could usually have his way in a negative sense.

Britain, however, maintained its candidacy for entry, despite talk of a trade agreement between itself and the community. De Gaulle never succeeded in disposing finally of the question of relations between Britain and the Six. It remained in the path of his own European ambitions despite all his attempts to push it aside.

VII

During this second phase of his European policy—when his 'concert of Europe' seemed unattainable—de Gaulle set in motion a wider,

*A curious instance of the prickly nature of Franco-German relations was the appearance in December 1967 of a study produced by the *Centre d'Etudes de*

global design aimed at gaining prestige for France in the Third World, but also directed against the United States.

As for the United States, this was the time when America became increasingly committed to the war in Vietnam. In February 1965 American aircraft bombed North Vietnam and, during the spring, massive reinforcements of troops were sent to the south. The unpopularity of this war in Europe, its denunciation in France both on the left and on the right (for nationalist reasons) made it an obvious first target for Gaullist attacks on American policy in the world at large.

In a television appearance on April 27, 1965, de Gaulle spoke of "our reprobation" of the widening war in Asia.[106] On September 1, 1966, in the course of a visit to Cambodia, he repeated this condemnation of American policy in far harsher terms. This was the famous Phnom-Penh speech—perhaps the sharpest of all de Gaulle's onslaughts on the United States—in which he denounced "increasingly extensive escalation in Asia, increasingly closer to China, increasingly provocative in the eyes of the Soviet Union, increasingly censured by numerous peoples of Europe, Africa and Latin America and, in the final analysis, increasingly menacing for the peace of the world." He predicted that "there is . . . no chance that the peoples of Asia will subject themselves to the law of the foreigner who comes from the other shores of the Pacific . . . "[107]

These thrusts at a vulnerable sector of American world policy were intended to have their positive side. The building up of a French position in Southeast Asia was to be based on the recognition of China and the establishment of France's old colony of Indochina as a neutral group of states. Already in the summer of 1963 de Gaulle had called for "domestic peace and unity" in Vietnam,[108] and the French government (much influenced by Jean Sainteny, the original negotiator with Ho Chi Minh in 1946 and subsequently the head of the French délégation-générale in Hanoi) apparently envisaged a Vietnam (flanked by Cambodia and Laos) willing to maintain economic and cultural ties with France and serving as an entrepôt from which trading relations with South China might be established.

Politique Etrangère. The study developed the ideas about Germany and a European security system suggested by de Gaulle in his Moscow speech. Its appearance at that particular moment seems to have been a gentle hint to the Germans that it would be best for them to keep in line with French policy.[105]

If that was the plan, it hardly got off the ground. Like other countries which had recognized Peking, France found that little that was constructive could be achieved, especially in view of the 'cultural revolution' which began in 1966. Further, the continuance of the Vietnam war destroyed all possibility of a neutral Vietnam enjoying preferential relations with France. Cambodia, which was to some degree in that position, was itself drawn into the conflict in May 1970 following the overthrow of the Francophil Prince Norodom Sihanouk. As for Laos, the remaining Indochinese state, France took part in the 1962 Laos Conference, and its subsequent policy wavered between cooperation with other powers to maintain the settlement reached there and efforts to demonstrate its capacity to take independent initiatives, culminating in a meeting of the Laotian factions (the so-called three princes) in Paris in the summer of 1964.[109] Apart from this, French diplomacy in Southeast Asia confined itself to withdrawal from the Southeast Asia Treaty Organization (SEATO) and some aid and encouragement to those local forces who, like the South Vietnamese Buddhists, might be deemed to represent an anti-American brand of neutralism.

Another distinctly anti-American line of policy unveiled in 1965 was the transfer by France of its monetary reserves from dollars into gold. It was at this point that de Gaulle himself began to use monetary policy as a political weapon. His adviser was Jacques Rueff whose devotion to gold dated from the time of the Poincaré franc. In his press conference on February 4, 1965, the French President spoke of "gold, which does not change in nature ... which has no nationality, which is considered in all places and at all times, the immutable and fiduciary value *par excellence.*"[110] As monetary theory this was somewhat old-fashioned. As an attack on American military and political activity overseas, financed by a deficit in the United States balance of payments, it was an irritatingly effective gambit.

France's purchases of gold put the dollar under a pressure which, had it been imitated by other countries, would have forced its devaluation. Whether this would have done anyone any good is a moot point, but, for de Gaulle, the 'hegemony' of the dollar as a reserve currency was inseparable from the political 'hegemony' of the United States and just as objectionable. He wished to destroy both. Thus France opposed the 'special drawing rights' (SDRs) proposed by the International Monetary

Fund (IMF) to increase the level of international liquidity, because it was felt in Paris that they would aid the dollar and the pound and act as a substitute for the financial discipline which Great Britain and the United States were failing to impose upon themselves.* At the 1967 London and Rio meetings of the fund, France was nevertheless forced to go a certain distance towards the creation of the SDRs. However, at the Stockholm meeting in March 1968, following a statement by de Gaulle reserving France's freedom of action, Debré dissociated himself from the final communiqué. Once again the President had imposed inflexibility on a minister. But France was isolated in this action even from its EEC partners, and the same was true of both its withdrawal from the 'gold pool' of the central banks and its negative attitude toward aid to Great Britain during the 1967 crisis of the pound. After May 1968 the franc was in difficulties itself, and little more was heard of the merits of stricter control of international liquidity.

The Gaullist 'Third World policy' was described succinctly by a commentator who often voiced official views:

> Outside Europe in a world which . . . is becoming increasingly diversified, the Fifth Republic means to intensify France's influence. (*le rayonnement français*.)[112]

This meant journeys to Latin America, Ethiopia, Cambodia and Canada on de Gaulle's part, visits to other foreign countries by French ministers, the sending of the Mona Lisa to Japan, and numerous state receptions of the leaders of the Third World in Paris. It meant attempts to spread the teaching of the French language and the use of France's cultural inheritance to political advantage. It meant economic and technical aid to underdeveloped countries—'cooperation'**—and more

---

*See the speech by Debré, then minister of finance, at the IMF meeting in September 1966: "I have heard of *paper-gold,* and this expression . . . would have the effect . . . of delaying the return to equilibrium of the balance of payments in the reserve currency countries, thus aggravating the threat of world-wide inflation."[111]

**The attempt to diversify French aid to countries outside the franc zone formed part of this policy, but in 1968 France's ex-colonies still received 64 percent of the total. The 'public aid' to countries outside the franc zone was running at $123.2 million. Compare this to the $240 million for Francophone Africa and Madagascar.[113]

profitably, the sale of arms to them.* It was, in fact, very largely cultural politics (the expression *rayonnement français* is most habitually used to describe French cultural preponderance in the *siècle des lumières*) and, as such, was most effective in Francophone countries.

In his visit to Latin America in the autumn of 1964, however, de Gaulle could appeal to a common Latin inheritance as well as making play with the necessity for the independence of states—a phrase which, in a Latin American context, necessarily had anti-United States overtones. The most spectacular manifestation of this showing of the Gaullist flag was de Gaulle's "Vive le Québec libre!" at the end of a speech from the balcony of the town hall of Montréal during his visit to Canada in July 1967.[115] This episode, which produced a strong reaction from the Canadian government and led to the French President's return home without going to Ottawa as had been intended, is the most extreme instance of the romantic linguistic nationalism which represents one side of Gaullism. The vehemence of de Gaulle's hostility to the Canadian federal system shocked many people in France, and, while French encouragement of *Québecois* autonomy might produce internal difficulties for the Canadian government, no very solid gains could be expected from it for the French themselves. It remained a policy tangential to France's main interests, but passionately felt by some Gaullists.**

French support for Biafra, the Ibo state which tried to secede from the Nigerian federation was a more serious affair. It was inspired by a mixture of motives: a desire to diminish British influence in West Africa by dividing the largest English-speaking African state, the hope of economic gains in the shape of oil concessions, the fact that the Ibos were largely Christians (French policy in West Africa has always been apprehensive of the influence of Islam), the opinion of some Francophone African leaders (especially Houphouët-Boigny who recognized Biafra in May 1968). But French attention was distracted from West

*French aerospace sales amounted to $600 million in the first quarter of 1970 alone, and France now ranks as the third largest seller of arms. Customers include Latin American and African countries, Libya, Spain, Belgium and South Africa.[114]

**It seems that moral support and some actual assistance was given to extremist groups in Québec following André Malraux's visit there in October 1963. The Canadian government later had the occasion to expel a French diplomat for activities considered to be beyond the scope of his official duties.

Africa at a crucial moment by the "events of May" and their consequences. By the time Biafra was once more the subject of consideration in Paris, Port Harcourt had fallen, and the secession state was cut off from the sea. When de Gaulle (in a press conference on September 9, 1968) declared that French recognition of Biafra was not excluded, the military position of the new state was hopeless, and the net result of France's policy was to prolong a forlorn defense of the Ibo heartland.[116] It had all been something of an adventure which might have produced dividends, but which, in the end, damaged France's position in West Africa.

The years 1967 and 1968 also saw a development of Gaullist interest in the Middle East. Not without reason de Gaulle attached importance to a reassertion of French influence in the Levant.[117] Like most of Western Europe, France was supplied with oil from the Arab countries (including Algeria), and the prudence imposed on French foreign policy by this fact has been one of the more lasting features of French foreign policy under the Fifth Republic. When it came to Arab-Israeli relations, however, de Gaulle seems to have regarded Israel as an American client state and been unfavorably impressed by Israeli willingness to disregard his advice. In any case, one of his first actions was to put an end to the close collaboration between the Israeli and the French armed forces which had existed since 1956 and included French help in the construction of a plant to produce plutonium.[118] Thus, when, in the summer of 1967, the Arab-Israeli conflict flared up into the six-day war, a strict interpretation was placed on the French government's previous statement that "the State that would be the first—wherever it might be—to take up arms will not have either [France's] approval and even less her support [sic]."[119] (June 2, 1967.)

After the fighting had ended, an official French government communiqué put the blame for the crisis on the climate of world affairs created by American intervention in Vietnam.[120] Inasmuch as this meant anything precise, it was a suggestion that the end of the Vietnam war should be part of the price paid by the United States for the stabilization of the Middle East. But, though Kosygin flew to New York via Paris, he nonetheless met Johnson at Glassboro, and the French government had to content itself with forbidding the delivery to Israel of fifty Mirages, which had already been paid for, and with voting at the U.N. on July 5 for the Yugoslav resolution, which put the onus of the six-day war on Israel. On this occasion only four Francophone African states could be induced to follow France in opposition to the United States.

France's attitude towards Israel caused a good deal of unhappiness even among veteran Gaullists—a Debré, a Chalandon, a Baumel, a Sanguinetti—and de Gaulle's description of the Jews in his press conference of November 27, 1968, as "an elite people, sure of itself and dominating" raised a storm of protest.[121]* Meanwhile, within the Arab world, France reaped some rewards in the shape of arms sales and oil agreements—notably with Iraq.

VIII

The Middle Eastern policy adopted by de Gaulle illustrates well enough the strength and weakness of French diplomacy under the Fifth Republic. It was probably realistic to believe that France must steer away from its post-Suez special relationship with Israel and seek to extend its influence in those Arabic-speaking states in the Middle East and the Maghreb from which its energy supplies were drawn. But, by accompanying this *rapprochement* with a sharp attack on Israel and publicly blaming the Middle East crisis on American intervention in Vietnam, de Gaulle appeared—not least to French public opinion—to be playing an extravagant and even brutal form of power politics, shocking to anyone who recalled the circumstances in which the Jewish state had been founded.

Moreover, the Glassboro meeting had shown that, when it came to the pinch, it was the United States to which the Soviet Union addressed itself. The attempt to insert France into the dialogue of the super-powers had failed.

All the beautifully adjusted machinery of French diplomacy, so responsive to the firm will that controlled it from the Elysée, could not lift France to the pre-eminent role which de Gaulle had chosen for his country. The global policies of 1967 in Canada or the Middle East were

*It is improbable that de Gaulle was giving way to anti-Semitism. These phrases are more likely to have been regarded by him as a veiled compliment. But he was certainly irritated by the sympathy enjoyed by Israel within official France, while totally neglecting the existence of an anti-Semitic tradition which his words could only encourage.

striking enough to the eye of the beholder, but remained pure exercises in diplomacy on their political side.

De Gaulle's attachment to the politics of prestige went far beyond a reasonable desire to establish contact with French Canada or restore France's position in the Levant. The dramatic gestures, the cutting remarks at press conferences had their resonance, but the echo was heard inside France rather than abroad. Perhaps that was what was intended. "The French people," de Gaulle remarked to Adenauer, "for centuries had been accustomed to being the mastodon of Europe, and it was the feeling it had of its greatness, and consequently of its responsibility, which maintained its unity, when by nature since the Gauls it had been perpetually addicted to divisions and delusions."[122] It was necessary, therefore, to hold their international mission before the eyes of Frenchmen and, to that end, not to shrink from any means, however theatrical, that might bring it home to them. What appeared from outside to be the politics of prestige was transformed in domestic terms into the politics of national cohesion. Large sections of Gaullist foreign policy were 'happenings' played, it was hoped, before an attentive audience—nothing more.

The more serious side of the Fifth Republic's foreign policy during de Gaulle's presidency clearly was its relations with European countries. Here immediate French interests were at stake, and here too France enjoyed a degree of real power. But that power was expressed in the negative sense of preventing policies from being put into effect or abstaining from concerted action with partners and allies. As to de Gaulle's own concept of a concert of Europe in which France would be *primus inter pares,* the decisive moment for that came with the failure of the Fouchet Commission in 1962. This made it clear that France's partners in EEC could not be mobilized for a Gaullist Europe. Later the same lesson was to emerge from the attempt to impose French leadership by means of a Franco-German axis. Gaullist diplomacy was, indeed, the victim of its own ideological preconceptions.

There were (and still are) forces in Western Europe to be mobilized against an American 'hegemony,' but, however non-Frenchmen may feel on this point, they would certainly not be willing to exchange it for a French one which would be incapable of supplying the same degree of protection from Russian pressure. Had de Gaulle been willing to be more flexible on the question of European integration through supranational institutions, there is no question but that France would have found itself in a position of leadership within the community and been able to carry its partners with it toward a West European foreign policy largely swayed by Gaullist ideas of greater freedom of maneuver between East and West. But flexibility on a basic philosophical point was not one of de Gaulle's characteristics, however pragmatic he might be in his choice of tactics, and the moment of possible French leadership passed. Despite the help afforded to it by a diminution of the real power of America and Russia during the sixties, the effects of Gaullism in Europe were negative. It was Germany, not France, which would embark on the delicate European dialogue with Russia.

By the beginning of 1968 it was clear that the disappearance of de Gaulle himself would leave any successor in a position of some difficulty. It required the same personal style to carry on the dazzling exhibition of conjuring that had been begun. A successor would also have to face nationalist reactions awakened by Gaullist appeals to the principle of the nation state. A harvest of prestige had been reaped, but it was questionable whether this was of real value or simply fairy gold that would turn to dust in the hands of anyone other than the old magician himself. Maurice Faure once asked in the National Assembly "What is your influence in Washington, in London, in Bonn, in Rome and the capitals of Benelux? What is your role as mediator in the Congo, in Cyprus and in South Vietnam? "[123] And to this there might have been added another question: "Do the French people attach as much importance to this task of greatness as you think? "

The answers were to be clear after May 1968. The last few months of de Gaulle's presidency saw the shattering of the prestige on which all had been based, and the events of May showed that "divisions and chimaeras" could not be kept at bay by even the most spectacular assumption of global power. Frenchmen were not to be distracted from their everyday needs by even the most Quixotic tilting at American windmills. Nor did a hectic political activity abroad compensate, in the eyes of the young, for the sleep of politics at home.

CHAPTER VII

Gaullism at Home:
The Domestic Policy of the Fifth Republic

*En fait, nous sommes établis sur des institutions
solides et qui viennent d'être confirmées, sur
des finances et une économie assainies de fond
en comble . . .*
        —*Charles de Gaulle*

*Il faut admettre en ce pays un essor soudain de
la prospérité publique, pareil à celui de la
Renaissance ou du siècle de Colbert. Cette
année, on fait 3,000 kilomètres de chemins de
fer. L'Empereur entend mieux la France et son
siècle qu'aucun de ses prédécesseurs.*
        —*Hippolyte Taine*

In writing of the political and social life of the Fifth Republic under
de Gaulle's presidency there is a temptation to make of each event the
forerunner of the crisis of May 1968. The causes of that upheaval will
be discussed in the next chapter (though it is, no doubt, too soon to
adopt any final explanation). But it would be too easy to view in

retrospect all the achievements of the Gaullist régime as so many preparatory steps towards the final catastrophe. Something more than specific achievements, or their lack, is involved. Certainly, the brittleness displayed by a system which had survived the turmoil of the Algerian war and its termination is not easily explicable in purely political terms. Indeed, it may be the absence of a genuine political life which is the most significant feature of the period from 1962-1968. Political movement largely took place within the Gaullist party itself. The emergence of a Gaullism separate from the person of de Gaulle was symbolized by the achievement on the part of Pompidou of a position of independent political power.

Economic expansion and social change, both part of the Gaullist period, were not accompanied by any corresponding political mutation and, still less, by any alteration in the habits of an administrative machine which, proud of its own efficiency, tended to be arbitrary in its dealings with the individual citizen. Nor did Gaullism escape those police scandals, frequent at other periods of French history, which led a distinguished English observer to write of "that twilight of legality which was one hall-mark of the Fifth Republic."[1] All in all, it is probably the atmosphere of the middle sixties which is most important for understanding the sudden convulsion which changed the course of French life and ended the triumphant period of Gaullism.

II

The background throughout the sixties was the economic expansion of France. It is something of a paradox that the economic and social side of Gaullism is both its most concrete and its most vulnerable achievement. De Gaulle denied having used a famous phrase attributed to him—"L'Intendance suit" ("the supply column follows")—but the feeling that economic problems were secondary and could be solved by the exercise of political will-power was undoubtedly deep-rooted in him.[2]

During his presidency, interventions from the Elysée in economic and financial affairs were usually on the side of a rigorous orthodoxy—a fact in which it is hard not to see some regret on de Gaulle's part for his own choice of an insufficiently severe financial policy immediately after the war. But in this area the prime minister and ministers of finance enjoyed considerable autonomy. While Debré was prime minister, it has been noted, he considered the national economy as his particular domain—one to which he would return as minister of finance in early 1966. The arrival of Pompidou in power resulted in closer collaboration on economic questions between the Elysée and the prime minister's office, but, as Minister of Finance, Giscard d'Estaing was very much identified with his own policies and created for himself an independent position.[3]

The first Minister of Finance of the Fifth Republic, Pinay, found himself at grips with a balance of payments crisis which had been still further worsened by lack of confidence following the threat of civil war after May 13th. In 1958 France's deficit on the current account rose to $300 million. For the moment the new Minister confined himself to launching a loan and declaring an amnesty destined to encourage the return of illegally exported capital. New taxes and a rise in the price of petrol were intended to restrict consumption. But the major decisions concerning France's economy were elaborated by a committee of experts headed by Jacques Rueff. The "Pinay-Rueff" plan, whose austere decisions taken on December 27, 1958, caused the withdrawal of the Socialists from the government, included a devaluation of the franc of 17.50 percent and the creation of a 'new franc' (= 100 old francs), the suppression of the connection between agricultural and industrial prices (*indexations*), a rise in taxes and in the cost of various consumer goods and services, social service contributions, etc. These measures were accompanied by a liberalization of trade and investment from abroad. Some 90 percent of the quotas were suppressed (the rest disappeared by April 1961), and the convertibility of currency gained in current transactions was restored. This was a harsh dose of deflation accompanied by a liberation of exchanges intended to make French industry more competitive. As such, it was a success. In the first months of 1959 industrial production began to pick up again, and the 'new' franc started on its career as a hard currency which was to last until the 'events' of May 1968.[4]

The Pinay-Rueff measures implied modifications in the objectives of the Third Plan (1957-61). This was now replaced by an "intermediary plan" (1960-61) which succeeded in its aim of raising the rate of growth to 11 percent in the last two years before the inception of the

Fourth Plan (1961-65). The yearly rate of growth required by this was 6 percent for a period of four years, and this was very nearly reached. The target of the Fifth Plan (1966-70) was slightly more modest: 5 percent growth per year. In the ten years between 1958 and 1968, therefore, France underwent a considerable economic expansion. By 1968 the Gross National Product was 29 percent above what it had been in 1963 (in 1958 it had stood at an index of 76 and, by 1968, was 129*)–a bigger increase than that of any other EEC country except the Netherlands. The background of Gaullist economic policy was a successful attempt to achieve rapid growth.

And growth was accompanied by a corresponding increase in the standard of living of the average Frenchman. Between 1962 and 1967 real wages rose by an average of 3.6 percent per year. This improvement was reflected in consumption. By 1969, for instance, there were 223 cars in use per 1,000 of the population–a greater proportion than in Great Britain. In 1967 there were 118 French doctors per 100,000 of the population–again more than in Britain. In the possession of television sets and telephones Frenchmen continued to lag behind, but were quickly closing the gap with their EEC partners.** Also the number of students attending schools or universities increased from 7.85 million in 1958-59 to 9,511 million in 1966-67 (from 17.3 percent of the population to 19.2 percent). There were increases in attendance rates at schools and universities for practically all the upper age groups–a fact that brought its own problems with it.[7]

These very real results were not achieved without some difficulties. The rise in wages and prices was a subject of constant concern to the authorities. In March 1961 Debré addressed a stern letter to the president of the *Comité national du patronat français* (CNPF) recalling that government policy required that wage rises should be held to 4 percent. In 1962-63 various factors, including the return to France of some million North African settlers, combined to cause inflationary pressure on the economy. Prices rose, and the minimum industrial wage (SMIG) had to be raised twice in June and November 1962. This potentially threatening situation forced Pompidou and Giscard

*The absolute figures at current prices were: 1958: $53.9 billion; 1968: $126.6 billion.[5]

**Taking 1959 = 100, the indexes for the possession of some consumer durables in 1968 were as follows: cars: 279.1; television sets: 476.8; refrigerators: 252.9; washing machines: 386.7.[6]

d'Estaing to introduce the "stabilization plan" of September 1963. These draconian measures, launched with some ceremony, included the blocking of prices, the discouragement of wage increases and restrictions on credit. A policy of budgetary rigor between 1963 and 1965 led to the elimination of any real deficit by 1964. Public expenditure was limited to an increase of 7 percent per year, and the government undertook not to ask for supplementary credits. This figure was maintained in the 1966 budget, though by that time the Ministry of Finance was beginning to think of re-expanding the economy. The year 1965 had been a bad one for growth: an increase of only slightly more than 3 percent and a distinct slowing down of consumption.[8]

No more than most other governments of industrialized countries did the French government in the sixties succeed in evolving a satisfactory prices and wages policy. The problem in France, however, was easier than in, say, Great Britain, since it was posed in a context of steady economic expansion which increased the size of the national cake and allowed rises in the standard of living that were not simply at someone else's expense. Industrial difficulties were mainly generated by the disproportion between the private and the public sectors of industry—those large sections of French industry which were owned and managed by the state were less responsive to wage demands than was private industry. The most bitter industrial clash of the Fifth Republic came at the beginning of 1963 with a six-week miners' strike. On March 3 de Gaulle signed a requisition order calling the miners up—the traditional French method of dealing with serious industrial unrest—but public opinion was on their side, the bishops of Arras and Autun spoke out in their favor, and the President's popularity sunk to the lowest point in the opinion polls it ever reached during his presidency.[9] The strike, which was eventually settled, resulted in the voting of a new law on strikes in the public sector, but this was no answer to the real problem of how to avoid the chain reaction set off by any rise in wages in part of the public sector. A committee of 'three wise men' was appointed to consider the question and, in due course, its report allowed the development of procedures for dealing with such claims, which seem to have worked well.

The industrial unrest of 1963 also caused a certain amount of heart-burning inside the government. The year of the stabilization plan was the one chosen by the Minister of Labor, Grandval (a left-wing

K

Gaullist), for agreeing to a fourth week of holidays with pay—a decision which was clearly unwelcome to some of his colleagues and which may have contributed to his leaving the government at the beginning of 1966.

The policies of the Pompidou government did become slightly more expansionist with the arrival of Debré at the Rue de Rivoli at the beginning of 1966, but, in general, the atmosphere continued to be one of caution and strict financial orthodoxy. A modest encouragement to investment and some concessions to disadvantaged social groups in 1966 (the "Debré plan") was followed, in 1967, by the more general attempt at the modernization of economic and social structures contained in the controversial "ordinances." Some of these were measures intended to prime the economy and combat rising unemployment. Others dealt with workers' participation in the profits of business. The package was by no means directed against the interests of the working class, as was claimed by its critics. Even the reform of the social security system was needed to prevent its financial collapse—the rise in industrial workers' contributions was intended to help pay for the new peasants now brought under the system for the first time. But the manner in which the new plan was made law suggested that these were solutions imposed on the working class by a right-wing government, nor was this impression contradicted by a drastic rise in fares on Parisian public transport—in some cases by as much as 300 percent.

The resentment and suspicion that were created at this time were to become visible in the attitude of the trade unions in May 1968. Meanwhile, Gaullists could point to a sound financial administration and a favorable balance of payments which had produced reserves in gold and currency of $6.674 billion in 1967. The liberalization of foreign exchange and banking operations introduced in January 1967 was intended to take advantage of this situation and to make of Paris a money market in its own right.

The weak point in the general economic picture of France was agriculture. A farm population too large to be either fully employed or economically viable as producers was slowly being whittled down by departures to the towns (140,000 per year in 1968). But despite attempts to raise the standard of living of the peasants, their level remained as far below that of industrial workers at the end of the sixties as at the beginning. And since real farm prices actually fell from an index of 100 to 94 between 1960 and 1967, they were becoming more economically disadvantaged throughout this period. Much of French farming was inefficient in its methods, too small in scale and too often hampered by bad soil and lack of equipment. To cope with some of these problems a law of 1960 had created the *Société d'aménagement foncier et d'équipement rural* (SAFER), which aided the merging of holdings and, if necessary, the adaptation to new trades of those who were leaving the land. However, by 1968, though the number of holdings had shrunk to 1,700,000 (by comparison with 2,300,000 in 1955), the average size was still only twenty hectares (as compared with the thirty-five hectares which Common Market experts have estimated as the size at which a holding becomes economically viable). By 1968 only 15 percent of the active population of France were farmers, and the movement to the towns was still continuing. But this was producing an insufficient easing of the position. Throughout the sixties, there have been constant peasant demonstrations of a more or less violent kind (the blocking of roads, occupation of prefectures, etc.). Areas where trouble was especially rife included Brittany and the wine-growing districts of the south. This agitation took on political importance during the presidential election campaign of 1965 when a farming protest vote for Lecanuet helped to rob de Gaulle of election on the first ballot. The Fifth Republic has not so far succeeded in settling France's agricultural problems, despite efforts in Brussels to obtain special advantages for French farmers, and it seems likely that the potential clash between the need of industry for a cheap food policy and the political weight of rural France will only be resolved by a rapid diminution of the latter's population.[10]

This perennial problem (which is the more difficult in that it is primarily a human problem) contrasts strangely with French achievements in advanced technology during this period. Here the Fifth Republic continued, and improved upon, the successes of the Fourth. To well-known instances of success in this area, such as the extraction of sulfur from the Lacq natural gas deposits (thus rendering them usable) or the use of tidal power to produce electricity at the mouth of the Rance, can be added the creation of a chemical industry which produces petrochemicals, plastics and synthetic rubber. The sales of French military aircraft and other weapons, whatever may be thought of them in the context of international relations, testify to highly efficient designers and manufacturers, and, if the *Concorde* fulfills the expectations placed in it, it too will bear witness to the effectiveness of France's aircraft industry. Great progress has also been made in the application of nuclear energy to peaceful purposes, though, until quite recently, the possession of other sources of energy (including Algerian oil) tended to keep down the number of nuclear power stations constructed. The creation of the Saharan oil and natural gas industry is also a feat of French technology, whose merit is unaffected by the fact that the companies which realized it have now been expropriated.[11]

It is interesting to note that in France, technological innovation has mostly been inspired by the state, thus continuing a long tradition started by Sully and Colbert. By and large, these efforts have been remarkably successful. Only in the field of computers has the stimulus so far been ineffective. The take-over by the American General Electric Company of *La Compagnie des Machines Bull,* to which French hopes had been pinned as far as a share of the European computer market was concerned, produced attempts at resistance by the government, fearful of the consequences for its nuclear weapons program. There was nothing to be done, however, and the government fell back on the *Plan Calcul* (announced in 1966) which provided for the fusion of two French computer companies into the *Compagnie Internationale pour l'Informatique* (CII). This would receive government help in the shape of funds and contracts, and there would be an effort to provide the basic research and training facilities needed to back a computer industry.[12] It is too early to say what success this effort will have, but the episode shows the difficulty of national autonomy in this field.*

France's rate of economic growth during the sixties has implied constant social change accelerated by an expanding population. The 1968 census showed the population of France to be 49.8 million (3.3 million more than in 1962), and, despite a slight drop in the birthrate after 1965, its present rate of growth (from natural increase and immigration) is about half a million per year. These additions to the population have taken place in sharply defined areas of the country: around Paris, along the Mediterranean coast and the valley of the

---

*The attitude of the Gaullist régime to American investment in France or take-overs of French firms has been variable. Some investments have been permitted or even encouraged (Libby's tomato-canning plant is a case in point). Others have been rejected. The inter-European merger between Citroën and Fiat was subject to stringent control by the French government.[13]

Rhône, in the Pyrenees. The rural departments of the northwest and southwest either lost population or remained static. People under twenty—the so-called new wave—were now 33.7 percent of the population (in 1946 they had been 29.5 percent).[14]

This changing population structure was accompanied by the onset of those habits which usually go with modern industrialism. Supermarkets are cutting into the numbers of small grocers and butchers that swarm in any French town. Self-service restaurants have begun to appear where customers formerly would have rejected meals cooked in the mass. The motor-car has made French households more mobile and reduced something of the strangle-hold exercised by the bourgeois family over its young. Frenchmen have also begun to travel in large numbers outside their own frontiers, thereby lessening a provincialism which was often evident in an older generation. It is, of course, easy to exaggerate these changes of manners. France remains an extremely traditional country, but, none the less, it is true to say that French society has become more mobile and that horizons have opened for the coming generation which were not available for their parents. The revolution of rising expectations has been under way since the fifties, bringing with it social restlessness and greater and more varied demands on the public authorities. New schools, new roads, better housing, more efficient medical services—all these requirements imposed a strain on a state apparatus which had not previously been subjected to the pressures of mass society. Its response was often that of a benevolent authoritarianism, echoing all too faithfully the ethos of a régime where decisions were not only handed down from on high, but were also seen to be so.[15]

With some of these demands Gaullism did its best. Between 1958 and 1968 the yearly number of dwellings completed rose from 290,000 to 409,700—a considerable onslaught on a major social problem.[16] Sundry social abuses, such as the hereditary privileges of the *bouilleurs de cru* (the local alcohol distillers), were cleaned up. A start was made on a network of motor-ways and an improved *métro* for the Paris region.

In education the achievement was less satisfactory. The *loi Debré* in 1959 had settled once again the vexed question of the relationship of the private (religious) schools to the state system—at the cost of the resignation of the Minister of Education, Boulloche, who felt that too many concessions had been made to clericalism. Subsequently, little was done to reform an overloaded educational system. It was only with the advent of Christian Fouchet at the ministry of education towards the end of 1962 that a plan of reform was worked out. This included modifications in the curriculum of secondary education with the aim of diminishing the role of classical studies in favor of more modern studies and, at the university level, the establishment of *Instituts universitaires de Technologie* (IUT) to fill the gap in higher technical education. Some 25 percent of the 793,000 students expected to be undergoing higher education in 1972 were supposed to pass through these institutes. But not enough was done in the way of providing new staff and budgetary resources to make the reforms work or cope with the flood of new students pouring into the schools and universities. By 1968 the government was discussing limited entry into the universities—a step hotly opposed by student organizations—but little had been done to change the rigid structure of French education. Some new equipment had been provided: a new science faculty had been constructed for the University of Paris, and a duplicate faculty of arts established at Nanterre in an isolated and disagreeable suburb of Paris. But the net result of the Fouchet reform was to put a further strain on a system already strained to breaking-point. No one foresaw that the crisis of the French university was also to be the crisis of the régime.[17]

III

Politically speaking, the Gaullists seemed in an impregnable position after the 1962 elections. In the National Assembly the Gaullist UNR nearly possessed an absolute majority, and control of parliament was assured by an alliance with Valéry Giscard d'Estaing's Independent Republicans. (These men were the pro-Gaullist elements that had defected from the *Centre national des Indépendants* [CNI] . Pompidou, the prime minister, had neglected the advice of Debré and others that they should be taken into the ranks of the official Gaullist party—a missed opportunity which he was to regret later.[18]) The relationship of political forces was expressed in the composition of the government itself, where fourteen Gaullists (UNR or UDT) faced three of Giscard d'Estaing's followers. In addition, ministers such as Couve de

Murville at the Quai d'Orsay, Messmer at the ministry of defense, and Joxe, minister of state responsible for the reform of public administration, though officials, were, in practice, even more faithful to de Gaulle's ideas than some of their political companions. Only one important ministry was held by a non-Gaullist: Giscard d'Estaing was minister of finance and economic affairs. (Another appointment should be noted: Fouchet, after his disagreeable experiences as chairman of the Fouchet Commission and the liquidator of Algeria, became minister of education—the sixth in four years.[19])

Almost immediately political interest was directed toward the presidential election due to take place at the end of 1965, when for the first time the president would be elected by direct popular vote. De Gaulle himself, for tactical reasons, was reticent about whether he intended to stand again, but there seemed little doubt that he would be the Gaullist candidate. For the scattered anti-Gaullist forces the choice of a likely candidate to put up against him became the subject of fevered cogitation. At this point the anti-Gaullist forces can be broken down into four sections. There were the Communists who had no chance of getting a candidate of their own elected, but who were in control of a substantial section of the electorate and whose consent would be necessary for any candidacy of the left to have a reasonable chance. On the extreme right there were the irreconcilable partisans of French Algeria, reinforced by the immigration of *pieds-noirs* into the south and southwest of France and headed by the indefatigable Tixier-Vignancourt, a brilliant lawyer who had been a pillar of every reactionary movement in France for thirty years and had defended Salan. This fraction of the right was small enough in numbers, but could, in certain circumstances, become a necessary part of a right wing coalition. Thirdly, there were the 'Centrists,' whose right and left wings were represented by Pflimlin and Maurice Faure (MRP and Radical). Lastly, there were the Socialists, still under the control of a party machine directed by Mollet, but increasingly restive over their defeats at the polls. In terms of the presidential election, it was they who were in the position of pivot. On their decision depended which alternative possibility would be pursued—a left-wing coalition with Communist participation or the revival of the center coalition with the MRP and Radicals which had dominated the early years of the Fourth Republic under the name of 'Third Force.'

It seemed, at the outset, that the second course had the greatest likelihood of success. It was characteristic of the fragmented nature of the political parties at this point in French political life that the initiative in building up a candidate of the center should have been taken by a weekly paper, *L'Express*, and by a number of political clubs and intellectual discussion groups (the Club Jean-Moulin in Paris, the Cercle Tocqueville in Lyon and, later, the *Convention des Institutions républicaines*). *L'Express* led off, in September 1963, by asking its readers what should be the qualifications of the "Monsieur X" who was to bear the banner of the anti-Gaullist forces in the presidential election. By the gradual unveiling of the conditions "Monsieur X" would have to fulfill—a politician but not one involved in the *débâcle* of the Fourth Republic, an effective administrator but a man of the left—the public was made aware that Gaston Defferre, the moderate Socialist mayor of Marseille, was the man for the job. In December 1963 he announced that he would be a candidate.[20]

This way of proceeding in disregard of the political parties bore the marks of an adaptation to France of transatlantic politics. It was the first instance of the impact on French political life of presidential election by direct universal suffrage. Given the new conditions, it was natural that the journalists and intellectuals behind the Defferre candidacy should have devoted their efforts to a "making of the President" in the so-called Kennedy style which has misled so many European politicians.[21]

But, quite apart from the clashes of personality involved (primarily between Mollet and Defferre), there was the distrust of the party hierarchies for a candidate imposed on them from outside and also Mollet's own desire not to give too much importance to a presidential institution which he disliked. The ultimate failure of the Defferre candidacy revealed the distaste felt by party militants and organizers for the kind of dominating figure needed to contest a presidential election.

It was also clear that this candidacy of the center had little chance of gaining Communist support. On January 12, 1964, Defferre defined his own attitude towards the Communist party:

I will not envisage conversations with the Communist party, I will not negotiate with it, I will not accept a common program.[22]

This was understandable in a candidate wishing to unite the center, but hardly calculated to produce a victory over the Gaullists. In February 1964 the Congress of the Socialist Party endorsed the candidacy, but without much unanimity or enthusiasm. Although Defferre wished to make certain constitutional changes (for instance, to reduce the presidential term from seven to five years), his view of the president's role was still far too active a one not to offend older party members, for whom a restoration of government by deputies was an instinct as much as a dogma.

Despite his own considerable activity during 1964, Defferre was not able to induce other parties to pronounce in his favor. Only his victory at the municipal elections in Marseille during March 1965 gave a new impetus to his campaign. His re-election as mayor had been due to a center coalition against Gaullists on the right and Communists on the left, and this seemed a good omen for a similar national effort. In May both the MRP and the Socialists agreed to form a "socialist democratic federation." However, the discussions in a committee of sixteen broke down on June 17-18. Mollet and the leaders of the MRP were distinctly cool about the whole business, the question of religious education reared its ugly head, and Defferre was forced to withdraw his candidacy on June 25. The episode, with all its complicated calculations, personal rivalries and party intrigues, had shown how unresponsive to new political forces the old political hands remained and how self-destructive their feuds could be. It seemed impossible to renew French political life either with or without the remnants of the old parties. From this situation the Gaullists naturally profited.[23]

Since it now seemed to be proved that no 'third force' candidature was possible, the alternative was a left-wing candidate receiving Communist support. After some uncertainty the choice fell on François Mitterand (backed by the left-wing clubs grouped in the *Convention des Institutions républicaines*) who gained the unconditional support of the Communists at the price of losing the men of the right center. These, after some vain attempts to induce Pinay to run, finally endorsed Jean Lecanuet, the president of the MRP, a figure from whom little was expected, but who proved surprisingly attractive to the electorate.*

*There were also three other candidates: Tixier-Vignancourt representing the irreconcilable right, Pierre Marcilhacy who originally hoped to attract the votes of the center, and a totally unknown figure, Marcel Barbu.[24]

K*

Before the 1965 presidential campaign opened in earnest, however, there had been a curtain-raiser in the shape of the March municipal elections. These had been preceded by the passage of a new law on voting in towns with over 30,000 inhabitants. It was hoped by the Gaullists that the law would help to polarize the non-Communist vote, thereby enabling the UNR to install itself at what has traditionally been considered the grassroots of French politics. Pompidou defined his intentions clearly enough in a broadcast on March 9:

> The first thing that characterizes the spirit of the Fifth Republic, the fundamental point, is to eliminate the régime of the parties at all levels of public affairs.[25]

This point of view was emphasized by another remark after the elections, which had been disappointing as far as the UNR was concerned: "In face of the Communists Gaullism, as a movement, represents the only real force in the country."

De Gaulle himself seems to have wished to modify this interpretation in his own commentary on the results.[26] In the individual outlooks of de Gaulle and Pompidou there were in fact two different conceptions of Gaullism. Pompidou and the party managers saw the movement as a vast party of the center-right which, since effective opposition to it was impossible without the aid of the Communists, would gradually change France's political structure into a two-party system. De Gaulle, on the other hand, still saw himself as an arbitrator, representing France as a whole and standing above the political parties—even the one which acted in his name. His distaste for politics in the party sense meant that the management of the Gaullist political machine increasingly fell into the hands of the Prime Minister, Pompidou, whose own peculiar skills led him to create an independent power relationship with the party faithful. Gaullists often repeated that their party (the UNR or its successors) was not a party "like the others." But, of course, it was, and, in Pompidou, it found, as time went by, a party manager of great ability.[27]

The tone of the Gaullist presidential campaign was set by de Gaulle himself in his opening announcement of his candidature on November 4, the day of St. Charles:

Should the massive and open support of the citizens pledge me to remain in office, the future of the new Republic will be decidedly assured. If not, no one can doubt that it will collapse immediately, and that France will have to suffer—but this time with no possible recourse—confusion in the State even more disastrous than that she experienced in the past.[28]

Even apart from the failure of this apocalyptic approach to deal with the issues of everyday life, the presentation of a possible return to the horrors of the Fourth Republic had two major defects as a main electoral theme. In the first place, the voter might well ask himself what a régime was worth which depended for its stability on the continued presence at its head of a man seventy-five years old. If Malraux was right in saying that "it is a question of choosing between a man of history who has assumed France and whom France will not find again tomorrow, and the politicians whom one always finds again,"[29] what would become of the much-vaunted institutions of the Fifth Republic when de Gaulle disappeared (we know now that he would not have lived out his seven-year term)? Secondly, neither Lecanuet nor Mitterrand corresponded to the chaotic picture painted by de Gaulle.

French voters were having their first taste of presidential politics, and, on television, the rival candidates were visible to a far greater proportion of the electorate than had ever been the case in any previous election. The Gaullist monopoly of state broadcasting was breached to the extent of allowing each of the other candidates two hours of time during the last fortnight of the campaign. Despite the existence of a control commission, the Gaullists could not resist the temptation to exploit their administrative advantages. Still, the sight of Lecanuet and Mitterrand on the screen did not suggest that they were about to reduce France to chaos.[30] In fact, the immediate result was to contrast the aging President with his more youthful rivals. This comparison was particularly favorable to Lecanuet who proved to be an impressive television personality.

Combined with an uninspiring Gaullist campaign, the appeal of the other candidates was reflected in the public opinion polls (another new feature of a French election) which, from a decisive lead for de Gaulle (69 percent) in October, sunk to only 43 percent in the first days of

December. The Gaullist reaction to this was some disarray and a flurry of attacks on the other candidates, Lecanuet more especially being resented as attracting votes which would otherwise have gone to de Gaulle. The success of the themes of renewal and change proposed by Lecanuet and Mitterrand were a warning to the governing party—which, however, was not heeded until the results of the first ballot had shown just how unreliable appeals to the past achievements of Gaullism and predictions of future chaos were. On December 5 de Gaulle received only 43.7 percent of the votes cast and 36.7 percent of the total of those eligible to vote and was forced into a run-off with Mitterrand two weeks later.*

His reaction to this was bitter, but his conclusion that, on the first ballot, Frenchmen had voted as though the occasion were elections rather than a referendum, was accurate.[32] Taken like this, de Gaulle's 36.78 percent might seem to lie somewhere between the 21 percent received by the UNR-UDT in the 1962 elections and the 46 percent *Yes* vote in the almost simultaneous referendum. In electoral terms, therefore, the figures might not seem so bad. But the number of abstentions had more than doubled since 1962, and, on this occasion, de Gaulle's whole prestige had been thrown into the balance. The result of the first ballot, therefore, meant a real decline in his personal hold over the voters, and the psychological impact of his not winning immediately was considerable.

The correct conclusions were drawn by Gaullist strategists, and redoubled efforts were made between December 5 and 19 to stem the tide of opinion. The desisting candidates mostly gave their support to Mitterrand, Lecanuet advising his followers to spoil their voting papers if they could not bring themselves to vote for a man of the left. To draw votes from the left Malraux coupled de Gaulle and the French Revolution, and the President himself, in three television interviews with Michel Droit, showed himself at his most seductive. The final result, in which de Gaulle received 54.5 percent of the votes cast and 44.7 percent of eligible voters, was something less than a triumph, but it was enough.[33]

However, the final impression of the 1965 presidential election was

*The percentages of those eligible to vote received by other candidates were: Mitterrand, 27.1; Lecanuet, 13.3; Tixier-Vignancourt, 4.4; Marcilhacy, 1.4; Barbu, 0.9; Abstentions, 14.9; Void, 0.8.[31]

one of a check for de Gaulle's personal authority. After the Algerian drama France had returned to normal, and its rulers would be judged, not on their own estimate of their indispensability, but on more everyday issues and the desire for normal political change. Moreover, the Lecanuet candidacy had shown that the right could be divided as well as the left. A combination of the European issue with the difficulties of French farmers had helped to rob de Gaulle of a victory on the first ballot. He had received a large number of left-wing votes—between two and three million according to one expert—but it was unlikely that any successor would be able to rely on support from this direction.[34] One day it would be necessary for the Gaullists to assemble the whole of the right, despite the bitterness caused by Lecanuet's candidature and the gulf separating them from the followers of Tixier-Vignancourt. As for the left, in spite of Mitterrand's relatively successful attempt to align Communists and non-Communists under the same banner, it had been revealed as a minority. The geographical distribution of the Mitterrand vote on the second ballot showed that it came largely from the more traditional areas of France (south of the Loire) whose political structures might be expected to alter under the impact of economic and social change.[35]

The governmental shuffle after the election saw the replacement of Giscard d'Estaing as minister of finance by Debré and the entry of Edgar Faure into the government as minister of agriculture. Pompidou may have wished to get rid of Giscard d'Estaing—a possible rival—but the return of Debré seems to have been imposed on him by the Elysée. This was the moment at which de Gaulle himself took control of French monetary policy, and he may have wished to have a more devoted minister at the Rue de Rivoli than Giscard d'Estaing. Once an atmosphere of national crisis or a danger of political defeat were removed the Gaullist coalition would reveal itself as composed of several elements.

The most active and disturbing of these were the left-wing Gaullists of the old UDT (Capitant, Hamon, Vallon). They exercised their influence chiefly through intellectual means (the weekly *Notre République*, for example), although the "Vallon amendment" of May 1965, which called upon the government to pass a law by which workers would enjoy a proportion of the benefits from the expansion of firms where they were employed, was a major example of their influence on social policy.[36] On the right and forming a bridge toward the 'Centrists' were the Independent Republicans of Giscard d'Estaing, a well-organized elite party with a leader whose ambitions were hardly concealed.[37] During 1966 an attempt was made by the Gaullist party leadership to reduce to order these somewhat disparate elements, with an eye to the parliamentary elections due to take place in 1967. A *Comité d'action pour la Ve République* was created in May, and, by July, an agreement was reached with the unwilling Giscard d'Estaing according to which single candidates would be presented at the first ballot by all the groups of the majority.

Meanwhile a somewhat different process of coalition building was taking place on the left. Mitterrand's *Fédération de la gauche démocrate et socialiste* (FGDS) included radicals, Socialists and the *Convention des institutions républicaines*. The problem once again was to come to an agreement with the Communists. On December 20, 1966, an electoral pact was concluded which provided for candidates of each party to stand down on the second ballot in favor of the most promising left-wing candidate. In January the *Parti socialiste unifié* (PSU), a splinter left-wing party notable for its intellectual connections, joined the pact. As for Lecanuet's *Centre démocrate* (CD), it was unable to make alliances and found itself badly placed at the polls.[38]

The campaign for the 1967 elections produced few surprises. De Gaulle's anti-American foreign policy, then reaching its height, with France's withdrawal from NATO and the attacks on American actions in Vietnam, made things very difficult for Mitterrand's *Fédération* and its Communist allies. Not only had de Gaulle cut the ground from under their feet, but the entire question of relations with the United States and the Atlantic alliance was a divisive theme within the *Fédération* itself. The hottest debate at the polls, erupting in confrontations between Pompidou and Mitterrand and Mendès-France, centered on a constitutional point: what would happen if an anti-Gaullist majority were elected to parliament? Would de Gaulle call on a non-Gaullist as prime minister? The Gaullist response to this was ambiguous and gave the impression that the decision of the electorate might simply be ignored.

This impression of willingness to deal cavalierly with constitutional principles may have been reinforced by memories of the Ben Barka affair and its sequel as revealed throughout 1966 (see chapter 6). In his press conference of February 21, 1966, de Gaulle, speaking of the case, had claimed that "what happened was only vulgar and second-rate."[39]

But the fact that General Jacquier, the head of French intelligence, was removed from his post, and a commission under the ex-president of the Constitutional Council, Léon Noël, formed to study the reform of the police suggested rather more extensive responsibilities. In any case, the Fifth Republic now had its own *affaire ténébreuse* of a type all too familiar in French history. The result was to make it appear a little more dingy than it had before—a régime like the others.[40]

However this may have affected the issue, the results of the elections of March 1967 did not fully correspond to Gaullist hopes. In the first ballot the Gaullists, whose political party was now called the *Union des démocrates pour la Ve République* (UDVe), received 37.7 percent of the votes cast—a high proportion. The nearest figure to it was the 22.4 percent of the Communists. The Federation had 18.7 percent; the 'Centrists' only 13.4 percent.* This flying start was expected to be enough to secure the Gaullists a substantial majority, but the second ballot resulted in a surprising reversal of fortunes. While the alliance of the Communists and the Federation worked well, many 'Centrists' switched their votes to a left-wing candidate, so that there was an unexpected concentration of votes on opposition candidates, and a number of prominent UDVe figures were defeated. These included Couve de Murville, Messmer and Sanguinetti—all of them ministers. The government ended up with a majority of two in the assembly which it owed to seats won in French overseas territories (Polynesia, the West Indies, etc.). The Communists gained 32 seats and the Federation and the PSU 31. Of the UDVe's 244 seats, 200 were Gaullist properly speaking (a loss of some 35 seats) and the Independent Republicans had 44 (a gain of 9).**

For the Gaullists this result was undoubtedly an awkward disappointment. Although their proportion of the vote had continued to increase, they had not won as many seats as they had hoped, and their Independent Republican allies had done better than they themselves. During the election campaign Giscard d'Estaing had defined his relationship to Gaullism in a much-quoted phrase: "Yes but ... "[43] This stance of support for the majority, while at the same time criticizing it and its leader, foreshadowed the line to be followed by Giscard d'Estaing throughout 1967 and early 1968. More and more sharply he was to attack de Gaulle's arbitrary conduct of affairs, and 1967, with the crisis in the Middle East and the President's Canadian visit, provided plenty of

*The percentages expressed in terms of eligible voters were as follows: Communists, 17.7; Extreme left, 1.7; Federation, 14.8; UDVe, 29.8; Dissident Gaullists, 0.3; Centrists, 10.6; Miscellaneous, 3.1; Extreme right, 0.6; Abstentions, 19.1; Invalid votes, 1.7.[41]

**The complete figures were: Communists, 73; Federation, 121; *Groupe*

occasions for such a policy. In this way Giscard d'Estaing made himself a candidate for the succession to de Gaulle. If anyone was the winner of the elections, it was he.

Pompidou, on the other hand, while remaining Prime Minister, had been damaged by the result. It was he who had prepared the elections, taking the opportunity to increase his hold over the UDVe, and after the March disappointment the reconstruction of the government showed a weakening in his position. Frey, who by now was one of the prime minister's closest associates, left the ministry of the interior to be replaced by Fouchet, whose loyalty was given solely to de Gaulle. Pompidou was only able to advance one protégé: Jacques Chirac, who had earlier belonged to his personal cabinet, now became secretary for employment.

Once again there was a change at the ministry of education: Fouchet, whose plan of reform had hardly got under way, was followed by Alain Peyrefitte, a young, ambitious, but, as things turned out, unfortunate Gaullist. Couve de Murville and Messmer were maintained in their posts despite their defeat at the polls.[44]

Immediately after the meeting of the new National Assembly Pompidou announced that the government would ask for "special powers" under article 38 of the Constitution in order to promulgate a number of ordinances dealing with economic and social affairs. The official explanation of this way of proceeding was that 1968 was the date fixed for the full freeing of exchanges within the Common Market, but the true reason seems to have had more to do with the narrowness of the parliamentary majority than anything else. The demand for special powers cost the government both the resignation of one of its more able ministers, Pisani, and some fifty days of parliamentary debate, during which three votes of censure were rejected by small majorities. And the ordinances—a word of ill omen in French history—gave Giscard d'Estaing (who, although the leader of a section of the majority, had not been consulted) an opportunity of redoubling his criticisms of the Gaullist style of government.

The ordinances themselves, promulgated between August and October, bore on three main sets of problems. First came a group of measures designed to stimulate the economy and deal with problems of employment (these included laws to help the concentration of

---

Progrès et Démocratie moderne (PDM)—the old *Centre démocrate*, 41; UDVe (Gaullists), 200; Independent Republicans, 44; Others, 8.[42]

businesses, industrial decentralization and the retraining of redundant workers). Second came a group of ordinances that carried through a reform of France's social insurance system (including a rise in the proportion of costs met by those insured). Thirdly there were the decrees giving the employees in a business the right to participate in its profits. (These latter ordinances, however, did not go as far as the "Vallon amendment" and, in general, the economic and social policy of the Pompidou government left the left-wing Gaullists dissatisfied. In the autumn, they refused to go to the Lille 'assizes' of the UNR-UDT, now to be officially transformed into the UDVe.[45])

As for Mitterrand's Federation and its allies, the rest of 1967 was spent in settling problems of organization and in negotiating with the Communists. Finally, on February 24, 1968, a common declaration was published which listed points of agreement and divergence (the latter principally on foreign policy) between the partners. The success of the left at the cantonal elections in the previous autumn and the common struggle against the ordinances probably helped this evolution. Also a split in the ranks of the PDM between the followers of Lecanuet and those of Jacques Duhamel meant that there was no alternative for the Federation to an alliance with the Communists.[46]

Quarrels within the Gaullist coalition and the consolidation of the opposition on the left made it clear that, in 1967-68, the post-de Gaulle (if not necessarily the post-Gaullist) period was setting in. The attitude of Giscard d'Estaing was explicable only by a wish to dissociate himself from what he felt to be a declining régime. As for Pompidou, his immediate aim was to transform the Gaullist party into a modern organization, unencumbered with too many historical memories or too personal a fidelity to de Gaulle and firmly under his own control. This task was a difficult one. As the political correspondent of *Le Monde* wrote at the end of 1967:

To brandish the Communist scarecrow, speak of the post-Gaullist period, get rid of cumbersome or compromising old companions, in order to place his own men and give the movement a more technocratic air—all this is to question the principle of the unity of the "assembled" nation, the dogma of the infallibility of its leader . . . and refuse the myth of absolute fidelity.[47]

For, though it may be exaggerating to talk of a 'struggle' between de Gaulle and Pompidou at this point, it remains true that their relationship was such as to carry them further apart even had 'the May events' not occurred.

In 1967-68 Pompidou appeared as the natural successor to de Gaulle—the only figure in the Gaullist ranks with a considerable political following of his own—at a time when the President still had five years of his mandate to run. And, inasmuch as Pompidou's position had become independent of de Gaulle, its mere existence diminished the latter's freedom of action. Pompidou provided a credible alternative to de Gaulle, thereby disproving the stark choice "de Gaulle or chaos" so often presented to the French voter. But Pompidou's own prospects of the presidency could be seriously affected by de Gaulle's actions and by his power to change the head of government. Nor were voices lacking in the Gaullist ranks to complain of the exclusively right-wing orientation given to Gaullism by Pompidou. As the left-wing Gaullists put it when explaining their reasons for not going to the Lille 'assizes':

> As long as De Gaulle is there, we have nothing to fear: he will not allow himself to be imprisoned by any parliamentary majority. The problem will only be posed on the day when universal suffrage will have to give him a successor. May the French people then choose a President which it knows to be as attached to the Constitution as detached from the parties.[48]

Nor was Pompidou especially popular with those who, like Debré or Couve de Murville, owed their allegiance directly to de Gaulle and shared a background of wartime activity from which the Prime Minister had stood apart. His strength was in the manipulation of the pieces on the political board, his arts those of the accomplished party leader. But he was a stranger to the heroic world of Free France and had no claim on the loyalties springing from common memories and common risks which formed so much of the emotional background of the Gaullist movement.

At the same time, de Gaulle and the 'unconditionally' faithful Gaullists were beginning to grow out of touch with a France where no one under thirty-five could remember much of the war. Pompidou's vision of a great modern conservative party based on economic interest and political stability was correct politically. Still it was bound to bring him into conflict with de Gaulle, since it meant discarding the ideology lying behind the latter's political career, preferring the flesh-pots of a consumer society to the task of grandeur set before France.

A more rigid, more Jacobin side of Gaullism was represented by Debré, a more social trend by Capitant, Vallon and their followers. These were possible alternatives to the Pompidou line, and, after May 1968, de Gaulle made use of them.

As has become clear at various points in this study, the position of the Gaullist party within the Fifth Republic was never devoid of ambiguity. De Gaulle's hostility to parties and his view of himself as an arbitrator between divergent forces in French society meant that at first he was unwilling to commit himself to its support. In the 1958 election not only was the UNR not backed by de Gaulle, but he actively tried to limit its electoral success—probably because he feared the emergence of a powerful right-wing party committed to a "French Algeria" and also because he wished to keep the Socialists in the government.* In 1959 he decreed that ministers should not sit on the controlling committees of the UNR. Frey, then a minister, was replaced as UNR secretary-general by Albin Chalandon. At this point de Gaulle was prepared to say "The UNR does not interest me." The other ministers in fact stayed at their party posts, but the uneasiness of relations between the Elysée and the Gaullist party persisted.[50]

The tension finally eased after the 'unconditional' Gaullists within the UNR had fought off Delbecque's attempt to carry the party against de Gaulle's Algerian policy (see chapter 6). On April 25, 1960, Soustelle was excluded from the party. Henceforward the danger, feared by de Gaulle, of a party that would restrict his freedom of action no longer existed. The role of the UNR would be that defined by Debré in a letter to Soustelle before the latter's expulsion: "The UNR has no value, no meaning, no legitimacy except insofar as its action totally follows the political directives of General de Gaulle."[51] Chalandon, secretary-general of the movement from February 1959 to November 1959, had indeed wanted the party to play the part of candid friend to the government with the secretary-general as its spokesman, but he soon found that this was to the taste neither of Debré nor of de Gaulle. The central committee of the party, whose business it was to decide the

*The Socialists wanted one type of electoral system (the *scrutin d'arrondissement*), the UNR another (the *scrutin départemental*). De Gaulle took the side of the Socialists.[49]

political line, prepare elections and meetings of the 'assizes' and national council of the movement, soon saw its powers transferred to a political commission of its own members. Even this, however, seemed rather to provide occasion for debate between ministers and Gaullist leaders than to be a decision-making body.[52]

The 'assizes' of Strasbourg, in March 1961, marked the final shaping of the UNR as a party of government pure and simple. During the election campaign of November 1962, de Gaulle rewarded its fidelity by identifying himself with it.[53] Despite his dislike of political parties, the realities of politics forced him to rely on the only formation that could provide parliamentary support for the government and align public opinion throughout France behind his own policies. One aspect of the political history of the Fifth Republic was the more and more voluntary assumption by de Gaulle of the role of party chief.

However, relations between de Gaulle and the deputies and militants of the Gaullist party were always distinguished by an absence of precise directives from above. Loyal Gaullists were reduced to behaving as they believed that their leader wished them to behave, and this attempt to achieve a sort of instinctive symbiosis was the easier in that the upper echelons of Gaullism were composed of men who had known each other a long time. As Jean Charlot has demonstrated, practically all the leading Gaullists had been associated during the war. "At the end of 1945, the Gaullist team of the Fifth Republic was almost complete."[54] Pompidou was an acquisition of the immediate postwar period, and Chalandon was one of the few outstanding figures of the Fifth Republic to be a late-comer. Even relatively junior Gaullists had personal ties with prominent participants in wartime Gaullism. Only at a late stage were 'new men' to appear on the scene. The first of them was Alain Peyrefitte, and his appearance was followed in the late sixties by that of some younger protégés of Pompidou: a Jacques Chirac or a Robert Poujade. But for most of de Gaulle's presidency the top ranks of Gaullism were filled with men who, as Frey put it, had followed the General for twenty years. In May 1958, ten telephone calls, according to one witness, were enough to reconstitute the whole network of Gaullism.[55]

In these conditions it is understandable that the atmosphere prevailing in the upper echelons of Gaullism was one of personal friendship and similar habits of thought—cliquishness almost. Hence the heart-burning when it came to expelling old comrades like Soustelle or

Raymond Dronne. Hence the somewhat forced ritual surrounding much of Gaullism, the emotive use of the cross of Lorraine and of the musical signal of *Radio Londres* during the war. Hence the rhetoric of fidelity and comradeship symbolized by the use of the form of address "dear companion." Hence the fact that power in the UNR and its successors never really resided in the organs created to exercise it. Chalandon, as we saw, did his best to make a party leader of the secretary-general, but failed: While it is true that the Gaullist parliamentary group played a rather more prominent role than the central committee, here too personal relationships and tenacious loyalties largely blunted the edge of criticism or desire to dispute government decisions.

For their part, the prime ministers of the Fifth Republic did their best to foster the ties between themselves and the deputies. Undoubtedly, the most successful in his attempts to attach them to him was Pompidou, but Debré had also made himself accessible to Gaullist parliamentarians, though there were complaints during his prime-ministership about the insufficient attention paid to the parliamentary party. A large part of Pompidou's success in propagating his candidacy for the succession to de Gaulle reposed on the clientele he had built up in this way—a lesson which has not been lost on Chaban-Delmas who, as president of the assembly for many years, had already constructed his own network of relationships in that body.[56]

In fact, as the closest student of political Gaullism has written, up to 1967, "the UNR was practically reduced to a ministerial circle plus a parliamentary group."[57] In terms of membership it was hardly a mass party. From about 7,000 in early 1959, its numbers had risen to 86,000 by the end of 1963, showing little change thereafter.[58] It was only in 1967, after the disappointing election results, that Pompidou undertook its renewal. The secretary-general (at that time Jacques Baumel) was replaced by five "national secretaries" who met every week in the prime minister's office together with Frey (now minister in charge of parliamentary relations) and the presidents of the Gaullist parliamentary groups (assembly and senate). Every two weeks there was a meeting of the new executive bureau.*

These changes, which implied a more direct and continuous relation-

---

*The executive bureau ended up with twenty-eight members, nine of them non-elected. These were: the prime minister, a minister designated by him (usually the one handling parliamentary business), ex-prime ministers and the presidents of the Gaullist parliamentary groups, the president of the assembly, the party secretary-general and two other functionaries.[59]

ship between government and party leadership, were accompanied by a restructuring of the party. In future the electoral district rather than the department would be the basis of its organization, and a plan was set afoot for regional councils. Much of this was, of course, unwelcome to older party members, and, at the 'assizes' of Lille in November, 1967–which the left-wing Gaullists did not attend–the organizers also found themselves faced with a revolt of the traditionalists who succeeded in getting the institution of a single secretary-general restored. A mixture of motives inspired this resistance–dislike of change, dislike of Pompidou, a desire to "democratize" the movement and, hence, to have a secretary-general who could speak as an equal to the prime minister.[60] More generally, however, the plans for the reform of what was now the UDVe went forward. Just before 'the events of May' a new membership campaign was launched which, powerfully aided by the fear of 'revolution,' carried the party to almost double its 1963 numbers.[61]

Who were the Gaullist voters and where did they come from? Inquiries by public opinion polls give a picture of the Gaullist which contrasts with that of his opposite number, the left-wing voter. The composite portrait that emerges from the 1967 and 1968 legislative elections (referendums and presidential elections usually attracted a certain number of left-wing sympathizers to the Gaullist side and were therefore less representative) is one of an electorate older than that of the left, containing more women, more farmers and professional men, but far fewer industrial workers. Gaullists are more often to be found among both the richest and the poorest categories of Frenchmen. There are many more of them who practice the Catholic religion. Gaullism finds more voters than the left in communes of under 20,000 inhabitants, while the left finds its supporters in towns of between 20,000 and 100,000 inhabitants and in the Paris region.

In terms of electoral geography, maps of the different votes during the Fifth Republic show Gaullist strength continuing in roughly the same areas of France. There is a bastion in the east based on Alsace-Lorraine and one in the west including Brittany and the Vendée. These are linked by a zone of strong Gaullist support running across the whole of the north of France and seriously eroded only by the 'red belt' around Paris. To the south of the Loire Gaullism has succeeded in implanting itself on the southern edge of the Massif Central and, to the east, in Savoy and the Alps. These last areas, indeed, appear to correspond to regions of strong practicing Catholicism. Thus Gaullism, as well as profiting from the pace of economic change in the 'dynamic' north of France, has also managed to exploit the more traditional right-wing inclinations of the 'static' south.[62]

The history of the Gaullist party under its changing insignia has been one of steady and deliberate progress, as has that of its Independent Republican allies. In the legislative elections of 1958 the proportion of votes cast received by the Gaullists was 20.4 percent; in 1962: 31.9 percent; in 1967: 37.7 percent; in 1968: 43.6 percent. Meanwhile votes in which de Gaulle's own personal authority was more directly involved (referendums and the presidential election) saw his proportion of votes cast diminish from 90.6 percent in April 1962 to 61.7 percent in October 1962 to 54.5 percent on the second round of the 1965 presidential election to 46.81 percent in the final referendum of April 1969. Thus while de Gaulle's own personality and prestige showed, during the sixties, all the marks of a historical phenomenon diminishing as time went on, the party that had been founded in his name was reaping the full benefits of his achievements as well as of more traditional features of French political life. At the presidential election in June 1969 Pompidou was to do significantly better than de Gaulle, receiving 57.6 percent of the votes cast.* This would seem to suggest that Pompidou now had more appeal than the General to the real Gaullist party electorate—a fact confirmed by the different profile of his electoral support revealed by the opinion polls.[63] The distinction between 'Gaullist' and 'Gaullien' (the latter term being used to denote the personal political impact of de Gaulle) appears to be born out by the facts of electoral sociology.

At the end of the sixties the Gaullists and their Independent Republican allies (to whom most of the 'Centrists' were added in 1969) appeared as a great party which had gradually absorbed most of the elements of the French right into an effective coalition. De Gaulle himself had always received large numbers of votes from normally left-wing voters and also had bitter enemies on the right. But the *Union des*

---

*It should be added that, in the 1969 election, abstentions were double (30.9 percent) the figure of 1965. With de Gaulle running, a presidential election seems to have been more interesting.

démocrates pour la République (UDR–the most recent title of the Gaullist party) can be seen as representing practically the whole of the traditional French right, and the number of industrial workers voting for Pompidou was significantly smaller than that voting for de Gaulle. Gaullism, René Rémond has written, has become "the federator of the rights." (In the same article, he has drawn attention to the resemblance of the crowds taking part in the massive Gaullist demonstrations of May 30, 1968, on the Place de la Concorde to those who, in the last years of the Third Republic, participated in the marches of the *Parti social français.*[64])

The UDR has benefited and will continue to benefit from the incapacity of the left to unite–an incapacity caused in the first place by the rigidity of the Communist party. The same conditions that produced a right-of-center majority in the political life of the Fourth Republic are now bringing about a similar conjuncture under the Fifth Republic. May 1968 notwithstanding, the Gaullists seem to have had some success in reaching the goal set before them by Frey in February 1965 when he called for a renewal of the UNR which would insure its attractiveness to the young and its survival in a future less and less affected by common memories of wartime Gaullism or the Resistance.[65]

Just how lasting this achievement is and just how far its content corresponds to what has usually been thought of as 'Gaullism' is another question and will be discussed in the conclusion. But it should be recognized that the Gaullist party leaders have taken advantage of a trend in French politics toward a broad right-wing coalition (PSF or CNI) set against a disunited left, which has existed for many years. This gives their construction a certain durability. Many observers have asked themselves recently whether France is not on the way to a two-party system. In that case, the threat to the preponderance of the right (and hence to Gaullism) would come from a left-wing coalition concentrating its fire on economic and social issues.

IV

It is perfectly probable that no other French government would have done better than the Gaullists in dealing with the social consequences of rapid economic growth and an expanding population. But it was the very lack of a political alternative to Gaullism during these years which made its failures on the domestic front particularly frustrating. Incidents like the Ben Barka case, the blatant use of the *Office de la Radio et Télévision française* (ORTF) for political propaganda in favor of the governing party, the pressures exercised by officials in the provinces on local newspapers—all this somewhat seamy side of Gaullism contrasted ill with the grandiose rhetoric from the Elysée imitated, with far less style and intelligence, by ministers and deputies. For as well as loyalty and reverence for the person of de Gaulle, servility and opportunism were also not lacking in the Gaullist ranks, and the President's occasional expression of angry rancor against opponents was followed by others in many an act of minor spitefulness.

By 1968 the atmosphere of French political life had become oppressive—a fact recognized by Viansson-Ponté in a famous phrase: "France is bored."[66] But it was not so much boredom as the sense of a certain staleness pervading French society and an unformulated desire for a more open type of politics. The increasingly arbitrary behavior of de Gaulle himself, the apparent lack of political change to match economic and social transformations, the difficulty of adjusting grievances against an unbending administrative machine combined to form a psychologically repressive environment which has been described by a sociologist, Michel Crozier, as "la société bloquée"—"the blocked society."[67] Something new was needed, and, in 1968, something new came. The Gaullist reign was to be shattered in a strange manner which has its lessons for other advanced industrial countries and which, whatever the future of the political party that has assumed the inheritance of Gaullism, brought to an end a period of French history.

The 'May movement' was not the future itself—in many respects it looked backwards—but it announced a future in which de Gaulle's "certain idea of France" was no longer a credible image of a country whose power could not be restored to its nineteenth century level or of the preoccupations of a people busy about their daily tasks. De Gaulle's romanticism could only impose itself on France for so long. But, curiously enough, its spell was to be broken not by everyday realities, but by another, no less romantic conception of the world, drawing equally upon the historical past of France.

CHAPTER VIII

The Decline of Gaullism:
May and the End of a Regime

L'ordre est le plaisir de la raison, le désordre le délice de l'imagination.
—*Paul Claudel*

L'année 1968, je la salue avec sérénité . . .
—*Charles de Gaulle*

On Friday, May 3, 1968, a demonstration of some 400 students of varying shades of left-wing opinion took place in the great courtyard of the Sorbonne, the building in the middle of the Quartier Latin on the left bank of the Seine which, since the Middle Ages, has been the heart of the University of Paris. Ostensibly to prevent any attack by the right-wing student organization *Occident* (which was thought to be responsible for a fire in the Sorbonne on the previous day), the demonstrators had placed guards armed with iron bars and cudgels. The purpose of the demonstration was to protest against the closing of the duplicate faculty of letters at Nanterre and the disciplinary appearance of 6 students before the council of the university. The closure of Nanterre had been ordered the day before by the Dean, Pierre Grappin, following a series of violent incidents which, since March, had reached a level of disruption that prevented the proper functioning of the university.

The leaders of the demonstration refused to leave the Sorbonne when asked to do so, and the Rector of the university thereupon called in the police to expel them. At a quarter to five a force of police with shields and truncheons entered the gates and, without using violence, herded the students outside and into police vans and buses. At this point crowds of students outside the Sorbonne began to attack the gendarmes. Before very long there were police charges up the Boulevard Saint-Michel, attempts by the demonstrators to build barricades, exchanges of stones and tear gas grenades. By 10:30 in the evening the fighting began to die away. Some 600 arrests were made, and 27 students held in custody. These included a German student leader from Nanterre, Daniel Cohn-Bendit, and Jacques Sauvageot, the vice-president of the official student organization, the *Union nationale des étudiants français* (UNEF). On the side of the police there were 5 injured—one seriously.[1]

The day of May 3 marked the real beginning of what came to be known as "the May events." Within a week even heavier clashes took place in the Quartier Latin, and the barricades became a reality which it required all the available forces of police and *Compagnies républicaines de sécurité* (CRS) to storm. What might be called the student phase of "the May events" acted as a detonator for the whole crisis—it led to an unexpectedly maladroit reaction from the government and then set off a chain reaction which spread to industrial and white-collar workers.

II

The student movement had begun at Nanterre, reaching its full proportions on March 22 with the occupation by protesting students of the hall in which the university senate met. Its causes have been variously defined. One Nanterre professor believed that "the first cause, the profound cause . . . was the discredit of knowledge."[2] The Ministry of the Interior saw the motivating force as being the action of a small number of extremist groups and the example set by Berkeley and

Berlin.* A foreign observer has pointed to the fragmentation of the UNEF and the government's (mild) persecution of it, which left French students without any effective representative body at a time when the universities were overcrowded and disorganized by the Fouchet reforms.[4]

In fact, these explanations are different facets of the same reality: a university system where physical conditions were almost unbearable and where authority exercised from above promulgated changes without consultation with the interested parties and without ascertaining whether it was possible to put them into effect. The huge mass of students—160,000 in the University of Paris alone—were left with little say and in conditions that took away all pleasure or interest in intellectual work. Nor was it university students alone that suffered: the creation of the *Comités d'action lycéens* (CAL) at the end of 1967 testified that the malaise was widespread in secondary education. As for the professors, the *Syndicat national de l'enseignement supérieur* (SNE. Sup.), under the leadership of its extremist Secretary-General, Alain Geismar, was willing to take part in any attempt to dissolve the existing structures of the French university.

In these circumstances, it is not surprising that small, determined groups of ideologues were able to extend their influence over wide sections of the student body. Whether influences from outside France played much part in this is more doubtful. The agitation against the Vietnam war certainly had an important part in creating the atmosphere within which such groups could operate profitably. The April 18 attempt on the life of Rudi Dutschke, the radical student leader from Berlin, combined with the activities of *Occident,* also had its influence on events by persuading the leaders of the *groupuscules,* always subject to paranoia, that their own lives might be in danger. But even though some German members of the *Sozialistische Demokratische Studentenbund* (SDS) do seem to have been active in France during May, direct

---

*These small extremist groups (or *groupuscules*) were: *La Jeunesse Communiste révolutionnaire* (JCR), a 'Trotzskyist' organization led by Alain Krivine: *L'Union des Jeunesses Communistes (marxistes-léninistes)* (UJC-ML), a Maoist group excluded from the Communist Party: *Le Comité de liaison des étudiants révolutionnaires* (CLER), another 'Trotzskyist' group: *Le Mouvement du 22 Mars* emanating from Nanterre and composed of a mixture of anarchists and members of the JCR under the leadership of Cohn-Bendit.[3]

influences were probably confined to a simple perception of Berkeley and Berlin.[5]

The mechanism of what happened at Nanterre and subsequently in Paris is, in any case, fairly clear, whatever dispute there may be about the causes that set it in motion. The extremist leaders, by provoking the authorities, were able to bring down on themselves reprisals, either on the part of the university authorities or the police, which swung many students to their side. On May 3 about 2,000 students were involved in the demonstrations. By May 13 the number had grown to 25,000, though this was still only a fraction of the student population of Paris.*

The first reflex of the government after May 3 was that firmness was required. The next day the Sorbonne was closed, and, the day after, 3 students were sentenced to two months imprisonment for attacking the police. These sanctions only served to spread the agitation in the student body. On May 6 and 7, in response to an appeal from the UNEF, the student organization, there were renewed demonstrations in the Quartier Latin, Montparnasse and along the Champs Elysées. Fighting again broke out between the demonstrators and the police. Barricades were built in the Quartier Latin and parked cars burned. On Monday (May 6) alone, there were more than 600 wounded among students and police, 422 arrests were made, and 31 of those arrested were detained. The demands of the demonstrators were an amnesty for those arrested, the withdrawal of security forces from the Quartier Latin and the reopening of the faculties of letters at Nanterre and the Sorbonne.

The attitude of the ministers in face of these new disorders and the students' ultimatum was hesitant. De Gaulle himself did not appreciate the threat. Pompidou, the only real politician among them and also the only one capable of influencing de Gaulle, was absent on a visit to Afghanistan. His place was occupied by Joxe, and the two ministers most nearly concerned with the crisis were Fouchet at the Interior (his reforms as minister of education having been a cause of problems) and Peyrefitte as minister of education. The former, while strongly in favor of a firm hand, recognized that there must be no bloodshed, and his orders to that effect were ably carried out by the Prefect of police, Grimaud.** Peyrefitte, on the other hand, having first provoked a

*These figures are estimates on the part of the Ministry of the Interior and may be on the low side.[6]

**It is worthy of note that, despite the fierceness of the fighting in the Quartier Latin only one death occurred during the riots in Paris. Compare this with

protest from five Nobel prize-winners (including the almost excessively Gaullist François Mauriac) by denouncing "fanaticism and violence" at a cabinet meeting on the morning of May 8, on the same evening, under the pressure of debate in the National Assembly, seemed to promise the reopening of the faculties—something which had neither been mentioned to the President nor to his colleagues in the government. To add to Peyrefitte's difficulties, on the same day Alain Geismar, who headed the left-wing organization of professors (SNE. Sup.), had declared: "this evening the Sorbonne will belong to us, students and teachers." Next day the Sorbonne remained closed, and Peyrefitte received a majestic rebuke from de Gaulle. Meanwhile, demonstrations, marches and student strikes showed the sympathy felt by those attending provincial universities for their Parisian brothers.[8]

Up to this moment it looks very much as though neither de Gaulle nor his ministers had fully realized the threat to the régime contained in the student agitation. But the night of May 10-11, the "night of the barricades," dispelled all doubts. Throughout that evening more than sixty barricades were constructed in the Quartier Latin by thousands of young people while the security forces watched them. Then, after some vain attempts at negotiation, the order was given for the police to attack the barricades. At 2:15 A.M. large forces of security police (CRS) and gendarmes began to clear the streets, firing tear-gas grenades to which the students replied with Molotov cocktails and paving stones. As the battle went on, the reaction of the police became more violent. Individual students were beaten in a way which excited compassion and indignation on the part of the other inhabitants of the district. The Archbishop of Paris broadcast an appeal for "a just solution," and distinguished scholars asked for one more attempt at mediation. But the police continued to storm barricade after barricade. By morning the university quarter of Paris had the air of a town devastated by war:

> torn up paving stones, rocks, beams borrowed from houses in the process of demolition, pieces of fences, iron grills still bar the streets . . . . Almost everywhere in this chaos . . . can be seen the remains of burned cars, of vehicles with their windscreens in fragments—with their bodies caved in when they were used to construct barricades.[9]

incidents like that at Kent State College in the United States. The explanation is that the French security forces were well trained in the control of crowds, and the temptation of bringing in the army was resisted.[7]

The government had appeared as brutal and inept, and a call for a general strike on Monday, May 13—the tenth anniversary of Gaullist power—was made by the trade unions and the leaders of the left-wing political parties: Communists, Federation and PSU.

It was at this moment, on May 11, that Pompidou returned from his journey to Afghanistan and Iran. His arrival was a turning-point, though this was not realized at the time. So far the reaction of the Gaullists to the student disorders had succeeded in making the worst of both worlds: the Gaullists had neither appeased the rioters nor successfully quelled them. Their rigidity had produced no results, and their lack of political sense was mobilizing public opinion against the government. Pompidou, therefore, believed that a new departure was necessary. Confident in his own powers of negotiation (not without reason), he proposed a plan which included the release of student demonstrators, an amnesty to be voted by the National Assembly, the re-opening of the Sorbonne, and the withdrawal of the police. This was tantamount to an unconditional acceptance of the students' demands, and Pompidou's policy—announced in a short broadcast on the evening of his return—was vehemently opposed by Fouchet and Peyrefitte.* The latter went so far as to write a letter of resignation which Pompidou kept, but did not acknowledge.

However, it was de Gaulle's decision that counted, and the Prime Minister was able to obtain his consent to the plan.** From now on Pompidou exerted an almost dictatorial control over the government, excluding ministers from matters that concerned them and replacing them by his own staff without any hesitation.[12] A state visit by de Gaulle to Rumania from May 14 to 18 left the way free for Pompidou to handle the crisis as he thought fit, and, in doing so, he displayed a self-confidence all the more revealing in that it betrayed his own consciousness of his political strength—something which, until that moment, had been hidden from the general public. By an untiring show of activity and skill he made himself the hero of the crisis.

In the short term, however, his attempt to calm the storm was

*In his memoirs Fouchet has denounced the decisions of May 11. At the time, he seems to have kept silent as to his real opinion.[10]

**De Gaulle's agreement seems to have been given grudgingly. Later on he apparently considered these gestures of conciliation as an error, and this played its part in the replacement of Pompidou as prime minister.[11]

unsuccessful and even appeared to have made matters worse. The one-day general strike on May 13 was rapidly followed by strikes and occupations of factories all over France, until, by the end of the week, the entire country was paralyzed. As for the students, the reopening of the Sorbonne had simply led to its occupation by them, and they were now able to indulge themselves in what became almost a collective orgy of continuous discussion. The scenes inside the Sorbonne and other occupied university buildings recalled, in turn, a political rally, a university lecture and a Bohemian free-for-all. As anarchists, Maoists and Trotskyists peddled their ideological wares and groups of students argued about every subject on earth, others among them coupled on the floor of the corridors beneath a banner proclaiming "We fear nothing, we have the pill".[13] The Odéon theatre–occupied four days after the Sorbonne–was the scene of something not unlike a continuous production of the *Marat-Sade* as students, actors and intellectuals crowded on to the stage to say their piece. 'Contestation' was the order of the day, and the symbolic 'happenings' staged by the students were more decorously imitated in factories and offices all over France. Even the journalists of the state broadcasting organization, ORTF, usually so submissive to the dictates of the government, announced in a general assembly their intention of being more objective in their presentation of news in future.[14] In a debate in the National Assembly, on May 14, the Prime Minister himself went so far in his policy of concessions as to admit student participation in the administration of the universities.

However, the student phase of "the May events" had come to an end. The more or less general strike which now reigned in France presented a problem fundamentally far more serious than the dramatic events in the Quartier Latin that had set it off. More than ten million workers were out, the foodshops were emptying, the pavements unswept and the garbage uncollected. But (and Pompidou's political sense enabled him to grasp this) the aims of the trade unions were basically unconnected with those of the students. What they wanted was not revolution but improved living conditions–the bourgeois comfort which was so repugnant to the ideologists of the *groupuscules*. Indeed, the Communist-controlled CGT, anxious not to be outbid on the left, was deeply suspicious of a left-wing movement uncontrolled by the party. Georges Séguy, the CGT's secretary-general, abounded in warnings against 'leftists' and '*provocateurs*,' and the Confederation followed the strike movement rather than led it. The Communist party itself was scared of being blamed for the disorders by the electorate, bitterly hostile to Cohn-Bendit and his like and anxious to reach a settlement which would guarantee substantial advantages to the working-class. The Christian trade unions (CFDT) were more ready to have contacts with the students, but little resulted from what few meetings there were.

This difference between workers and students gave Pompidou his chance to separate the two wings of the May movement. After twenty-five hours of discussion at the Ministry of Social Affairs in the Rue de Grenelle, the so-called Grenelle protocol was agreed on May 27. It provided for an average increase of 10 percent in wages, an increase in the minimum wage (SMIG), a diminution of hours of work and increases in some social security benefits. Despite this, it was almost immediately rejected by the strikers. But the final terms of an industrial settlement had now been sketched.* The Minister of Finance, Debré, who had not been consulted throughout the negotiations and saw in the terms the ruin of France's financial position, resigned.

Meanwhile the general situation had seemed to have deteriorated. De Gaulle cut short his visit to Rumania and, on his return to Paris (May 18), expressed his view of the matter in two phrases: "Reform, yes; mess, no".** On May 21-22, a motion of censure in the National Assembly failed by eleven votes, but, before the debate, the leader of the left-wing Gaullists, Capitant, announced that he was resigning as a deputy in order not to have to vote for it. A former Gaullist minister, Pisani, did vote for the censure and then resigned with the intention of fighting for his seat again. On the same day Cohn-Bendit was expelled from France—a decision which led to further rioting in the Quartier Latin. On May 24 de Gaulle, in a long-delayed broadcast, told France that a referendum would be held on "a draft law giving the State and, primarily, its head a mandate for renewal."[17] "Participation" was to be the Gaullist answer to "contestation," but the effect of the President's speech was far from what he had hoped or expected. The ultimatum to the French people implied by the holding of a referendum was ill suited to the situation, and de Gaulle's weary and wooden delivery did not

*The unions were to win rather more. Ultimately, the rises in wages went to 13-15 percent in the public sector and well over 10 percent in private industry.[15]

**"La réforme, oui; la chienlit, non." "*Chienlit*" means the act of excreting in one's bed.[16]

make it any more seductive. As he spoke, more rioting was beginning in
Paris, Lyon, Nantes, Bordeaux and Strasbourg. In Paris the demonstrators succeeded in crossing to the right bank of the Seine and tried to set
the Bourse on fire. The night's toll of injured included 1 dead and more
than 500 wounded. In Lyon a police officer was killed.

For five days it looked as if the government had totally lost control
of events. With de Gaulle's speech the Gaullists had played their trump
card, and it had turned out to be a blank. Committed to a referendum
which would be almost impossible to hold and which, in Pompidou's
opinion, would be lost in any case, the régime appeared to have no way
of escape. The opposition drew the consequences. In a meeting at the
Stade Charléty on May 27 organized by the student UNEF and the
left-wing PSU, one speaker proclaimed that "today revolution is
possible".[18] Next day Mitterrand held a press conference in which he
announced that, if necessary, he would form a provisional government.
Mendès-France also declared that he would not refuse responsibilities
which might be placed on him "by the whole united left."[19] When, on
May 29, it was learned that de Gaulle had disappeared after leaving
Paris by helicopter, he made known his availability to head the
provisional government suggested by Mitterrand (the latter presumably
becoming President).

In fact, de Gaulle had gone to Baden-Baden to meet Massu, now
commanding the French forces in Germany. Just why he did so remains
something of a mystery, but two factors probably dictated his decision.
First, there was a long tradition, dating at least from the sixteenth
century, that the correct thing to do when faced by disorders in Paris
was to leave the city. This had been the tried recipe which had
succeeded at the time of the League, the Fronde and the Commune. It
was Louis XVI's failure to leave in time which had led to his fate as a
helpless prisoner of the Revolution. De Gaulle, no doubt, also wished to
regain his calm away from the beleaguered Elysée which he may have
considered a weak enough stronghold in the circumstances of May
1968–earlier he had wanted to change the seat of the presidency but
had been unable to find any suitable alternative.[20] But his purpose in
flying to Baden-Baden was also to ascertain whether or not the French
army would obey if called upon to restore order. Implicit in the
journey was a threat to the rioters. According to some accounts, de

Gaulle was ready to call in the army and transfer the seat of government outside Paris.*

In fact, May 29 turned out to be something of a day of dupes. On his return to Paris next day de Gaulle had recovered his vigor and sureness of political touch. After a cabinet meeting he made his decisions public: postponement of the referendum, the dissolution of the National Assembly and new elections, the continuance of Pompidou as prime minister. He also denounced in his broadcast "the intimidation, the poisoning of opinion and the tyranny exercised by groups organized accordingly long ago and by a party which is a totalitarian enterprise, even if it already has rivals in this respect," and threatened to assume 'special powers' under Article 16 of the Constitution.[22] A massive Gaullist demonstration on the Place de la Concorde and the Champs Elysées in which nearly a million people took part showed that the idea of restoring order was far from being unpopular. A government reshuffle eliminated those ministers associated with "the May events" (Fouchet, Joxe and Peyrefitte) and brought the leader of the left-wing Gaullists, Capitant, into the government as minister of justice. Marcellin, an Independent Republican, became minister of the interior, and Ortoli, a technocrat, was made minister of education. Soon a trend toward a return to work began to make itself felt. The secretary-general of the CGT asserted that his organization did not wish to disturb the elections in any way, and his statement was echoed by Duclos on behalf of the Communist party.[23]

In fact, de Gaulle had caught the students, the unions and the opposition politicians off balance. They could not reasonably complain about the holding of elections, but it was at once clear that these would take place in very unfavorable circumstances for them. Student demonstrators might have been able to influence the result of a referendum where all anti-Gaullist forces could agree to vote *No*, but they were helpless in a contest between parties. As for the politicians, they saw themselves associated in the minds of conservative Frenchmen with the violence of small extremist groups who were by now visibly trying the patience of most of their fellow-citizens. In his broadcast de Gaulle set the theme on which the elections would be fought by his

---

*On at least two occasions de Gaulle seems to have questioned his ministers as to whether the army should not be brought in.[21]

followers: France was threatened with a dictatorship inspired by totalitarian communism. For those middle-class people who saw their cherished cars being set on fire by the bearded anarchists of the left bank this summary view of the situation was quite enough. France was tired of the students and their disorders, and they could no longer call upon public sympathy in their battles with the police. By calling for elections de Gaulle had made possible an appeal to 'the silent majority' of Frenchmen. By basing himself on the need to maintain public order he had responded to their fears and made sure of their allegiance. No referendum on "participation" would have been half as effective in attracting support from conservative France.

Meanwhile a new 'social' Gaullism was being unveiled. In a television interview on June 7 de Gaulle emphasized once again that "participation" offered a "third solution" between capitalism and socialism.[24] Capitant even drew a formal protest from the employers organization, the CNPF, by suggesting a tripartite organization of industry (capital labor, management). But the Gaullists did not neglect those to the right of them. Salan and other OAS officers were amnestied (it was widely believed that this was the price paid by de Gaulle at Baden-Baden for assurances of army support), and Bidault was allowed to return to France.[25] Some right-wing Gaullists had already been active in forming *Comités pour la défense de la République* (CDR) which were to have some political influence during the coming year—principally in acting as a pressure group against a number of schemes dear to left-wing Gaullists.

The results of the elections were what might have been expected. Under the skillful leadership of Pompidou the Gaullist *Union pour la défense de la République* (UDR) pursued its advantage. The efforts of the Communists and the Federation to get rid of the label which de Gaulle had attached to them were unavailing.

On June 23 the first ballot showed that the UDR (including the Independent Republicans) had received 43.6 percent of the votes cast as against 20 percent for the Communists (the next biggest party), 16.5 percent for the Federation, and 3.9 percent for PSU. The Centrists received 10.3 percent.* On the second ballot a week later the

*The percentages in terms of eligible voters were as follows: Communists, 15.7; PSU, 3.1; Federation, 13; PDM, 8.1; UDR, 34.3; Abstentions, 20; Invalid, 1.4.[26]

bi-polarization which seemed to be imposing itself on French party politics brought with it even worse results in terms of seats for the left. The Gaullists had 294 deputies with 64 of their Independent Republican allies. The centrist PDM had 33, the Federation 57 and the Communists 34. There was, therefore, an absolute Gaullist majority in the new parliament, and the forces of the left, in comparison with 1967, had been routed.

During the campaign the country had been getting back to normal. There was a gradual return to work, and the student 'contestation' petered out in disillusionment and the evacuation of filthy buildings. The Sorbonne was once again in the hands of the authorities on June 16. The Odéon had been cleared two days earlier. The small left-wing groups were banned, and a number of foreigners deported. The Quartier Latin slowly resumed its everyday appearance. The "May movement" was over.

What was it and why did it happen? De Gaulle himself was to speak of "the alliance of vain imaginings, blackmail and cowardice".[27] His Minister of the Interior, Marcellin, pointed to an international conspiracy as the cause.[28] But this general attribution of responsibility to the powers of darkness is hardly a sufficient explanation. The industrial strikes, of course, can be seen as the result of suppressed anger at the ordinances and a feeling that the time had now arrived when the government was vulnerable to working-class pressure. The original student troubles too had their particular reasons which have been discussed above. But there were more elements to "the May events" than these. The chain reaction to the first disorders and the apparent inability of the government to influence events require more explanation.

No doubt, French revolutionary tradition had something to do with it. Barricades had been up before in the Quartier Latin, and their appearance had a resonance which awakened historical memories. The Gaullist government found itself faced by the kind of insurrectional movement which had ended the reigns of Charles X and Louis-Philippe. The students, behind their piles of paving-stones and shattered Renaults, were conscious that their defenses were constructed on the very spot where the Communards had built theirs and died. History played its part by making a symbol of the barricades: the traditional prelude to the fall of régimes.

In that sense "the May events" looked backwards toward historical episodes and nineteenth century ideologies which, while they called forth powerful echoes in the French mind, were hardly relevant to an advanced industrial society. To replace the rigid centralized structure of the French state by a kind of anarcho-syndicalism was no solution. Perhaps the May upheaval was the final convulsion of an intellectual tradition under threat from economic and social change. As such it may have been of more intellectual than political significance. The black and red flags hoisted over the Sorbonne seemed to have come from the pages of Victor Hugo. The barricades recalled a painting by Delacroix. A whole romantic revolutionary tradition found release and satisfaction in those days—perhaps for the last time.[29]

But the 'contestation' which called the structure of the French state into question easily demonstrated how ill-adapted this state was to sudden change. For the Gaullist régime also looked backwards into the past from which it had inherited the bureaucratic tradition of the great functionaries of the *ancien régime*. As Michel Crozier has pointed out, to the centralizing bureaucratic state of Louis XIV and Napoleon was opposed the other great stream of French history, the spectacle of a Paris seething with revolt.[30] The positive result of "the May events" was the clear indication they gave that a benevolently paternalistic government supported by the rhetoric of an historic symbol was not enough. The stiff fabric of a system, which de Gaulle had made even more unyielding by ending the political crises that had acted as a safety-valve under the Fourth Republic, could not easily bend, but it could break. In the end, that was what happened, and the explosion which made the breach had behind it the force of historical memories and of social and economic change seeking new political expression.

III

Whatever the causes of "the May events," their effect on Gaullism is not in doubt. As Crozier puts it:

The crisis revealed not only the general's temporary powerlessness, but the underlying failure of the style of action and system of government he had brought to France. In June, Frenchmen did not vote for him, but for order . . . [31]

"Gaullien" Gaullism had been badly damaged by the temporary collapse. Not only had the President himself been seen, for the first time, to be ineffective in his appeal to Frenchmen, but the ministers who had failed to cope with the students were all closely associated with de Gaulle himself. Pompidou, on the contrary, had come out of the whole episode with his reputation much enhanced. It was he who had negotiated the Grenelle protocol. It was he who had managed the massive electoral success. It was he who now understood, better than de Gaulle himself, the wishes of conservative France and of the mass of the Gaullist electorate. The release of Salan and the other OAS conspirators had extended the majority toward the right, and the anti-Communist electoral rhetoric expressed its views unequivocally. "The May events" had hastened the evolution of Gaullism towards a federation of the French right, a great conservative party. Of this kind of party Pompidou was the obvious representative and leader. May 1968 made his independent political position a reality where before it had been merely potential.

Understandably, this result of the crisis was not particularly welcome to de Gaulle. The difficulty inherent in having an obvious successor on the scene was infinitely greater now that Pompidou had emerged with honors from a confrontation in which, as de Gaulle himself confessed later: "everything slipped through my fingers. I no longer had any hold over my own government."[32] Moreover, the President was now convinced that a new departure was essential. 'Participation,' the nostrum of the left-wing Gaullists, and decentralization would be the heart of the reform which once again would crown the monarch of the Elysée with the approval of his people. But a turn in this direction would certainly be disapproved by Pompidou who, for good reasons, had incurred the hostility of the left-wing Gaullists. It is also possible that a touch of rancor may have influenced de Gaulle.* During his disappearance on May 28, Pompidou had taken measures which suggested that he neither expected nor especially desired de Gaulle's return.[34] This was not the attitude of 'unconditional fidelity' to which the latter was accus-

*The description of Pompidou's character and abilities given in the second volume of *Mémoires d'Espoir* is ungenerous and unfair, since it implies that any success the Prime Minister may have had was due to his good fortune in having de Gaulle as President of the Republic.[33]

tomed on the part of his followers. The temptation to deflate
Pompidou's pretensions must have been strong, quite apart from the
political reasons for a change.

The dismissal of the Prime Minister and the choice of Couve de
Murville in his place became known at the beginning of July. After
the resignation of the Pompidou government on July 10 the new
prime minister was officially named next day. There were also two
notable new appointments: Ortoli was changed from minister of
education to finance and Edgar Faure became minister of education.
They were to figure heavily in the policies of the next months.

In an exchange of letters with Pompidou, de Gaulle expressed the
hope that he would hold himself ready "to accomplish any mission
and assume any charge" which might one day be confided to him by
the nation.[35] This was widely taken as a reference to Pompidou's
future candidacy for the presidency—an impression confirmed by de
Gaulle's later remark that Pompidou had been "placed in the reserve
of the Republic" (a phrase that might be used of soldiers, but also of
bottles of wine).[36] There was, in fact, more than a touch of irony in
this way of announcing the change, and it seems unlikely that it was
borne with equanimity by Pompidou.

Couve de Murville, in his opening declaration to the National
Assembly, set himself three objectives: educational reform, "the
opening of a dialogue between employers and workers" in industry,
and regional reform and a transformation of the senate.[37]

It was soon apparent that this program was not universally popular.
On the educational side, Faure's plan for "a democratization of
teaching from the nursery school to the university" was received
coolly by Gaullist deputies. Still less did they like his advocacy of
"liberty of political expression" within the university.[38] At the
beginning of September the political bureau of the UDR declared
itself against any politicization of the university, and, at the party's
conference at La Baule (September 10-12), Pompidou was among
those who implicitly criticized the new minister. However, Faure
received strong support from de Gaulle in the council of ministers
against attacks from Debré and Jeanneney, and, soon afterwards, the
new law dealing with higher education was voted by parliament.[39]

Its spirit was liberal. It provided for the setting-up of councils to administer academic institutions in which all university participants (teachers, students, research fellows, etc.) would be represented. Universities would no longer be governed by a rector nominated by the government, but by an elected head, and they would also become freer to decide their own methods of teaching and curricula without reference to the center. Entry to higher education would not be limited, and a far wider definition of education itself was adopted, taking in sport, the arts, and "an apprenticeship in liberty and responsibility". Finally, political discussion was allowed (even in the *lycées*) and the ban on the political activities of student unions was lifted. The new law was a fairly drastic step in the direction of decentralization and participation. As such it continued to excite the fears of Gaullists who felt that it gave too much to the rebels of May. At the end of 1968, Robert Poujade, the secretary-general of the UDR was to excite an attack on Faure's policy by the CDR, the right-wing Gaullists) of Dijon, and, during the vote in the National Assembly, several right-wing Gaullists (Fouchet, Sanguinetti, Tribou-let) abstained.[40]

Workers' 'participation' in industry was criticized both from the left and the right. The left-wing Gaullists naturally found that it did not go far enough. Both trade unions and employers were suspicious of it for different motives. In reality, profit-sharing and the sharing of increases in the capital value of firms were already in force. What remained was what de Gaulle called "to organize . . . regular informa-tion for everyone about the position and the future of the business to which they contribute their work."[41] All this did not go any further than the ideas of 'social' Catholicism in the early part of the century, but right-wing Gaullists and employers feared that it would be a step toward the *co-gestion* (joint control) of businesses which was felt to be the ultimate objective of the left-wing Gaullists.

But the major political battle of the last nine months of de Gaulle's presidency was to be fought around the establishment of regional councils and the abolition of the senate in its previous form. The second chamber of parliament had always been a stronghold of opposition to the Gaullist régime. Monnerville, the president of the senate, had been one of de Gaulle's main opponents at the referendum of October 1962 and, though he had been replaced by Alain Poher in the autumn of 1968, the tone of the house remained unaltered. It was de Gaulle's intention to end this state of affairs by reducing the senate to a purely consultative role, combining it with the economic and social council and making it into a corporate body connected with regional councils to be formed out of deputies, local dignitaries and representatives of economic and social groups.[42] Thus the unpopular quietus of the senate as a legislative body was associated with the far more welcome creation of a measure of regional autonomy. However, it was also clear that the main purpose served by the referendum, as always under the Fifth Republic, would be that of confounding de Gaulle's critics and vindicating his personal authority. Once again it was a plebiscite for or against a whole régime, and, by connecting with regional reform the reduction of a hostile political fortress, de Gaulle made sure that his intentions were not misunderstood. Once more he "incurred the hostility of the whole political class, local as well as national."[43]

Among the hostile seems to have been numbered Pompidou. His public position during these months was that of a party leader who loyally supports the government, while having secret doubts about its policies. He had criticized the educational policy of Faure, as an ex-banker can be presumed to have had reservations about too strong a dose of 'participation,' and he did not regard a trial of strength on the issue of the regions or the senate as good political tactics. Among the UDR deputies he took the lead in extracting assurances from the government to soothe the fears of his colleagues. By the end of the year he was in a more commanding position within his party than ever. But he was faced with the problem of keeping his name before the general public, since it was only in this way that his candidacy to the succession could be kept alive. His solution was to seek publicity for his claims. On January 17, 1969, while visiting Rome—instructions had been given to the French embassy to seek no special facilities for him—he declared to a group of journalists assembled for the purpose: "Everyone, I think, knows that I will be a candidate in an election for the presidency of the Republic when there is one." Five days later, de Gaulle replied in a declaration to the council of ministers: "In the accomplishment of the national task which devolves upon me I was re-elected, on December 19, 1965, as President of the Republic by the French people for seven years. I have the duty and the intention of fulfilling this mandate to its end."[44]

By this time the two men were in almost open conflict, and the tension was not eased by attempts on the part of some left-wing Gaullists in the Ministry of Justice to involve Pompidou and his wife in the *affaire Markovitch*. This concerned the murder of Stefan Marko-vitch, the bodyguard of the actor Alain Delon. The lawyers of Marcantoni, a dubious figure arrested during the inquiries, demanded the interrogation of Pompidou and his wife by the examining magistrate. The request was not granted.[45] But whoever was respon-sible for this intrigue, miscalculated. De Gaulle could not let his former prime minister be slandered in a manner that recalled the worst precedents of the Third Republic. On March 12 he invited Pompidou and his wife to dinner at the Elysée, thereby showing that he himself gave no credence to the flood of unsavory rumor current in Parisian political circles. This apparent reconciliation was sealed by an ostenta-tious display of loyalty on the ex-Prime Minister's part during the referendum campaign. It was, indeed, his best tactic.

Pompidou's assumption of the position of heir-apparent in the eyes of public opinion had been made all the easier in that there were many signs of the approaching end of a régime. The last nine months of de Gaulle's presidency were dreary ones marked by failure. The Russian invasion of Czechoslovakia at the end of August 1968 appeared to make nonsense of the Gaullist conception of a Europe stretching from "the Atlantic to the Urals." Debré, the foreign minister, might speak of it as "a road accident," but French policy was forced to take account of the consequences. On December 5, Messmer told the National Assembly "We are in the Atlantic alliance, and we will remain in it."[46] It was at this time that General Fourquet, Ailleret's successor as chief-of-staff, in an article in the *Revue de défense nationale*, buried the "all-azimuths" strategy and reinstated the distinction between the Western and Eastern blocs which it had been a purpose of Gaullist policy to remove. At the end of February 1969 the visit of President Nixon to Paris also allowed some reconstruction of the bridges to Washington.

In this context of a mild *rapprochement* with the Anglo-Saxons, the conversation between de Gaulle and the British Ambassador, Christo-pher Soames, on February 4, 1969, may have indicated a new turning in French policy. In the course of the conversation, de Gaulle suggested that there should be bilateral talks between France and Great Britain "to see if the two governments could resolve their differences of conception." He also threw out a hint that the Common Market might be transformed in a way which would take account of British interests—possibly into a free-trade area—and that there should be closer cooperation in European affairs between France, Germany, Great Britain and Italy. Essentially, this was a proposed return to 1958. Instead of France using the European community as a power-base from which Britain had to be excluded, Britain would be used to help destroy a community which had ceased to be politically useful to France.

This was, no doubt, a genuine attempt to find an alternative European policy, but suspicions of de Gaulle were by now so deeply rooted in England's Foreign Office that fear of a trap was the first British reaction. It was feared in London that acceptance of the proposals would be followed by France using them to torpedo support for British entry into the community. De Gaulle was the victim of the mark of his own past devious diplomacy, and it is hard to blame the British government for itself hastening to inform the other EEC members of the conversation. Naturally, the result was a worsening of Anglo-French relations.

The last diplomatic land-mine exploded by de Gaulle was France's withdrawal from the meeting of the Western European Union (WEU) because it was feared in Paris that discussions within that body on the harmonization of Western European foreign policies might lead to talks on British entry and circumvent France's veto in the community.[47]

The 'De Gaulle-Soames' conversation was probably motivated on de Gaulle's part by a conviction of the need to restore a balance in Western Europe or, more bluntly, to find a countervailing force to Germany. In a sense, therefore, it was the direct result of the crisis of the franc in November 1968, which had revealed German economic power and how little the French government could manage to influence even a Francophil administration in Bonn when something really important was at stake.

The economic consequences of "the May events" had been serious. Not only had a rise in the average wage—estimated by one authority as being of 13-14 percent—damaged France's competitive position, but the disorders and the consequent uncertainty had caused massive losses of currency reserves. These losses amounted to $3.5 billion during 1968.[48] Already, on May 29, 1968, $745 million had been drawn from the International Monetary Fund, and this was followed by a further sum of $138 million on June 12. The loss of production and revenue to the treasury due to the strikes was also serious. The budgetary deficit for 1968 was raised from 5.3. billion francs to 12.8.

To meet this situation the Pompidou government and its successor took a series of measures during the summer: currency control, the reintroduction of quotas on some imports, the raising of the bank-rate to 5 percent, attempts to keep prices and wages from rising, heavier taxation and higher charges for public services, aids to exporters. But the currency drain continued, and the abolition of currency control in September combined with the announcement, in the coming budget, of a far heavier inheritance tax served to drive capital abroad.

The size of the deficit in the budget and the general expectation that the differential between French and foreign prices would make devaluation inevitable carried speculation against the franc to a crescendo in November. On November 20 the finance ministers and the governors of the central banks of the so-called Group of Ten (United States, Canada, Japan, Germany, France, Great Britain, Italy, Belgium, Netherlands, Sweden) met in Bonn, and the Paris Bourse was shut from the 20th to the 25th to await the result of this conclave. America, France and Great Britain pressed Germany to revalue the mark and put an end to the wave of speculation. Germany, however, in the person of Franz-Josef Strauss, refused,* All the Germans would do was put a 4 percent tax on exports and give a similar tax rebate to imports.

At this point it seemed certain that the franc would be devalued— probably by less than 10 percent. De Gaulle, however, had other ideas. After a cabinet meeting on November 23, it was announced that there would be no devaluation. The reason for this was put succinctly by Malraux: "Devaluation is contrary to the Gaullist myth. I am against devaluation."[50] This was magnificent, but hardly economics. Nine months later when devaluation had finally been carried through, Giscard d'Estaing, once again minister of finance, revealed that losses of reserves during the first six months of 1969 had run at $300 million a

*The symbolic impact of this refusal can be seen in the headline in *Bild-Zeitung*: "Now the Germans are number 1 in Europe."[49]

month and that, at this rate, France would have had no reserves left by the end of the year had the drain continued.[51] Plainly, the world of international finance had not been impressed by de Gaulle's 'non possumus.'

Meanwhile, Ortoli put into effect a new series of austerity measures. The deficit in the budget was reduced from 11.96 billion francs to 6.35 billion through cuts in government (including military) expenditure. The value-added tax was raised, and more measures taken to discourage price increases. Currency control was reintroduced on November 25 in a more sweeping form than before.[52]

The political results of this hopeless fight to save the franc were disastrous. Such a policy was unpopular with employers, who saw themselves subject to greater and greater fiscal pressure, and with labor, which was affected by the rise in prices allowed for the products of public enterprises (electricity, coal, transport, etc.). Both sides of industry looked askance at public expenditure amounting to some 30 percent of France's GNP. As for the Gaullists, they were irritated by Ortoli and said so in no uncertain terms. The comparison with the Pompidou government was all to the latter's advantage.

Thus de Gaulle and his government approached the referendum against a background of discontent and with diminished prestige. The reform of the senate did not excite much enthusiasm even on the part of Gaullists (not even Gaullist senators were willing to defend it when it was debated).[53] Moreover, the question to be answered by the electorate "Do you approve the attached draft law concerning the creation of regions and the renewal of the Senate?" seemed to make a mockery of the referendum procedure (the law consisted of 68 complex articles). The *Conseil d'Etat* too was once again of the opinion that to submit the law on the senate to a referendum was unconstitutional.

In March a public opinion poll showed that while 54 percent of Frenchmen were favorable to regional reform, only 26 percent wanted to change the senate. It is small wonder that Gaullist commentators (including Jeanneney, the minister of state who had drafted the law) tried to suggest that a negative vote would not necessarily mean a rejection of de Gaulle by the electorate. This interpretation, however, was firmly set aside by the President himself in a television interview with Michel Droit on April 10: "From the country's answer to what I ask of it will naturally depend either the continuation of my mandate, or else my immediate departure."[54]

It was now evident that a large section of French opinion was hostile to de Gaulle's continued presence at the head of affairs. The left, despite a perennial tendency to split (the transformation of the Federation into the *Parti Socialiste* had caused the withdrawal of the radicals) could at least agree to say no. Giscard d'Estaing had declared the hostility of himself and the Independent Republicans to a referendum as far back as December, and, at the official opening of the campaign, announced that he would vote *No*. The Faure reforms had not conciliated the left or the students who continued to agitate (often violently), but they had profoundly annoyed some of the Gaullists and many officials. For the first time the official caste, the *Polytéchniciens* and graduates of the *Ecole nationale d'administration* (ENA), began to desert the Gaullist banners. They had been for de Gaulle as long as he could insure the execution of measures they deemed administratively necessary, but "the May events" and, even more, the refusal to devalue had convinced them that he had lost his touch. Together with the world of business, they had concluded that there must be a change. Moreover, a change was now possible. The existence of Pompidou provided an alternative without risks, a return to a leader of proven ability, whose conservatism now appeared more in tune both with the times and with bourgeois France than did that of de Gaulle. Fundamentally, those left-wing Gaullists who held Pompidou responsible for de Gaulle's defeat and resignation in April 1969 were not wrong. But it was the ex-Prime Minister's very plausibility as an alternative which did the damage.

As April 27 approached, the public opinion polls became steadily more threatening. Poher, the president of the senate, had proved unexpectedly effective as leader of the opposition to the changes, and pressure to get Pompidou to announce his refusal to stand as president in the event of de Gaulle's defeat brought no results. The tried remedy of a television interview, again with Michel Droit, failed to turn the tide of opinion, and a last-minute broadcast appeal was no better received. By the afternoon of April 25 de Gaulle himself had no illusions. "Tout est foutu," he remarked to one of his staff and gave orders for the Elysée files to be removed the moment the victory of the

No's was confirmed.[55] The last public opinion poll published in *Le Figaro* on April 25 showed 53 percent *No* against 47 percent *Yes*. In the event, the results were slightly worse: 53.18 percent *No* and 46.81 percent *Yes* of votes cast.* A statement from Colombey immediately announced the resignation of the President of the Republic. He was temporarily succeeded, as the Constitution provided, by Poher, the president of the senate, who found empty files and bare offices in the Elysée and a government some members of which refused to shake hands with him.

On June 15, 1969, Georges Pompidou was elected President of the Republic on the second ballot with 57.6 percent of the votes cast against Poher's 42.4 percent. He chose Jacques Chaban-Delmas as his first prime minister, and the new government included men of the center such as Pleven and Duhamel. A new political era had begun—an era which de Gaulle himself had done much to bring about, but which was hardly to be conducted in his spirit. The ex-President, however, saw little enough of the reign of his successor. On November 9, 1970, he died of a heart attack in his home at Colombey a few days before his eightieth birthday. After all, he was not fated to play the part, under the new régime, of the Commander's statue in *Don Giovanni*.[57]

---

*In terms of eligible voters the percentage results were: No: 41.68; Yes: 36.68; Abstentions: 19.41; Invalid: 2.21.[56]

Conclusion and Aftermath

*On doit savoir... que je suis étranger à ce qui
se passe. Ça ne me concerne aucunement. Ce
n'est pas ce que j'ai voulu. C'est autre chose.*
— Charles de Gaulle. 1969.

*Une chose connue de tout le monde est la
facilité avec laquelle notre pays se réorganise.*
— Ernest Renan.

After the departure and death of the creator of Gaullism two
questions remain to be answered about the nature of this considerable
phenomenon. First, what was Gaullism in terms of French history and
political categories? Secondly, can it be said to have continued in a real
sense under the successor régime of President Pompidou? Of course,
the two questions are really one and the same. On the definition given
to Gaullism will depend whether or not we believe its main characteristics to have survived, and to be likely to continue to survive the
disappearance of its founder. If we regard as Gaullist a political party
calling itself by that name and appealing vociferously to the sacred
memory of a heroic national figure, then there is little doubt that the
UDR, under Pompidou as under de Gaulle, is Gaullist. If Gaullism is
thought to imply a comradeship established by history and, hence, a
tendency to indulge in the nostalgia and grumbling of the old soldier,
there has been plenty of occasion for that since 1969, and a section of
Gaullists seem in danger of becoming what the political pamphleteer

Emmanuel Berl once called "le parti de la rouspétance" (*rouspétance* = grumbling in a strong sense). If the *force de frappe* is one of the pillars of Gaullist policy, it still exists, sustained by a loyal caryatid in the shape of Michel Debré.

Naturally enough, there is plenty of continuity between the two presidencies of the Fifth Republic. But the task of the political analyst is not to state the obvious, but to detect trends that may dominate the future, distinguishing them carefully from the flotsam left behind by the past. Nor should he be deceived by the banners under which parties do battle. The Second Empire was Bonapartist if we consider its ostentatious evocation of a great historical ghost. It was hardly Bonapartist at all if the phrase is to be taken as implying the continuation of Napoleon I's policies. Similarly, no successor to de Gaulle could be expected not to take advantage of a familiar, emotive label, but it would appear unlikely, *a priori*, that the content of his policies would be precisely the same.

Gaullists themselves have given varying expression to what they believed their political principles to be. For the Gaullist minister Edmond Michelet, the heart of Gaullism was "a state of mind made up of permanent enthusiasm, of irreducible confidence in the destinies of France." For an intellectual pamphleteer like Jacques Bloch-Morhange, it was "the national pride." Olivier Guichard has spoken of "a fidelity towards the state, an acute sense of our responsibilities towards that state ... , " and Robert Poujade, a *protégé* of Pompidou, of "a mystique of national unity." On the right wing of Gaullism, Alexandre Sanguinetti has identified its mission as "preparing France to meet the 21st century in good conditions"; on the left, Louis Vallon as that of "suppressing the alienation suffered by the working class and overcoming the contradictions of classical capitalism." André Malraux once defined Gaullism in terms of the contrast between the historical figure of de Gaulle and the common run of politicians, and in his last conversation with the General, the latter answered him with his own personal interpretation of the movement as "the élan of our country, the rediscovered élan."

Behind all these phrases with their varying emphasis lies a common nationalism springing originally from the seering experience of 1940.

Left-wing and right-wing Gaullists might disagree about the nature of the tasks to which their patriotic fervor should address itself, but they were agreed on the supreme importance of holding "a certain idea of France." It was this which, during de Gaulle's term of office, made them, as Guichard put it, "belong to the same flock" in the evangelical sense of the word. Gaullism, therefore, is primarily a form—the latest form—of French nationalism, and, as such, it has connections with Jacobinism, Bonapartism and the nationalist right of the Third Republic.

But, unlike that of the doctrinaire nationalism of *Action française* and its followers, the spirit of Gaullism has never been narrowly sectarian. De Gaulle's own temperament and the experience of the Second World War prevented him from imitating the mass excommunication of whole classes of Frenchmen, to which the French right, under the influence of Maurras, was so prone before 1940. The necessities of wartime Gaullism meant that it had its roots in republican France as well as in the more obvious tradition of French nationalism. The rancor that might be felt by Gaullists towards a Lecanuet or the Communist "separatists" did not, theoretically at least, change the feeling that all categories of Frenchmen ought to be Gaullists in so far as they were Frenchmen. The fact that they were not could be put down to contingent circumstances—to the perversity of journalists and intellectuals or the resentment of baffled politicians—but made no difference to the attempt to assemble all sorts and conditions of Frenchmen into one common movement which, ideally, would be the national community itself. Gaullism was not exclusive of social or racial groups or of sections of French history. So far as France was concerned the movement was oecumenical, and, in this, faithfully reflected the inclinations of its leader.

To view Gaullism as a nationalist movement assembling Frenchmen of widely differing political persuasions behind a prestigious leader is to recall similar previous episodes in French history—in particular that of the great "assembler" who overcame the divisions of Frenchmen after the revolution: Napoleon Bonaparte. The historian of the French right, Professor Rémond, has demonstrated convincingly the continuity of Gaullism with the Bonapartist tradition of nationalism and plebiscitary democracy. (The claim made by Gaullists like Malraux, or even Debré, to be the heirs of the Jacobin revolutionary tradition would in itself be enough to distinguish them from other French right-wing figures whose beliefs were formed in opposition to those of Robespierre and Saint-Just.) The practical expression of the willingness to merge conflicting currents of French history was de Gaulle's ability to attract left-wing votes when his own person was in question.

But France's 'rank' was as important as its unity. A Jacobin readiness to go to any lengths to insure the safety of the state, the centralizing traditions of the *ancien régime*, a Gallican approach to religion and a confident reliance on the innate superiority of French culture all blended together in Gaullism in a synthesis aimed at producing both national unity at home and the most striking assertion possible of France's mission abroad. Once the sterile contradiction between right and left was overcome, so Gaullist doctrine maintained, it would be possible to release the energies of the nation for the task of establishing France's position in the world at large. Behind the Bonapartist feeling of unification, which runs like a thread in French nineteenth century history from Napoleon to Boulanger, can be felt this aspiration to set internal feuds aside the better to assert the national destiny.

It was also of the essence of Bonapartism that this national feeling should be incarnated in a leader/saviour who could appear as the expression of the popular will. The plebiscitary procedure of the referendum, which on so many occasions sealed the 'compact' between de Gaulle and the French people, circumvented the 'intermediary' powers of parties and parliament and assured the triumph of the 'general will.' As in many Latin countries, nationalism in France is most effective when personified in some outstanding individual. In one of its aspects Gaullism is a version of that Mediterranean tendency toward *caudillismo*, seen at its most baroque in Latin America.

The institutions of a personified nationalism were inevitably government by referendum and the election of the head of state by direct popular vote. The Constitution which de Gaulle gave to France has so far proved to be one of his most solid achievements, surviving both the crisis of May 1968 and the difficult transition of April 1969. But it remains to be seen whether the double-edged weapon of the referendum can be used by a successor and, if not, whether the president of the republic will not become more and more dependent on the possession of an adequate parliamentary majority to support his chosen government. A diminution in the plebiscitary character of Gaullism would imply a transition toward a more parliamentary form of democracy which would profoundly change the nature of the régime and, in effect, restore the conditions of the Third or Fourth Republics.

As an expression of nationalism Gaullism could naturally be all things to all men, satisfying widely different requirements on the part of adherents whose individual views of France's future conflicted with one another. In terms of economics, for a right-wing Gaullist the emphasis in industrial policy could be on expansion and modernization, while on the left, the followers of Capitant or Vallon could point to "participation" and the necessity of bridging the crevasse between capital and labor. Thus an uneasy balance was established which de Gaulle himself could arbitrate.

Yet those Marxists who saw in Gaullism a movement of the right expressing a "neo-capitalist infrastructure" were not entirely wrong. 'Participation' was always unwelcome to the average French worker, and the left-wing Gaullists, except for a brief period from May 1968 to April 1969, enjoyed little power as anything other than an intellectual pressure group. Gaullism, as François Goguel has pointed out, found its electoral clientele in the "industrially advanced" areas of France. In some sense Gaullism was the political expression on the right of that modernization, although it never received much support from a *patronat* which preferred a more traditional type of conservatism.

In terms of foreign affairs, however, both the right and the left wings of Gaullism could unite in supporting a policy whose striking gestures satisfied the chauvinism of the one and the desire for moral superiority of the other. Under de Gaulle the far-ranging diplomacy of the Fifth Republic was the principal banner around which Gaullists could assemble. This fact was, of course, hardly coincidental: nationalism invariably defines itself most clearly vis-à-vis foreign competitors. For de Gaulle himself foreign policy (in which national defense was included) was the palladium of the Fifth Republic—the shrine to whose service the whole national effort was directed. It is a striking fact that "the May events" took place at precisely the moment when Gaullist foreign policy appeared to have run out of steam and its real failure (stemming from de Gaulle's inability either to dissolve the Europe of the Six or carry it with him) had begun to become apparent. The primacy he had attributed to foreign affairs made a loss of momentum in this domain especially dangerous.

Gaullism, therefore, can be defined as French nationalism personified in the figure of a national saviour and inheriting the streak of plebiscitary democracy which runs through French history from Bonaparte onward and blurs the distinction between right and left. Although Gaullism might be associated with economic expansion and a new industrial revolution (a legacy from the Fourth Republic), it also had as its ambition the reconciliation of capital and labor in the name of a united national community—an ideal handed down from the 'social' Catholicism of earlier days. And this newly recreated national unity—the "great people brought together" of de Gaulle's imagination—was to be placed at the service of a foreign policy which would both offer it an enterprise commensurate with its greatness and assert for it a place in the contemporary world analogous to that which it had once known in history.

What has been described here is the 'presidential', the 'Gaullien' Gaullism of the General's own presidency. It was an irony of history that, as we have seen, these aspirations could only find a suitable political instrument in a *party* whose electoral clientele and many of whose leaders came to be less and less in sympathy with the loftier elements of the Gaullien vision, however deep a respect they themselves might feel for the President of the Republic. From being a movement which claimed to unite Frenchmen of the left and the right Gaullism became a political party of the right and was, indeed, pushed farther in that direction by "the May events" at the very moment when de Gaulle himself felt the time had come to emphasize the social aims of the movement. Out of 'presidential' Gaullism emerged an 'electoral' Gaullism whose real leader was Pompidou and whose concerns were very different from the 'heights' toward which de Gaulle saw himself as encouraging the French people. To be the federator of the French right was a far remove from being the unifier of France. De Gaulle had wished to be the latter and, almost unconsciously, had become the former. As for Pompidou, he was quite willing to assume the inheritance of a modernized conservatism without attempting to elevate this solid achievement on to the messianic level at which the policies of his predecessor existed.

It was, therefore, quite natural that what seemed at first a divergence in style between de Gaulle and Pompidou should gradually have developed into a divergence in policies. The Pompidou presidency is both more political and more conservative in a traditional sense than that of de Gaulle. Parliament has begun once again to play a role as something other than the loyal supporter of government policies. The different factions of Gaullism have sprung to life from the torpor in which the presence of the General at the Elysée had kept them slumbering.

The left-wing Gaullists were the first to suffer from the change. 'Participation' had been rejected in the April referendum and was thus conveniently buried, and the dropping of Edgar Faure as minister of education from the new Chaban-Delmas government marked both the abandonment of Faure's attempt to introduce this principle into the university and the beginning of a gradually tougher attitude on the part of the authorities towards dissident students. With the deaths of Capitant and Michelet and the expulsion from the party of Vallon (after his publication of a virulent pamphlet directed against the new President), the left-wing Gaullists saw their influence reduced to a vanishing-point and themselves condemned to nostalgia.

On the right, too, a group of true-blue Gaullists, including such figures as Couve de Murville, Messmer, Fouchet and Jacques Vendroux (de Gaulle's own brother-in-law), watched suspiciously for signs of deviation from policies hallowed by association with the General himself. When, in March 1971, the UDR party managers decided to ally themselves, during the municipal elections in Lyon, with a list containing the name of Soustelle, Fouchet and Vendroux resigned from the party in protest. Debré, however, remained in the government watching over the *force de frappe*, and without him, the right-wing *purs des purs*—the purest of the pure—lacked a leader, Couve de Murville's failure to secure a seat in the assembly seriously handicapping him for the position. Almost immediately afterwards there was another incident involving an old Gaullist. René Tomasini, the secretary-general of the UDR and an old associate of Debré, attacked the judiciary for being insufficiently harsh with students and members of violent left-wing splinter groups and had to be rebuked by the government—an incident which did not exactly improve the position of the 'hard-line' Gaullists.

If the UDR showed signs of remembering that it was a coalition composed of many different nuances of political belief, there were also symptoms of change in other directions—notably in that of foreign policy. Some of de Gaulle's more personal policies—the ostentatious attacks on the United States or the support for a 'free' Quebec—were quietly dropped. Others, like the concept of a Mediterranean policy based on a 'special relationship' with Algeria, collapsed or, like the veto on negotiations between Great Britain and the European Economic Community, were changed. At the Hague conference in the autumn of 1969 Pompidou was prepared to end France's boycott of further European integration, and at the time of writing (May 1971), it looks as though the issue of British entry into the Common Market may be the occasion for a collision between him and the hard core of the Gaullist faithful. Another difference with the previous régime was underlined when the new President visited black Africa where de Gaulle had not appeared after 1958.

But the greatest difference was in tone rather than in specific policies. Under Pompidou the Fifth Republic no longer seemed to accord that absolute priority to its external relations which had been the case under de Gaulle. Defense and foreign affairs were no longer the *'partie noble'* of government. That title increasingly seemed to fall to economic policy. Giscard d'Estaing at the ministry of finance was a more powerful figure than Maurice Schumann at the Quai d'Orsay, partly because of his independent party support, but also because this distribution of influence reflected the preoccupations of the President of the Republic.

Under Pompidou's presidency the Fifth Republic's device was to be "prosperity and order." These, in fact, were the achievements which the French electorate had always valued in Gaullism. De Gaulle's return to power in 1958 had been based on his ability to bring order out of potential civil war, and economic prosperity had been the measure by which his administration was most commonly judged by Frenchmen after the Algerian crisis was over. But, in addition to these politically attractive concepts, there was under de Gaulle the priority given to France's place in the world and the distinctly unpopular expenditure of money on nuclear armaments to maintain it. Gaullism, in fact, always contained within itself a potential conflict between a policy of *grandeur* and a policy of *interests*—a conflict which recalls the similar tug-of-war under the Second Empire of Louis-Napoléon. Even de Gaulle himself could not decide the debate purely in favor of *grandeur*. France's immediate *interests* for example, dictated that it should remain within the European community on economic grounds, whereas de Gaulle's own instincts might have led him to favor withdrawal. But the realistic element in his political thought never allowed him totally to neglect facts or to make the ultimate concessions to the national myth which he had evoked.

Pompidou, on the other hand, has only been restrained in his abandonment of *grandeur* by the opinions of other Gaullists whose reverence for past glories made them ready to denounce any change as a departure from orthodoxy. His has been a policy of *interests*—of order and prosperity—all the more welcome to the Gaullist electorate in that May 1968 had seemed to threaten both. It was only among the faithful who remembered the heroic days of wartime Gaullism that these limited objectives failed to satisfy. The main ingredient of 'integral' Gaullism is now nostalgia, and, though there may be sudden acts of rebellion against the present leadership of the movement, any permanent reversion from the new line seems unlikely.

In the long run the Gaullism of de Gaulle himself seems bound to disappear as a major political element in French life, remaining only as a current of intellectual intransigence, a touchstone of national sentiment which will, no doubt, be used against French presidents and prime ministers by all those who feel that something is rotten in the state of France or in a Europe where France does not receive its 'due.' Pure Gaullist feeling may, indeed, retreat to the periphery of politics—to an area where the use of English within the European community appears as more important than the European balance of power. Powerlessness leads to cultural, if not to ideological, politics, and there are already signs of a stiffening in the intellectual joints of the most orthodox among the Gaullists.

As to the French party system, the most likely area of change will be within the present majority party itself. The creation of a federation of the right ought to produce an answering phenomenon on the left, but for any such left-wing coalition to be effective, there would have to be a great deal more flexibility on the part of the Communists, and this process, while perhaps already in motion, has a long way to go yet. Pompidou's brand of modern conservatism, moreover, has considerable freedom of maneuver. It can appeal to the 'Centrists' and, on the left, to some of the Radicals, and, while enlarging its parliamentary base and adopting less rigid policies, it need not lose the support of more than a few hard-line Gaullists. The UDR and its Independent Republican allies remain a loose coalition which is bound to become looser, but which will not necessarily fall apart unless very grave mistakes are made by its leaders. "Moroseness"—the fashionable name in France for party discontent—will hardly bring the régime down, and there is wide scope for adroit politicians to play off factions against one another, producing alternative combinations of power which will act as safety valves for the repressed feelings of the politically minded. (Much of the trouble which Pompidou has so far had with his own party is due to the fact that the average party 'militant' is usually less intelligent than the average member of the general public. In the CDRs of the provinces undoubtedly lurk Gaullist neanderthalers who, were their advice heeded, would have a disastrous effect on the fortunes of the régime.)

It is, therefore, possible to imagine that the conservative coalition which, at present, calls itself Gaullist will become receptive to new influences from the center and left and, in so doing, will lose many of the traces of its origins. The name of de Gaulle will continue to be inscribed upon its banners, but as time takes its toll of surviving wartime Gaullists, the principles of de Gaulle will have less and less influence upon its behavior. The movement might, of course, be split by a sudden schism. If a considerable number of hard-line Gaullists behaved like Fouchet and Vendroux, then the present supremacy of the

UDR might be endangered. But too many sentimental memories—not to speak of more material attractions—bind Gaullists, even of the strictest sect, to the idea that the president's government must be carried on for such a brutal rupture to appear probable. Moreover, Pompidou is almost certainly too skillful a politician not to be able to divide his right-wing opposition. The defection of Fouchet and Vendroux, the indiscretion of Tomasini were answered by taking Messmer into the government. Meanwhile the UDR continues to extend its electoral grip even if (as in the local elections of March 1971) the results are not always up to the expectations of its leaders.

It should now be possible to estimate just how far the Fifth Republic has moved away from what de Gaulle had made of it. France is no longer governed by plebiscite. Politics in the party and parliamentary sense are coming to life again. A party chieftain has replaced a president whose desire originally was to be an arbitrator. French policy is no longer geared to the primacy of foreign affairs over all the other activities of government. More modern economic doctrines have replaced the devotion to the supreme value of gold as a measure of successful national housekeeping, and this change from Poincaré to Keynes has been symbolized by the devaluation of the franc—a fact noted, not without bitterness, by de Gaulle in his *Mémoires d'Espoir*. The atmosphere of the Fifth Republic has changed. Where before the tone was one of grandeur, frequently falling into grandiloquence, bread and butter politics are now the order of the day. Negotiation, intrigue even, have replaced obedience to imperious commands. The eagles and kettle-drums of the First Empire have been transformed into the furniture of the bourgeois monarchy of Louis Philippe (which, it is true, placed the inscription "A toutes les gloires de la France" upon the pediment of Versailles) or even into the moneyed radicalism of the Third Republic. The reign of normality has begun again after an episode during which exemplary drama appeared to be the customary mode of political action.

For it is now possible to see that the Gaullism of de Gaulle was an episode. With all its faults and all its myth-making, it represented a perceptible aspiration toward a greater degree of national unity, a more dynamic form of political cohesion, an aspiration which may inspire respect as an ideal. But for better or for worse, there are limits to the ability of political leaders to breathe their spirit into their fellow-countrymen. At moments of crisis men will devote themselves to an ideal or a country with passion and self-abnegation, but, in ordinary times, they will remember their ordinary interests and find the air of the summits chill. It is a mistake to forget either the Don Quixote or the Sancho Panza who, as George Orwell once remarked, lurk in all of us. There are moments when the giants of historical destiny seen by the national saviour appear to the citizen as windmills, and the historian may be allowed the comment that it is good that they should so appear. Gaullism was prevented from falling into the excesses of other modern, myth-inspired movements both by the disillusioned and self-critical character of its leader and by the circumstances in which it arose, but a return to everyday politics can hardly be regretted. That the transition has brought about no more than "morosity" is a final tribute to the adaptability of the institutions with which de Gaulle endowed France.

When all is said and done, the story of Gaullism remains astonishing and paradoxical. Of de Gaulle himself it might be said that if, during the thirty odd years of his active political life, he often failed to obtain what he wished, it was because he was fighting history—a combat few politicians have cared to undertake. His statement to Malraux "But I was not mistaken about the destiny of France" resounds like a cry of triumph—or of defiance. As for the men he first gathered about him and then led for three decades, it is possible now to see how much they depended on him for inspiration and direction. The Gaullism which survived de Gaulle, the great party of the right which is his incongruous monument, is but one example of the paradox of history which has so often decreed that a swan's egg should hatch some different, less noble, but ultimately more edible bird.

France was lucky to have a de Gaulle on the two occasions when it desperately needed him, but he himself would not have regarded it as luck, assured as he was that his presence at the crucial hour was only one more example of a national destiny ever *in extremis*—staggering from misfortune to triumph with the aid of leaders doomed to redress a balance which had turned against their country.

Notes

Abbreviations used in Reference to Works often Quoted

Charles de Gaulle: *La Discorde chez l'ennemi*. Paris, 1924. (Berger-Levrault) *DE*

Charles de Gaulle: *Le Fil de l'Epée*. Paris, 1964. (Collection 10/18) *FE*
The Edge of the Sword. Translated by Gerard Hopkins. New York, 1960. (Criterion Books)

Charles de Gaulle: *Vers l'armée de métier*. Paris, 1963. (Presses Pocket). *AM*
The Army of the Future. Foreword by Walter Millis. New York, 1941. (J.B. Lippincott Company)

Charles de Gaulle: *La France et son armée*. Paris, 1965. (Collection 10/18). *FA*

Charles de Gaulle: *Trois Etudes*. Paris, 1945. (Berger-Levrault) *TE*

Charles de Gaulle: *Mémoires de Guerre: L'Appel 1940-1942*. Paris, 1954. (Plon) *MI*
Mémoires de Guerre: L'Unité 1942-1944. Paris, 1956. (Plon) *MII*
Mémoires de Guerre: Le Salut 1944-1946. Paris, 1959. (Plon) *MIII*
War Memoirs: The Call to Honour 1940-1942. Translated by Jonathan Griffin. London, 1955. (Collins)
War Memoirs: Unity 1942-1944. Translated by Richard Howard. New York, 1959. (Simon & Schuster)
War Memoirs: Salvation 1944-1946. Translated by Richard Howard. New York, 1960. (Simon & Schuster)

Charles de Gaulle: *Discours et Messages*. Vol.I: *Pendant la Guerre* (Juin 1940–Janvier 1946). Vol.II: *Dans l'Attente* (Février 1946–Avril 1958). Vol.III: *Avec le Renouveau* (Mai 1958–Juillet 1962). Vol.IV: *Pour l'effort* (Août 1962–Décembre 1965). Vol.V: *Vers le Terme* (Janvier 1966–Avril 1969). Paris, 1970. (Plon). *DM.I.II.III.IV.V.*

Charles de Gaulle: *Mémoires d'Espoir: Le Renouveau 1958-1962*. Paris, 1970. (Plon) *MEI*
Mémoires d'Espoir: L'effort 1962 . . . Paris, 1970. (Plon) *MEII*

André Passeron: *De Gaulle parle*. Paris, 1962. (Plon) *PI*

André Passeron: *De Gaulle parle 1962-1966*. Paris, 1966. (Fayard) *PII*

Note on Translations

The translations of de Gaulle's works used in the test are the official ones noted above. Where the meaning needed to be made clearer I have occasionally amended them. In other cases I have made my own translation, though for the speeches, I have sometimes used the official English text put out by the information services of the French embassy (*Major Addresses, Statements and Press Conferences of General Charles de Gaulle.* May 19th, 1958–January 31st, 1964 and March 17th, 1964–May 16th, 1967. New York: French Embassy, Press and Information Division). In the notes the page numbers refer to the original French text of the book in question.

I. De Gaulle's Doctrine:
The Roots of Gaullism

1. "Toute ma vie, je me suis fait une certaine idée de la France. Le sentiment me l'inspire aussi bien que la raison. Ce qu'il y a, en moi, d'affectif imagine naturellement la France, telle la princesse des contes ou la madone aux fresques des murs, comme vouée à une destinée éminente et exceptionelle. J'ai, d'instinct, l'impression que la Providence l'a créée pour des succès achevés ou des malheurs exemplaires. S'il advient que la médiocrité marque, pourtant, ses faits et gestes, j'en éprouve la sensation d'une absurde anomalie, imputable aux fautes des Français, non au génie de la patrie. Mais aussi, le côté positif de mon esprit me convainc que la France n'est réellement elle-même qu'au premier rang; que, seules, de vastes entreprises sont susceptibles de compenser les ferments de dispersion que son peuple porte en lui-même . . . "(*MI*, p. 1.)

2. "Vieille France, accablée d'Histoire, meurtrie de guerres et de révolutions, allant et venant sans relâche de la grandeur au déclin, mais redressée, de siècle en siècle, par le génie du renouveau! "(*MIII*, p. 290.)

3. "qui sont, certes, très différents les uns des autres, qui ont chacun son âme à soi, son Histoire à soi, sa langue à soi, ses malheurs, ses gloires, ses ambitons à soi, mais . . . qui sont les seules entités qui aient le droit d'ordonner et l'autorité pour agir." (*DMIII*, pp. 244-245.)

4. "l'intérêt supérieur de l'espèce humaine commande que chaque Nation soit responsable d'elle-même . . . . " (*DMIII*, p. 356.)

5. "La vie est la vie, autrement dit un combat, pour une nation comme pour un homme." (*DMIV*, p. 319.)

6. "La France fut faite à coups d'épée." (*FA*, p. 9.)

7. "quand il avait vu en moi la France comme un Etat ambitieux qui paraissait vouloir recouvrer sa puissance en Europe et au delà des mers, Churchill avait, naturellement, senti passer dans son âme quelque souffle de l'âme de Pitt." (*MIII*, p. 204.)

8. "C'est la raison qui dicte les pactes." (*DMI*, p. 488.)

9. "Une fois de plus, il est prouvé que pour un peuple, si résolu et puissant qu'il soit, l'ambition effrénée de dominer les autres peut arracher des succès plus ou moins éclatants et plus ou moins prolongés, mais que le terme est l'effondrement." (*DMI*, p. 548.)

10. "nous ne croyons pas du tout que l'intérêt, l'honneur, l'avenir de la France soient liés au maintien . . . de sa domination sur des populations dont la grande majorité ne fait pas partie de son peuple et que tout porte et portera de plus en plus à s'affranchir et à s'appartenir." (*DMIII*, p. 339.)

11. J-R. Tournoux, *La Tragédie du Général* (Paris: Plon, 1967), pp. 307-308.

12. "le corps militaire est l'expression la plus complète de l'esprit d'une société." (*AM*, p. 184.)

13. "Sans la force, en effet, pourrait-on concevoir la vie? Qu'on empêche de naître, qu'on stérilise les esprits, qu'on glace les âmes, qu'on endorme les besoins, alors, sans doute, la force disparaîtra d'un monde immobile. Sinon, rien ne fera qu'elle ne demeure indispensable. Recours de la pensée, instrument de l'action, condition du mouvement, il faut cette accoucheuse pour tirer au jour le progrès. Pavois des maîtres, rempart des trônes, bélier des révolutions, on lui doit tour à tour l'ordre et la liberté. Berceau des cités, sceptre des empires, fossoyeur de décadences la force fait la loi aux peuples et leur règle leur destin." (*FE*, pp. 10-11.)

14. "un inéluctable élément, comme la naissance et comme la mort . . . " (*AM*, p. 86.)

15. "Nulle sorte de lutte n'est, au total, plus sanglante que celle des nations armées." (*AM*, p. 86.)

16. "se gardant d'abstractions mais goûtant les réalités, préférant l'utile au sublime, l'opportun au retentissant, cherchant, pour chaque problème particulier, la solution non point idéale mais pratique, peu scrupuleuse quant aux moyens, grande, toutefois, par l'observation d'une juste proportion entre le but poursuivi et les forces de l'Etat." (*FA*, p. 59.)

17. *Rôle historique des places françaises* is to be found in *TE*, pp. 3-58.

18. Cf. his remarks in *AM*, p. 18.

19. "cette Sarre à qui la nature des choses, découverte par notre victoire, désigne une fois de plus sa place auprès de nous . . . " (*DMII*, p. 9.)

20. "Il s'agit de répondre, en effet, au souhait obscur des hommes à qui l'infirmité de leurs organes fait désirer la perfection du but, qui, bornés dans leur nature, nourrissent des voeux infinis et, mesurant chacun sa petitesse, acceptent l'action collective pourvu qu'elle tende à quelque chose de grand." (*FE*, p. 86.)

21. "Il faudrait savoir, en effet, si quelque grand rêve national n'est pas nécessaire

M

à un peuple pour soutenir son activité et conserver sa cohésion." (*AM*, p. 76.)

22. "Le bandeau lui couvrant les yeux, il frappe à faux de grands coups, se prodigue à contresens, charge héroïquement les murs. Puis, déconfit, mais redressé par l'amour-propre, il se trouve face à face avec la réalité et lui arrache ses voiles. Alors il l'étreint, la domine, la pénètre, en tire toutes les délices de la gloire." (*AM*, p. 30.)

23. "Dans le jardin à la française, aucun arbre ne cherche à étouffer les autres de son ombre, les parterres s'accommodent d'être géométriquement dessinés, le bassin n'ambitionne pas de cascade, les statues ne prétendent point s'imposer seules à l'admiration. Une noble mélancolie s'en dégage parfois. Peut-être vient-elle du sentiment que chaque élément, isolé, eût pu briller davantage. Mais c'eût été au dommage de l'ensemble, et le promeneur se félicite de la règle qui imprime au jardin sa magnifique harmonie." (*DE*, p. x.)

24. "le goût caractéristique des entreprises démesurées, la passion d'étendre, coûte que coûte, leur puissance personelle, le mépris des limites tracées par l'expérience humaine, le bon sens et la loi." (*DE*, p. viii.)

25. "sa marque d'équilibre dans les nuances et d'union dans la diversité." (*AM*, p. 29.)

26. "rien ne pourrait nous faire oublier que sa grandeur est la condition *sine qua non* de la paix du monde. Il n'y aurait pas de justice si justice n'était pas rendue à la France! " (*DMI*, p. 136.)

27. "Notre pays de ciel nuancé, de relief varié, de sol fertile, nos campagnes du beau blé, du bon vin, de la viande de choix, notre industrie des objets fins, des produits achevés, des articles de luxe, nos dons d'initiative, d'adaptation, d'amour-propre, font de nous, par excellence, la race des actions d'éclat et des groupements sélectionnés." (*AM*, pp. 92-93.)

28. "Rêve français, par excellence, celui d'un monde organisé, où la rigueur des lois, la modération des désirs, l'ubiquité des gendarmes, garantiraient à tous la paix et à chacun son domaine." (*AM*, p. 26.)

29. "Confondre l'intérêt permanent de la France avec un grand idéal humain, voilà qui serait beau et, en même temps, profitable." (*AM*, pp. 78-79.)

30. "Vieux monde, toujours nouveau, qui reçut, de siècle en siècle, la marque profonde de la France et qui attend en secret qu'elle vienne encore montrer le chemin! " (*DMII*, p. 373.)

31. "Que la France ait été exposée aux plus grands périls possibles, il n'en pouvait être autrement . . . cette conjonction de facteurs géographiques, matériels, spirituels, qui a fait de la France ce qu'elle est, la vouait . . . à rester en vedette des événements et à courir d'insignes dangers." (*DMI*, p. 548.)

32. "la loi éternelle qui fait de nous l'avant-garde d'une civilisation fondée sur le droit des peuples et le respect de la personne humaine." (*DMI*, p. 549.)

33. "Ils confessaient la France, ils ne confessaient que la France." (*DMI*, p.470.)

34. "l'intérêt supérieur de la France,–lequel est tout autre chose que l'avantage immédiat des Français . . . " (*MIII*, p. 28.)

35. Jacques Dumaine, *Quai d'Orsay (1945-1951)* (Paris: Juillard, 1956), pp. 282-283.

36. André Malraux, *Antimémoires* (Paris: Gallimard, 1967), p. 140.

37. "un grand peuple rassemblé . . . " (*DMI*, p. 646.)

38. "le ciment de l'unité française, c'est le sang des français . . . " (*DMI*, p. 236.)

39. "l'unité nationale signifie . . . que l'intérêt commun doit s'imposer à tout le monde." (*DMI*, p. 658.)

40. "Ah! je sais bien que pour répandre et maintenir dans les masses d'hommes et de femmes, si divers par leurs caractères, leurs activités, leurs intérêts, dont se compose éternellement la France, l'esprit auquel elles aspirent, il faut un puissant et constant appel, il faut un grand mouvement des âmes." (*DMI*, p. 531.)

41. Robert Sherwood, *Roosevelt and Hopkins: An Intimate History* (New York: Harper and Bros., 1948), p. 956.

42. "Nous avons vu se créer en France une sorte de mystique dont nous sommes le centre et qui unit, peu à peu, tous les éléments de résistance. C'est ainsi que nous sommes, par la force des choses, devenus une entité morale française." (*MII*, p. 383.)

43. "Que voulez-vous . . . ? Il est un fait dont ils ne se décident pas à tenir compte, un fait essentiel pourtant et qui fait échec à tous leurs calculs; ce fait c'est de Gaulle. Je ne le comprends pas toujours bien moi-même . . . mais j'en suis prisonnier." (Robert Buron. *Carnets politiques de la guerre d'Algérie* [Paris: Plon, 1965], p. 159.)

44. "Car les féodalités . . . sont d'accord pour s'opposer à l'établissement d'un Etat qui les dominerait toutes et gênerait leurs combinaisons. Or, c'est à un Etat de cette sorte que j'entends conduire la nation." (*DMII*, p. 341.)

45. "Dans l'histoire de la France, il y a toujours eu, sous une forme ou sous une autre, des féodalités. Aujourd'hui, elles ne sont plus dans les donjons, mais elles sont tout de même dans des fiefs. Ces fiefs sont dans les partis, dans les syndicats, dans certains secteurs des affaires . . . de la presse et de l'administration, etc . . . " (Tournoux, *La Tragédie du Général*, pp. 44-45.)

46. "organiser la division des Français." (*DMII*, p. 156.)

47. "Les Français sont des veaux . . . . La France entière est un pays de veaux . . . " (Tournoux, *La Tragédie du Général*, p. 89.)

48. *MIII*, p. xx.

49. Emmanuel d'Astier, *Sept fois sept jours* (Paris: Editions de Minuit, 1957), p. 138.

50. Ibid., p. 179.

51. "Ce que vous avez à faire c'est d'acquérir les esprits à l'unité nationale, à la réforme française, à l'appui au Général de Gaulle, sans d'ailleurs lui forcer la main, mais dans le cadre que je vous fixe." (*PI*, p. 155.)

52. *PI*, p. 241. On this subject see Alfred Grosser, *La Politique extérieure de la Vème république* (Paris: Editions du Seuil, 1965), pp. 25-26.

53. "Face à l'événement, c'est à soi-même que recourt l'homme de caractère. Son mouvement est d'imposer à l'action sa marque, de la prendre à son compte, d'en faire son affaire .... La difficulté attire l'homme de caractère, car c'est en l'étreignant qu'il se réalise lui-même .... Il y cherche, quoi qu'il arrive, l'âpre joie d'être responsable." (*FE*, pp. 53-55.)

54. "L'homme de caractère incorpore à sa personne la rigueur propre à l'effort. Les subordonnés l'éprouvent et, parfois, ils en gémissent. D'ailleurs, un tel chef est distant, car l'autorité ne va pas sans prestige, ni le prestige sans éloignement." (*FE*, p. 55.)

55. "il ... se montre bon prince, du moment qu'on l'invoque." (*FE*, p. 57.)

56. "un parti pris de garder par devers soi quelque secret de surprise qui risque à toute heure d'intervenir." (*FE*, p. 79.)

57. "splendeur des forts et refuge des faibles, pudeur des orgueilleux et fierté des humbles, prudence des sages et esprit des sots." (*FE*, p. 80.)

58. D'Astier,*Sept fois*, p. 146.

59. "L'homme d'action ne se conçoit guère sans une forte dose d'égoïsme, d'orgueil, de dureté, de ruse." (*FE*, p. 87.)

60. D'Astier, *Sept fois*, p. 77.

61. "Même le roi de Bourges, la Restauration de 1814 et celle de 1815, le gouvernement et l'assemblée de Versailles en 1871, ne se sont pas subordonnés." (*MII*, p. 321.)

62. *TE*, pp. 147-150.

63. "A présent, le peuple et le guide, s'aidant l'un l'autre, commencent l'étape du salut." (*MII*, p. 322.)

64. René Rémond, *La droite en France: de la première Restauration à la Vème*

République (Nouvelle édition revue et augmentée) (Paris: Aubier, 1963), pp. 289-290.

65. "Maurras a eu tellement raison qu'il en est devenu fou." (Dumaine, *Quai d'Orsay*, p. 138.)

66. Tournoux, *La Tragédie du Général*, p. 236.

II. The Third Republic:
Prelude to Failure

1. *AM*, pp. 77-78.

2. On the subject of the Maginot line and its proposed continuation see Guy Chapman, *Why France Collapsed* (London: Cassell, 1968), chap. 2.

3. *MI*, p. 16.

4. Major-General Sir Edward Spears, *Assignment to Catastrophe, Prelude to Dunkirk July 1939–May 1940*; and *The Fall of France 1940* (London: Heinemann, 1954), I: 147-148.

5. Quoted in Eugen Weber, *Action Française: Royalism and Reaction in Twentieth-Century France* (Stanford: Stanford University Press, 1962), p. 418.

6. Quoted in John T. Marcus, *French Socialism in the Crisis Years 1933-1936* (New York: Praeger, 1960), p. 116.

7. "A peine en fonction, le Président du Conseil était aux prises avec d'innombrables exigences, critiques et surenchères, que toute son activité s'employait à dérouter sans pouvoir les maîtriser. Le Parlement, loin de le soutenir, ne lui offrait qu'embûches et défections. Ses ministres étaient ses rivaux. L'opinion, la presse, les intérêts, le tenaient pour une cible désignée à tous les griefs. Chacun, d'ailleurs,–lui-même tout le premier–savait qu'il n'était là que pour une courte durée. De fait, après quelques mois, il lui fallait céder la place," (*MI*, p. 4.)

8. *Tableau des partis en France* (Paris: Grasset, 1931), p. 89.

9. *La République des professeurs* (Paris: Grasset, 1927), p. 182.

10. For the economic weaknesses of the *Front populaire* see the second volume of Alfred Sauvy's great *Histoire économique de la France entre les deux guerres* (Paris: Fayard, 1965, 1967), vol. 1, 1918-1931; vol. 2, 1931-1939, chaps. 17-18.

11. Dieter Wolf, *Die Doriot Bewegung: Ein Beitrag zur Geschichte des Französischen Faschismus* (Stuttgart: Deutsche Verlags-Anstalt, 1967), p. 167.

12. Marcus, *French Socialism*, p. 81.

13. Ibid., p. 119.

14. Jacques Fauvet, *Histoire du parti communiste français* vol. 1, *De la guerre à la guerre 1917-1939* (Paris: Fayard, 1964), p. 281.

15. Rémond, *Droite en France*, p. 225.

16. Ibid., pp. 221-225.

17. Sauvy, *Histoire économique*, vol. 1, chap. 1.

18. On the reparations and the debt question see Sauvy, *Histoire économique*, vol. 1, chaps. 7-9.

19. The figures in this paragraph are taken from Sauvy, *Histoire économique*, vol. 1, tables on pp. 445 and 464.

20. Another way of putting the stagnation of French industry would be to say that France's annual rate of growth between 1929 and 1938 gives a figure of -2 as the average yearly diminution of the national product. See J.M.Jeanneney, *Forces et faiblesses de l'économie française 1945-1959 (seconde édition revue et augmentée)* (Paris: Colin, 1959), p. 215.

21. Spears, *Assignment to Catastrophe*, 2:212.

III. The War Years:
The Founding of Gaullism

1. See the Brazzaville manifesto of October 27, 1940. *MI*, pp. 303-304.

2. The expression is used by Professor Jacques Chapsal in his *La Vie politique en France depuis 1940*, 2nd ed. (Paris: Presses Universitaires de France, 1966), p. 35.

3. Edmond Michelet, *Le Gaullisme passionante aventure* (Paris: Fayard, 1962), p. 47.

4. Robert Aron, *The Vichy Régime 1940-1944* (London: Putnam, 1958), pp. 314-317.

5. Quoted in William L. Langer, *Our Vichy Gamble* (New York: Norton, 1966), p. 72. This important book was originally published in 1947, but I quote from the paperback edition.

6. Eberhard Jäckel, *Frankreich in Hitlers Europa: Die Deutsche Frankreichpolitik im zweiten Weltkrieg* (Stuttgart: Deutsche Verlags-Anstalt, 1966), p. 57.

7. Aron, *Vichy Régime*, pp. 231-283.

8. On the attitude of Catholics see Jacques Duquesne, *Les Catholiques français sous l'occupation* (Paris: Grasset, 1966), Valentin's appeal is reproduced on pp. 332-333.

9. Aron, *Vichy Régime*, p. 475.

10. *MI*, p. 270.

11. *MI*, pp. 278-282.

12. *MI*, pp. 282-283.

13. Langer, *Vichy Gamble*, p. 290. On the question of security see M.R. D. Foot, *SOE in France; An Account of the Work of the British Special Operations Executive in France 1940-1944* (London: H.M.Stationery Office, 1966), p. 151.

14. Jacques Soustelle, *Envers et contre tout. I: De Londres à Alger. II: D'Alger à Paris* (Paris: Robert Laffont, 1947 and 1950), I:163.

15. *MI*, p. 304.

16. "Leur jeu . . . visait à instaurer, dans tout l'Orient, le *leadership* britannique." (*MI*, p. 159.)

17. For the history of the Resistance see: Henri Michel, *Histoire de la Résistance* (Paris: Presses Universitaires de France, 1969).

18. "Le Général de Gaulle et le Comité national français pensent qu'il leur appartient de prendre effectivement la direction de cette résistance en territoire français occupé par l'ennemi ou contrôlé par lui." (*MI*, p. 625.)

19. *MI*, p. 648.

20. This report is published in Foot, *SOE in France*, pp. 489-498.

21. "L' 'Intelligence,' qui est, pour les Anglais, une passion, autant qu'un service . . . " (*MI*, p. 124.)

22. *MII*, p. 340.

23. William L. Langer and S. Everett Gleason, *The Challenge to Isolation* (New York: Harper and Brothers, 1952), p. 733.

24. The labyrinthine intrigues of this period, the preparation of the putsch before the Anglo-American landings and the assassination of Darlan are exhaustively recounted in Yves Maxime Danan, *La Vie politique à Alger de 1940 à 1944* (Paris: R. Pichon and R. Durand-Auzias, 1963).

25. *MII*, pp. 407-408.

26. Winston S. Churchill, *The Hinge of Fate* (New York: Houghton-Mifflin, 1950), p. 632.

27. For the so-called Anfa memorandum see Arthur Layton Funk, *Charles de Gaulle, the Crucial Years, 1943-1944* (Norman: University of Oklahoma Press, 1959), pp. 78-79.

28. For this decree see Danan, *Vie politique à Alger*, p. 204.

29. *MII*, p. 475.

30. Soustelle, *Envers et contre tout*, 2:20.

31. Quoted in Funk, *Crucial Years*, p. 201.

32. For a perceptive account of Roosevelt's attitudes toward France see ibid., pp. 83-91 and pp. 265-272.

33. Ibid., p. 248.

34. "le refus de nous reconnaître comme l'autorité nationale française couvrait, en réalité, l'idée fixe du président des Etats-Unis d'instituer en France son arbitrage." (*MII*, p. 211.)

35. "L'unité nationale exige que tous les Français suivent leur Gouvernement. Où qu'ils soient et quoi qu'il arrive, les Français n'ont d'ordre à recevoir que de lui . . . Aucune autorité n'est valable si elle n'agit pas en son nom. Aucun effort français dans la guerre ne peut compter pour la France s'il n'est accompli sous son autorité." (*DMI*, p. 394.)

36. Soustelle, *Envers et contre tout*, 2:308.

37. Quoted in Robert Aron, *Histoire de la Libération de la France* (Paris: Fayard, 1959), p. 122.

38. Michel, *Histoire de la Résistance*, pp. 105-106.

39. *MII*, pp. 176-177.

40. For the differences in concept of the future role of the CDL between Algiers and the CNR, see Henri Denis, *Le Comité Parisien de la Libération* (Paris: Presses Universitaires de France, 1963), p. 15.

41. For these cross-currents see ibid., pp. 25-27.

42. *MII*, p.676.

43. Funk, *Crucial Years*, p. 223.

44. Ibid., p. 241.

45. *MII*, p. 224.

46. "Ce n'était point que je n'eusse hâte de prendre contact avec les chefs de l'insurrection parisienne. Mais je voulais qu'il fût établi que l'Etat . . . rentrait d'abord, tout simplement, chez lui." (*MII*, p. 303.)

47. "rendre . . . service à l'intérêt publique." (*MIII*, p. 101.)

48. See Aron, *Histoire de la Libération*, pp. 651-655. Peter Novick's criticism is contained in *The Resistance Versus Vichy: The Purge of Collaborators in Liberated France* (London: Chatto & Windus, 1968), pp. 202-208.

49. See Paul Farmer, *Vichy: Political Dilemma* (London: Oxford University Press, 1955), p. 333.

50. For France's economic plight see Yves Trotignon, *La France depuis 1939* (Paris, n.d.; a duplicated series of lectures delivered at the Ecole des Hautes Etudes Commerciales), pp. 16-22.

51. "Depuis toujours, je l'attendais. Parmi les ambitions nationales qui s'enrobaient dans le conflit mondial, il y avait celle des Britanniques, visant à dominer l'Orient. Que de fois j'avais rencontré cette ambition passionée, prête à briser les barrières! " (*MIII*, p. 185.)

52. On the Syrian crisis see A.W.DePorte, *De Gaulle's Foreign Policy: 1944-1946* (Cambridge: Harvard University Press, 1968), pp. 126-152.

53. "la chère et puissante Russie . . . " (*DMI*, p. 405.)

54. See Herbert Feis, *Churchill, Roosevelt, Stalin* (Princeton, New Jersey: Princeton University Press, 1957), pp. 531-532.

55. *MIII*, pp. 274-275.

56. "Il y a des Allemands, il y a même des Allemagnes. Mais où est aujourd'hui l'Allemagne? " (*DMI*, p. 630.)

57. "Vous aurez à vous défendre, non seulement contre les pressions . . . des puissances . . . mais encore contre le désir naturel de nos propres négociateurs. Ce désir, en effet, est de s'accorder avec leurs partenaires et, comme on dit, d'aboutir. J'insiste sur le fait qu'une telle disposition risque de jouer, dans la période où nous sommes, à notre détriment. C'est dire qu'il n'y faut pas céder, lors même qu'un tumulte orchestré de presse et radio étrangères, voire françaises, se déchaînerait pour vous entraîner. Depuis que nous sommes malheureux, ce que nous avons fait de plus fructueux fut en même temps ce qui provoqua les plus violents orages." (*MIII*, p. 506.)

58. Dumaine, *Quai d'Orsay*, p. 71.

59. "Je crois que chaque territoire sur lequel flotte le drapeau français doit être représenté à l'intérieur d'un système de forme fédérale dans lequel la Métropole sera une partie et où les intérêts de chacun pourront se faire entendre." (*DMI*, p. 418.)

M*

60. For all these events see Donald Lancaster, *The Emancipation of French Indochina* (London:Oxford University Press, 1961), and Dennis J. Duncanson, *Government and Revolution in Vietnam* (London: Oxford University Press, 1968).

61. "le combat mené depuis quatre ans en Indochine par la France et l'Union Français fait partie de cette même lutte [contre la domination communiste]. Les malveillants qui accusent la France de colonialisme, tandis qu'elle combat Ho Chi-Minh, feront bien d'entrer dans le silence." (*DMII*, p. 375.)

62. "Edouard Herriot déclina mon offre de faire partie du gouvernement. Je lui demandai d'aider à la reconstruction de la France; il me déclara qu'il se consacrerait à restaurer le parti radical." (*MIII*, p. 261.)

63. On the referendum and the elections for the Constituent Assembly see Chapsal, *Vie politique*, pp. 99-109.

64. These and subsequent electoral figures are taken from François Goguel and Alfred Grosser, *La Politique en France*, 3rd ed. (Paris: Colin, 1967), pp. 289-298.

65. "je reconnus que, décidément, la cause était entendue, qu'il serait vain et, même, indigne d'affecter de gouverner, dès lors que les partis, ayant recouvré leurs moyens, reprenaient leurs jeux d'antan, bref que je devais maintenant régler mon propre départ." (*MIII*, p. 279.)

66. *MIII*, p. 286.

67. Dumaine, *Quai d'Orsay*, p. 71.

68. Tournoux, *La Tragédie du Général*, p. 26.

69. "Avec de Gaulle s'éloignaient ce souffle venu des sommets, cet espoir de réussite, cette ambition de la France, qui soutenaient l'âme nationale." (*MIII*, p. 287.)

70. "Dans le chef tenu à l'écart, on continuait de voir une sorte de détenteur désigné de la souveraineté, un recours choisi d'avance. On concevait que cette légitimité restât latente au cours d'une périod sans angoisse. Mais on savait qu'elle s'imposerait, par consentement général, dès lors que le pays courrait le risque d'être, encore une fois, déchiré et menacé." (*MIII*, p. 287.)

71. Henri Michel, *Les Courants de Pensée de la Résistance* (Paris: Presses Universitaires de France, 1962), p. 27.

IV. The Fourth Republic and the RPF

1. "Sans qu'on puisse prévoir encore quel facteur ou quels événements

provoqueront le changement du régime, on peut croire que la secousse viendra." (*DMII*, p. 637.)

2. For some examples of the antagonism of the MRP and Mendès-France see Alexander Werth, *France 1940-1955* (London: Robert Hale, 1956), pp. 711-712.

3. Chapsal, *Vie politique*, p. 251.

4. Ibid., p. 123.

5. Dumaine, *Quai d'Orsay*, p. 190.

6. See pp. 85-86.

7. "C'est donc du chef de l'Etat, placé au-dessus des partis, élu par un collège qui englobe le Parlement mais beaucoup plus large et composé de manière à faire de lui le Président de l'Union Française en même temps que celui de la République, que doit procéder le pouvoir exécutif. Au chef de l'Etat la charge d'accorder l'intérêt général quant au choix des hommes avec l'orientation qui se dégage du Parlement. A lui la mission de nommer les ministres et, d'abord, bien entendu, le Premier, qui devra diriger la politique et le travail du Gouvernement. Au chef de l'Etat la fonction de promulguer les lois et de prendre les décrets, car c'est envers l'Etat tout entier que ceux-ci et celles-là engagent les citoyens. A lui la tâche de présider les Conseils du Gouvernement et d'y exercer cette influence de la continuité dont une nation ne se passe pas. A lui l'attribution de servir d'arbitre au-dessus des contingences politiques, soit normalement par le conseil, soit, dans les moments de grave confusion, en invitant le pays à faire connaître par des élections sa décision souveraine. A lui, s'il devait arriver que la patrie fût en péril, le devoir d'être le garant de l'indépendance nationale et des traités conclus par la France." (*DMII*, p. 10.)

8. *DMII*, pp. 22-23.

9. "Rien n'est plus nécessaire pour notre pays que d'organiser l'Etat de telle manière qu'il dispose, dans sa structure, d'assez de force; dans son fonctionnement, d'assez d'efficience; dans ses hommes, d'assez de crédit, pour diriger la nation et assurer son salut, quoi qu'il puisse arriver." Declaration of August 27, 1946. (*DMII*, p. 18.)

10. *DMIII*, p. 3.

11. On this movement which may be considered as a curtain-raiser for the RPF see Christian Purtschet, *Le Rassemblement du People Français 1947-1953* (Paris: Editions Cujas, 1965), pp. 43-50.

12. Dumaine, *Quai d'Orsay*, p. 368.

13. For more details see Peter Campbell, *French Electoral Systems and Elections since 1789* (London: Faber, 1965), pp. 113-120.

14. Chapsal, *Vie politique*, p. 189. Author's italics.

15. Goguel and Grosser, *La Politique en France*, pp. 290-91 and 295-96.

16. François Goguel, *France Under the Fourth Republic* (Ithaca, New York: Cornell University Press, 1952), p. 113.

17. Purtschet, *Rassemblement du Peuple*, p. 355.

18. André Siegfried, *De la IVe à la Ve République* (Paris: Grasset, 1958), p. 70.

19. "Je n'ai pas sauvé la France pour la donner à un tanneur" (Jean Ferniot, *De Gaulle et le 13 Mai* [Paris: Plon, 1965], p. 55.)

20. Lancaster, *French Indochina*, p. 336; Georges Bidault, *Resistance* (London: Weidenfeld and Nicolson, 1967), p. 204.

21. Siegfreid, *IVe à la Ve République*, pp. 90-91.

22. See Alfred Grosser, *La IVe République et sa politique extérieure* (Paris: Colin, 1961), p. 332.

23. Philip M. Williams, *Crisis and Compromise: Politics in the Fourth Republic* (London: Longmans, 1964), p. 44.

24. François Goguel et al., eds., *Les Elections du 2 Janvier 1956* (Paris: Colin, 1957), p. 489.

25. Quoted in Chapsal, *Vie politique*, pp. 259-260.

26. For relations between Faure and Mendès-France see Francis De Tarr, *The French Radical Party from Herriot to Mendès-France* (London: Oxford University Press, 1961), pp. 182-183.

27. Editorial by Pierre Poujade in *Fraternité française* of 10 September 1955, quoted in Rémond, *Droite en France*, p. 372.

28. See André de Lattre, *Politique économique de la France depuis 1945* (Paris: Sirey, 1966), pp. 480-485; and Henri Brousse, *Le niveau de vie en France*, 2nd ed. (Paris: Presses Universitaires de France, 1962), p. 26.

29. Brousse, ibid., pp. 98-99.

30. The figures in this paragraph are taken from Jeanneney, *L'économie française*, pp. 9-18; and Trotignon, *France depuis 1939*, pp. 75-78.

31. Trotignon, ibid., p. 126.

32. Ibid., p. 127.

33. Trotignon, ibid., p. 144; and de Lattre, *Politique économique de la France* (Paris: Cours de Droit, 1968-1969), Fascicule III, p. 81.

34. Brousse, *Le niveau de vie en France*, p. 26.

35. Jeanneney, *L'économie française*, p. 64.

36. Ibid., p. 65.

37. For more detail about inflation and deflation under the Fourth Republic see de Lattre, *Politique économique de la France depuis 1945*, pp. 444-486; and Trotignon, *France depuis 1939*, pp. 50-58, and (for monetary policy), pp. 59-63.

38. "Il y a eu, hélas! depuis trois ans, la défaillance chronique de notre politique officielle, de celle que prétendent vaguement défendre nos réprésentants... Cette faiblesse a été l'un des éléments qui ont fait écarter la solution française, européenne, humaine, du grand problème allemand. On en est donc venu à ce qu'on appelle la solution de Bonn. Ne nous faisons pas d'illusion, c'est la reconstitution du Reich! " (*DMII*, p. 292.)

39. Bidault, *Resistance*, pp. 147-148.

40. For this evolution see Grosser, *Politique extérieure*, pp. 193-213.

41. John T. Marcus, *Neutralism and Nationalism in France* (New York: Bookman Associates, 1958), p. 37.

42. Ibid., p. 86.

43. Dumaine, *Quai d'Orsay*, p. 497.

44. Raymond Aron et al., eds., *France Defeats EDC* (New York: Praeger, 1957), p. 4.

45. "des faux-semblants tels que le pool charbon-acier et le project d'armée européenne." (*DMII*, p. 483.)

46. Grosser, *Politique extérieure*, pp. 45-46.

47. *DMII*, pp. 523-524.

48. Aron, *France Defeats EDC*, p. 21.

49. Grosser, *Politique extérieure*, pp. 213-214.

50. Michel Debré, *Ces Princes qui nous gouvernent...* (Paris: Plon, 1957), pp. 126-127.

51. Grosser, *Politique extérieure*, p. 47.

52. Ellen J. Hammer, *The Struggle for Indochina, 1940-1955* (Stanford: Stanford University Press, 1966), p. 224.

53. Robert Buron, *Les Dernières années de la IVe République. Carnets politiques* (Paris: Plon, 1968), pp. 27-28.

54. Grosser, *Politique extérieure*, p. 282.

55. See de Lattre, *Politique économique*, p. 461.

56. Henri Navarre, *Agonie de l'Indochine (1953-4)* (Paris: Plon, 1956), p. 67.

57. For what followed the evacuation, see Lancaster, *French Indochina*, pp. 359-367.

58. Hammer, *Struggle for Indochina*, pp. 355-356.

59. Grosser, *Politique extérieure*, p. 265.

60. Ibid., p. 275.

61. Bidault, *Resistance*, pp. 182-183.

62. Gilbert Grandval, *Ma Mission au Maroc* (Paris: Plon, 1956), p. 128.

63. Navarre, *Agonie de l'Indochine*, p. 321.

64. For this and other instances of the effect of World War II on the French army see John Steward Ambler, *Soldiers Against the State: The French Army in Politics* (New York: Anchor Books, 1968), chap. 3.

65. Raoul Girardet, "Problèmes moraux et idéologiques," in *La Crise militaire française 1946-1962: Aspects sociologiques et idéologiques*, Girardet, ed. (Paris: Colin, 1964), p. 161.

66. Quoted in Tournoux, *La Tragédie du Général*, p.284.

67. "Le Rassemblement du Peuple Français a pour objet de promouvoir au-dessus des partis, en matière économique, sociale, impériale, extérieure, les solutions que j'ai esquissées et, dans le cadre d'un Etat rendu capable de les appliquer, de soutenir la politique qui viserait à les réaliser." (Press conference of April 24, 1947. *DMII*, p. 66.)

68. Purtschet, *Rassemblement du Peuple*, p. 338.

69. "Tant que la masse française pourra vivre sur sa substance, ou bien de la mendicité internationale, elle n'éprouvera pas le besoin de recourir à nous. Mais lorsqu'elle touchera au drame, lorsqu'elle arrivera près de la catastrophe,

elle fera appel à celui qui a déjà sauvé la France dans des circonstances encore plus dramatiques. C'est dans le drame que les régimes s'effondrent." (Tournoux, *La Tragédie du Général*, pp. 118-119.)

70. For these and for an analysis of the movement's structure see Purtschet, *Rassemblement du Peuple*, pp. 67-85.

71. Ibid., p. 60.

72. For all this see Purtschet's chapter on "Manifestations extérieures du Rassemblement du Peuple français," ibid., pp. 175-245.

73. Ibid., pp. 104-115.

74. See Williams, *Crisis and Compromise*, p. 65.

75. Purtschet, *Rassemblement du Peuple*, pp. 296-298.

76. Chapsal, *Vie politique*, pp. 191-193.

77. See Tournoux, *La Tragédie du Général*, pp. 127-130.

78. "Avant tout [le Rassemblement] doit s'écarter d'un régime qui est stérile et qu'il ne peut, pour le moment, changer." (*DMII*, p. 582.)

79. Quoted in Purtschet, *Rassemblement du Peuple*, p. 138,n.72.

80. See the findings of the *Institut français d'opinion publique* (IFOP) published in Williams, *Crisis and Compromise*, appendix VII, p. 509.

81. Purtschet, *Rassemblement du Peuple*, pp. 121-122.

82. *La France sera la France: ce que veut Charles de Gaulle* (Paris: Rassemblement du Peuple français, 1951) p. 120.

83. RPF brochure on *L'Association Capital-Travail*, p. 6. quoted by Purtschet, *Rassemblement du People*, p. 270. The summary of the Soustelle-Vallon proposal is also taken from Purtschet.

84. "Les avant-gardes cosaques . . . campent à 158 kilomètres du Rhin." (Tournoux, *La Tragédie du Général*, p. 106.)

85. "les Etats-Unis doivent être désormais liés à l'Europe" (Ibid., p. 106.)

86. *DMII*, p. 98.

87. Marcus, *Neutralism*, p. 86.

88. Tournoux, *La Tragédie du Général*, p. 105.

89. *DMII*, pp. 326-327 and 219-220.

90. *DMII*, p. 524.

91. Marcus, *Neutralism*, p. 91.

V. The Founding of the Fifth Republic:
Gaullism and Algeria

1. Général d'Armée Paul Ely, *Mémoires II. Suez . . . Le 13 Mai* (Paris: Plon, 1969), p. 274.

2. Merry and Serge Bromberger, *Les 13 Complots du 13 Mai* (Paris: Fayard, 1959), p. 395.

3. Siegfried, *IVe à la Ve République*, p. 261.

4. Ferniot, *De Gaulle et le 13 Mai*, p. 146.

5. On general Gaullist intentions see Paul-Marie de la Gorce, *De Gaulle entre Deux Mondes* (Paris: Fayard, 1964), pp. 534-537.

6. Ibid., p. 535.

7. "Une entreprise d'usurpation." (*DMIII*, p. 421.)

8. "Il est vrai que deux ou trois personnages entreprenants, qui avaient participé à mon action au temps où j'en exerçais une, séjournaient en Algérie pour répandre l'idée qu'il faudrait bien, un jour, me charger du salut public. Mais ils le faisaient en dehors de mon aval et sans m'avoir même consulté." (*MEI*, p. 21.)

9. Quoted in Ferniot, *De Gaulle et le 13 Mai*, p. 219.

10. Roger Trinquier, *Le Coup d'Etat du 13 Mai* (Paris: Editions Esprit Nouveau, 1962), p. 99 and p. 130.

11. For the activities of the "Grand O" and other small conspiratorial groups see Ferniot and the Brombergers.

12. See Ely, *Mémoires II*, pp. 291-307 for his own account of his resignation.

13. Ibid., p. 277.

14. Trinquier, *Coup d'Etat*, p. 173.

15. "La légitimité nationale que j'incarne depuis vingt ans." (*DMIII*, p. 166.)

16. Buron, *Les dernières années*, p. 245.

17. "l'aventure, débouchant sur la guerre civile, en la présence et, bientôt, avec la

participation en sens divers des étrangers." (*MEI*, p. 22.)

18. De la Gorce, *Entre Deux Mondes*, p. 569.

19. "Naguère, le pays, dans ses profondeurs, m'a fait confiance pour le conduire tout entier jusqu'à son salut. Aujourd'hui, devant les épreuves qui montent de nouveau vers lui, qu'il sache que je me tiens prêt à assumer les pouvoirs de la République." (*DMIII*, p. 3.)

20. Chapsal, *Vie Politique*, p. 322.

21. "L'ai-je jamais fait? . . . Croit-on, qu'à 67 ans, je vais commencer une carrière de dictateur? " (*DMIII*, p. 10.)

22. For the texts of these letters see Ferniot, *De Gaulle et le 13 Mai*, pp. 422-425.

23. De la Gorce, *Entre Deux Mondes*, pp. 565-566.

24. "J'ai entamé hier le processus régulier nécessaire à l'établissement d'un gouvernement républicain capable d'assurer l'unité et l'indépendance du Pays . . . . Dans ces conditions, toute action, de quelque côté qu'elle vienne qui met en cause l'ordre public, risque d'avoir de graves conséquences. Tout en faisant la part des circonstances, je ne saurais l'approuver." (*DMIII*, p. 11.)

25. See *MEI*, pp. 28-29. For the details of "Operation Resurrection" see Ferniot, *De Gaulle et le 13 Mai*, pp. 397-404.

26. "si le Parlement vous suit, je n'aurai pas autre chose à faire que vous laisser vous expliquer avec les parachutistes et rentrer dans ma retraite en m'enfermant dans mon chagrin." (*MEI*, p. 30.)

27. Chapsal, *Vie politique*, pp. 327-328, Ferniot, *De Gaulle et le 13 Mai*, pp. 462-473.

28. Ferniot, ibid., p. 471.

29. Louis Terrenoire, *De Gaulle et l'Algérie: Témoignage pour l'Histoire* (Paris: Fayard, 1964), p. 78.

30. Chapsal, *Vie politique*, p. 333.

31. Quoted in Association française de Science politique, *L'établissement de la Cinquième République: Le Référendum de Septembre et les Elections de Novembre 1958* (Paris: Colin, 1960), p. 14.

32. The translation of the 1958 Constitution is quoted from Philip M. Williams and Martin Harrison, *De Gaulle's Republic* (London: Longmans, 1960), pp. 232-249.

33. "Disons, si vous le voulez, que notre Constitution est à la fois parlementaire et présidentielle, à la mesure de ce que nous commandent, à la fois, les besoins de notre équilibre et les traits de notre caractère." (*DMIII*, p. 301.)

34. Williams and Harrison, *Republic*, p. 123.

35. See François Goguel et al., eds., *Le Référendum d'Octobre et les Elections de Novembre 1962* (Paris: Colin, 1965), pp. 10-13.

36. In a speech to the *Conseil d'Etat* on August 27. Quoted in Chapsal, *Vie politique*, p. 373.

37. *PI*, p. 67.

38. See D'Astier, *Sept fois*, p. 223.

39. Association française de Science politique, *L'établissement de la Cinquième République*, p. 235.

40. Tournoux, *La Tragédie du Général*, p. 220.

41. Michel Debré, *Refaire une démocratie, un état, un pouvoir* (Paris: Plon, 1958), p. 61.

42. In an interview to *L'Express*, 29 June–5 July 1970.

43. See de Gaulle's declaration on Algeria of 18 August 1947. *DMII*, pp. 106-109.

44. "Une vague qui emporte tous les peuples ver l'émancipation. Il y a des imbéciles qui ne veulent pas le comprendre; ce n'est pas la peine de leur en parler." (Terrenoire, *De Gaulle et l'Algérie*, p. 41.)

45. "Il est impossible d'accueillir au Palais-Bourbon cent vingt députés algériens." (Tournoux, *La Tragédie du Général*, pp. 243-244.)

46. Ibid., p. 284.

47. See the text of this letter in Jacques Soustelle, *Vingt-Huit Ans de Gaullisme* (Paris: La Table Ronde, 1968), p. 446.

48. "En premier lieu, j'excluais du domaine des possibilités toute idée d'assimilation des musulmans au peuple français." (*MEI*, p. 49.)

49. "cela reviendrait à maintenir la France enlisée politiquement, financièrement et militairement dans un marécage sans fond . . . " (*MEI*, p. 49.)

50. "Quoi qu'on ait pu rêver jadis ou qu'on pût regretter aujourd'hui, quoi que j'aie moi-même, assurément, espéré à d'autres époques, il n'y avait plus, à mes yeux, d'issue en dehors du droit de l'Algérie à disposer d'elle-même." (*MEI*, p.50.)

51. "l'Algérie de l'avenir, en vertu d'une certaine empreinte qu'elle a reçue et qu'elle voudrait garder, demeurerait, à maints égards, française." (*MEI*, p. 51.)

52. "Quant à la tactique, je devrais régler la marche par étapes, avec précaution." (*MEI*, p. 51.)

53. Merry and Serge Bromberger et al., *Barricades et Colonels: 24 Janvier 1960* (Paris: Fayard, 1960), p. 371.

54. *PI*, p. 156.

55. *DMIII*, p. 16.

56. For all these incidents see *PI*, pp. 154-161.

57. "l'on veut se comporter comme un Français à part entière et que l'on croit que l'évolution nécessaire de l'Algérie doit s'accomplir dans le cadre français." (*DMIII*, p. 40.)

58. "J'ai parlé de la paix des braves. Qu'est-ce à dire? Simplement ceci: que ceux qui ont ouvert le feu le cessent et qu'ils retournent, sans humiliation, à leur famille et à leur travail! " (*DMIII*, p. 55.)

59. *PI*, p. 179.

60. See *MEI*, pp. 64-65.

61. See Ambler, *French Army in Politics*, pp. 271-272.

62. "Ce qu'ils veulent c'est qu'on leur rende 'l'Algérie de papa', mais l'Algérie de papa est morte, et si on ne le comprend pas on mourra avec elle." (*PI*, p. 194.)

63. "La Sécession, où certains croient trouver l'indépendance . . . . Je suis, pour ma part, convaincu qu'un tel aboutissement serait invraisemblable et désastreux. L'Algérie étant actuellement ce qu'elle est, et le monde ce que nous savons, la sécession entraînerait une misère épouvantable, un affreux chaos politique, l'égorgement généralisé et, bientôt, la dictature belliqueuse des communistes." (*DMIII*, p. 121.)

64. "Le Gouvernement des Algériens par les Algériens, appuyé sur l'aide de la France et en union étroite avec elle, pour l'économie, l'enseignement, la défense, les relations extérieures." (*DMIII*, p. 121.)

65. For this episode see Jean Charlot, *L'U.N.R.: Etude du pouvoir au sein d'un parti politique* (Paris: Colin, 1967), pp. 61-67.

66. Ambler, *French Army in Politics*, p. 270.

67. See Bromberger et al., *Barricades et Colonels*, p. 176.

68. Ambler, *French Army in Politics*, p. 274.

69. "un mauvais coup porté à la France." (*DMIII*, p. 160.)

70. Ely, *Mémoires II*, pp. 437 and 445.

71. For the attitude of ministers see Tournoux, *La Tragédie du Général*, pp. 350-355.

72. "Ceux qui ont pris les armes contre l'Etat ne peuvent pas être absous. Les militaires ne veulent pas faire couler le sang, comme s'ils n'étaient pas là pour ça! L'Armée n'est quand même pas faite pour avoir peur du sang. L'Armée est faite pour obéir." (Ibid., p. 354.)

73. "ce qui reviendrait à la bâtir elle-même comme la seule représentation valable et à l'ériger, par avance, en gouvernement du pays. Cela, je ne le ferai pas." (*DMIII*, p. 163.)

74. For a journalist's report of *la tournée des popotes* see *PI*, pp. 232-233 where de Gaulle is reported using the words given in the text: "La France ne doit pas partir. Elle a le droit d'être en Algérie. Elle y restera." For Gaullist versions see Terrenoire, *De Gaulle et l'Algérie*, pp. 175-178; and *MEI*, p. 92.

75. Buron, *Carnets politiques de la guerre d'Algérie*, p. 119.

76. *PI*, p. 70.

77. Jacques Soustelle, *L'Espérance Trahie (1958-1961)* (Paris: Editions de l'Alma, 1962), p. 160.

78. Ambler, *French Army in Politics*, p. 277.

79. Text in *PI*, pp. 236-238.

80. Soustelle, *L'Espérance Trahie*, pp. 187-188.

81. For de Gaulle's account of the Si Salah episode see *MEI*, pp. 104-105. For the Melun meeting ibid., pp. 94-95.

82. Tournoux, *La Tragédie du Général*, pp. 396-397.

83. "Tout ce que [la France] demande, c'est qu'avant d'entrer dans la salle on ait déposé son couteau." (*PI*, p. 255.)

84. "le gouvernement de la République algérienne, laquelle existera un jour ... " (*DMIII*, p. 259.)

85. Ely, *Mémoires II*, pp. 485-486.

86. For the text of the question and the law see François Goguel, ed., *Le Référendum du 8 Janvier 1961* (Paris: Colin, 1962), pp. 109-110.

87. Ely, *Mémoires II*, p. 499.

88. These figures are taken from Goguel and Grosser, *La Politique en France*, p. 292.

89. Goguel, ed., *Le Référendum du 8 Janvier 1961*, p. 51.

90. Ibid., p. 189.

91. Terrenoire, *De Gaulle et l'Algerie*, p. 223.

92. Ambler, *French Army in Politics*, p. 278.

93. Tournoux, *La Tragédie du Général*, p. 371.

94. "Voici l'Etat bafoué, la nation défiée, notre puissance ébranlée, notre prestige international abaissé, notre place et notre rôle en Afrique compromis. Et par qui? Hélas! hélas! par des hommes dont c'était le devoir, l'honneur, la raison d'être, de servir et d'obéir." (*DMIII*, p. 307.)

95. Tournoux, *La Tragédie du Général*, p. 377.

96. *DMIII*, p. 292.

97. "dans tout sujet débattu, il voit, de notre part, l'intention de garder une emprise directe sur l'Algérie ou, pour le moins, des prétextes à y intervenir, alors qu'au contraire c'est de cela que nous voulons nous débarrasser." (*MEI*, p. 121.)

98. De la Gorce, *Entre Deux Mondes*, pp. 663-665; Terrenoire, *De Gaulle et l'Algérie*, pp. 238-239.

99. "Pour ce qui est du Sahara, notre ligne de conduite est celle qui sauvegarde nos intérêts et qui tient compte des réalités. Nos intérêts consistent en ceci: libre exploitation du pétrole et du gaz . . . disposition de terrains d'aviation et droits de circulation pour nos communications avec l'Afrique noire. Les réalités, c'est qu'il n'y a pas un seul Algérien, je le sais, qui ne pense que le Sahara doive faire partie de l'Algérie . . . " (*DMIII*, p. 340.)

100. *OAS Parle* (Paris: Julliard, 1964), p. 85.

101. Ibid., p. 318.

102. *MEI*, p. 129. However, the figures given by Janin, the director of the Sûreté Nationale in Algeria at Salan's trial were 1,200 Moslems and 200 Europeans killed up to April 1962.

103. For the text of the Evian agreements contained in the *Déclaration générale du 19 Mars rélative à l'Algérie* see François Goguel, ed., *Le Référendum du 8 Avril 1962* (Paris: Colin, 1963), pp. 216-221.

104. Tournoux, *La Tragédie du Général*, p. 401.

105. Chapsal, *Vie politique*, pp. 460-462; also Guy de Carmoy, *The Foreign Policies of France 1944-1968*, trans. Elaine P. Halperin (Chicago & London: University of Chicago Press, 1970), pp. 232-236.

106. For results see Goguel and Grosser, *La Politique en France*, p. 128.

107. Goguel, ed., *Le Référendum du 8 Avril 1962*, pp. 129 and 149.

108. "On peut penser que je ne le ferais pas, comme on dit: de gaieté de coeur. Pour un homme de mon âge et de ma formation, il était proprement cruel de devenir, de son propre chef, le maître d'oeuvre d'un pareil changement." (*MEI*, p. 41.)

109. See *Le Monde*, 7 February 1970.

110. "Le président de la République, j'y insiste, est essentiellement un arbitre." (Quoted in Goguel, ed., *Le Référendum d'Octobre et les Elections de Novembre 1962*, p. 14.)

111. For relations between the President and parliament, see Chapsal, *Vie politique*, pp. 395-396 and pp. 405-408.

112. For this conversation with Mollet see Tournoux, *La Tragédie du Général*, pp. 408-413.

113. *DMIII*, p. 423.

114. Chapsal, *Vie politique*, p. 464.

115. On de Gaulle's disagreement with Debré on the holding of the elections see Goguel, ed. in *Le Référendum d'Octobre et les Elections de Novembre 1962*, p. 27.

116. "le Président a besoin de la confiance directe de la nation. Au lieu de l'avoir implicitement, comme c'était mon propre cas en 1958 pour une raison historique et exceptionelle ... il s'agit que le Président soit élu, dorénavant, au suffrage universel." (*DMIV*, p. 31.)

117. Text in *PII*, p. 31.

118. Quoted in Rémond, *Droite en France*, p. 370.

119. For an analysis of the question of form see Chapsal, *Vie politique*, pp. 467-471.

120. Quoted in ibid., p. 469.

121. Results in Goguel and Grosser, *La Politique en France*, p. 292.

122. Results in ibid., p. 293.

123. André Malraux, *Les chênes qu'on abat* . . . (Paris:Gallimard,1971), pp. 49-50.

VI. Gaullism Abroad:
The Foreign Policy of the Fifth Republic

1. "Ce désir . . . de s'accorder avec leurs partenaires et, comme on dit, d'aboutir." (*MIII*, p. 506.)

2. See Général Charles Ailleret, *L'Aventure Atomique Française* (Paris: Grasset, 1968), pp. 176-177 for the planning bureau; and Wolf Mendl, *Deterrence and Persuasion: French Nuclear Armament in the Context of National Policy, 1945-1969* (New York, Praeger, 1970), pp. 146-149 for Pierrelatte.

3. "La conséquence, c'est qu'il faut, évidemment, que nous sachions nous pourvoir . . . d'une force capable d'agir pour notre compte, de ce qu'on est convenu d'appeler 'une force de frappe' susceptible de se déployer à tout moment et n'importe où. Il va de soi qu'à la base de cette force sera un armement atomique—que nous le fabriquions ou que nous l'achetions—mais qui doit nous appartenir. Et, puisqu'on peut détruire la France, éventuellement, à partir de n'importe quel point du monde, il faut que notre force soit faite pour agir où que ce soit sur la terre." (*DMIII*, p. 127.)

4. *Revue de défense nationale*, December 1967.

5. "Hourra pour la France!" (*PI*, p. 365.)

6. Some of the facts in this paragraph are taken from The Institute for Strategic Studies, *The Military Balance 1970-1971* (London: the Institute, 1970); and others from Mendl, *Deterrence and Persuasion*, pp. 111-112; and an article by Pierre Messmer in the July 1967 issue of *Le Républicain Indépendent* (New York: Ambassade de France, Service de Presse et d'Information, August 1967).

7. See Jacques Isnard in *Le Monde*, 4 January 1969.

8. See Messmer's article in the *Revue de défense nationale*, March 1968.

9. Robert Gilpin, *France in the Age of the Scientific State* (Princeton, New Jersey: Princeton University Press, 1968), p. 271-273.

10. Figures taken from Institute for Strategic Studies, *The Military Balance* 1970–1971.

11. The arguments for and against the *force de frappe* are outlined in Mendl, *Deterrence and Persuasion*, passim.

12. Ambler, *French Army in Politics*, p. 321.

13. See Grosser, *Politique extérieure*, pp. 351-353.

14. See Title XII of the Constitution given in Williams and Harrison, *Republic*, pp. 246-247.

15. "Chaque Territoire, s'il le juge bon . . . a le droit de répondre 'non' à la question qui sera posée par le référendum. S'il répond 'non', s'il refuse pour son compte de faire partie de la Communauté, avec la Métropole et ses frères africains, eh bien! il prendra son destin entre ses seules mains, il suivra sa route, isolément. Bien entendu . . la Métropole et les autres Territoires africains tireraient toutes les conséquences d'un tel choix." (*PI*, p. 457.)

16. Jean Lacouture, *Cinq Hommes et La France* (Paris: Editions du Seuil, 1961), pp. 364-365.

17. Alfred Grosser, *La politique extérieure de la Ve République* (Paris: Editions du Seuil, 1965), p. 72.

18. Carmoy, *Foreign Policies*, pp. 222-225; and Grosser, ibid., pp. 72-74.

19. *MEI*, pp. 107-108.

20. "les réunions des Nations Unies ne sont plus que des séances tumultueuses et scandaleuses . . . " (*DMIII*, p. 296.)

21. For France's military forces in Africa see Institute for Strategic Studies, *The Military Balance 1970-1971*, pp. 54-55.

22. For a balanced assessment of the present French situation in Africa see an article by Kaye Whiteman in the December 1968 number of *Interplay* magazine.

23. Figures from *French Aid to the Developing Countries in 1968* (New York: Ambassade de France, Service de Presse et d'information).

24. Ibid.

25. For the details of the Ben Barka case see the study by Philip M. Williams, *Wars, Plots and Scandals in Post-War France* (Cambridge: Cambridge University Press, 1970), pp. 78-125.

26. Carmoy, *Foreign Policies*, pp. 232-236.

27. Figures from *French Aid to the Developing Countries in 1968*.

28. *PII*, p. 157.

29. "Amener à se grouper, aux points de vue politique, économique et stratégique, les Etats qui touchent au Rhin, aux Alpes, aux Pyrénées. Faire de cette organisation l'une des trois puissances planétaires et, s'il le faut un jour, l'arbitre entre les deux camps soviétique et anglo-saxon. Depuis 1940, ce que j'ai pu accomplir et dire ménageait ces possibilités." (*MIII*, pp. 179-180.)

30. "Ma politique vise donc à l'institution du concert des Etats européens, afin qu'en développant entre eux des liens de toutes sortes grandisse leur solidarité." (*MEI*, p. 182.)

31. Jean-Paul Palewski, president of the commission of finances of the National Assembly writing in *Politique Etrangère* 29 (1964): p. 130.

32. On this agreement see John Newhouse, *De Gaulle and the Anglo-Saxon* (New York: Viking, 1970), pp. 16-17 and p. 66. This book is by far the best and most detailed study of de Gaulle's European policy.

33. Quoted in Grosser, *La Politique extérieure de la Ve République*, p. 99.

34. *Politique Etrangère* 30 (1965): p. 241. Author's italics.

35. Newhouse, *De Gaulle and the Anglo-Saxons*, p. 70.

36. *MEI*, pp. 214-215.

37. Ibid., p. 215.

38. Ibid.

39. Ibid.

40. On this point see Carmoy, *Foreign Policies*, p. 276.

41. "l'acceptation des faits accomplis pour ce qui est des frontières, une attitude de bonne volonté pour les rapports avec l'Est, un renoncement complet aux armements atomiques, une patience à toute épreuve pour la réunification." (*MEI*, p. 187.)

42. *MEI*, p. 188.

43. On Adenauer's outlook see Waldemar Besson, *Die Aussenpolitik der Bundes-Republik* (München: Piper, 1970), pp. 56-61.

44. Konrad Adenauer, *Erinerungen 1955-1959* (Stuttgart: Deutsche-Verlags-Anstalt, 1967), p. 426.

45. *MEI*, p. 188.

46. Adenauer, *Erinerungen*, p. 434.

47. Besson, *Die Aussenpolitik*, pp. 242-245 and p. 304.

48. "nous n'admettrions pas que Berlin-Ouest soit livré au système de Pankow." (*DMIII*, p. 84.)

49. "ne point négocier sur Berlin, ni sur l'Allemagne, tant que l'Union Soviétique n'aura pas cessé ses menaces et ses sommations . . . " (*DMIII*, p. 385.)

50. *DMIV*, pp. 14-15.

51. Fred Luchsinger, *Bericht über Bonn 1955-1965* (Zürich: Fretz & Wasmuth, 1966), pp. 316-317.

52. See Mendl, *Deterrence and Persuasion*, p. 61; and Newhouse, *De Gaulle and the Anglo-Saxons*, pp. 86-87.

53. On Franco-American nuclear relations see Mendl, ibid., pp. 56-61.

54. "les réalités profondes qui font de la Fédération canadienne un Etat perpétuellement mal à son aise, ambigu et artificiel." (*MEI*, p. 251.)

55. *MEI*, pp. 268-269.

56. "Si cela mène à la guerre, ce sera bien par votre faute." (*MEI*, p. 241.)

57. *DMIII*, pp. 84-85.

58. *MEI*, pp. 261-265.

59. On the Bonn declaration see Miriam Camps, *Britain and the European Community 1955-1963*

60. Besson, *Die Aussenpolitik*, p. 243-244.

61. "Se figurer qu'on peut bâtir quelque chose qui soit efficace pour l'action et qui soit approuvé par les peuples en-dehors et au-dessus des Etats, c'est une chimère." (*DMIII*, p. 245.)

62. "un concert organisé régulier des Gouvernements responsables et puis, aussi, le travail d'organismes spécialisés dans chacun des domaines communs, organismes subordonnés aux Gouvernements . . . " (*DMIII*, p. 245.)

63. See Camps, *European Community*, p. 417.

64. Carmoy, *Foreign Policies*, p. 387.

65. Camps, *European Community*, pp. 418-419.

66. "le porte-parole de toutes les négations." (*MEI*, p. 209.)

67. *DMIII*, pp. 406-407.

68. *MEI*, p. 199.

69. See on this point Richard Mayne, *The Recovery of Europe: From Devastation to Unity* (New York: Harper & Row, 1970), pp. 265-266.

70. Grosser, *La Politique extérieure de la Ve République*, p. 108. On the Château de Champs meeting see Newhouse, *De Gaulle and the Anglo-Saxons*, pp. 176-179.

71. Henry Kissinger, "Strains on the Alliance," *Foreign Affairs* (January, 1963).

72. Jacques Vernant in *Politique Etrangère* 27 (1962): p. 511.

73. *PII*, pp. 207 and 271.

74. "il apparaîtrait une Communauté atlantique colossale sous dépendance et direction américaines . . . " (*DMIV*, p. 69.)

75. See Mayne, *Recovery of Europe*, p. 271.

76. Camps, *European Community*, pp. 471-472

77. Text in *The Bulletin*: A weekly survey of German affairs issued by the Press and Information Office of the German Federal Government. Bonn, 29 January 1963.

78. *Politique Etrangère* 28 (1963): p. 453.

79. Text in *The Bulletin*, 21 May 1963.

80. "Les traités . . . sont comme les jeunes filles et comme les roses: ça dure ce que ça dure." (*PII*, p. 340.)

81. See Besson, *Die Aussenpolitik*, pp. 324-325.

82. *DMIV*, p. 230.

83. Quoted in Miriam Camps, *European Unification in the Sixties: From the Veto to the Crisis* (New York: McGraw-Hill, 1966), p. 5.

84. On the details of all this see ibid., pp. 6-28.

85. For the Commission's proposals see ibid., pp. 38-46.

86. Text in *PII*, pp. 308-309.

87. For the French ten points and the results of the Luxembourg meetings see Camps, *European Unification*, pp. 104-115.

88. Ibid., p. 115.

89. Text of Couve de Murville's speech issued in English translation by Ambassade de France, Service de Presse et d'Information, New York.

90. See *L'Election Présidentielle des 5 et 19 Décembre 1965* (Paris: Colin, 1970). p. 402.

91. "que l'Allemagne soit désormais un élément certain du progrès et de la paix." (*DMIV*, p. 339); and "la politique nouvelle des relations franco-allemandes repose sur une base populaire incomparable." (*DMIV*, p. 77.)

92. "nous multiplions enfin nos rapports avec les Etats européens de l'Est à mesure que leur évolution interne les oriente vers la paix." (*DMIV*, p. 319.)

93. "pour la France, sans qu'elle méconnaisse aucunement le rôle essentiel que les

Etats-Unis ont à jouer dans la pacification et la transformation du monde, c'est le rétablissement de l'Europe en un ensemble fécond, au lieu qu'elle soit paralysée par une division stérile, qui en est la première condition. Aussi, l'entente entre des Etats jusqu'à présent antagonistes est-elle surtout, suivant les Français, un problème européen . . . . C'est le cas pour le règlement qui, un jour, devra fixer le sort de l'ensemble de l'Allemagne et la sécurité de notre continent." (*DMV*, p. 43.)

94. Adam B. Ulam, *Expansion and Coexistence. The History of Soviet Foreign Policy, 1917-67* (New York: Praeger, 1968), p. 736.

95. The text of the Franco-Soviet communiqué is taken from the *Bulletin Mensuel d'Information* (Ambassade de France à Londres, Service de Presse et d'Information, July 1966).

96. "Il s'agit aussi de mettre en oeuvre successivement: la détente, l'entente et la coopération dans notre Europe toute entière . . . " (*DMV*, p. 58.)

97. "modifier successivement les dispositions actuellement pratiquées . . . " (*DMV*, p. 19.)

98. For the effects on NATO of France's withdrawal see Brigadier K. Hunt, *NATO without France: The Military Implications*, Adelphi Papers Number 32 (London: The Institute for Strategic Studies, December 1966).

99. Alfred Fabre-Luce, *L'homme journal* (Paris: Gallimard, 1967), p. 229.

100. Text in *French Foreign Policy: Official Statements, Speeches and Communiqués 1966.* (New York: Ambassade de France, Service de Presse et d'Information), p. 50

101. See *Le Monde* 30 January 1968.

102. For the new notes struck by the 'great coalition' see Besson, *Die Aussenpolitik*, chaps 19 and 20.

103. "une sorte de Zone de libre-échange de l'Europe occidentale, en attendant la Zone atlantique qui ôterait à notre continent toute réelle personnalité." (*DMV*, p. 173); and "une certain évolution intérieure et extérieure . . . " (*DMV*, p. 174.)

104. Carmoy, *Foreign Policies*, p. 442.

105. In *Politique Etrangère* 32 (1967): pp. 519-541.

106. *DMIV*, p. 356

107. "une escalade de plus en plus étendue en Asie, de plus en plus proche de la Chine, de plus en plus provocante à l'égard de l'Union Soviétique, de plus en plus réprouvée par nombre de peuples d'Europe, d'Afrique, d'Amérique latine, et, en fin de compte, de plus en plus menaçante pour la paix du monde." "il n'y a . . . aucune chance pour que les peuples de l'Asie se sou-

mettent à la loi de l'étranger venu de l'autre rive du Pacifique . . . " (*DMV*, pp. 76-77.)

108. *PII*, pp. 386-387.

109. On French policy in Laos see Newhouse, *De Gaulle and the Anglo-Saxons*, pp. 257-265.

110. "l'or, qui ne change pas de nature . . . qui n'a pas de nationalité, qui est tenu, éternellement et universellement, comme la valeur inaltérable et fiduciaire par excellence." (*DMIV*, p. 333.)

111. *French Foreign Policy 1966*, p. 120.

112. Jacques Vernant in *Politique Etrangère* 28 (1963), p. 466.

113. *French Aid to Developing Countries in 1968*, n.p.

114. See article by Robert E. Farrell, *Interplay Magazine*, October 1970.

115. *DMV*, p. 192.

116. Ibid., p. 332.

117. *MEI*, p. 277.

118. Ibid., p. 279.

119. *French Foreign Policy: Official Statements, Speeches and Communiqués January–June 1967* (New York: Ambassade de France, Service de Presse et d'Information), p. 81.

120. Ibid., p. 103.

121. "un peuple d'élite, sûr de lui-même et dominateur . . . " (*DMV*, p. 232.)

122. "Le peuple français . . . avait, pendant des siècles, pris l'habitude d'être le mastodonte de l'Europe et c'est le sentiment qu'il avait de sa grandeur, par conséquent de sa responsabilité, qui maintenait son unité, alors, qu'il est par nature, et cela depuis les Gaulois, perpétuellement porté aux divisions et aux chimères." (*MEI*, p. 189.)

123. Quoted in Grosser, *La Politique Extérieure de la Ve République*, p. 188.

VII. Gaullism at Home:
The Domestic Policy of the Fifth Republic

1. Williams, *Wars, Plots and Scandals in Post-war France*, p. 125.

2. *DMIV*, p. 414.

3. Chapsal, *Vie politique*, pp. 499-501.

4. For the Pinay-Rueff plan see de Lattre, *Politique économique de la France depuis 1945*, pp. 491-493.

5. See *Basic Statistics of the Community 1968-1969* (Brussels and Luxembourg: Statistical Office of the European Communities, 1970), pp. 22-23.

6. Figures from the *Annuaire statistique de la France. Résultats de 1968* (Paris: Institut national de la Statistique et des études économiques, 1969).

7. These figures are taken either from *Five Years of Peace under the Fifth Republic: An Economic Balance Sheet* (New York: Ambassade de France, Service de Presse et d'Information, March 1968); or from *Basic Statistics of the Community 1968-1969*.

8. On the 1963 stabilization plan see de Lattre, *Politique économique de la France depuis 1945*, pp. 497-499.

9. See the diagram in Jean Charlot, *Le Phénomène Gaulliste* (Paris: Fayard, 1970), pp. 44-45.

10. On the present problems of French agriculture see de Lattre, *Politique économique*, Fascicule III, pp. 105-115.

11. On the modernization of French industry see John Ardagh, *The New French Revolution* (New York and Evanston: Harper & Row, 1968), pp. 46-66.

12. On the Bull affair and the *plan calcul* see Gilpin, *France in Age of Scientific State*, pp. 49-51 and 331-333.

13. See Ardagh, *New French Revolution*, pp. 38-40.

14. Figures taken from *The Population of France* (London: Ambassade de France, Service de Presse et d'Information, n.d.).

15. For general change in habits see Ardagh, *New French Revolution*, chaps. 5, 6 and 9.

16. See de Lattre, *Politique économique*, p. 209; and *Basic Statistics of the Community 1968-1969*, p. 68.

17. On the Fouchet reforms see *L'Année Politique en France 1965* (Paris: Presses universitaires de France, 1966), pp. 397-407; also Ardagh, *New French Revolution*, chap. 10.

18. On the Independent Republicans see Jean Charlot, *Le Phénomène Gaulliste*, pp. 112-123.

19. Chapsal, *Vie politique*, pp. 480-481. For details of government changes up to the end of 1965 see *PII*, pp. 415-418.

20. Chapsal, *Vie politique*, pp. 536-540.

21. See: *L'Election Présidentielle des 5 et 19 Décembre 1965*, p. 25.

22. Quoted in Chapsal, *Vie politique*, p. 541.

23. For the fate of the Defferre candidacy see Chapsal, ibid., pp. 559-562; and *L'Election Présidentielle des 5 et 19 Décembre 1965*, pp. 45-70.

24. *L'Election Présidentielle des 5 et 19 Décembre 1965*, pp. 135-139 for other candidates.

25. Quoted in Chapsal, *Vie politique*, p. 554.

26. *PII*, pp. 102-103.

27. For the rise of Pompidou and his gradual assumption of authority see Werner F. Koeng, *Duell im Schatten: Der Sturz de Gaulle* (Bern and Stuttgart: Verlag Hallwag, 1969), pp. 100-105.

28. "Que l'adhesion franche et massive des citoyens m'engage à rester en fonctions, l'avenir de la République nouvelle sera décidément assuré. Sinon, personne ne peut douter qu'elle s'écroulera aussitôt et que la France devra subir—mais cette fois sans recours possible—une confusion de l'Etat plus désastreuse encore que celle qu'elle connût autrefois." (*DMIV*, p. 401.)

29. Quoted in Jean Charlot, *Le Gaullisme* (Paris: Colin, 1970), p. 183.

30. On the Gaullist use of television see Monica Charlot's study of "Le Journal télévisé," in *L'Election Présidentielle des 5 et 19 Décembre 1965* pp. 175-179.

31. Figures in Goguel and Grosser, *Politique en France*, p. 293.

32. *PII*, p. 130.

33. Figures in *L'Election Présidentielle des 5 et 19 Décembre 1965*, p. 404.

34. François Goguel quoted in Charlot, *Le Phénomène Gaulliste*, p. 84.

35. See *L'Election Présidentielle des 5 et 19 Décembre 1965*, pp. 407-409 and maps 17 and 18 on p. 418.

36. On the left-wing Gaullists see Charlot, *Le Phénomène Gaulliste*, pp. 104-111.

37. Ibid., pp. 112-123.

38. Chapsal, *Vie politique*, pp. 578-582.

39. "Ce qui s'est passé n'a rien eu que de vulgaire et de subalterne." (*DMV*, p. 14.)

40. Williams, *Wars, Plots and Scandals in Post-war France*, p. 100.

41. Figures taken from Goguel and Grosser, *La Politique en France*, pp. 293-294.

42. Ibid., p. 298.

43. For this speech see *L'Année Politique en France 1967* (Paris: Presses Universitaires de France, 1968), p. 2.

44. Koeng, *Duell im Schatten*, p. 159.

45. For the ordinances see *L'Année Politique en France 1967*, pp. 111-124.

46. For all this see Chapsal, *Vie politique*, pp. 587-592.

47. Pierre Viansson-Ponté in *Le Monde*, 29 December 1967.

48. Text in Charlot, *Le Gaullisme*, pp. 131-132.

49. Terrenoire, *De Gaulle et l'Algérie*, p. 108.

50. On the relations between de Gaulle and the UNR see Charlot, *L'U.N.R.*, chap. 10, passim.

51. Quoted in ibid., p. 80.

52. Ibid., pp. 140-141.

53. See *Le Référendum d'Octobre et les Elections de Novembre 1962*, pp. 77-78.

54. Charlot, *L'U.N.R.*, p. 302.

55. Ibid., pp. 303-304.

56. See Charlot, *Le Phénomène Gaulliste*, pp. 146-148.

57. Ibid., p. 130.

58. Charlot, *L'U.N.R.*, p. 116.

59. See Charlot, *Le Phénomène Gaulliste*, pp. 131 and 134. Also p. 193 n.75.

60. Ibid., pp. 132-133.

61. Estimate in ibid., p. 135.

62. For analysis of the Gaullist electorate see ibid., tableau no. 15, p. 75 and carte no. 1, pp. 80-81. Also electoral maps in Goguel and Grosser, *Politique in France*, pp. 285-287. Compare with map of practicing Catholicism on p. 284.

63. See Charlot, *Le Phénomène Gaulliste*, pp. 73-76 for differences between the electoral 'profiles' of de Gaulle and Pompidou.

64. René Rémond, "Le Gaullisme à la lumière du printemps 68," *France-Forum* 90-91 (Octobre-Novembre 1968): p. 28.

65. Text in Charlot, *Le Gaullisme*, pp. 123-124.

66. *Le Monde*, 15 March 1968.

67. Michel Crozier, *La Société Bloquée* (Paris: Editions du Seuil, 1970).

VIII. The Decline of Gaullism: May and the End of a Regime

1. *Le Monde*, 5-6 May 1968.

2. Epistémon, *Ces idées qui ont ébranlé la France* (Paris: Fayard, 1968), p. 18.

3. See the report of "the May events" addressed by the Minister of the Interior, Raymond Marcellin, to the prefects on June 24, 1968 in J-R. Tournoux, *Le mois de Mai du Général* (Paris, Plon, 1969), pp. 364-386.

4. See the essay by David Goldey, "The Events of May 1968" in Philip M. Williams, *French Politicians and Elections 1951-1969* (Cambridge: Cambridge University Press, 1970), pp. 226-260. This is the best account of the crisis.

5. See *Tournoux, Le mois de Mai*, p. 378, for the ministry of the interior's estimate of these.

6. Ibid., p. 379.

7. For Fouchet's concern to avoid bloodshed see Philippe Alexandre, *L'Elysée en péril: 2/30 Mai 1968* (Paris: Fayard, 1969), p. 28. For the attitude of the minister of defense and the army to a military intervention to suppress the rioting see ibid., pp. 274-277; and Tournoux, *Le mois de Mai*, pp. 263-265.

8. On Peyrefitte's difficulties see Alexandre, *L'Elysée en péril*, pp. 21-23. For Geismar's statement see *Le Monde*, 9 May 1968.

9. *Le Monde*, 12-13 May 1968.

10. Christian Fouchet, *Au service du Général de Gaulle* (Paris: Plon, 1971), pp. 256-259.

11. On de Gaulle's attitude towards Pompidou's policy see Tournous, *Le Mois de Mai*, pp. 329-330; and Claude Paillat, *Archives Secrètes 1968/69: les coulisses d'une année terrible* (Paris: Denoel, 1969), p. 141.

12. For some examples of his cavalier treatment of ministers see Paillat, ibid., p. 142.

N

13. Epistémon, *Ces idées qui ont ébranlé la France*, p. 57.

14. *Le Monde*, 19-20 May 1968.

15. For the terms of the Grenelle protocol see *L'Année politique en France 1968* (Paris: Presses Universitaires de France, 1969), pp. 166-167. On the final wage settlement, p. 170.

16. *L'Année Politique 1968*, p. 40.

17. *DMV*, p. 290.

18. *L'Année Politique 1968*, p. 43.

19. Ibid., pp. 43-44.

20. *MEI*, pp. 307-308.

21. Tournoux, *Le mois de Mai*, p. 66 and p. 221; and Alexandre, *L'Elysée en péril*, p. 298.

22. "l'intimidation, l'intoxication et la tyrannie exercées par des groupes organisés de longue main en conséquence et par un parti qui est une entreprise totalitaire, même s'il a déjà des rivaux à cet égard." (*DMV*, p. 293.)

23. *Le Monde*, 1 June and 4 June 1968.

24. *DMV*, pp. 302-303.

25. *L'Année Politique 1968*, p. 47.

26. Figures in Chapsal, *Vie politique*, pp. 609-610.

27. "l'alliance des chimères, des chantages et des lâchetés . . . " (*MEI*, p. 144.)

28. See his statement before the National Assembly in *Le Monde,* 16 November 1968.

29. To get some sense of this side of "the May events" see Alain Schnapp and Pierre Vidal-Naquet, *Journal de la Commune étudiante: Textes et Documents Novembre 67–Juin 68* (Paris: Editions du Seuil, 1969).The texts contained in this collection give a good idea of the ideological spectrum.

30. Crozier, *Société bloquée*, pp. 177-178.

31. Ibid., p. 243.

32. "Tout m'échappait. Je n'avais plus de prise sur mon propre gouvernement." (André Malraux, *Les chênes qu'on abat* . . . [Paris: Gallimard, 1971], p.28.)

33. *MEII*, pp. 112-115.

34. For these see Koeng, *Duell im Schatten*, pp. 225-226.

35. Text in Tournoux, *Le mois de Mai*, pp. 333-334.

36. "placé en réserve de la République." (*DMV*, p. 323.)

37. See *L'Année Politique 1968*, p. 56.

38. Ibid., p. 59.

39. *Le Monde*, 13 and 21 September 1968.

40. For the provisions of the law see *L'Année Politique 1968*, pp. 367-369.

41. "organiser . . . l'information régulière de tous sur la situation et les perspectives de l'affaire à laquelle ils apportent leur travail . . . " (*DMV*, p. 328.)

42. For de Gaulle's conception of the reformed Senate see *DMV*, pp. 324-326.

43. Williams, *French Politicians and Elections 1951-1969*, pp. 282-283.

44. For these statements and Pompidou's attitude towards the referendum see *Le Monde*, 15 February 1969.

45. Koeng, *Duell im Schatten*, pp. 341-342 and 386-391.

46. *L'Année Politique 1968*, p. 100.

47. See the article by André Fontaine in *Le Monde*, 11 March 1969.

48. De Lattre, *Politique économique*, Fascicule III, p. 11.

49. Besson, *Die Aussenpolitik*, p. 421.

50. Charlot, *Le Phénomène Gaulliste*, p. 179.

51. *Le Monde*, 10-11 August 1969.

52. For the austerity plan see *L'Année Politique 1968*, pp. 134-135.

53. *L'Année Politique 1968*, p. 97.

54. "De la réponse que fera le pays à ce que je lui demande va dépendre évidemment, soit la continuation de mon mandat, soit aussitôt mon départ." (*DMV*, p. 401.) See note 1 on the same page for previous Gaullist statements to the contrary.

55. Koeng, *Duell im Schatten*, p. 436.

56. Figures in Charlot, *Le Gaullisme*, p. 158. Opinion poll in Koeng, *Duell im Schatten*, p. 426.

57. Malraux's remark in *Les chênes qu'on abat . . .*, p. 46.

A Selective Bibliographical Note

For the whole period of this book and especially from 1940 onwards a main source is clearly the works of Charles de Gaulle listed on p. 331. Among these the five volumes of *Discours et Messages* (Paris, Plon, 1970) are particularly important. They contain a useful-chronology and notes by François Goguel. It should be noted that the English translation of the *Mémoires de Guerre* (Paris, Plon, 1954-1959) does not contain the selection of documents added to the French edition. *La France sera la France: ce que veut Charles de Gaulle* (Paris, Rassemblement du Peuple français, 1951) gives a useful selection of de Gaulle's utterances chosen by Georges Pompidou under the author's own supervision. The two volumes by André Passeron also listed on p. 311, *De Gaulle Parle* (Paris, Plon, 1962) and *De Gaulle Parle 1962-1966* (Paris, Fayard, 1966), perform much more than they promise, giving many texts supplementary to de Gaulle's own speeches.

Among biographies of de Gaulle one might single out: Jean Lacouture, *De Gaulle* (Paris, Editions du Seuil, 1969); and, Paul-Marie de La Gorce, *De Gaulle entre deux Mondes: une vie et une époque* (Paris, Fayard, 1964). Both of these are written from what might be called a left-wing Gaullist point of view.

Of general studies of French politics which deal with the period covered in this book by far the most useful is: Jacques Chapsal, *La Vie Politique en France depuis 1940*, deuxiéme édition revue et complétée par Alain Lancelot (Paris, Presses Universitaires de France, 1969). A useful reference work is François Goguel and Alfred Grosser, *La Politique en France*, troisième édition entièrement revue et mise à jour (Paris, Colin, 1967). A study in English is Pierre Avril, *Politics in France* (Harmondsworth, Penguin Books, 1969). An economic history which goes up to around 1965 is Yves Trotignon, *La France depuis 1939* (Paris, a duplicated series of lectures delivered at the Ecole des Hautes Etudes Commerciales, n.d.). There is also the authoritative work by André de Lattre: *Politique Economique de la France depuis 1945*, (Paris, Sirey, 1966).

For foreign policy during the Fourth and Fifth Republics there are the excellent studies by Alfred Grosser: *La IVe République et sa Politique extérieure* (Paris, Colin, 1961), and *La Politique extérieure de la Ve République* (Paris, Editions de Seuil, 1965). The latter, however, needs to be complemented by a much fuller work which goes right up to 1968 and is distinctly critical of Gaullist policies: Guy de Carmoy, *The Foreign Policies of France 1944-1968.* Translated by Elaine P. Halperin (Chicago, University of Chicago Press, 1970).

Gaullism itself is most conveniently first studied in the collections of documents assembled by Jean Charlot: *Le Gaullisme* (Paris, Colin, 1970). Another quite indispensable book by M. Charlot is *Le Phénomène Gaulliste* (Paris, Fayard, 1970) which, with the aid of the public opinion polls, analyzes in depth the movement as it finally emerged under the Fifth Republic. A longer historical perspective is provided by René Rémond's great book, so revealing of the traditional elements in French political life: *La Droite en France: de la première restauration à la Ve République.* Nouvelle édition revue et augmentée (Paris, Aubier, 1963).

CHAPTER I: DOCTRINE OF GAULLISM

In addition to de Gaulle's own writings and speeches mentioned above, J-R. Tournoux, *La Tragédie du Général* (Paris, Plon, 1967), contains many revealing traits of a character which has also been discerningly analyzed by André Malraux in *Antimémoires* (Paris, Gallimard, 1967) and *Les Chênes qu'on abat...* (Paris, Gallimard, 1971), and by Emmanuel d'Astier in *Sept fois sept jours* (Paris, Editions de Minuit, 1957). There is unfortunately no adequate study of de Gaulle's intellectual background, but the materials for one will not exist until we have a good deal more knowledge of his earlier life, the influences upon him and his reading.

CHAPTER II: THE THIRD REPUBLIC: PRELUDE TO FAILURE

The best general picture of politics in the closing years of the Third Republic is still André Siegfried, *Tableau des Partis en France* (Paris, Grasset, 1931). A more detailed historical account is to be found in François Goguel, *La Politique des Partis sous la IIIe République* (Paris, Editions du Seuil, 1946). Other works which give insights into various sectors of French political life at this time are: Eugen Weber, *Action*

Française: Royalism and Reaction in Twentieth-Century France (Stanford, California, Stanford University Press, 1962); John T. Marcus, *French Socialism in the Crisis Years 1933-1936* (New York, Praeger, 1960); Jacques Fauvet, *Histoire du Parti Communiste Français.* Vol. I *De la guerre à la guerre 1917-1939* (Paris, Fayard, 1964); Annie Kriegel, *Les Communistes Français. Essai d'ethnographie politique* (Paris, Editions du Seuil, 1968); Dieter Wolf, *Die Doriot Bewegung: Ein Beitrag zur Geschichte des Französischen Faschismus* (Stuttgart, Deutsche Verlags-Anstalt, 1967). This last work is far more than a biography of Doriot. It illumines the whole structure of French politics in the thirties – in particular the reasons for the failure of the *Front Populaire.* There is also a history of the *Front Populaire* – Georges Lefranc, *Histoire du Front Populaire 1934-1938* (Paris, Payot, 1965).

The economic history of France between the two wars has now been written on a suitable scale by Alfred Sauvy, *Histoire économique de la France entre les deux guerres.* Vol. I. 1918-1931. Vol. II. 1931-1939 (Paris, Fayard, 1965 and 1967), which, again, shows fairly clearly where the *Front Populaire* went wrong.

For French defense policy there is Guy Chapman, *Why France Collapsed* (London, Cassell, 1968), and the best witness of the 1940 campaign and the dissolution that followed it is still Major-General Sir Edward Spears, *Assignment to Catastrophe:* Vol. I. *Prelude to Dunkirk July 1939-May 1940* and Vol. II. *The Fall of France* (London, Heinemann, 1954).

CHAPTER III: THE WAR YEARS: THE FOUNDING OF GAULLISM

For Vichy see Robert Aron, *The Vichy Régime 1940-1944* (London, Putnam, 1958) and Paul Farmer, *Vichy: Political Dilemma* (London, Oxford University Press, 1955), neither of which is really adequate. An entirely new light has been thrown on the relations of Vichy with the occupying power by Eberhard Jäckel, *Frankreich in Hitlers Europa: Die Deutsche Frankreichpolitik im zweiten Weltkrieg* (Stuttgart, Deutsche Verlags-Anstalt, 1966). There are, of course, many other works which throw light on different aspects of Vichy as well as numerous memoirs by participants.

On the London Gaullist movement a main source is the documents supplied in de Gaulle's *Mémoires de Guerre*. The history of Free France has been briefly written by Henri Michel, *Histoire de la France Libre* (Paris, Presses Universitaires de France, 1963) and the Gaullist struggle for recognition by the allies magistrally recounted by Arthur Layton Funk, *Charles de Gaulle, the Crucial Years, 1943-1944* (New York, Norman and University of Oklahoma Press, 1959). This excellent work, to which every other writer about wartime Gaullism must be indebted, is a great deal harder on American policy than William L. Langer in *Our Vichy Gamble* (New York, Norton, 1966). A French account of the struggle between de Gaulle and Giraud and the intrigues of the Algerian period of Gaullism can be found in Yves-Maxime Danan, *La Vie politique à Alger de 1940-1944* (Paris, R. Pichon et R. Durand-Auzias, 1963). Among Gaullist writers of memoirs the most important is Jacques Soustelle, *Envers et contre Tout. I: De Londres à Alger. II: D'Alger à Paris* (Paris, Robert Laffont, 1947 and 1950).

The Resistance has not had a full-scale history devoted to it. There is Henri Michel's small *Histoire de la Résistance* (Paris, Presses Universitaires de France, 1950), but a longer work is badly needed. The evolution of the institutions of the Resistance and de Gaulle's struggle to control it are recounted in: René Hostache, *Le Conseil national de la Résistance* (Paris, Presses Universitaires de France, 1958); and Henri Denis, *Le Comité Parisien de la Libération* (Paris, Presses Universitaires de France, 1963). A good idea of how clandestine action was carried on is given by M.R.D. Foot, *SOE in France: An Account of the Work of the British Special Operations Executive in France 1940-1944* (London, H.M. Stationery Office, 1966). The ideas generated by the Resistance are studied in Henri Michel, *Les Courants de Pensée de la Résistance* (Paris, Presses Universitaires de France, 1962).

Robert Aron has written a *Histoire de la Libération de France* (Paris, Fayard, 1959), but the provisional government of de Gaulle has received less attention than other periods of wartime Gaullism. For foreign policy see A.W. DePorte, *De Gaulle's Foreign Policy: 1944-1946* (Cambridge, Harvard University Press, 1968). Accounts of de Gaulle's policy in Indochina can be found in: Donald Lancaster, *The Emancipation of French Indochina* (London, Oxford University Press, 1961); Ellen J. Hammer, *The Struggle for Indochina, 1940-1955* (Stanford, California, Stanford University Press, 1966); and Dennis J.

Duncanson, *Government and the Revolution in Vietnam* (London, Oxford University Press, 1968). An interesting witness of events, whose journal begins in 1945, is the head of protocol at the Quai d'Orsay, Jacques Dumaine, *Quai d'Orsay (1945-1951)* (Paris, Julliard, 1956).

CHAPTER IV: THE FOURTH REPUBLIC AND THE RPF

There are several works which give good general descriptions of the political life of the Fourth Republic. The most authoritative and massive of all is that by Philip M. Williams, *Crisis and Compromise: Politics in the Fourth Republic* (London, Longmans, 1964), which is required reading for anyone interested in the period. To this may be added two collections of articles by the same author, some of which deal with the Fifth Republic as well: *Wars, Plots and Scandals in Post-War France* (Cambridge, Cambridge University Press, 1970); and *French Politicians & Elections 1951-1969* (Cambridge, Cambridge University Press, 1970). Other works include: Jacques Fauvet, *La IVe République* (Paris, Fayard, 1959); Raymond Aron, *Immuable et Changeante, de la IVe à la Ve République* (Paris, Calmann-Levy, 1959); Alexander Werth, *France 1940-1955* (London, Robert Hale, 1956) – this is written from a neutralist' point of view and is sometimes untrustworthy; and André Siegfried, *De la IVe à la Ve République* (Paris, Grasset, 1958). The last is a collection of articles, including prefaces written to each year's *Année Politique*. It provides one of the most lucid and intelligent commentaries to the politics of the Fourth Republic. There is also an early work by François Goguel, *France Under the Fourth Republic* (Ithaca, New York, Cornell University Press, 1952). General aspects of the political, economic and social life of the Fourth Republic will be found in Stanley Hoffmann, et al., *In Search of France* (Cambridge, Mass., Harvard University Press, 1963).

Special political themes have been studied by Stanley Hoffmann, *Le Mouvement Poujade* (Paris, Colin, 1956) and by Francis de Tarr, *The French Radical Party from Herriot to Mendès-France* (London, Oxford University Press, 1961). There is an excellent study of the 1956 elections: Maurice Duverger, et al. ed., *Les Elections du 2 Janvier 1956* (Paris, Colin, 1957). Among the governments of the Fourth Republic that of Mendès-France has received special treatment in Pierre Rouanet,

Mendès-France au pouvoir 1954-1955 (Paris, Lafont, 1965).

In addition to the works mentioned above by de Lattre and Trotignon, economic problems are dealt with in J-M. Jeanneney, *Forces et Faiblesses de l'Economie française 1945-1959,* seconde édition revue et augmentée (Paris, Colin, 1959), and in Henri Brousse, *Le Niveau de Vie en France* (Paris, Presses Universitaires de France, 1962).

The foreign policy of the Fourth Republic is well served by the works of Grosser and Carmoy mentioned above. For the Indochinese war see the various works listed under the last chapter. On the struggle around the European Defense Community (EDC) and French neutralism in general see: Daniel Lerner, et al. ed, *France Defeats EDC* (New York, Praeger, 1957); and John T. Marcus, *Neutralism and Nationalism in France* (New York, Bookman Associates, 1958). This is a very perceptive book and an important one for anyone interested in Gaullism. Much about events in North Africa can be found in Grosser. Other works include: Germaine Tillion, *L'Algérie en 1957* (Paris, Editions de Minuit, 1957); and Raymond Aron, *La Tragédie algérienne* (Paris, Plon, 1957). On the reactions of the French army to the Algerian war see: Raoul Girardet, ed., *La Crise militaire française 1946-1962: Aspects sociologiques et idéologiques* (Paris, Colin, 1964); and John Ambler, *Soldiers Against the State: The French Army in Politics* (New York, Anchor Books, 1968).

There are a number of books of memoirs which illustrate the history of the Fourth Republic. Scanty but significant are the two volumes of Robert Buron: *Les Dernières Années de la IVe République: Carnets politiques* (Paris, Plon, 1968), and *Carnets politiques de la Guerre d'Algérie* (Paris, Plon, 1965). There are also two important witnesses to the painful process of "decolonization": Gilbert Grandval, *Ma Mission au Maroc* (Paris, Plon, 1956); and Henri Navarre, *Agonie de l'Indochine (1953-1954)* (Paris, Plon, 1957). Georges Bidault has written his memoirs under the deceptive title of *Resistance* (London, Weidenfeld and Nicolson, 1967), and Vincent Auriol's diaries will be a very important source when published in their entirety. So far we have a selection: *Mon Septennat 1947-1954* (Paris, Gallimard, 1970). Dumaine is also an interesting witness.

On the RPF the essential book is: Christian Purtschet, *Le Rassemblement du Peuple Français* (Paris, Editions Cujas, 1965).

CHAPTER V: GAULLISM AND ALGERIA:
THE ESTABLISHMENT OF THE FIFTH REPUBLIC

The events of May 13th, 1958, and the end of the Fourth Republic
have been the subject of many works. The best essay on the subject is
by Philip M. Williams in *Wars, Plots and Scandals in Post-War France.*
His remarks there should make us cautious about so-called secret
history by journalists, but the best of this kind of book is Jean Ferniot,
De Gaulle et le 13 Mai (Paris, Plon, 1965). The judgments of Merry and
Serge Bromberger, *Les 13 Complots du 13 Mai* (Paris, Fayard, 1959)
seem much less reliable. On the events themselves we have the testi-
mony of de Gaulle himself *(ME 1),* of Buron, and of Jacques Soustelle,
L'Espérance trahie 1958-1961 (Paris, Editions de l'Alma, 1962). There
is a revealing book by one of the colonels concerned, Roger Trinquier,
Le Coup d'Etat du 13 Mai (Paris, Editions Esprit, 1962), and the essen-
tial second volume of the memoirs of General Paul Ely, *Mémoires II.*
Suez . . . Le 13 Mai (Paris, Plon, 1969).

On the Constitution there is a good account in Chapsal and in
Maurice Duverger, *Les Institutions Françaises* (Paris, Presses Universitaires de France, 1962). There is also a discussion of it in Philip M.
Williams and Martin Harrison, *De Gaulle's Republic* (London, Longmans, 1960), a book which gives an interesting account of the first
years of the Fifth Republic (I have not been able to see the recently
published enlarged edition of this work).

The various referendums and elections of the Fifth Republic have
been studied in a series of works published under the auspices of the
Association française de Science politique: L'Etablissement de la
Cinquième République: Le Référendum de Septembre et les Elections
de Novembre 1958 (Paris, Colin, 1960); François Goguel, ed., *Le*
Référendum du 8 Janvier 1961 (Paris, Colin, 1962); François Goguel,
ed., *Le Référendum du 8 Avril 1962* (Paris, Colin, 1963); and François
Goguel, ed., *Le Référendum d'Octobre et les Elections de Novembre*
1962 (Paris, Colin, 1965). The material contained in these works is
essential for an understanding of French politics during this period.

De Gaulle's Algerian policy is best studied in his own speeches and
press conferences, but there is much in the two books by Passeron
mentioned above that cannot be found elsewhere. On the episode of
the barricades there is Merry and Serge Bromberger, Georgette Elgey, and

J-F. Chauvel, *Barricades et Colonels: 24 Janvier 1960* (Paris, Fayard, 1960). On the generals' putsch, Jacques Fauvet and Jean Planchais, *La Fronde des généraux* (Paris, Arthaud, 1961). The state of mind of the OAS is shown in the documents published in *OAS Parle* (Paris, Julliard, 1964). See also the trials of Raoul Salan and Edmond Jouhaud. Buron's *Carnets politiques de la Guerre d'Algérie* are also of great interest for this period, since he was a signatory of the Evian treaty, and Louis Terrenoire, *De Gaulle et l'Algérie: témoinage pour l'histoire* (Paris, Fayard, 1964), provides a good counterbalance to Soustelle. The effect of the Algerian crisis on the Gaullists is dealt with at length by Jean Charlot in his excellent book *L'U.N.R.: étude du pouvoir au sein d'un parti politique* (Paris, Colin, 1967). What followed the Evian agreements is recounted in Carmoy. It is interesting, in the light of what came later, to glance at Michel Debré's various pamphlets written before he became prime minister. Two examples are *Ces Princes qui nous gouvernent . . .* (Paris, Plon, 1957) and *Refaire une démocratie, un état, un pouvoir* (Paris, Plon, 1958).

For de Gaulle's alteration of the Constitution in the autumn of 1962 see Chapsal and the various contributions to *Le Référendum d'Octobre et les Elections de Novembre 1962.*

CHAPTER VI: GAULLISM ABROAD:
THE FOREIGN POLICY OF THE FIFTH REPUBLIC

General works are those by Grosser and Carmoy mentioned above. On de Gaulle's European policy there is an excellent work by John Newhouse, *De Gaulle and the Anglo-Saxons* (New York, The Viking Press, 1970). And for Franco-German relations this can usefully be supplemented by a German work by Waldemar Besson, *Die Aussenpolitik der Bundesrepublik* (München, Piper, 1970). The evolution of French policy can best be traced in the utterances of de Gaulle and Couve de Murville. There is much useful information – especially on French relations with the underdeveloped countries – in the documents put out by the French embassy's *Service de Presse et d'Information* in both London and New York. Particularly useful are the Ambassade de France series, *French Foreign Policy: Official Statements, Speeches and Communiqués* (Service de Presse et d'Information, New York).

On France's nuclear force see the various publications of the Institute for Strategic Studies – particularly the yearly *The Military Balance* and *Strategic Survey*. The most up-to-date book on the subject is Wolf Mendl, *Deterrence and Persuasion: French Nuclear Armament in the Context of National Policy, 1945-1969* (New York and Washington, Praeger, 1970). There is also some interesting information on the technological and budgetary aspects of this in Robert Gilpin, *France in the Age of the Scientific State* (Princeton, N.J., Princeton University Press, 1968).

On France and the European Economic Community see two works by Miriam Camps: *Britain and the European Community 1955-1963* (Princeton, N.J., Princeton University Press, 1964); and *European Unification in the Sixties: From the Veto to the Crisis* (New York, McGraw-Hill, 1966). For the military consequences of France's withdrawal from NATO see Brigadier K. Hunt, *NATO Without France: The Military Implications, Adelphi Papers Number Thirty-Two* (London, Institute for Strategic Studies, December 1966).

On France's African policy under the Fifth Republic there is no complete work. There is a good summary in an article by Kaye Whiteman in *Interplay Magazine* (December 1968).

In general there is much interesting material for the study of French foreign policy during these years both in the monthly review *Politique Etrangère* and in *L'Année Politique*.

CHAPTER VII: GAULLISM AT HOME
THE DOMESTIC POLICY OF THE FIFTH REPUBLIC

The same general works of political history can be used here: Chapsal, Goguel, Grosser, etc. For the presidential election of 1965 we have another massive study produced under the auspices of the *Centre d'Etude de la Vie politique française: L'Election présidentielle des 5 et 19 décembre 1965* (Paris, Colin, 1970). There is as yet nothing of this sort for the 1967 elections, but the works of Jean Charlot mentioned above are essential for an understanding of the gradual rise of a Gaullism divorced from the person of de Gaulle. The rise of Pompidou is also recounted (with a hostile bias) in a book by a Swiss journalist, Werner F. Koeng, *Duell im Schatten: Der Sturz de Gaulles* (Bern and

Stuttgart, Hallwag, 1969). In general, for these years *Le Monde* and *L'Année Politique* are the most valuable sources. There is also the *Révue française de Science Politique* where many studies of contemporary politics appear.

For economic facts and figures there are once again official French documents of various kinds supplied by the Service de Presse et d'Information, the *Basic Statistics of the Community 1968-1969* (Brussels and Luxembourg, Statistical Office of the European Communities, 1970), and, as a reference book, the *Annuaire Statistique de la France* (Paris, Institut national de la Statistique et des études économiques, 1969). The basic work is still that by de Lattre mentioned above, and it is completed by a course of lectures, *Politique Economique de la France* (Paris, Les Cours de Droit, n.d) which carries events up to 1968. Social change in France is dealt with by John Ardagh, *The New French Revolution* (New York and Evanston, Harper & Row, 1968), and technology is analyzed by Gilpin in *France in the Age of the Scientific State.*

CHAPTER VIII: THE DECLINE OF GAULLISM: MAY AND THE END OF A RÉGIME

Much has been written about "the May events," but by far the best way of getting an impression of what happened is to read through *Le Monde* for May and June 1968. Among books on the subject there is a good one on the student discontent by a professor at Nanterre: Epistémon, *Ces idées qui ont ébranlé la France* (Paris, Fayard, 1968). The ideological turmoil is well reproduced in Alain Schnapp and Pierre Vidal-Naquet, *Journal de la Commune étudiante: Textes et documents Novembre 67-Juin 68* (Paris, Editions du Seuil, 1969). But the best diagnosis is in a brilliant book by Michel Crozier, *La Société Bloquée* (Paris, Editions du Seuil, 1970). As to the events themselves and their political and economic consequences, there is a good analysis in *L'Année Politique 1968* and also in an essay by David Goldey in Philip M. Williams's *French Politicians and Elections 1951-1969*, mentioned above. Otherwise there are the 'secret' histories which can be used when they more or less agree: J-R. Tournoux, *Le Mois de Mai du Général* (Paris, Plon, 1969); Philippe Alexandre, *L'Elysée en Péril: 2/30 Mai 1968* (Paris, Fayard, 1969); and Claude Paillat, *Archives Secrètes*

1968/69: les coulisses d'une année terrible (Paris, Denoel, 1969).

For the economic results of the crisis there are the works by de Lattre already mentioned.

There is no satisfactory work on the last months of de Gaulle's presidency. I have used Koeng, and Jean Charlot's *Le Phénomène Gaulliste* illustrates well enough what happened in electoral terms. De Gaulle's own view of May 1968 can be found in André Malraux's *Les chênes qu'on abat . . .*

These bibliographical indications are, of course, by no means exhaustive. Some subjects are only touched upon, but this is inevitable in a wide-ranging study of this kind. I have mostly listed works that I myself found useful and I'm sure that a number of excellent books have been omitted.

A.H.

Index

A

Abadie, Jules, 70-71*n*.
Abbas, Ferhat, 132, 175,181
Abetz, Otto, 56
Acre, negotiations at, 62, 63
Action française, 39, 45, 57, 111*n*., 301
Action Républicaine et Sociale (ARS), 106
Added value tax (TVA), 117
Adenauer, Konrad, 121, 209, 212, 213, 214, 215, 218, 220, 225, 226
"Affaire des généraux," 127
Africa, 306; "decolonization" of, 201-206 (*see also* Algeria; Morocco; North Africa; Tunisia)
Afrique francophone, 201, 202, 204, 227, 238*n*., 239, 241
Agriculture, problems in, 116, 250-251
Ailleret, General Charles, 198, 233
Aimée et souffrante Algérie 166*n*.
Ait Ahmed, Hocine, 131*n*.
Algeria, 147-193, 206, 217, 240, 306; French integration with, 8, 49, 86; rebellion in, 96, 103, 106, 109, 111, 112, 117, 118, 125, 131-135
Algerian army of national liberation (ALN), 132
Algerian National Liberation Front (FLN), 25*n*.
Alibert, Raphael, 54, 56
"All-azimuth," theory, 233, 292
Allard, General Jacques, 170*n*.
Allied Control Commission for Italy, 73*n*.
Allied Control Council (Berlin), 119
Allied Military Government (AMGOT), 74, 76
Alsace-Lorraine, 35, 42, 46; Allied victories in, 79
Altmann, Georges, 64
American aid (Vietnam), 127-128 (*see also* Southeast Asia; Vietnam)

American leadership in Europe, 120-121
Anti-Semitism, 241*n*.
Arab-Israeli relations, 240
Argoud, Colonel Antoine, 172, 174, 178*n*.
Armée de libération nationale (ALN), 184
Aron, Raymond, 188
Aron, Robert, 55*n*., 80*n*.
Arrighi, Pascal, 153, 171, 187
Assises Nationales ("Assizes"), 138
Atlantic alliance, French integration in, 9
Auboyneau, Philippe-Marie, 63*n*.
Auriol, Vincent, 17, 99, 102, 122*n*., 127, 154, 156
Austria, 84
Austria-Hungary, 37

B

Balance of power, European, 37
Banque de France, 42, 46
Boa Dai, 87, 126, 128
Barbu, Marcel, 247*n*., 260*n*.
Bardo, treaty of (1881), 86
Barrachin, Edmond, 140
Barrès, Maurice, 13, 32
Bastien-Thiry, Colonel Jean-Marie, 190
Baudoin, Paul, 54, 56
Baumel, Jacques, 241, 269
Bayet, Albert, 64
Belgium, 37, 38*n*., 219, 239*n*., 294 (*see also* Benelux Countries)
Ben Arafa, Mulay Mohammed, 130, 131
Ben Barka, Mehdi, 205-206
Ben Bella, Ahmed, 131*n*., 133, 180, 184, 206
Ben Khedda, Ben Youssef, 181
Ben Youssef, Sidi Mohammed, 130, 131

Benelux Countries, 120, 124, 218
  (see also Belgium; Luxembourg;
  Netherlands)
Benoist-Méchin, Jacques, 56
Benouville, Guillain de, 141
Berkeley (University of California)
  riots, 276-277, 278
Berl, Emmanuel, 299-300
Berlin Wall, 214
Berthouin, Jean, 164
Beynet, General Paul Emile, 82
Biafra, secession of from Nigeria,
  205n., 239-240
Biaggi, Jean-Baptiste, 171, 187
Bichelonne, Jean, 56
Bidault, Georges, 78n., 85, 88, 91,
  98, 104, 108n., 113, 119, 130,
  147, 150, 177, 182, 197n., 285
Billotte, Pierre, 142
Billoux, François, 73, 78n.
Bloch, Marc, 24, 64
Bloch-Morhange, Jacques, 300
Blum, Léon, 42-43, 45, 88, 100-101,
  116
Bonapartism, 300, 301, 302
Bonn agreements, 107, 122
Bonnet, Henri, 70-71n.
Bordeaux, intrigue of, 48, 49
Bougrenet de la Tocnaye, Alain, 190n.
Boukharrouba, Mohammed (see
  Boumédienne, Houari)
Boulanger, Georges E.J.M., 35, 302
Boulloche, André, 253
Boumédienne, Houari (Mohammed
  Boukharrouba), 206
Bourgès-Maunoury, Maurice, 134,
  164, 177
Bourguiba, Habib, 128, 129, 202-203
Boutemy, André, 139n.
Bouthillier, Yves, 54
Brandt, Willy, 234
Brazzaville Conference (1944), 85, 86
Briand, Aristide, 38, 40
Broizat, Colonel Joseph, 174, 178n.
Brussels (European) Commission,
  227, 228, 229

Brussels talks (1961-1963), 221-222
Bucard, Marcel, 45n.
Bureau central de Renseignements et
  d'Action militaires (BCRA), 65
Buron, Robert, 145, 153, 172, 174,
  179, 183

C

Caillaux, Eugène A., 47
Caillaux, Joseph, 95
Cambodia, 237, 238 (see also
  Southeast Asia)
Camps, Miriam, 228
Canada, 120, 216, 238, 239, 241-242,
  294
Capitant, René, 68, 71n., 78n., 102,
  141, 261, 267, 282, 284, 285, 303,
  305
Carpentier, Marcel, 127
Cartel des Gauches, 38, 41, 42
Cartier, Raymond, 204
Casablanca Conference (1943), 70
Cassin, René, 60, 61n., 63n., 94
Catholic right, the 35, 41, 55, 57, 102
Catholicism, role of in French history,
  33
Catroux, Georges, 60, 61n., 63n.,
  70n., 71n., 78n., 131, 134
Caziot, Pierre, 54
Central African Republic, 203-204
Centre démocrate (CD), 191, 262, 263
Centre national des Indépendants
  (CNI), 45, 254
Centre national des Indépendants et
  Paysans, 113
Cercle Tocqueville, 256
Chaban-Delmas, Jacques, 112, 145,
  148, 162, 187, 196, 269, 297, 305
Chad (Tchad), 204
Chalandon, Albin, 187n., 241, 267,
  268, 269
Challe, Maurice, 151, 169, 171, 174,
  177, 178, 179, 185
Chapsal, Jacques, 157, 189

Charlot, Jean, 268
Chassin, Lionel, 150
Chatenet, Pierre, 164
Cherrière, Paul, 150
Chevigné Pierre de, 126n.
Chiang Kai-shek, 126n.
China, 83, 87, 128 (see also People's Republic of China)
Chirac, Jacques, 264, 268
Chou En-lai, 127
Churchill, Winston, 7, 38, 59, 60n., 66, 69, 70, 73n., 83, 84 (see also Great Britain)
Ciano, Galleazzo, 56
Clark, Mark, 69
Claudel, Paul, 275
Clemenceau, Georges, 7n., 36
Club Jean-Moulin, 256
Cohn-Bendit, Daniel, 276, 277n., 282
Colonial affairs, 85-88
Combat, 64, 65
Comité d'Action Militaire (COMAC), 74, 75
Comité d'action pour la Ve République, 262
Comité d'Algérie-Sahara, 168
Comité de liaison des étudiants révolutionnaires (CLER), 277n. (see also Groupuscules)
Comité de Vincennes, 182
Comité Française de Libération nationale (CLFN), 52, 70, 71, 74, 76, 77, 86; transformation to government, 72-73
Comité Général d'Études (CGE), 75
Comité National de Résistance, 185
Comité national du Patronat français (CNPF), 139, 248
Comité National pour la défense de l'Intégrité du Territoire, 177
Comité Parisien de la Libération (CPL), 78
Comités d'action lycéens (CAL), 277
Comités départementaux de Libération (CDL), 76

Comités pour la défense de la République (CDR), 285, 290, 308
Commissaires de la République, 75
Commissariat Général du Plan, 36, 114
Committee of Vigilance (Algeria), 149
Committees of Public Safety (Algeria), 147, 148, 152
Commune, the, 35, 283
Communist Party, 43-44, 46, 74-75, 76, 79, 84, 89, 90, 98, 101, 104, 112, 144, 180, 184, 186, 191, 255, 285, 308; and the 1958 constitution, 163; and the referendum of January 8, 1961, 177 (see also Elections)
Compagnie des Machines Bull, 252
Compagnie Internationale pour l'Informatique (CII), 252
Compagnies républicaines de sécurité (CRS): in Algiers, 152; in "the May events," 276, 279
Concert of Europe, 207-209, 213, 218, 220, 227, 228, 235, 242
Conseil de Direction, 141
Conseil de la République, 139
Conseil National de la Résistance (CNR), 65, 72, 74, 75, 78
Conseil national de la Résistance, le (Hostache), 53n.
Conservative Moderates, 163 (see also Elections)
Constantine Plan, 168
Constituent Assembly, 89-90, 98
Constitution of 1958, 158-163 (see also Elections; Fifth Republic; French Community)
Constitutional Council (1958), 160
Constitutional theory, de Gaulle's, 21-22, 99-100
Convention des Institutions républicaines, 256, 257, 262
Cornut-Gentille, Bernard, 172, 174
Corsica: capture of, 152; liberation of, 71

Coty, René, 112, 155, 156, 164
Coulet, François, 77
Council of Defense (1940), 61
Counterterror, postliberation, 79-80
Couve de Murville, Maurice, 70n.,
    73, 94, 156, 188, 196-197, 222,
    224n., 228, 229n., 230, 233n.,
    254-255, 264, 266, 289, 305
Crazafor, Colonel, 170n.,
Croix de Feu, 45n., (see also Leagues,
    the)
Crozier, Michel, 273, 287
Czechoslovakia, 37, 39, 292

D

Dakar, 59; defeat at, 60-61; "the
    lesson of," 63
Daladier, Edouard, resignation of the
    government of, 44
Dalton, Hugh, 65
Damnosa hereditas, 46
Darlan, Jean L.X.F., 54, 55, 56, 69,
    73
Dawes, Charles G., 38, 47
D'Argenlieu, George Thierry, 60, 61n.,
    63n., 87
D'Astier, Emmanuel, 27, 29, 64, 71n.,
    78n.,
De Broglie, Jean, 183
De la Vigerie, Emmanuel d'Astier
    (see D'Astier, Emmanuel)
De Lattre de Tassigny, Jean, 55, 79,
    94, 107, 126
Debré, Michel, 24, 75, 124n., 145, 148,
    156, 158, 161, 164, 165, 176, 179,
    187, 188, 238, 241, 247, 248, 250,
    261, 266, 267, 269, 282, 292, 300,
    302, 305, 306
Défense "tous azimuths" (see "All-
    azimuths" theory)
Defferre, Gaston, 113, 125, 158n., 164,
    201, 256, 257
Dejean, Maurice, 63n.
Delbecque, Léon, 24, 149, 151, 165,
    171, 187, 267

Délégation-Générale, role of, 75
Délégué militaire national, in the
    resistance, 75
Délégués militaires régionaux (DMR),
    in the resistance, 75
Delouvrier, Paul, 169, 172, 176
Denmark, 120
Dentz, Henri, 62, 133n.
Deuxième Bureau, 64
Devers, Jacob, 82
Dien Bien Phu, 108, 109, 127, 133n.
Diethelm, André, 63n., 70-71n., 141, 144
Discorde chez l'ennemi, la, (de Gaulle),
    14, 29
Domestic policy, 245-273 (see also
    Fifth Republic)
Doriot, Jacques, 45n.
Dreyfus, Alfred, 35
Drieu La Rochelle, Pierre, 195
Droit, Michel, 260, 295-296
Dronne, Raymond, 88, 269
Duchet, Roger, 113, 150
Duclos, Jacques, 284
Duhamel, Jacques, 265, 297
Dulac, General André, 153n.
Dulles, John Foster, 203, 211, 214
Dumaine, Jacques, 85n., 91n.,
    99n., 104, 121n.
Dunkirk, Treaty of (1947), 120
Dutschke, Rudi, 277

E

East Germany (see German Democratic
    Republic)
Eboué Félix, 60, 61n., 94
Echo d'Alger, 150
École nationale d'administration
    (ENA), 296
Economy: after "the May events,"
    293-295; problems (1945), 80-81;
    recovery (1946), 81-82
Eden, Anthony, 123
Education, 253-254
Eisenhower, Dwight D., 70, 71, 72,
    74, 76, 77, 211n.

El Glaoui, 130
Elections: (1946), 97-98, 101-102;
    (1951), 104-106; (January 1956),
    111-113; (November 1958), 163-
    164; (November 1962), 191-192
    268; (December 1965), 258-261;
    (March 1967), 262-264; (June
    1968), 285-286; (June 1969),
    296-297
Electoral system (1945), 89
Ely, Paul Henri, 148n., 150, 151,
    152, 172, 176
Envers et contre tout (Soustelle), 53
Erhard, Ludwig, 209, 226, 234, 235
Erler, Fritz, 209
Esprit, 58
Ethiopia, 238
European Atomic Energy Authority
    (EURATOM), 124
European (Brussels) Commission, 227,
    228, 229
European Coal and Steel Community,
    144, 213
European Defense Community (EDC),
    97, 106, 107, 108, 109, 110, 121,
    122, 123, 124, 144, 145, 206-207,
    213
European Economic Community
    (EEC), 46, 113, 204, 207, 208,
    212, 213, 215, 218, 221, 224, 226,
    228, 234, 242, 306, 307; French
    integration in, 9; veto on British
    entry, 25
"Europeans," in the government, 122
Evian agreements (1962), 157, 180-
    181, 183-185, 186, 197
Executions, postliberation, 79-80
Express, L', 108, 111n., 256

                              F

Faisceau, 45n. *(see also* Leagues, the)
Farès, Abderrahmane, 169, 184
Fascism, 39, 44, 45-46
Faure, Edgar, 110, 111, 112, 117,
    130, 164, 261, 289, 290, 296, 305

Faure, Maurice, 243, 255
Fédération de la gauche démocrate et
    socialiste (FGDS), 262, 263, 265
Federation of Mali, 171n., 202
Fellaghas, 129, 132
Feudalities, in French history, 21n.,
    23, 100
Fifth Republic, 36, 43, 45, 46, 49, 53,
    79, 85, 94, 99, 125, 137, 142;
    changes in structure of, 187-192;
    characteristics of, 101; diplomacy
    of, 303-340; domestic policy of,
    245-273; foreign policy of, 195-
    243; founding of, 147-193; and
    French history, 299-310 *passim;*
    1958 constitution, 158-163;
    reactions to, 101
Figaro, Le, 297
Fil de l'épée, Le (de Gaulle), 9, 12,
    26, 27, 32
First Empire, 309
Flandin, Pierre-Etienne, 55, 73
Foccart, Jacques, 145, 148, 204
Force de frappe, 198-201, 208, 209,
    210, 215-216, 223, 232, 300, 305,
    (see also Nuclear weapons)
Force, in national will, 9
Forces de manoeuvre, 204
Forces françaises de l'Intérieur (FFI),
    75, 78; incorporation in the
    regular army, 79
Foreign policy: of the Fifth Republic,
    195-243; (1951-1958), 106-107;
    (1944-1946), 83-88; toward
    Germany, 118
Fouchet, Christian, 183, 218, 219,
    254, 255, 264, 278, 280, 284,
    290, 305, 308, 309
Fourquet, General Michel, 234, 292
Fourth Republic, 36, 43, 44, 45, 46,
    49, 71, 79, 85, 87, 88, 94, 157,
    303, 304; achievements of, 96,
    113-116; European policies of,
    124-125; fall of, 134-135; move-
    ment to the right, 98, 102; and
    the RPF, 95-145

Franc-Tireur, 64, 65
Franc-Tireurs et Partisans français
   (FTPF), 64
France Combattante, 51, 66
France et son armée, La (de Gaulle),
   7, 29
France sera La France, La, (de Gaulle),
   101*n.,* 138, 143
Francisme, 45*n.,* 80 (*see also* Leagues,
   the)
Franco-German Coal and Steel
   Community, 121
Franco-German Treaty of Friendship
   (1963), 225-226
Franco-Soviet agreement (1965),
   231-232
Franco-Soviet Alliance (1935), 39, 44
Franco-Prussian War, 35
Frédéric-Dupont, Edouard, 140
Free France, 20, 49; armed forces of
   (1940), 59; first military engage-
   ments of, 61-63; history of, 51-78;
   legitimacy of the government of,
   53, 66, 93; territories of (1940),
   60-61
"Free Zone," 55, 57
Frenay, Henri, 64, 71*n.*
French Army, and Algeria, 132-133,
   150-151, 170-173, 178-179, 183,
   185-186
French Community, 201-201 (*see also*
   Constitution of 1958)
Frey, Roger, 141*n.,* 145, 148, 164,
   187, 264, 267, 268, 269
Front de libération nationale (FLN),
   131, 132, 133, 134, 168-169, 171,
   173, 175, 176, 178, 180, 181, 184,
   185
Front national, 64
Front national Française (FNF), 172
Front populaire, 39, 41, 42-43, 44,
   48, 163

G

Gabon, 60, 203-204

Gaillard, Félix, 114, 117, 134
Gamelin, Maurice G., 38*n.*
Gardes, Jean, 171, 172, 174, 178*n.*
Gaullist voters, 270-272
Geismar, Alain, 277, 279
Generals' putsch (22 April 1961), 178
Geneva conference (1954), 108,
   127-128
Georges, Alphonse-Joseph, 70
German Democratic Republic (East),
   231
German Federal Republic (West),
   120, 208-209, 212, 226, 229
Germany, 35, 36, 37, 38, 47, 48, 52,
   59, 83, 84, 118, 223, 225, 230, 234,
   243, 293, 294; new position of,
   121-123; surrender of, 79 (*see also*
   German Democratic Republic;
   German Federal Republic)
Gerow, Leonard T., 78
Gingembre, Maurice, 182*n.*
Giraud, Henri, 66, 68, 69, 70, 71,
   72, 73, 86
Giscard d'Estaing, Valéry, 188, 191,
   247, 248-249, 254, 255, 261, 262,
   263, 264, 265, 294, 296, 306
Glassboro meeting (1967), 240, 241
Glory, aspects of, 13
Godard, Yves, 174, 178*n.*
Goguel, François, 105, 161, 303
Gouin, Félix, 98
Gouraud, General Henri, 179
Goussault, Colonel Michel, 170*n.*
Gouvernement provisoire de la
   république Algérienne (GPRA),
   132, 169, 175, 176, 177, 180, 181,
   182
Gouvernement provisoire de la
   république française (GPRF), 52,
   73, 77
"Grand O," the, 150
Grandval, Gilbert, 130, 145, 249-250
Grappin, Pierre, 275
Great Britain, 37, 38, 39, 47, 48, 49,
   58, 59, 62, 66, 75, 77, 83, 87, 93,
   119, 120, 121, 208, 215, 216, 218,

221, 223, 224, 234-235, 249, 293,
  294, 306 (*see also* Churchill,
  Winston)
Grenelle protocol, 282, 288
Grenier, Fernand, 25, 73
Gribius, Colonel André, 152
Gromyko, Andrei, 230
Gross National Product, 248, 295
Grosser, Alfred, 17, 29, 123, 173, 202,
  209
Group of Ten, 294
Groupe d'action républicaine et sociale
  (ARS), 136, 140, 142
Groupuscules, 277, 281
Guichard, Olivier, 145, 148, 165*n.,*
  300, 301
Guillaumat, Pierre, 172, 174
Guillaume, Augustin, 130

H

Ha Long Bay agreement (June
  1948), 126
Hached, Ferhat, 129
Hadj, Messali, 131*n.,* 132, 178
Hague conference (1969), 306
Hallstein, Walter, 214*n.,* 226
Hamon, Léo, 261
Harrison, Martin, 160
Hassan II, 206
Hauteclocque, Jean de, 129
Heath, Edward, 221, 224*n.*
Herriot, Edouard, 42, 47, 88, 90
Historicism, 28-31
Hitler, Adolph, 37, 39, 44, 55, 56
Ho Chi Minh, 87, 128, 236
Hoare-Laval agreement (1935), 39
Hoover, Herbert, and economic
  moratorium, 48
Houphouët-Boigny, Félix, 167, 201,
  239
Hull, Cordell, 72, 73, 76

I

Iceland, 120

Independent Republicans, 191, 254,
  262, 263, 271, 286, 296 (*see also*
  Elections)
Independents, 191 (*see also* Elections)
Indochina, 82, 86-88, 97, 106, 107,
  108, 109, 118, 125-128, 133, 134
Inflation, 118
Instituts universitaires de Technologie
  (IUT), 254
Integration, de Gaulle on, 8, 9
International Monetary Fund (IMF),
  237-238
Israel, 240, 241 (*see also* Middle East)
Italy, 39, 73, 120, 218, 220, 293, 294
Ivory Coast, 201, 204

J

Jäckel, Eberhard, 56
Jacobinism, 301
Jacquier, General, 263
Jacquinot, Louis, 71*n.,* 156
Japan, 86, 87, 294
Jeanneney, Jules, 78*n.,* 116*n.*
Jeanson Network, 175
Jeunesse Communiste révolutionnaire
  (JCR), 277*n. (see also Groupuscules)*
Jeunesses Patriotes, 45*n. (see also*
  Leagues, the)
Johnson, Lyndon B., 240
Jouhaud, Edmond, 169, 178, 183,
  185, 190*n.*
Journées des barricades, les, 172
Joxe, Louis, 176, 178, 179, 183,
  187, 278, 284
Juin, Alphonse, 129, 130, 171, 177

K

Katanga, 203 (*see also* United Nations)
Kennedy, John F., 214, 216, 223-224,
  225, 226-227
Kent State College, 278-279*n.*
Keynes, J.M., 5, 7*n.,* 309
Khider, Mohammed, 131*n.*
Khrushchev, Nikita, 214, 216-217

Kiesinger, Georg, 234, 235
Kissinger, Henry, 222n.
Koenig, Joseph Pierre, 68, 75, 94
Korean,War, 117, 143
Kosygin, Aleksei, 232, 240
Krivine, Alain, 277n.

L

La Rocque, François de, 45n.
Lacheroy, Colonel Charles, 170n.,
    178n.
Lacoste, Robert, 78n., 134, 151,
    164, 177
Laffont, Robert, 170
Lagaillarde, Pierre, 147, 151, 171,
    173, 177
Laniel, Joseph, 106, 130n., 164
Laos, 237 (see also Southeast Asia)
Larminat, Edgard de, 60, 61n.; and
    German enclaves on the
    Atlantic Coast, 79
Latin America, 238, 239
Laval, Pierre, 39, 44, 51; execution
    of, 80; and the Vichy régime,
    54-56
Le Troquer, André, 71n., 155
Leadership: French, 15; German,
    14; Russian, 15
Leagues, the, in politics, 45
Lease-Lend, 67
Lebanon, 73, 83
Lebrun, Albert, 49
Lecanuet, Jean, 229, 257, 259, 260,
    261, 262, 265, 301
Leclerc, General (Philippe de
    Hautecloque), 60, 61n., 77, 78,
    94; operations in Vietnam, 87
Lefèvre, Bernard, 150
Legentilhomme, Paul Louis, 60,
    62, 63n.
Lehideux, François, 56
Lemaigre-Dubreuil, Jacques, 130
Lepercq, Aimé, 78n.
Les-Bouches-du-Rhone, 158n.
Lévy, J-P., 64

Libération, in the resistance, 64, 65
Libération-Nord, 64
Libya, 239n.
Little Entente, 37
Locarno, treaty of (1925), 38, 39
Loi Barangé, 96, 103, 105, 140,
    143
Loi-cadre, 134, 201
Louis Philippe, 309
Lugrin negotiations, 181
Luns, J.M.A.H., 220
Luxembourg, treaty of (1956),
    113, 123
Luxembourg agreement (1966),
    228, 229
Lyttleton, Oliver, 62

M

MacArthur, Douglas, 143
MacMahon, Marie Edme Patrice
    Maurice de, 160
Macmillan, Harold, 211n., 213, 214,
    221, 222, 223
McNamara, Robert S., 216, 222
Madagascar, 68n., 69, 125, 204, 238n.
    (see also Malagasy Republic)
Maginot, André, 37
Maginot line, 38n.
Mahammad V, 202 (see also Morocco)
Malagasy Republic, 204 (see also
    Madagascar)
Mali, Federation of, 171n., 202
Malleret-Joinville, General, 75
Malraux, André, 13, 17, 91, 141, 145,
    156, 172, 182, 239n., 259, 260,
    294, 300, 302, 310
Manifesto of 121, the, 175
Mao Tse Tung, 126n.
Marcellin, Raymond, 284, 286
Marcilhacy, Pierre, 257n., 260n.
Marin, Louis, 39, 88
Markovitch affaire, 292
Marquet, Adrien, 54
Marshall Plan, 103-104, 119, 120
Martel, Robert, 150, 151

Massigli, René, 63n., 70n., 94
Massu, Jacques, 133, 147, 151, 171, 172, 283
Mast, General Charles, 127 (*see also* "Affaire des généraux")
Maudling negotiation, 213, 221
Mauriac, Francois, 279
Maurin, Félix, 38
Maurras, Charles, 24, 32, 39, 56, 100, 301
"May events," 275-289, 293, 296
Mayer, Daniel, 65
Mayer, René, 70n., 78n., 106, 117, 122, 140, 145
Melouza massacre, 132
Mémoires d'Espoir (de Gaulle), 149, 166, 167, 186, 207, 210n., 211, 212n., 216, 218, 220, 288n., 309
Mémoires de Guerre (de Gaulle), 5, 6, 7, 16, 18, 20, 24, 29, 31n., 78, 84n., 88, 92, 207
Mendès-France, Pierre, 65, 71n., 78n., 94, 97, 103, 108, 112, 122, 123, 128, 129, 130, 156, 163, 164, 262, 283; and the French economy (1945), 81; political downfall of, 109-110
Menthon, François, de, 71n., 78n.
Messina conference (1955), 123
Messmer, Pierre, 174, 187, 188, 199, 255, 264, 292, 305
Michelet, Edmond, 140, 141, 145, 172, 187, 300, 305
Middle East: and oil, 240; policies in, 241-242
Millerand, Alexandre, 100, 101
Miners' strike (1963), 249
Miquel, General Roger, 152
Mitterrand, François, 112, 130, 156, 257, 259, 260, 261, 262, 283
Moderates, the, 104, 105, 112 (*see also* Elections)
Mollet, Guy, 124, 134, 154, 156, 188, 255, 256, 257; achievements of 112-113
Molotov, Viasheslav, 108n., 119, 127

Monnerville, Gaston, 190, 290
Monnet, Jean, 36, 70, 96, 114, 121
Mons, Jean, 128, 129
Morice, André, 113, 150, 177
Morin, Jean, 176
Morocco, 106, 107, 109, 129-131, 134, 202, 205-206
Moscow conference (1947), 119
Moulin, Jean, 65, 72, 94
Mounier, Emmanuel, 58
Mouvement du 22 Mars, 277n. (*see also Groupuscules)*
Mouvement national algérien (MNA), 132, 178
Mouvement pour le triomphe des libertés démocratiques (MTLD), 131n.
Mouvement républicaine populaire (MRP), 88, 90, 91, 96, 97, 98, 103, 104, 105, 106, 122, 126n., 134, 136, 139, 142, 163, 186, 191, 255, 257; and the referendum of 8 January 1961, 177 *(see also* Elections)
Mouvements Unie de Résistance (MUR), 65
Multilateral force (MLF), 223, 225
Murphy, Robert, 69
Muselier, Emile-Henry, 60, 61n., 63n.
Mussolini, Benito, 44
Mysticism, in de Gaulle's role, 20

N

Napoleon I (Napoleon Bonaparte), 300, 301, 302, 304
Napoleon III (Louis Napoleon), 307
Nassau conference (1962), 223-224
National Assembly, 101, 113, 123, 139, 254; and de Gaulle, 155-157; in the "May events," 275-292 *passim*; after the 1958 elections, 188, 191
National-Socialists, 45-46

Nationalism: under the Fifth
Republic, 196; nineteenth-
century romantic, 31
NATO Air Defense Ground
Environment (NADGEO),
232-233
Navarre, Henri, 127, 133n.
Netherlands, the, 219-220, 294
(see also Benelux countries)
Niger, 204
Nigeria, Biafran secession from, 205n.,
239-240
"Night of the barricades," 279
Nixon, Richard M., 292
Noël, Léon, 263
Normandy, Allied landings in, 73, 77
North Africa, 61, 68, 73, 75
(see also Africa; Algeria; Morocco;
Tunisia)
North Atlantic pact, 120
North Atlantic Treaty Organization
(NATO), 83n., 109, 123, 206,
210, 211, 215, 219, 223, 231,
232-234, 262; France's with-
drawal from, 26
Norway, 120
Notre République, 261
Novick, Peter, 80n.
Nuclear non-Proliferation Treaty
(NPT), 200, 234
Nuclear Test Ban Treaty (1963), 200,
226
Nuclear weapons, 197-201, 222, 233
(see also Force de frappe)

O

Occident, 275, 277
Office de la Radio et Télévision
française (ORTF), 273, 281
Olié, Jean, 179
"Operation Resurrection," 153, 155
Operation Torch, 68 (see also North
Africa)
Oran Committee of Public Safety, 25

Organisation Armée Secrète (OAS),
133, 178, 179, 180, 182-183,
285, 288
Organisation civile et militaire (OCM),
64
Organisation de Sécurité (OS), 131n.
Organization for European Economic
Cooperation (OEEC), 120
Ortiz, Joseph, 150, 171, 172, 173
Ortoli, Francois-Xavier, 284, 289, 295
Orwell, George, 310
Oufkir, Muhammad, 205

P

Palewski, Gaston, 60, 141
Panama, 35
Paris, liberation of, 77-78; de Gaulle's
symbolic gestures in, 78
Paris summit conference (1960), 217
Paris, Treaty of, 207 (see also
European Defense Community)
Parodi, Alexandre, 75, 78n.
Parti populaire français (PPF), 45n.
(see also Leagues, the)
Parti social français (PSF), 45, 272
Parti socialiste unifié (PSU), 262
Passy, Colonel (André de Wavrin), 60,
64, 65, 94
Péguy, Charles P., 13, 24, 32
People's Republic of China, 226
(see also China)
Pétain, Henri Philippe, 29, 37, 38n.,
41, 48, 52, 53, 80; and the Vichy
régime, 54-58
Peyrefitte, Alain, 228, 264, 268, 278,
279, 280, 284
Pflimlin, Pierre, 134, 148, 151, 154-155,
156, 188, 255
Philip, André, 63n., 65, 70n., 135n.,
165
Pinay, Antoine, 94, 97, 105, 106, 117,
131, 156, 164, 174n., 247, 257
Pineau, Christian, 64, 65, 164
Pisani, Edgar, 264, 282

Plan de Modernisation et d'Equipement,
  114-115
Plan XVII, 37
Plebiscitary democracy, 90, 93; in
  French history, 21, 302, 304
Pleven, René, 60, 63*n.*, 70-71*n.*, 78*n.*,
  85, 91, 122, 144, 148, 297; and
  the French economy (1945), 81
Poher, Alain, 290, 296, 297
Poincaré, Raymond, 38, 39, 41, 47,
  107, 309
Poland, 37, 39, 67, 234
Political organization, de Gaulle on,
  158-159
Polytéchniciens, 296
Pompidou, Georges, 24, 101*n.*, 138,
  145, 160, 178, 188, 193, 224*n.*,
  247, 248-249, 258, 261, 262, 264,
  265, 266, 268, 269, 271, 272,
  299-309 *passim;* and the decline
  of Gaullism, 278-297 *passim*
Population expansion, 252-253
Portugal, 120
Potsdam, 118
Poujade, Pierre, 97, 111, 112, 141-142,
  177
Poujade, Robert, 268, 290, 300
ler Commandement Aérien tactiques
  (1 CATAC), 233*n.*
Professional army, character of, 9-10
Progrès et Démocratie moderne
  (PDM), 263*n.*, 265
Pucheu, Pierre, 56, 57, 80

Q

Quebec, 239
Queuille, Henri, 65, 71*n.*

R

Radicals, 98, 104, 105, 112, 139,
  163, 191, 255, 308; and the
  Constitution of 1875, 90; and

the referendum of 8 January
  1961, 177 (*see also* Elections)
Ramadier, Paul, 102
Rassemblement démocratique, 191
  (*see also* Elections; Radicals)
Rassemblement des gauches
  républicaines (RGR), 111, 112,
  139
Rassemblement du peuple français
  (RPF), 45, 92, 94, 187; de
  Gaulle's interpretation of, 135-
  136; in elections (1947-1956),
  139-141; and the Fourth
  Republic, 95-145; sources of
  support for, 141-142
Referendums, in the Fifth Republic,
  160, 163, 168, 177, 191, 192,
  302-303
Regroupement National pour
  l'Unité de la République, 177
Rémond, René, 32, 272, 301
Rémy (Gilbert Renaud), 141
Renan, Ernest, 299
Renaud, Gilbert (Rémy), 141
Renaud, Jean, 45*n.*
Reparations Commission, 38
Républicaines-Sociaux, 111
Republicans, Independent (*see*
  Independent Republicans;
  see also Elections)
Resignation of de Gaulle (1946),
  91-92
Resistance movement, 64-66, 74, 75
Return to power (by de Gaulle,
  1958), 97
Revel, Jean-François, 22
Revers, Georges, 127 (*see also*
  "Affaire des généraux")
Reynaud, Paul, 39, 48, 49, 184, 190
Rhineland, the, 37, 39, 118
Rhine River, 44, 78, 84, 143
Robespierre, Maximilien F.M.I. de, 302
Role historique des places françaises
  (de Gaulle), 11*n.*
Rome, treaty of (1957), 113, 124,
  212, 213

Roosevelt, Franklin D., 19, 60n., 67, 69, 70, 72, 76, 77, 83, 84; attitudes of toward France (1943-1944), 73-74, 93
Romanticism, in de Gaulle's role, 20
Roziers, Etienne Burin des, 85n.
Rueff, Jacques, 107, 237, 247
Ruhr: occupation of the, 38, 47; postwar, 84, 118, 119
Rumania, 234, 280
Russia (see Union of Soviet Socialist Republics)
Russo-German pact (1939), 40

S

Saar, the, 84, 118, 119, 123
Sahara, 181-182, 184 (see also Algeria; Morocco; North Africa; Tunisia)
Saillant, Louis, 64
Sainteny, Jean, 236
Saint-Exupéry, Antoine de, 13, 17
Saint-Just, Louis A.L. de, 35, 302
Salaire minimum interprofessionel garanti (SMIG), 117, 282
Salan, Raoul, 147, 148, 150, 151, 152, 168, 169, 177, 178, 183, 185, 190n., 285, 288
San Francisco Conference (1945), 85
Sanguinetti, Alexandre, 241, 290, 300
Sartre, Jean-Paul, 175-176
Sauvageot, Jacques, 276
Schmittlein, Raymond, 165n.
Schröder, Gerhard, 226, 229, 235
Schuman, Robert, 60, 96, 121, 129
Schumann, Maurice, 306
Second Empire, 300, 307
Séguy, Georges, 281
Self-determination, Algerian, 166-167, 170, 175, 176
Sembat, Marcel, 100
Senegal, 171n., 201, 202, 204 (see also Federation of Mali)
Senghor, Léopold, 201
Sérigny, Alain de, 150, 167n.
Service de Renseignements (SR), 64

Seydoux, François, 225
Sicé, General, 61n.
Siegfried, André, 41, 106, 108, 148
Sihanouk, Norodom, 237
Skybolt missile, 222
Soames, Christopher, 292, 293
Socialism, 40, 43, 44
Socialist Party, 89, 90, 91, 96, 98, 102, 104, 112, 139, 163, 186, 188, 191, 257, 267n., 296; and de Gaulle, 158n.; and the Fifth Republic, 164; and the referendum of January 8, 1961, 177 (see also Elections)
Sokolovsky, Vassily Danilovich, 119
Solidarité française, 45n. (see also Leagues, the)
Sorbonne, the, 275-281
Soustelle, Jacques, 24, 28, 53, 60, 63n., 73, 94, 106, 109, 113, 134, 140, 141, 143, 145, 148, 150, 152, 156, 164, 165, 166n., 172, 174, 175, 177, 182, 187, 267, 268, 305
South Africa, 239n.
Southeast Asia, 236-237 (see also Cambodia; Laos; Vietnam)
Southeast Asia Treaty Organization (SEATO), 237
Sozialistische Demokratische Studentenbund (SDS), 277
Spaak, Paul-Henri, 219, 220
Spain, 239n., effect of the civil war in, 39
Special drawing rights (SDRs), 237-238
Special Operations Executive (SOE), history of (Foote), 53n.
Salah, Si, 175
Stalin, Josef, 44, 83, 84
Stark, Harold R., 18-19
Stresemann, Gustav, 38
Strikes, in "the May events," 281-286
Student demonstration, in the "May events," 275-281
Sudreau, Pierre, 172, 179, 190

Supreme Allied Commander Europe
  (SACEUR), 123
Susini, Jean-Marie, 172
Sweden, 294
"Synarchy," the (1941), 56
*Syndicat national de l'enseignement
  supérieur* (SNE. Sup), 277, 279
Syndicat national des instituteurs
  (SNI), 40n.
Syria, 61, 62, 66, 82, 83, 93, 133n.

T

Taine, Hippolyte, 245
Taittinger, Pierre, 45n.
Tanguy-Prigent, François, 78n.
Tardieu, André, 48
Tchad (*see* Chad)
Technology, achievements in, 251-252
Teitgen, Pierre-Henri, 78n.
Terrenoire, Louis, 145, 165, 171n.,
  174, 187
Thibaudet, Albert, 41n.
"Third Force," 97, 103, 104, 209
Third Republic, 35-49, 55, 61, 100,
  301, 303, 309
Third World, 196, 205, 236, 238
Thomazo, Colonel Robert, 150, 171,
  (*see also Unités Territoriales*
  [Algeria])
Thorez, Maurice, 24, 73, 79, 83, 90,
  91
Tillon, Charles, 78n.
Tixier, Adrien, 70-71n., 78n., 91, 92
Tixier-Vignancourt, Pierre, 255, 257n.,
  260n., 261
Tomasini, René, 306, 309
Touré, Sékou, 167, 202
Tournée des popotes, 173, 174, 175,
  185
Travail, Famille, Patrie, 54
Trianon, Treaty of (1920), 37
Triboulet, Raymond, 290
Trinquier, Roger, 150n., 170n.
Tripartisme, character of, 98-99

Tunisia, 71, 106, 107, 109, 128-129,
  134, 202-203, 205

U

U-2 incident, 217
*Union de Défense des Commerçants
  et Artisans* (UDCA), 111
Union démocratique du travail (UDT),
  187, 254, 265 (*see also Union
  démocratique pour la Ve
  République)*
*Union des démocrates pour la
  République* (UDR), 271-272,
  299, 305, 306, 308, 309
*Union des Jeunesses Communistes
  (marxistes-leninistes)* (UJC-ML),
  277n. (*see also Groupuscules*)
*Union des Républicaines d'Action
  Sociale* (URAS), 106, 141, 145
*Union Générale des Travailleurs
  Tunisien* (UGTT), 129
Union nationale, 41
*Union nationale des étudiants
  français* (UNEF), 276, 277, 278,
  283
Union of Soviet Socialist Republics,
  37, 67, 77, 79, 83, 120, 143, 144,
  214, 217, 230-232, 292
"Union of States," 219, 220
*Union pour la défense de la
  République* (UDR), 285, 289, 290,
  291
Union pour la nouvelle république
  (UNR), 45, 94, 141n., 162, 163,
  164, 171n., 177, 186, 191, 254, 258,
  265, 267, 268, 269 (*see also
  Union démocratique pour la Ve
  République* (UDVe), 263, 265, 270
*Union pour le Salut et le Renouveau
  de l'Algérie Français* (USRAF),
  113
United Nations, 73, 84, 129, 196; in
  the Congo, 203; disarmament
  conference, 200; in Katanga, 203

United States, 47, 48, 206-217 *passim*,
224, 231, 236, 240, 294, 306;
policies toward Free France, 66-68,
83, 119-120, 128
Unités Territoriales (Algeria), 150-151
(*see also* Thomazo, Colonel)

V

Valentin, François, 57
Valin, General, 63*n*.
Vallon, Louis, 64, 143, 261, 267, 300,
303, 305
"Vallon Amendment" (1965), 261,
265
Valois, Georges, 45*n*.
Vatican, the, 42
Vaudrey, Colonel Roland, 170*n*.
Véme Bureau, 171, 174 (*see also*
Gardes, Jean)
Vendroux, Jacques, 305, 308, 309
Vernant, Jacques, 223
Vers l'armée de métier (de Gaulle),
9, 13, 29
Versailles, Treaty of (1919), 35, 37,
38, 39, 40, 46
Vichy government, 45; and Free
France. 52-61, 79
Viet Minh, 87, 125-126, 127, 128
Vietnam, 87, 236, 237, 240, 241,
262; partition of, 127-128 (*see
also* Southeast Asia)
Viet Nam Doc Lap Dong Minh Hoi
(the League for the Independence
of Vietnam) 87*n*.

W

Wavrin, André de (*see* Passy, Colonel)
West Berlin, 213, 214
West Germany (*see* German Federal
Republic)
Western European Union (WEU),
123, 293
Weygand, Maxime, 38*n*., 48
Williams, Philip M., 160
Wilson, Harold, 234, 235
Wilson, Woodrow, 38
World War I, 37; French economic
losses after, 46-48; French man-
power losses in, 46-47
Women's suffrage, 73*n*.

X

Xuan, Ngoyen Van, 126

Y

Yalta conference (1945), 83-84, 118
Yaoundé convention 204, 227
Youlou, Abbé, 204
Young, Owen, D., 47

Z

Zeller, André, 178, 179